PONS

W0220882

Das große Übungsbuch
ENGLISCH

5.–10. Klasse

von
Christina Cott
Rebecca Davies
Jens Flach
Miriam Gensty
Philipp KalabisAnna Mielke
Susanne Scholten
Anne Weber
Verena Wróbel

PONS GmbH
Stuttgart

PONS

Das große Übungsbuch ENGLISCH

von
Christina Cott
Rebecca Davies
Jens Flach
Miriam Gensty
Philipp KalabisAnna Mielke
Susanne Scholten
Anne Weber
Verena Wróbel

Dieses Werk basiert in Teilen auf ISBNs:
978-3-12-561586-1, 978-3-12-561587-8, 978-3-12-561588-5,
978-3-12-561420-8, 978-3-12-561582-3, 978-3-12-561480-2

Auflage A1 6 5 4 3 / 2016 2015 2043 2013

PONS Produktinfos und Shop: www.pons.de
PONS Sprachenportal: www.pons.eu
E-Mail: info@pons.de

Redaktion: Canan Özdamar
Logoentwurf: Erwin Poell, Heidelberg
Logoüberarbeitung: Sabine Redlin, Ludwigsburg
Titelfoto: kate_sept2004, iStockphoto
Einbandgestaltung: Daniel Müller, Stuttgart
Illustrationen: Braingame Publishing GmbH, Michael H. Musal, Wiesbaden; Palmer-Lorenz Illustrationen, Rockenberg
Layout/Satz: Satzkasten Dollenbacher & Müller, Stuttgart
Druck und Bindung: Medienhaus Plump, Rheinbreitbach

Printed in Germany.
ISBN: 978-3-12-560730-9

Vorwort

Das **PONS große Übungsbuch Englisch** ist das Fitnessprogramm, das dich jede Klassenarbeit locker schaffen lässt.

Für die Klassen 5 - 10 sind alle wichtigen Disziplinen, die im Englischunterricht vorkommen, in einfache Übungseinheiten gepackt, die leicht zu verstehen und abwechslungsreich sind. Die Inhalte der **Klassen 8 - 10** sind dabei ein wenig anders aufgebaut. Mehr Informationen dazu findest du vor diesem Teil auf S. 228. Wie in einem sportlichen Wettkampf werden die Übungen langsam immer anspruchsvoller - das heißt trainieren, trainieren, trainieren! Und so sieht dein Training aus:

• Aufwärmen

Mit der Aufwärmübung zu Beginn jeden Kapitels kannst du ganz leicht einsteigen.

Im Boxenstopp werden die wichtigsten Regeln des Kapitels erklärt. Hier kannst du immer wieder nachschauen.

BOXENSTOPP

• • Pflicht

Nach dem Aufwärmen folgen die Pflichtübungen. Hier trainierst du die Grundlagen, die dich sicher ans Ziel führen.

• • • Kür

Die Kürübungen sind anspruchsvoller. Wenn du die Pflichtübungen gut durchgearbeitet hast, schaffst du sie ganz bestimmt!

Zwischen den Übungen findest du immer wieder wichtige Tipps, die das Lernern erleichtern.

Und nun - viel Spaß & viel Erfolg!

Auf Seite 399 beginnt der Teil **Referate halten**. Hier lernst du, wie du - von der Themensuche bis zur Durchführung - vorgehen musst, damit dein Referat ein voller Erfolg wird. Mit dem Sprechtraining kannst du zusätzlich die Aussprache hören, üben und verbessern.

Ein ausführliches **Inhaltsverzeichnis** findest du zu Beginn jeder Klassenstufe.

Hier hast du einen schnellen Überblick, auf welchen Seiten du welche Klassenstufen findest.

Übungen zu:

KLASSE 5

Inhalt

Grammatik

Wortschatz

KLASSE 6

Inhalt

Grammatik

Wortschatz

KLASSE 7

Inhalt

Grammatik

Wortschatz

KLASSE 8

Inhalt

Grammatik

Wortschatz

KLASSE 9

Inhalt

Grammatik

Wortschatz

KLASSE 10

Inhalt

Grammatik

Wortschatz

REFERATE HALTEN

Inhalt

Inhalt

Grammatik

Wortschatz

KLASSE 5

1 DAS VERB *TO BE*

1.1 Die Formen von *to be*

- Unterstreiche im folgenden Text alle Formen von **to be**, die du finden kannst.

Hello, I am Taylor. I'm twelve years old. My brother is only seven. We live in a very big house. It is green and there are four bedrooms. They are all very big, too. We're very happy to live here.

BOXENSTOPP

Jetzt kannst du dich selber testen. Ergänze in der folgenden Tabelle die fehlenden Formen von **to be**.

	Langformen		Kurzformen	
Singular	I	**am**	I	'm
	you	are	you	**'re**
	he	**is**	he	's
	she	is	she	's
	it	is	it	**'s**
Plural	we	are	we	're
	you	**are**	you	're
	they	are	they	**'re**

Nicht vergessen, Sportsfreunde: Aus zwei Gründen ist das Verb **to be** sehr wichtig! Als so genanntes Vollverb bedeutet es *sein*. Und als Hilfsverb kann man mit **to be** verschiedene Zeiten bilden. Daher solltest du dieses Verb genau lernen und sowohl die Lang- als auch die Kurzformen kennen.

•• Kannst du die folgenden Sätze mit der jeweils richtigen Form von **to be** ergänzen?

1. Marc is a good friend of mine.
2. Mum and Dad are in the office.
3. Our classroom is very nice.
4. Mrs Black is our new English teacher.
5. The weather is fantastic.
6. The bathrooms is / are on the right.

••• Wenn du jetzt noch die folgenden Sätze ins Englische übersetzen kannst, dann hast du die Formen von **to be** drauf!

1. Heute ist es sehr heiß.

Today is it very hot

2. Die Flaschen sind leer.

The bottles are empty.

3. Heute ist Montag.

Today it is monday.

4. Die Großeltern sind in den Ferien.

The grandparents are in the holidays.

1.2 Die Verneinung von *to be*

• Fällt dir hier etwas auf? Markiere in den folgenden Sätzen die verneinten Formen von **to be**.

1. Jane is not at home.

2. Kim and Delilah are not hungry. They are thirsty.

3. Sally isn't eleven. She is ten.

4. They aren't in my class.

BOXENSTOPP

Wie werden die Formen von **to be** verneint? Überlege dir eine Regel in deinen eigenen Worten und schreibe sie auf.

Nicht vergessen! Auch für die Verneinung gibt es Abkürzungen:

isn't = is not **aren't** = are not

•• Ergänze die folgenden Sätze mit der jeweils richtigen Form von **to be**. Aber aufgepasst auf die verneinten Formen!

1. Susan isn't (not be) eleven. She is (be) ten.
2. Jack isn't (not be) my best friend.
3. He isn't (not be) in my class.
4. Zoë is (be) from London. She isn't (not be) from Liverpool.
5. Lane and David aren't (not be) in my school.
6. I am not (not be) nine years old. I am (be) ten.

••• Die folgenden Sätze sind etwas durcheinander geraten. Kannst du sie wieder in die richtige Reihenfolge bringen? Denke dabei auch an die richtigen Formen von **to be**.

1. years / eleven / Tim / be / old / not
Tim isn't eleven years old
2. Linda / beautiful / very / be / girl / a
Linda is a gvery beautiful girl
3. interesting / this / be / book / not
This isn't book intressting This book isn't interesting.
4. New York / cities / London / big / be / and
New york and london are big cities
5. show / your / on / favourite / be / TV
Your are on favourile show TV Your favourite TV show is on.
6. old / very / grandparents / my / be / not
My grandparents isn't very old
aren't

1.3 Fragen mit *to be*

• Sieh dir die beiden folgenden Unterhaltungen einmal genau an.

Tim: Hi Betty, **how** are you?
Betty: I'm fine, thanks. And how are you?
Tim: I'm fine. **Who** is your German teacher?
Betty: It's Mrs Black.

Mrs Black: **Where** is my German book?
Tim: Hello, Mrs Black. Is this your book?
Mrs Black: Oh, yes it is. Thank you. **What**'s your name?
Tim: I'm Tim.

Und jetzt schreibe alle Fragen aus den beiden Dialogen auf, in denen das Verb **to be** vorkommt.

1. How are you?
2. And how are you?
3. Who is your German teacher?
4. Where is my German book?
5. Is this your book?
6. What's your name?

BOXENSTOPP

Ergänze die folgende Regel mit den angegebenen Begriffen.

how who to be Anfang to be what where

Nach den Fragewörtern how, who, what, where oder **when** steht immer eine Form von to be. Gibt es keine Fragewörter, steht die Form von to be gleich am Anfang des Fragesatzes.

•• Ordne den Fragen auf der linken Seite die jeweils richtige Antwort auf der rechten Seite zu.

1. Is this your book?
2. Are they new?
3. How are you?
4. Is Tom twelve years old?

a. I'm fine, thank you.
b. Yes, he is.
c. Yes, they are.
d. No, it isn't.

••• Du hast dir auf einem Notizzettel einige Fragen notiert, die du deinen Klassenkameraden stellen möchtest. Leider ist der Zettel zerrissen. Kannst du die Satzteile wieder zu sechs vollständigen Fragesätzen verbinden? Achte dabei auf die richtige Form von **to be** und schreibe deine Lösungen in die freien Zeilen.

Who		school	over
When		your sister's	name
What	**be**	the post office	too difficult
Where		the birthday party	teacher
How		your	
		the homework	

1. Who is your teacher?
2. When is school over?
3. Where is the post office?
4. Is the homework too difficult?
5. Where is the brithday party?
6. How is your sister's name?

2 PERSONALPRONOMEN

2.1 Personalpronomen als Subjekt

• Sieh dir an, was Nick zu erzählen hat und notiere anschließend alle Personalpronomen, die er benutzt. Welche Pronomen verwendet man im Singular und welche im Plural? Fallen dir noch weitere Personalpronomen ein?

Hello, I'm Nick. This is Joey the cat. She is from London and we are friends. Who are you?

Singular: I'm,

Plural: She is, We are

BOXENSTOPP

Subjektpronomen

Ordne die entsprechenden Formen von **to be (am, are** oder **is)** den Personalpronomen in der Tabelle zu.

Singular		Plural	
Langform	Kurzform	Langform	Kurzform
I am	I 'm	we are	we 're
you are	you 're	you are	you 're
he is	he 's	they are	they 're
she is	she 's		
it is	it 's		

Aufgepasst! Das Personalpronomen **you** hat mehrere Bedeutungen. Es kann *du, ihr, euch, Sie* oder *Ihnen* heißen! Die richtige Übersetzung kannst du dir aber meistens aus dem Satzzusammenhang erschließen.

•• Jetzt geht's richtig los. Kannst du die hervorgehobenen Satzteile durch die jeweils richtigen Personalpronomen ersetzen? Formuliere die folgenden Sätze um und schreibe sie noch einmal auf.

1. Where are Jacky and Tina? **Jacky and Tina** are in the garden.

They are in the garden.

2. There is Freddy. **Freddy** is Tina's brother.

He is Tina's brother.

3. Lea is there, too. **Lea** likes to play table tennis with Freddy.

She likes to play table tennis with Freddy.

4. Where is the table tennis ball? **The table tennis ball** is under the table.

He is under the table.

••• Ergänze die folgenden Sätze mit der jeweils richtigen Vorgabe in Klammern.

1. Are you (he / she / you) from England?
2. He (I / He / We) is going home.
3. Is she (she / he / you) Marc's sister?
4. We (He / We / It) are watching a film.
5. We/ ~~She/He~~ (She / We / He) speak English.
6. Am I (I / they / you) right?
7. Are they (I / he / they) in the cinema?
8. She (They / I / She) is playing soccer.
9. Are you (I / she / you) joking?
10. It (He / We / It) is a wonderful day.

2.2 Personalpronomen als Objekt

• Sieh dir die Unterhaltung von Kim und Sarah genau an und markiere darin alle Personalpronomen, die als Objekt stehen.

Kim: Hey Sarah, do you know where Jess is? I want to pick him up, but now he isn't there.
Sarah: No, I don't. Sorry, I can't help you. But you can come to the cinema with Sam and me.
Kim: Oh, that's a good idea! I come with you two. What's the name of the film? I hope I like it.
Sarah: I don't know. It's a nice film with Jim Black and Cathy Jones. I always like to see them.

BOXENSTOPP

Objektpronomen
Hier siehst du eine Übersicht der Personalpronomen in der Objektform, es fehlen nur noch einige Pronomen aus der Aufwärmübung oben. Kannst du die fehlenden Pronomen ergänzen?

Singular		Plural	
Subjektpronomen	Objektpronomen	Subjektpronomen	Objektpronomen
I	**me**	we	**us**
you	your	you	**you**
he	his	they	them
she	**her**		
it	it		

•• Ersetze die hervorgehobenen Satzteile durch das jeweils passende Personalpronomen und schreibe die Sätze dann noch einmal auf.

1. **Jane** wants to read **a book**.
   She wants to read it.
2. **Sarah and Sam** like **Marc**.
   They like him.
3. **The dog** sees **the ball** in the yard.
   He sees it in the yard.
4. **Mr Jackson** reads **a comic**.
   He reads it.
5. **Michael** wants to meet **Martha**.
   He wants to meet her.

•• Jetzt geht's noch einmal um Alles. Ergänze im folgenden Text die jeweils fehlenden Personalpronomen, dann hast du's geschafft!

1. **Sarah:** Hi, Mum. We're getting wet. Can you pick us up?
2. **Jane:** Look at these horse posters, Sally. You can put it on your wall.
3. **Sam:** Hey, Martha. Can you help me with my German homework? I can't do them.
4. **Lucy:** Hey Sarah, where is the cat? I can't find her.
5. **Marc:** Look, there's Sam with his skates. I can see him next to the tree.
6. **Sandy:** I'm sorry, Michael. I'm busy. I can't play tennis with your.
7. **Henry:** Hey, Tony and Sally. Can I come to the cinema with you?
8. **Mrs Burton:** What about your skateboard, Sarah? Put it in the garage, please.
9. **Jane:** There are so many things. I can't carry them all.
10. **Tony:** Wait for me, Sally. I'm coming.

3 DAS SIMPLE PRESENT

3.1 Bildung und Gebrauch des Simple Present

- Lies dir den folgenden Text aufmerksam durch und markiere darin alle Formen des Simple Present, die du finden kannst. Erkennst du auch schon ein paar Signalwörter, die dir verraten, dass es sich um eine Zeitform der Gegenwart handelt?

Jess gets up at half past six every day. The school bus arrives at a quarter past seven. School starts at eight o'clock. He and his friends always have lunch at half past eleven. Katie is one of his best friends. After school they often play basketball in front of her house.

BOXENSTOPP

Jetzt bist du gefragt. Kannst du die folgende Regel vervollständigen?

to Grundform oft **-s** **always** regelmäßig **often**

Das Simple Present ist die Grundform des Verbs ohne to. In der dritten (he, she, it) Person Singular wird ein S angehängt. Das merkt man sich am besten mit diesem kurzen Reim:

Bei **he, she** und **it**, das **-s** muss mit!

Man benutzt das Simple Present, wenn etwas gerade (oft) oder jetzt (regelmäßig) geschieht. Es wird aber auch bei Tatsachen verwendet, die alltäglich und üblich sind. Signalwörter zeigen die verwendete Zeit an. Beim Simple Present sind das zum Beispiel **every (day)**, always, often, **never, sometimes** oder **usually**.

Vorsicht beim Training! Es gibt 3 wichtige Ausnahmen:

1. Bei Hilfsverben wie zum Beispiel **can, must** und **would like to** wird auch in der 3. Person Singular kein **-s** angehängt.
2. Endet ein Verb auf einem Zischlaut, wie zum Beispiel **to watch**, dann wird in der 3. Person Singular ein **-es** angehängt (**she watches**). Dasselbe gilt für die Verben **to go** und **to do** (**he goes, she does**).
3. Verben, die auf Konsonant + **y** enden, wie zum Beispiel **to fly** oder **to cry**, haben in der 3. Person Singular die Endung **-ies** (**she cries**).

•• Ergänze die folgenden Sätze mit der jeweils richtigen Vorgabe in Klammern.

1. I visits (visit / visits / visited) her grandmother every day.

2. Sarah do always (always do / do always / always does) my homework.

3. Mr and Mrs O'Donnelly usually goes (are going / goes / go) to Ireland on holidays.

4. They stays normally (normally stay / stay normally / stays normally) at a youth hostel.

5. You sometimes like (sometimes likes / like sometimes / sometimes like) school.

•• Und jetzt musst du im folgenden Text nur noch die Verben an der richtigen Stelle einfügen, dann kennst du dich schon gut aus mit dem Simple Present! Achte dabei auch auf die richtige Endung in der dritten Person Singular.

like | get up | pick up | get | drive | take | fetch | be | take | find | ask | check

Every day Mr Barclay (1) ____________ at six o'clock and (2) ____________ his bus at the garage. Then he (3) ____________ the children from the villages around Nottingham and (4) ____________ them to Briggs High School.

The children (5) ____________ Mr Barclay because he (6) ____________ always nice to them. The children usually (7) ____________ to school at a quarter to eight. In the afternoon Mr Barclay (8) ____________ his bus to school again and (9) ____________ the children home. After that he (10) ____________ his bus and often (11) ____________ things on the floor. Sometimes the children (12) ____________ Mr Barclay when they can't find a pullover or a jacket.

3.2 Die Verneinung im Simple Present

• Verbinde die Fragen auf der linken Seite mit den passenden Antworten rechts.

1. Do you like to play on the computer?
2. When does he do his homework?
3. What does Emma usually do with her friend Kathy?
4. Does she like chocolate?
5. Where do they live?

a. They don't play cards.
b. No, she doesn't like it at all.
c. He doesn't do it in the morning.
d. They don't live near London.
e. No, I don't like computer games.

BOXENSTOPP

Kannst du die untenstehende Regel mit den folgenden Vorgaben ergänzen?

don't **Infinitiv** **does not**

Wenn du Aussagen im Simple Present verneinen möchtest, dann musst du **do not** (don't) oder does not (**doesn't**) vor den Infinitiv des Verbs setzen.

Die einzigen Verben, die nicht mit **do** oder **does** verneint werden, sind **to be** und die Hilfsverben **have got, can, could, should, would** und **must**.

•• Kannst du die folgenden Aussagesätze verneinen? Schreibe die Sätze noch einmal in verneinter Form auf.

1. Nick goes shopping.

Nick goesn't shopping

2. We write a lot at school.

3. In the evening Lucy watches TV.

4. The weather in England is sunny.

The weather in England isn't sunny

5. Sammy and Robert play football every Saturday.

Sammy and Robert don't play football every saturday.

•• Sieh dir das folgende Beispiel einmal genau an und bilde anschließend selbst Sätze nach dem vorgegebenen Schema, dann hast du's drauf!

1. ~~Sarah~~ / Kim / live in Nottingham
   Sarah doesn't live in Nottingham. Kim lives in Nottingham.
2. ~~Sarah's parents~~ / Sarah's grandma / make her birthday cake
   Sarah's parents don't make her birthday cake. Sarah's grandma makes her birthday cake
3. ~~Mrs O'Brien~~ / Sarah / come from Germany
   Mrs O'Brien dosen't come form Germany. Sarah comes form Germany
4. ~~German children~~ / English children / wear school uniforms
   German children don't wear school uniforms. English children wears go school uniforms
5. ~~Sarah~~ / Sam / play the guitar
   Sarah doesn't play the guitär. Sam plays the guitar.

3.3 Fragen im Simple Present

• Markiere in den folgenden Sätzen jeweils **do** oder **does** und das Fragewort.

1. Do I work?
2. Do you work?
3. Does he work?
4. When do we work?
5. Where do you work?
6. What do they work?

BOXENSTOPP

Wenn du jetzt die untenstehende Regel mit den folgenden Vorgaben ergänzen kannst, dann bist du gut vorbereitet!

do | **Infinitiv** | **does** | **Subjekt** | **where** | **Vollverbs** | **what**

Fragen im Simple Present werden gebildet, indem du Infinitiv oder Subjekt vor das Vollverbs des Fragesatzes und vor den do des does setzt. Fragewörter, wie zum Beispiel **when**, where oder what stehen übrigens noch vor **do** oder **does**.

•• Die folgenden Fragesätze sind durcheinander geraten. Kannst du sie noch einmal aufschreiben?

1. always / rain / England / does / in / it / ?

____

2. British people / do / a lot of tea / drink / ?

____

3. like / children / sweets / do / ?

____

4. Jeremy / do his homework / does / when / ?

____

5. grandparents / live / your / where / do / ?

____

••• Stell dir vor, du triffst einen unbekannten Jungen oder ein unbekanntes Mädchen. Was für Fragen kannst du ihm oder ihr stellen? Schreibe deine Fragen in die freien Zeilen. Das Beispiel zeigt dir, wie es funktioniert.

Where?	When?	How?	What?
come from want to go on vacation	do your homework play basketball	get home from school like your teacher	do on Saturday like to eat

1. *Where do you come from?*
2. ______________________________
3. ______________________________
4. ______________________________
5. ______________________________
6. ______________________________
7. ______________________________
8. ______________________________

4 DAS PRESENT PROGRESSIVE

4.1 Bildung und Gebrauch des Present Progressive

- Lies dir den folgenden Text aufmerksam durch und markiere darin alle Formen des Present Progressive, die du finden kannst. Aber aufgepasst: Das Present Progressive ist eine zusammengesetzte Zeitform! Erkennst du auch schon ein paar Signalwörter?

Kim and Delilah are at Martins Media, a big shop in London. Right now they are spending their pocket money. At the moment Delilah is buying a book and Kim is just looking at some DVDs.

Delilah: Let's go, Kim. Alicia is waiting outside.

Kim: Just a minute, Delilah.

Delilah: What are you doing? Are you buying that DVD?

Kim: No, I'm not. I'm just reading about it. Ok, now I'm ready. Let's go!

BOXENSTOPP

Leider ist die Regel nicht mehr vollständig. Kannst du die Wörter wieder an der jeweils richtigen Stelle einsetzen?

just Form von **to be (am - is - are)** gerade dabei ist **at the moment** **-ing**

Gegenwart Verbs **(right) now** Infinitiv **to**

Das Present Progressive ist eine Zeitform der ____________. Mit dem Present Progressive wird ausgedrückt, dass jemand ____________, etwas zu tun. Gebildet wird es mit einer ____________ (____________), dem ____________ des ____________ (ohne ____) und der Endung ____________. Signalwörter für das Present Progressive sind zum Beispiel ____________, ____________ und ____________.

Aufgepasst bei der Schreibweise der **ing**-Form:

1. Endet ein Verb auf ein stummes **e**, dann fällt dieses weg:

   Jacky is **making** a cake.

2. Bei Verben, die auf einen kurzen Vokal + Konsonant enden, wird der Konsonant verdoppelt:

   Tim is **getting** things ready for tea.
   Eve is **running** very fast.

•• Kannst du die Verben in den folgenden Sätzen in das Present Progressive umwandeln?

1. She talks to her friend. She is talking to her friend.
2. Luke swims in a lake. ______
3. We hide under the table. ______
4. Lane kisses Tom. ______
5. The grandparents watch TV. ______
6. You talk to Frances. ______
7. I ride my bike. ______

Wenn du das Present Progressive verneinen möchtest, dann setze einfach **not** hinter die Form von **to be**:

I'm **not** watching TV.

Im Deutschen gibt es übrigens keine Verlaufsform wie das Present Progressive. Daher wird diese Form oft mit den Begriffen *gerade*, *im Moment*, *im Augenblick* oder *jetzt* ausgedrückt.

••• Wenn du jetzt noch übersetzen kannst, was Sarah und Sam gerade tun, dann kennst du dich schon prima mit dem Present Progressive aus!

1. Sarah liest gerade ein Buch.

______

2. Sam macht gerade seine Hausaufgaben.

______

3. Sarah schläft im Augenblick nicht.

______

4. Sam spielt jetzt Tennis mit seinem Bruder.

______

5. Sarah spricht zurzeit nicht mit ihrer Großmutter.

______

6. Sarah und Sam essen im Moment keine Pizza.

______

4.2 Fragen im Present Progressive

- Kannst du die folgenden Sätze vervollständigen?

1. Is the boy sitting on the grass? Yes he is.
2. Is the boy reading a book? No, he ________. He is listening to music.
3. Are the three children ____________ football? Yes, they are.
4. ________ the two boys having a fight? Yes, they are.
5. Is the old man playing with his dog? Yes, ____________.
6. Is the girl sitting on a bench? ________, she is.

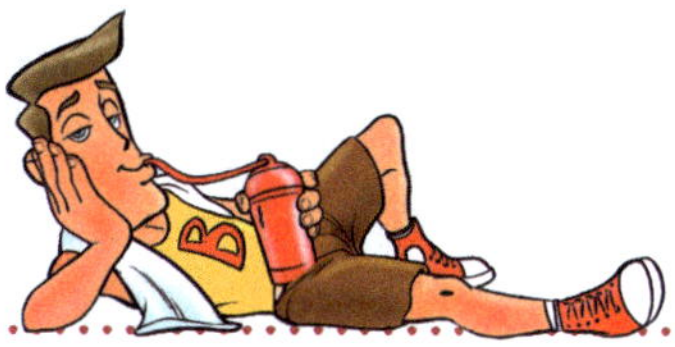

Hier noch einmal ein Beispiel:

The boy is lying on the sofa.

Is the boy lying on the sofa? – Yes, he is.

BOXENSTOPP

Wie bildet man eine Frage im Present Progressive? Formuliere eine Regel.

Eine Frage im Present Progressive stellst du, indem du

____.

Die Kurzantwort besteht dann nur aus

____.

• • Kannst du die folgenden Satzteile in die richtige Reihenfolge bringen?

1. game / he / is / a / playing / ?

____

2. they / visiting / London / are / ?

____

3. basket / its / sleeping / in / the cat / is / ?

____

4. the playground / she / is / going / to / ?

____

5. we / are / a test / writing / now / ?

____

• • • Wenn du jetzt noch aus den folgenden Vorgaben fünf Fragen im Present Progressive bilden kannst, dann hast du's geschafft!

			listen to rock music
Am	**I**	**it**	**play basketball**
Are	**you**	**we**	**read a book**
Is	**he**	**you**	**talk to a friend on the phone**
	she	**they**	**watch a film**

1. ______________________________

2. ______________________________

3. ______________________________

4. ______________________________

5. ______________________________

4.3 Simple Present und Present Progressive im Vergleich

- Unterstreiche im folgenden Dialog alle Formen des Simple Present blau und die Formen des Present Progressive rot.

Marc: Sarah, what is your brother doing?
Sarah: He is playing basketball with his best friend John right now.
Marc: Does he play basketball with John every Saturday?
Sarah: No, he doesn't.
Mrs O'Brien: And what are you two doing?
Marc and Sarah: We are studying for the maths test.

BOXENSTOPP

Welche Signalwörter deuten auf das Simple Present hin und welche auf das Present Progressive? Ordne die folgenden Ausdrücke richtig zu.

often | (right) now | sometimes | always | never | usually | at the moment | every ...

Simple Present	Present Progressive

Aufgepasst, Sportsfreunde: Das Present Progressive benutzt man, wenn etwas **jetzt im Moment** geschieht. Das Simple Present wird dagegen verwendet, wenn etwas **regelmäßig, immer wieder** oder **nie** passiert!

•• Simple Present oder Present Progressive? Ergänze die folgenden Sätze mit den Verben in Klammern in der jeweils richtigen Zeitform.

1. At the moment the boys ______________________ (swim) in the sea.
2. Every Sunday the O'Brien family ______________________ (go) to the zoo.
3. On Mondays Sam ______________________ (eat) lunch at his grandma's house.
4. Sarah sometimes ______________________ (play) computer games with her brother.
5. Marc and Sam never ______________________ (talk) during English lessons.
6. Our English teacher ______________________ (clean) the board at the moment.
7. We often ______________________ (ride) our bikes in the park.
8. Grandma Martha ______________________ (not bake) a cake at the moment.

Immer am Ball bleiben, okay? Auch wenn in einem Satz mal kein Signalwort steht, kannst du die richtige Zeitform herausfinden. Du musst dann einfach versuchen, dir die passende Zeit zu denken. Frage dich zum Beispiel, welches Signalwort am ehesten passen könnte.

••• Und jetzt musst du nur noch den folgenden Text mit der jeweils richtigen Form der Verben in Klammern ergänzen, dann weißt du bestens Bescheid, wann man das Simple Present und wann das Present Progressive benutzt!

Jack Burton (1) ________________ (live) in London. He (2) ________________ (work) at Heathrow airport. Jack usually (3) ________________ (get up) at six o'clock and (4) ________________ (go) for a walk with his dog. Then he (5) ________________ (have) breakfast and after that he (6) ________________ (walk) to the bus stop. Today it (7) ________________ (be) very cold, so he (8) ________________ (wear) a long anorak. Sometimes Jack (9) ________________ (go) by car, but today he (10) ________________ (take) the bus.

Now Jack (11) ________________ (stand) in the big hall at the airport. Some people (12) ________________ (walk) through the hall. Listen, two of the passengers next to Jack (13) ________________ (speak) German. Oh, dear! They (14) ________________ (not speak) English. Jack Burton (15) ________________ (help) them because he (16) ________________ (speak) German. He (17) ________________ (like) his job.

5 DAS SIMPLE PAST

5.1 Bildung und Gebrauch des Simple Past

- Tom erzählt dir, was er letzte Nacht geträumt hat. Unterstreiche in seinem Bericht alle Verben, die im Simple Past stehen.

Listen, I dreamed this crazy story last night: I was on my way to school. Suddenly I saw a big light in the sky. It came nearer and nearer. I saw that it was a small vehicle. It looked like a very funny little plane. It landed in the park. Two funny people came out. They said: "Hello, we are Huggy and Buggy, and who are you? We are on our way to Mars and we need some orange juice for our plane. It only works with orange juice!" It was no problem for me because I had a bottle of juice with me. So I gave it to them. They filled their tank with it and flew into the sky again. What a crazy dream that was.

BOXENSTOPP

Kannst du die folgende Regel vervollständigen?

Infinitiv | abgeschlossen | Ereignissen | lernen | **-ed** | Handlungen | Vergangenheit

Das Simple Past ist eine Zeitform der ______________. Es steht bei ______________ und ______________, die bereits ______________ sind.

Bei regelmäßigen Verben bildet man das Simple Past, indem man die Endung ________ an den ______________ des Verbs (ohne **to**) anhängt. Für unregelmäßige Verben gibt es keine Regel. Die muss man einfach ______________!

•• Trage die Verben aus Toms Traum in die folgende Tabelle ein und finde jeweils den passenden Infinitiv dazu. Aber aufgepasst: Welche Verben bilden das Simple Past regelmäßig und welche nicht? Wenn sich die Verben wiederholen, musst du sie nicht doppelt aufschreiben.

Regelmäßige Verben		Unregelmäßige Verben	
Infinitiv	Simple Past	Infinitiv	Simple Past
to dream	dreamed	**to be**	was

Aufgepasst, Sportsfreunde: Bei regelmäßigen Verben, die im Infinitiv auf **-y** enden, wird **y** zu **ie** im Simple Past! Hier ein Beispiel:

Infinitiv	Simple Past
to cr**y**	we cr**ie**d

••• Welche Form ist richtig? Entscheide jeweils, welche Verbform hier benutzt werden muss und schreibe den richtigen Satz dann noch einmal auf.

1. Yesterday he (went / go / going / goes) to school.

____

2. Last week Marc and Sam (putting / put / putted / puts) a drawing pin on Jess' chair.

____

3. In my last holidays I (carry / carried / carrying / carries) a lot of fish.

____

4. Two years ago I (win / wined / winning / won) a 400 metre race in a championship.

____

Es gibt eine ganze Reihe von Signalwörtern für das Simple Past. Hier einige Beispiele:

last week (Sunday / year / ...)	**in 1996**
yesterday	**on 24th December**
the day before yesterday	**two (three / four / ...) days ago**

5.2 Die Verneinung im Simple Past

• Kannst du die Satzanfänge auf der linken Seite mit dem jeweils richtigen Ende rechts verbinden?

1. Last year I played tennis,	**a.** but he didn't like maths.
2. The puppies weren't thirsty,	**b.** and I wasn't at school.
3. He liked his new teacher,	**c.** and I didn't play football.
4. Sally didn't do her homework,	**d.** but she did a lot of other things.
5. We went to the supermarket,	**e.** but they were hungry.
6. Yesterday I was at home,	**f.** and we didn't go to the shopping centre.

BOXENSTOPP

Jetzt musst du nur noch die Regel ergänzen, dann weißt du, wie man das Simple Past verneint!

wasn't | **gleich** | **didn't (did not)** | **to be** | **Infinitiv** | **weren't**

Vollverben werden im Simple Past verneint, indem man ____________ vor den ____________ des Verbs setzt. Das ist für alle Personen ____________. Eine Ausnahme bilden die verneinten Formen von ____________. Sie heißen im Singular ____________ und im Plural ____________.

•• Jetzt bist du gefragt. Ergänze die folgenden Sätze mit dem jeweils richtigen Verb in Klammern. Benutze dazu die verneinte Form des Simple Past.

1. We ____________ (not go) to school last Thursday.

2. Last week Sam and Sarah ____________ (not be) at school.

3. I ____________ (not get) a new computer yesterday.

4. The cat ____________ (not sleep) in the basket last night.

5. My English teacher ____________ (not be) happy about my last test.

6. Marc and Sally ____________ (not like) the music at our school party.

••• Jims Freunde erzählen ihm von ihrer Woche. Ergänze die Sätze mit dem jeweils richtigen Verb im Simple Past. Aber aufgepasst: Manche Verben müssen verneint werden, manche auch nicht!

Kim: Last Sunday we (1) ____________ (want) to have a picnic in the country. But the weather (2) ____________ (not be) good, so we (3) ____________ (go) to the cinema.

Sally: Sam (4) ____________ (make) me very angry the day before yesterday. He (5) ____________ (tell) stories about me to mum and dad. Of course the stories (6) ____________ (not be) true. I (7) ____________ (explain) this to mum and dad, but they (8) ____________ (not listen).

Sam: Yesterday we (9) ____________ (play) football in the park. After our game Marc (10) ____________ (feel) tired and (11) ____________ (not want) to walk. So dad (12) ____________ (carry) him all the way home!

Mary: I (13) ____________ (be) very happy on Saturday. I (14) ____________ (think) I (15) ____________ (not have) any money. But when I (16) ____________ (clean) my room I (17) ____________ (find) two pounds under my bed.

5.3 Fragen im Simple Past

• Marcs Freunde stellen ihm ein paar Fragen. Ordne diese Fragen Marcs Antworten auf der rechten Seite zu.

1. **Kim:** Did they look frightened?
2. **Jess:** Who saw them, too?
3. **Sarah:** How big was their plane?
4. **Laura:** When did you see them?
5. **Zoë:** Where did you meet them?
6. **Tom:** Were you frightened?

a. My dog saw them, too.
b. No, they looked funny.
c. I saw them on my way to school.
d. It was very, very small.
e. No, I was really cool.
f. I met them in the park.

BOXENSTOPP

Wie werden Fragen mit Vollverben im Simple Past gebildet? Vervollständige die Regel.

Subjekt **did** **was/were** **when** **where** **what** **who**

Bei Fragen ohne Fragewort steht im Simple Past __________ oder __________ vor dem __________ des Fragesatzes. Enthält ein Fragesatz jedoch ein Fragewort, wie z.B. __________, __________, __________ und __________, dann stehen diese vor **did** oder **was / were**.

Verneint werden Fragen im Simple Past mit dem Wörtchen **not** nach **did** oder **was/were**. Man verwendet dann allerdings meist die Kurzformen **didn't**, **wasn't** oder **weren't**. Hier ein paar Beispiele:

Didn't you go to school yesterday?	*Bist du gestern nicht in die Schule gegangen?*
Why **wasn't** he at home?	*Warum war er nicht zu Hause?*
Weren't they together at the shop?	*Waren sie nicht zusammen im Laden?*

•• Kannst du die folgenden Fragen wieder in die richtige Reihenfolge bringen? Achte auf die richtige Satzstellung!

1. he / did / play / the / this / piano / afternoon / ?

____

2. leave / they / did / when / house / the / ?

____

3. book / did / a / she / want / birthday / her / for / ?

____

4. did / where / stay / you / class trip / on / the / ?

____

••• Nach den Ferien unterhält sich Marc mit Sarah. Ergänze ihre Unterhaltung mit der jeweils richtigen Verbform im Simple Past, dann hast du's geschafft!

Marc: Hi Sarah. (1) ________ you ________ (get) my postcard?

Sarah: Yes, I (2) ________________ (do), thanks. I (3) ________________ (like) the picture on it. (4) ________ you ________ (stay) near that place?

Marc: Well, we (5) ________________ (not be) far from there, on Springfield Farm.

Sarah: Kim and I (6) ________________ (look) at a map and (7) ________________ (find) the place.

Marc: Kim? Oh – er – (8) ________ she ________ (see) my postcard?

Sarah: Well, I (9) ________________ (show) her the picture.

Marc: And – er – (10) ________ she ________ (read) what I (11) ________________ (write)?

Sarah: No, she (12) ________________ (not do). Don't worry, Marc. I (13) ________________ (not think) it (14) ________________ (be) a good idea to show her what you (15) ________________ (say) about Daniel!

6 DIE SATZSTELLUNG IN AUSSAGESÄTZEN

• Hier siehst du jeweils einen englischen Satz und die dazugehörige deutsche Übersetzung. Suche und markiere in beiden Sätzen das Subjekt des Satzes und das jeweilige Verb.

1. Every Saturday my sister reads a comic.	*Meine Schwester liest jeden Samstag einen Comic.*
2. We sometimes play tennis on Mondays.	*Montags spielen wir manchmal Tennis.*
3. Karen and Jenny must do their homework.	*Karen und Jenny müssen ihre Hausaufgaben machen.*
4. You're funny.	*Du bist lustig.*
5. I'm meeting Paul in front of the cinema at 6 o'clock.	*Ich treffe Paul um 6 Uhr vor dem Kino.*

BOXENSTOPP

Kannst du die folgende Regel vervollständigen?

Verb | Ortsangaben | allen | Objekt | Subjekt

In ____________ Aussagesätzen im Englischen gilt folgende Regel: Zunächst steht das ____________ des Satzes, danach das ____________, und schließlich das ____________. Die Formel dafür heißt also: **S V O**. Erst dann folgen ____________ und schließlich Zeitangaben in einem Aussagesatz.

Hier noch ein paar nützliche Tipps:

1. In englischen Aussagesätzen werden Verben in der Regel nicht voneinander getrennt:

   Daniel **can play** the guitar.

2. Adverbien der Häufigkeit, wie **often, sometimes, always, usually** und **never**, stehen zwischen dem Subjekt und dem Verb.

   She **never** goes to school by bus.

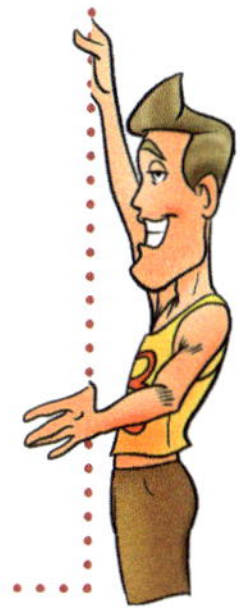

•• Jetzt kannst du dich selbst testen! Bringe die folgenden Sätze in die richtige Reihenfolge.

1. I / play / every Saturday / tennis

____

2. in the afternoon / our homework / do / we

____

3. often / listen / they / to music

____

4. to the city centre / go / I / by bus / always

____

5. never / go / my parents / to the cinema

____

••• Übersetze nun noch die folgenden Sätze ins Englische. Achte dabei vor allem auf die richtige Satzstellung. Na, hast du's gecheckt?

1. Sie frühstücken immer zusammen.

____

2. Jeden Samstag geht meine Schwester im Park spazieren.

____

3. Ich male gerade ein schönes Bild.

____

7 FRAGEWÖRTER

• Sieh dir die folgenden Fragen genau an. Markiere darin alle Fragewörter und versuche, diese ins Deutsche zu übersetzen.

1. **What** are your favourite pets? Was?

2. Where is my book? ______________

3. When is the meeting at the pool? ______________

4. How many pens are in your pencil case? ______________

5. Why is there so much homework, Mrs Black? ______________

6. Who is the new girl in our class? ______________

7. Which is your favourite colour? ______________

BOXENSTOPP

Wenn du den folgenden Satz ergänzt, dann hast du die Regel drauf!

die Form von to be | das Fragewort

Bei Fragen mit einem Fragewort und einer Form von **to be** gilt folgende Regel: Zuerst kommt ______________ und dann ______________.

Aufgepasst, hier lauern falsche Freunde: Verwechsle nicht die Fragewörter **who** und **where**! **Who** bedeutet auf Deutsch *wer*, und **where** bedeutet *wo*.

who = *wer*
where = *wo*

•• Ergänze in den folgenden Sätzen jeweils das richtige Fragewort. Du kannst **what, how, where** oder **who** einsetzen.

1. Your brother is not here. ______________ is he? – I have no idea.
2. ______________'s your name? – My name is Michael.
3. ______________ old is Sam? – He's eleven.
4. ______________ often do you play tennis? – I play every Monday.
5. ______________ can I do for you? – I need a blue pullover.
6. ______________ is Sarah? – She's still at school.
7. ______________ is playing with us? – Tony, Michael and Sandy.
8. ______________ long can we play? – For two hours.
9. ______________ is at the door? – I don't know.
10. ______________'s your telephone number? – It's 3-4-5-2.

••• Auf der rechten Seite siehst du einige Antworten. Findest du heraus, welche Frage jeweils dazu gestellt wurde? Das Beispiel zeigt dir, wie das geht. Viel Spaß beim Knobeln!

1. *Who are you?* **I'm Marc O'Brien.**
2. ______________________________ **I'm twelve.**
3. ______________________________ **She's from London.**
4. ______________________________ **The girl is ten.**
5. ______________________________ **Marc is at school.**
6. ______________________________ **His teacher is Mrs Black.**
7. ______________________________ **It's a biro.**
8. ______________________________ **The bag is on the table.**
9. ______________________________ **My pen is blue.**
10. ______________________________ **We're on page 10.**
11. ______________________________ **It's my homework.**

8 DIE MODALEN HILFSVERBEN

8.1 Bildung und Gebrauch der modalen Hilfsverben

- Lies dir das Gespräch zwischen Kim und Jess aufmerksam durch und markiere darin alle modalen Hilfsverben (**can/can't, must/mustn't, needn't**), die du finden kannst.

Kim: Can I listen to your new CD, Jess?
Jess: No, you can't. You can listen to your CDs.
Kim: They're at Delilah's house. I can't listen to them.
Jess: Maybe you can go to Delilah's house to get your CDs.
Kim: No, I can't. I must do my homework.
Jess: Kim! You can do your homework and listen to your CDs!
Kim: Oh Jess! My mother says I mustn't do my homework and listen to music at the same time.
Jess: Ok. You needn't go to Delilah's house. You can listen to my CDs now.

BOXENSTOPP

Jetzt bist du gefragt: Kannst du die folgenden Verben ins Deutsche übersetzen? Dann hast du schon einen guten Überblick über die Modalverben!

Kurzform	Langform	Übersetzung
can	-	____________
can't	**cannot**	____________
must	-	____________
mustn't	**must not**	____________
needn't	**need not**	____________

Noch ein kleiner Hinweis: Da die Verben **can, can't, must, mustn't** und **needn't** Hilfsverben sind, können sie **nicht** alleine stehen und werden **immer** von einem Vollverb begleitet!

•• Sieh dir die folgenden Sätze genau an und entscheide jeweils, ob die Satzstellung richtig oder falsch ist.

	Richtig	Falsch
1. I mustn't in the house play with my friends.	☐	☐
2. I can play in the garden with my friends.	☐	☐
3. I can't with my friends play in the house.	☐	☐
4. I must do my homework.	☐	☐
5. I needn't to your CDs listen.	☐	☐

•• Mit dieser Übung wirst du richtig fit! Ergänze die folgenden Sätze mit den Verben in Klammern und entscheide dabei jeweils, welches Modalverb (**can, can't, must, mustn't** oder **needn't**) du benutzen musst. Das Beispiel zeigt dir, wie's funktioniert!

1. Jimmy and Luke *can't write* (not write) a letter in English.

2. The children ______________ (not stay) in the woods after 9 o'clock at night.

3. Sally ______________ (jump) into the pool.

4. Delilah and Kim ______________ (not get up) early, they ______________ (sleep) until 10 o'clock.

5. The parents ______________ (bring) two camping chairs, so we can all have a picnic.

8.2 Die Bildung von Fragen mit *can*

• Jetzt wird's etwas knifflig: Schau dir die Beispielsätze mit **can** genau an und markiere darin jeweils das Subjekt, das Hilfsverb und das Vollverb mit unterschiedlichen Farben.

Aussagesatz	Frage	Frage mit Fragewort
Sally can give you the book.	Can Sally give you the book?	When can Sally give you the book?
Marc can buy the camera.	Can Marc buy the camera?	When can Marc buy the camera?

BOXENSTOPP

Ergänze nun die Regel zur Bildung von Fragen mit **can**. Na, alles klar?

vor zwischen nach

Im Aussagesatz steht **can** ______________ dem Subjekt des Satzes. Bei Fragen wird **can** ______________ das Subjekt des Satzes gestellt, und bei Fragen mit Fragewörtern steht **can** ______________ dem Fragewort und dem Subjekt des Satzes.

•• In jeder der folgenden Wortschlangen hat sich eine Frage mit **can** versteckt. Schreibe die richtigen Fragen auf und achte dabei besonders auf die richtige Satzstellung. Das Beispiel zeigt dir, wie's geht.

1. docanyourdancesdincewithtome?

Can you dance with me?

2. canhaveyoutheybeisnicebesttoaboutyouryousisterdelilah?

____

3. gocantheythemplayplayingintheasgarden?

____

4. doescanthemhesitsittingnexttoonmeourin?

____

••• Denke dir die jeweils passende Frage zu den vorgegebenen Antworten aus, dann hast du's geschafft!

1. *Can old people run 400 metres in one minute?*
   No, old people can't run 400 metres in one minute.
2. ______________________________
   No, I can't help you with your Maths homework.
3. ______________________________
   Yes, I can give you the bag from the table.
4. ______________________________
   No, I don't know when Sam can help you.
5. ______________________________
   Yes, I can carry so many books!

Übrigens: Fragen mit **must** werden genauso gebildet wie Fragen mit **can**.

9 DIE ARTIKEL

9.1 Der unbestimmte Artikel *a* oder *an*

• Sieh dir die folgenden Wörter genau an.
Kannst du hier einen Unterschied feststellen?

an exercise book

a pencil case

a CD

a book

an idea

an apple

BOXENSTOPP

Kannst du die folgende Regel zum unbestimmten Artikel ergänzen?

Konsonant

Vokal

ein

eine

Den unbestimmten Artikel **a** oder **an** übersetzt man ins Deutsche mit (1) __________ oder (2) __________. Man verwendet **a**, wenn das folgende Substantiv mit einem gesprochenen (3) ______________________ beginnt. **An** wird hingegen benutzt, wenn das folgende Wort mit einem gesprochenen (4) ______________________ beginnt.

Aufgepasst, Sportsfreunde: Es heißt **a uniform** und **a unit**, aber **an uncle**. Den Unterschied hört man beim Sprechen!

•• Ordne die Wörter auf der rechten Seite in die Tabelle ein. Entscheide jeweils, ob du **a** oder **an** verwenden musst.

a	an
funny uncle	

answer – right answer – easy question – old CD – ~~funny uncle~~ – silly exercise – swimming pool – great CD – orange folder – good idea – Indian friend – English book – tennis racket – empty bottle – brilliant game

••• So, und jetzt kannst du dich selbst testen. Ergänze die folgenden Sätze mit dem jeweils richtigen unbestimmten Artikel: **a** oder **an**?

1. Sarah and Sam have got ________ computer in their room.

2. The pupils in class 5a have got ________ extra sports day at school.

3. They have got ________ rabbit in ________ cage in the garden.

4. It has ________ apple in its mouth.

5. Helen has got ________ TV in her room.

6. We have got ________ English girl in our class, and she has ________ nice brother.

9.2 Der bestimmte Artikel *the*

- Sieh dir die folgenden Ausdrücke mit dem bestimmten Artikel **the** einmal genau an und spreche sie laut aus. Fällt dir etwas auf?

the best pizza **the classroom** **the ocean** **the girl from England**

the sea side **the answer** **the uniform** **the orange folder**

the tidy room **the example** **the unit**

BOXENSTOPP

Kannst du die Regel schon selbst ergänzen?

männliche | Vokal | weibliche | bestimmte | Plural

Der ____________ Artikel **the** wird im Englischen sowohl für ____________ als auch für ____________ Substantive im Singular und im ____________ verwendet. Aber aufgepasst bei der Aussprache: Vor einem gesprochenen ____________ spricht man **[ði:]** und vor einem gesprochenen Konsonant **[ðə]**.

•• Ordne die Ausdrücke aus der Aufwärmübung in die folgende Tabelle ein, je nachdem, ob man den bestimmten Artikel **[ðə]** oder **[ði:]** ausspricht.

[ðə]	[ði:]
____________	____________
____________	____________
____________	____________
____________	____________
____________	
____________	
____________	
____________	

••• Zum Abschluss kannst du dir noch die folgenden Sätze ansehen. Kreuze bei jedem Satz an, wie man den bestimmten Artikel **the** ausspricht.

	[ðə]	[ði:]
1. I have got the old books from Henry.	☐	☐
2. She has got the new film by Spike Jones.	☐	☐
3. Has she got the oranges for a drink?	☐	☐
4. This is the unit from our English book.	☐	☐
5. This is the new unit from our French book.	☐	☐

10 HAVE GOT UND HAS GOT

• Kannst du die Tabelle mit der jeweils richtigen Form vervollständigen?

Langformen	Kurzformen
I **have got** a new football.	I 've got
You **have got** a nice room.	you ______
He **has got** a sister.	he 's got
She **has got** a new book.	she ______
It **has got** 300 pages.	it ______
We **have got** a new English teacher.	we ______
You **have got** little puppies.	you ______
They **have got** a tree in their garden.	they ______

BOXENSTOPP

Ergänze die folgende Regel, dann weißt du, wie man **have got** und **has got** verwendet!

has got | **besitzt** | **she**

Wenn man ausdrücken möchte, dass man etwas hat oder ______________, dann benutzt man im Englischen **have got** oder (bei **he**, ________ und **it**) ______________.

Noch zwei wichtige Tipps:

1. Fragen mit **have got** und **has got** bildet man, indem man **have** oder **has** vor das Subjekt setzt.
2. Die Verneinung wird einfach mit **not** gebildet:

I **haven't got** a new football. She **hasn't got** a new book.

•• Jetzt bist du gefragt: Ergänze die folgenden Fragen mit **have got** oder **has got** und beantworte sie für dich.

1. Have you got a new school bag? No, I haven't. / Yes, I have.
2. ________ your family ________ a house? ________
3. ________ your friends ________ a dog? ________
4. ________ your mother ________ a car? ________
5. ________ your grandparents ________ pets? ________
6. ________ your father ________ a computer? ________

••• Schau dir die Hinweise genau an, und beantworte anschließend die untenstehenden Fragen. Die Beispiele zeigen dir, wie's funktioniert!

~~football magazines~~ / comics
~~sister~~ / brother
dog / ~~cat~~
new CD / ~~new DVD~~
~~car~~ / bicycle
~~folder~~ / book
~~tennis rackets~~ / inline skates

1. Have the boys got football magazines?
No, they haven't. They've got comics.
2. Has Kim got a dog?
Yes, she has. But she hasn't got a cat.
3. Have Marc's parents got a car?
____
4. Has Kim got a sister?
____
5. Has Marc got a new CD?
____
6. Have Kim and Delilah got tennis rackets?
____
7. Has Mrs Burton got a folder?
____

Aufgepasst bei den Kurzformen: Hier kann man **has** und **is** leicht verwechseln. Vergleiche:

She's **got** a nice room.	She **has got** a nice room.
She's nice.	She **is** nice.

11 WOULD LIKE TO UND WANT TO

- Lies dir den folgenden Dialog aufmerksam durch.

Waiter: Hello, a table for how many people, please?
Mr Burton: There are four of us.
Waiter: Here you are, a table for four. And here's the menu.
Mrs Burton: Thank you.
Waiter: What would you like to drink?
Sam: I want to drink a large orange juice!
Mrs Burton: Sam, that's not polite. Order again, please.
Sam: I would like to have a large orange juice, please. Is that ok, Mum?
Mrs Burton: Well done. Yes, that's ok.

BOXENSTOPP

Na, hast du herausgefunden, wie man **would like to** und **want to** benutzt? Ergänze die folgende Regel.

Ich will... | höflich | *Ich möchte gerne...*

Man benutzt **would like to**, wenn man ____________ sein will. **I would like to...** bedeutet ____________ und **I want to...** übersetzt man im Deutschen mit ____________.

Nach **would like to** und **want to** steht immer der Infinitiv des Verbs. Aber aufgepasst bei **want to:** Bei **he, she** und **it** nicht das **-s** vergessen!

She wants to drink a large orange juice.

•• Verbinde die deutschen Erklärungen auf der linken Seite mit den passenden englischen Sätzen rechts.

1. Deine Mama fragt deinen Freund, ob er etwas trinken möchte.
2. Die Lehrerin fragt, wer vorlesen möchte.
3. Jess möchte unbedingt die neue CD haben.
4. Die Kinder sitzen am Tisch und sind ziemlich hungrig.

a. Mum, we want to eat something.
b. Who would like to read?
c. Would you like to drink a lemonade, Daniel?
d. But dad, I really want to have this CD!

••• Jetzt bist du gefragt: Ergänze in den folgenden Sätzen entweder **would like to** oder **want to**, dann hast du auch dieses Kapitel geschafft!

1. Teacher: I ______________________ have some of your exercise books.

2. Marc: But Mum, I really ______________________ have chocolate.

3. Sarah to Kim: My brother ______________________ buy a computer.

4. In the café: My daughter ______________________ drink a hot chocolate, please.

12 SINGULAR UND PLURAL

• Sieh dir die folgenden Wörter genau an und überlege schon einmal, welche Substantive zusammen gehören.

Singular	Plural
foot postcard mouse sheep tooth sandwich woman potato box fish class knife child country	postcards countries feet mice sheep teeth classes children sandwiches fish potatoes women boxes knives

BOXENSTOPP

Und hier sind die wichtigsten Regeln zur Bildung von Pluralformen! Findest du zu jeder Regel ein Beispiel aus der Aufwärmübung?

1. Regelmäßige Pluralformen bildet man, indem man **-s** an die Singularform anhängt.

   Beispiel: ______

2. Wenn ein Substantiv im Singular auf **Konsonant + o**, auf **-ch, -s, -ss, -sh** oder **-x** endet, dann hängt man im Plural die Endung **-es** an:

   Beispiel: ______

3. Endet ein Substantiv im Singular auf **-y**, dann wird daraus im Plural **-ies**:

   Beispiel: ______

4. Viele Substantive, die im Singular auf **-f** oder **-fe** enden, werden im Plural mit **-ves** gebildet:

   Beispiel: ______

5. Einige Substantive haben im Singular und Plural die gleiche Form:

   Beispiel: ______

6. Und schließlich gibt es eine ganze Menge Substantive mit unregelmäßigem Plural, also mit völlig unterschiedlichen Formen:

   Beispiel: ______

•• Jetzt bist du gefragt: Kannst du die Wörter im Plural aus der Aufwärmübung in die folgende Tabelle einordnen? Die Rubriken entsprechen den Regeln im Boxenstopp. Wenn du möchtest, darfst du auch noch weitere Substantive ergänzen!

1. Regelmäßiger Plural	2. Plural auf -es	3. Plural auf -ies
______	______	______
	______	
	______	
	______	

4. Plural auf -ves	5. Singular = Plural	6. Unregelmäßiger Plural
______	______	______
	______	______
		______
		______
		______

Aufgepasst Sportsfreunde: Das Wörtchen **people** steht in der Bedeutung *Leute* bereits im Plural. Hier darf man also kein **-s** mehr anhängen!

••• Ergänze nun noch die folgenden Sätze mit dem jeweils passenden Wort. Achte aber darauf, dass du die vorgegebenen Wörter erst noch in den Plural setzen musst!

fish | foot | CD | child | sheep | mouse | cat | country

1. Look, there are two ____________________ in the pond.
2. Two black ____________________ are in their basket in the kitchen.
3. There are three ____________________ in my family.
4. My uncle has got a farm. He has got twenty ____________________.
5. Aaaaahhhh, there are four ____________________ on the floor.
6. We are three girls. Together we have got six ____________________.
7. I like to listen to my new ____________________.
8. Germany and France are two ____________________ in Europe.

13 THERE IS UND THERE ARE

• Sieh dir die folgenden Bilder genau an und ergänze darunter entweder **there is** oder **there are**.

1. ______________ four eggs on the table.

2. Look! ______________ a book on the chair.

3. ______________ a dog on the floor.

4. ______________ two mice under the bed.

BOXENSTOPP

Ergänze die Regel mit den angegebenen Begriffen. Na, hast du sie verstanden?

there is | **there are** | Dinge | *sind* | Singular | Personen | Plural | *ist*

Mit ________ oder **there are** kann man auf ________ oder ________ hinweisen. Im ________ benutzt man **there is** oder kurz **there's**. Im ________ benutzt man ________. Übersetzt ins Deutsche sagt man *es gibt*, (*es / da*) ________ oder (*es / da*) ________.

•• Jetzt kannst du dich selbst testen: Wie übersetzt man **there is** oder **there are** in den folgenden Sätzen ins Deutsche?

1. There is a new girl in our class.
   In unserer Klasse ________ ein neues Mädchen.
2. There's a monster in my room.
   In meinem Zimmer ________ ein Monster.
3. There are two green books on my bed.
   ________ *zwei grüne Bücher auf meinem Bett.*

Wenn man ausdrücken möchte, dass es etwas **nicht** gibt, dann verwendet man die verneinten Formen **there isn't** und **there aren't**.

••• Endspurt in diesem Kapitel, Sportsfreunde! Ergänze in den folgenden Sätzen **there is, there are, there isn't** oder **there aren't**, dann hast du schon wieder einiges geschafft!

Look at our house. (1) ________ four rooms downstairs and three rooms upstairs. (2) ________ (not) a room for me because I share a room with my sister. (3) ________ four people in our house and (4) ________ one dog. His name is Skippy. (5) ________ four cats, too. We love animals. In our garden behind the house, (6) ________ a pond. But (7) ________ (not) ten fish in the pond anymore, now (8) ________ twelve fish.

14 MUCH, MANY UND A LOT OF

• Kannst du den Fragen auf der linken Seite die jeweils passende Antwort rechts zuordnen?

1. Marc: Are there many nice girls in your class?	**a. Mum:** Yes dear, there are a lot of apples in the kitchen.
2. Sally: How much money have you got?	**b. Sarah:** There are twelve boys in my class.
3. Kim: Mum, have you got an apple for me?	**c. Sam:** Yes, there are a lot of nice girls in my class.
4. Jane: How many boys are in your class?	**d. Tony:** I've got a lot of money, I've got £2.

BOXENSTOPP

Aufgepasst, die Regel ist ein bisschen knifflig!
Kannst du sie trotzdem ergänzen?

a lot of | nicht zählbaren | zählbaren | lots of

Much steht vor ______________________ Substantiven, und **many** steht vor ______________________. Beide Mengenangaben werden hauptsächlich in **Fragen** und **verneinten Aussagesätzen** benutzt. In **bejahten Aussagesätzen** wird dagegen meistens ______________ oder ______________ verwendet.

Das solltest du dir merken: **Money** ist im Englischen nicht zählbar – genauso wie **time**! Man sagt also:

I don't have **much** money. *Ich habe nicht viel Geld.*
I don't have **much** time. *Ich habe nicht viel Zeit.*

•• Zählbar oder nicht zählbar? Ergänze in den folgenden Sätzen jeweils entweder **much** oder **many**.

1. Good. There aren't ______________ people in this shop.
2. Come on. We haven't got ______________ time.
3. There are so ______________ nice things here.
4. Don't spend too ______________ money.
5. How ______________ sweets are in the tin?
6. How ______________ is it? *(Wie viel kostet es?)*

••• Jetzt noch einmal volle Konzentration, einverstanden? Ergänze in den folgenden Sätzen entweder **much, many** oder **a lot of**, dann hast du's geschafft!

1. Sarah and Sam have got ______________ toys in their room.
2. Has Henry got ______________ animals on his farm?
3. Mrs Burton has got ______________ tea left.
4. Oh, that shirt is very expensive. That's too ______________ money for me.
5. I want to drink a glass of lemonade, but there's not ______________ left in the bottle.
6. Do you know how ______________ cats your aunt Jane has got?

15 DEMONSTRATIVBEGLEITER

• Sieh dir die folgenden Sätze einmal genauer an. Wie verwendet man die Demonstrativbegleiter?

1. That pullover over there is red, but **this** pullover here is green.
2. This book is about dogs, and **that** book there in the corner is about cats.
3. These apples here are red, but **those** apples are green.

BOXENSTOPP

Hier siehst du die Demonstrativbegleiter einmal im Überblick:

Singular	Plural
this	**these**
that	**those**

Kannst du jetzt die Regel selbst ergänzen?

Sprechers · that · Substantiven · these

This und __________ verwendet man zusammen mit ______________, die sich in der Nähe des ______________ befinden.
Und umgekehrt benutzt man ______________ und **those** bei Substantiven, die etwas weiter weg sind.

•• Welcher Demonstrativbegleiter ist hier richtig? Streiche jeweils die falschen Formen durch.

1. **Sally:** Marc, would you like **that / these** comics here or **these / those** over there?
2. **Marc:** I would like to have **these / this** comics, please.
3. **Sally:** Ok. And do you like **this / these** cake?
4. **Marc:** No, I like **that / those** cake over there.
5. **Sally:** Are **those / that** girls over there at your school?
6. **Marc:** No, **those / that** over there aren't. But this / these girl here is.

•• Und nun noch einmal volle Konzentration, dann hast du wieder ein Kapitel geschafft! Ergänze in den folgenden Sätzen die jeweils richtigen Demonstrativbegleiter.

1. ______________ pullover here is too big for you, but ______________ pullover is okay.
2. Oh look, right here! Aren't ______________ posters beautiful?
3. Just look over there! Can you see ______________ beautiful flowers?
4. I like ______________ green cap and ______________ blue sneakers much better than ______________ black cap and ______________ grey tennis shoes over there.

16 DER *S*-GENITIV UND DER *OF*-GENITIV

16.1 Der *s*-Genitiv

• Markiere in den folgenden Sätzen jeden **s**-Genitiv, den du finden kannst.

1. Tony's bike is blue and yellow.
2. This is the cat's biscuit.
3. These are the girls' books.
4. The Burtons' house is near a forest.

BOXENSTOPP

Kannst du die Regel zum **s**-Genitiv schon selbst vervollständigen?

gehört | Personen | Lebewesen | **'s** | Apostroph

Mit dem Genitiv kann man ausdrücken, wem etwas ______________. Der **s**-Genitiv wird bei ______________ und anderen ______________ verwendet.

Im Singular wird einfach ______________ (Sätze 1 und 2) angehängt, im Plural dagegen nur der ______________ ('), da ein Substantiv im Plural meist bereits auf **-s** endet (Sätze 3 und 4).

Bei Substantiven, die den Plural nicht auf **-s** bilden, benutzt man **'s**:

The **children's** toys are in the way.
Das Spielzeug der Kinder steht im Weg.

•• Ergänze in den folgenden Sätzen jeweils den **s**-Genitiv **'s** oder nur den Apostroph.

1. This is Marc _____ cat.
2. These are our neighbours _____ dogs.
3. This is the girls _____ hamster.
4. These are the dog _____ biscuits.
5. This is the boys _____ room.
6. These are the boys _____ skateboards.
7. This is the cat _____ toy.
8. These are Sam _____ pens.
9. This is the teacher _____ desk.
10. These are the children _____ lunchboxes.

••• Zum Abschluss wird's noch einmal etwas knifflig: Kannst du die folgenden Ausdrücke ins Deutsche übersetzen? Achte vor allem auf die Stellung des Apostrophs!

1. **my brother's friend** *der Freund meines Bruders*
2. **my brothers' friend** _____________________
3. **my brothers' friends** _____________________
4. **my brother's friends** _____________________
5. **the cats' basket** _____________________
6. **the cat's baskets** _____________________
7. **the cats' baskets** _____________________
8. **the cat's basket** _____________________

16.2 Der *of*-Genitiv

• Sieh dir die folgenden Sätze genau an und vergleiche sie miteinander. Fällt dir etwas auf?

1. I drink a bottle of water.
2. He gives me a box of candles.
3. There are three tins of dog food.
4. Sarah's picture is funny.
5. Sarah is Sam's sister.
6. The cat's bed is in the kitchen.

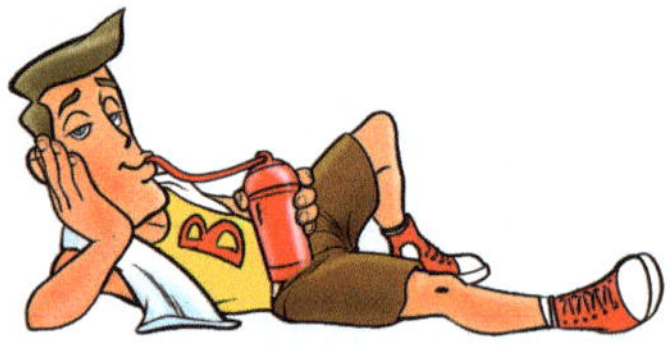

BOXENSTOPP

Na, hast du den Unterschied bei den Sätzen in der Aufwärmübung bemerkt? Prima, dann kannst du bestimmt die Regel selbst ergänzen!

Im Gegensatz zum **s**-Genitiv wird der **of**-Genitiv nur bei ______________________ verwendet,

sowohl im Singular als auch im ________________.

In der deutschen Umgangssprache hört man öfter Ausdrücke wie *der Sohn von Herrn Schmidt*. Das darfst du so aber auf keinen Fall ins Englische übersetzen, denn da Herr Schmidt eine Person ist, muss es **Mr Schmidt's son** heißen.

Übersetze die folgenden Sätze ins Deutsche.

1. The door of the house is green.

____

2. The chairs of class 5 are new.

____

3. The colour of the table is blue.

____

4. The prices of the t-shirts are high.

____

So, und jetzt kannst du selbst Sätze mit dem **of**-Genitiv bilden! Das Beispiel zeigt dir, wie's funktioniert.

1. C / third letter / alphabet

C is the third letter of the alphabet.

2. today / the first day / the week

____

3. the park / at the end / the road

____

4. the colour / the socks / green

____

5. the name / the street / Marble Lane

____

1 MEIN KÖRPER

- Marc hat seine Vokabeln nicht ordentlich aufgeschrieben. Nun sind sie völlig durcheinander geraten. Kannst du ihm helfen? Streiche alle Körperteile durch, die nicht zum menschlichen Körper gehören!

(1) **arm** (2) **head** (8) **eye** (15) **hand**
(16) **toe** (19) **wing** (4) **elbow** (17) **neck**
(6) **horn** (12) **knee** (13) **finger** (7) **beak**
(18) **foot** (10) **ear** (11) **tusk** (20) **tooth**
(5) **leg** (14) **fin** (3) **tail** (9) **belly**

Damit dir so etwas nicht auch passiert, kannst du neue Vokabeln zum Beispiel auf Karteikarten schreiben und in einen Karteikasten einsortieren!

BOXENSTOPP

Hier kannst Du noch einmal nachschauen, was an einem Menschen so alles dran ist:

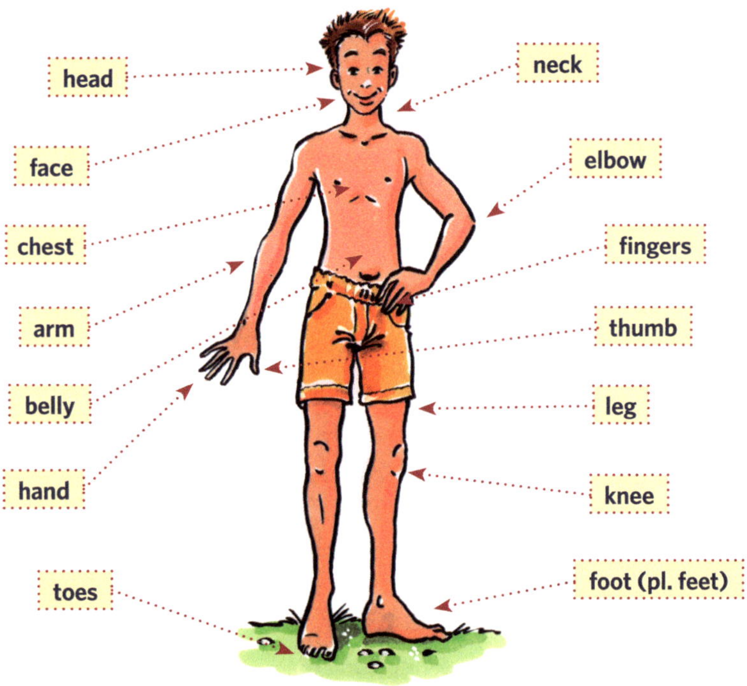

•• Am Kopf und im Gesicht gibt es eine ganze Menge wichtiger Dinge. Weißt du, wie sie auf Englisch heißen? Ordne die folgenden Wörter den jeweiligen Körperteilen in der Abbildung zu!

hair **mouth** **lips** **chin** **ears** **nose** **eyes** **teeth** **tongue** **cheek** **eyebrow**

1. ____________
2. ____________
3. ____________
4. ____________
5. ____________
6. ____________
7. ____________
8. ____________
9. ____________
10. ____________
11. ____________

Aufgepasst bei der Mehrzahl von **tooth** und **foot**: Es heißt **thirty-two teeth** und **two feet**!

••• Die verschiedenen Körperteile helfen dir, bestimmte Dinge zu tun. Ergänze die folgenden Sätze mit dem jeweils richtigen Verb.

kick | clap | shout | smell | run | hear | shake | watch

On the football field

1. My legs help me to ______________ very fast.

2. I ______________ the ball with one of my feet.

3. My parents ______________ me playing football with their eyes.

4. Sometimes they ______________ their hands.

5. I can ______________ that with my ears.

6. When I fall to the ground, I can ______________ the grass with my nose.

7. My father opens his mouth to ______________ "Come on, boy, get up!"

8. Then I get up, ______________ my whole body and go on playing.

••• Ordne nun noch die folgenden Verben den passenden Körperteilen in der Tabelle unten zu, dann kennst du dich bestens mit dem menschlichen Körper aus!

run **sing** **kick** **beat** **grasp** **eat** **stomp**

speak **dance** **write** **drink** **knock**

mouth	feet	hands

2 IN DER WELT DER TIERE

- In diesem Wortgitter haben sich insgesamt 20 verschiedene Tiere versteckt. Findest du sie alle? Du musst **von links nach rechts** und **von oben nach unten** lesen! Schau mal, der vorlaute Affe hat sich schon zu erkennen gegeben!

Y	E	L	E	P	H	A	N	T	J	B	I	R	D	R
C	A	R	K	A	N	G	A	R	O	O	R	U	H	A
A	C	O	W	C	O	C	K	H	I	P	P	O	O	T
T	H	E	N	T	D	U	C	K	Z	O	P	D	R	F
T	O	G	H	A	M	S	T	E	R	X	I	O	S	I
M	O	U	S	E	M	O	N	K	E	Y	G	G	E	S
D	G	I	R	A	F	F	E	R	A	B	B	I	T	H

Waagerecht	Senkrecht
1. ______	14. ______
2. ______	15. ______
3. ______	16. ______
4. ______	17. ______
5. ______	18. ______
6. ______	19. ______
7. ______	20. ______
8. ______	
9. ______	
10. ______	
11. ______	
12. ______	
13. ______	

BOXENSTOPP

Manchmal haben Tiere im Englischen einen sehr langen Namen. Weil das vielen Leuten zu umständlich ist, kürzen sie die Wörter einfach ab. Hier sind zwei wichtige Beispiele:

hippopotamus → **hippo** *Nilpferd*
budgerigar → **budgie** *Wellensittich*

Klingt doch gleich viel niedlicher, oder? Übrigens darfst du natürlich die Kurzform verwenden!

•• Die Tiere aus dem Wortgitter oben sind ja alle noch ganz wild durcheinander! Du weißt aber sicher, welche Tiere man zu Hause halten kann, welche auf einem Bauernhof leben und welche es im Zoo gibt, oder? Trage sie in die richtige Spalte ein und versuche, die Wörter ins Deutsche zu übersetzen!

pets *Haustiere*	**farm animals** *Tiere auf dem Bauernhof*	**animals in the zoo** *Zootiere*

Oh, hier laufen immer noch vier Tiere frei herum! Fange sie ein und bringe sie zu ihren Freunden in die richtige Spalte der Tabelle!

lion

guinea pig

crocodile

snake

Beim Spielen lernt man sehr schnell Vokabeln, wusstest du das? Du könntest dir mit deinen Freunden zum Beispiel ein Tier-Memory® basteln. Schreibt immer die englischen Tiernamen auf die Karten und sagt sie laut, wenn ihr die Kärtchen aufdeckt!

•• Heute war Kim mit ihrer Familie im Zoo. Jetzt möchte sie ihrer Cousine in Indien am Telefon erzählen, was sie alles gesehen hat. Leider kennt Kims Cousine nicht alle englischen Tiernamen. Kannst Du Kims Beschreibungen auf der rechten Seite dem jeweiligen Tier links zuordnen?

1. A tiger — **a.** walks slowly. On its back there is a hard shell.
2. A penguin — **b.** is a bird that can't fly. It lives in the Antarctic.
3. A zebra — **c.** has got two humps on its back.
4. A parrot — **d.** smells very, very badly!
5. A tortoise — **e.** can speak. It is a very colourful bird.
6. A seal — **f.** is a dangerous animal with yellow and black stripes.
7. A camel — **g.** looks like a tortoise but it lives under water.
8. A turtle — **h.** looks like a snake but it lives under water.
9. A skunk — **i.** looks a bit like a horse but it has got black and white stripes.
10. An eel — **j.** lives under water and eats fish. It is always smiling!

3 IN DER SCHULE

• Jetzt darfst du dir erst einmal einen Stundenplan ganz nach deinem Geschmack zusammenstellen. Achte dabei aber darauf, dass jedes Schulfach (**subject**) aus der Liste auf der nächsten Seite mindestens einmal vorkommt!

	Monday	Tuesday	Wednesday	Thursday	Friday
1st period					
2nd period					
3rd period					
4th period					
5th period					
6th period					

Subjects			
English	*Englisch*	**Biology**	*Biologie*
German	*Deutsch*	**Sports**	*Sport*
Mathematics	*Mathematik*	**Music**	*Musik*
History	*Geschichte*	**Art**	*Kunst*
Geography	*Erdkunde*	**free period**	*Freistunde*

BOXENSTOPP

Auch in der Schule werden lange Wörter abgekürzt. Wundere dich also nicht, wenn dir die folgenden **short forms** begegnen:

maths	=	**mathematics**	*Mathematik*
board	=	**blackboard**	*Tafel*
gym	=	**gymnasium**	*Turnhalle*
exam	=	**examination**	*Prüfung*
pen	=	**ballpoint pen**	*Kugelschreiber*

Schreibe dir auf deine Vokabelkärtchen immer die kurze und die lange Form! So bist du auf der sicheren Seite!

•• Marc hat viele verschiedene Stifte in seinem Mäppchen. Weißt du, welches Schreibgerät wie aussieht? Ordne die folgenden Sätze der jeweils richtigen Abbildung zu.

1.

2.

3.

There are many pens in Marc's pencil case.

a. At school he writes with his **fountain pen**.

b. He draws a picture with his **pencil**.

c. But he can't draw with the **felt-tip pen** – it is too thick!

d. He takes his **coloured pencil** to make the picture more colourful.

e. With his **wax crayon** he can make the picture more colourful, too.

f. At home he uses a **pen** to write notes to his brother.

4.

5.

6.

•• Das ist natürlich nicht alles, was Marc in seinem Schulranzen hat. Leider herrscht darin ein ziemliches Durcheinander. Kannst du die Dinge trotzdem erkennen? Schreibe sie in die mittlere Spalte der folgenden Tabelle.

1. burreb	______	*Radiergummi*
2. lurre	______	*Lineal*
3. licnep shenerarp	______	*Bleistiftspitzer*
4. rowkkobo	______	*Arbeitsbuch*
5. nulch obx	______	*Brotdose*
6. ecrexesi koob	______	*Heft*
7. corissss	______	*Schere*

••• Was du hier siehst, ist natürlich kein Wort, das du dir merken musst! In der Wortschlange haben sich aber insgesamt 10 Gegenstände und Personen versteckt, die du aus deinem Klassenzimmer kennst. Findest du alle Begriffe?

chalkteacherdustbinblackboardsatchelclassmatedeskspongechairpupil

1. ______________________ 6. ______________________
2. ______________________ 7. ______________________
3. ______________________ 8. ______________________
4. ______________________ 9. ______________________
5. ______________________ 10. ______________________

••• Die folgenden Sätze hast du bestimmt schon oft gehört. Daher fällt es dir sicher leicht, die passenden Verben an der jeweils richtigen Stelle zu ergänzen!

draw | write down | read | listen to | stand up | open | erase | wipe | sing | learn

1. ______________ and say "good morning"!
2. ______________ your books, please!
3. Who wants to ______________ the story?
4. Please be quiet and ______________ the CD!
5. Let's ______________ this song together!
6. The board is dirty. Please ______________ it with the sponge!
7. Don't ______________ pictures in your exercise book!
8. ______________ the picture with your rubber!
9. Don't forget to ______________ your homework!
10. ______________ the new vocabulary!

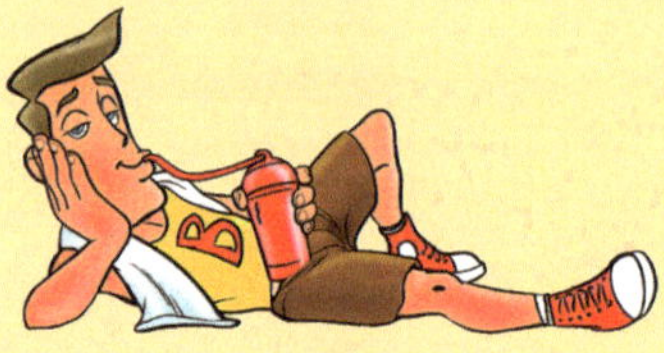

4 ZU HAUSE

- Kim teilt sich zu Hause ein Zimmer mit ihrer Schwester Delilah. Darin gibt es viele Sachen, die du bestimmt auch hast. Markiere im folgenden Text alles, was man auch in deinem Zimmer finden kann!

Kim's and Delilah's room

Kim and her sister have got a large room. It is nice and bright because there is a big **window** with pretty flowers on the **window sill**. There are also many **posters** and **pictures** on the **walls**. On the **floor** there is a very colourful **carpet** and on the **ceiling** there is a **lamp**. The two sisters do their homework at the **desk** that stands next to the **bookshelf**. They keep their clothes in the **wardrobe**. Next to the **door** there is Kim's and Delilah's **bunk bed**. Look, the **teddy bear** is still sleeping! But where are their **toys**? They are in the **cupboard**. This is a very tidy room!

BOXENSTOPP

Aufgepasst: Einige Substantive haben eine besondere Pluralform. Das Wort **shelf** gehört übrigens auch dazu:

one shel**f**	two shel**ves**	*Regal*
one kni**fe**	two kni**ves**	*Messer*
one hal**f**	two hal**ves**	*Hälfte*
one wol**f**	two wol**ves**	*Wolf*

Na, hast du die Regel gecheckt? Ergänze den folgenden Satz.

Immer wenn ein Wort im ______________ auf **-f** endet, wird die Mehrzahl mit ______________ gebildet.

Hier ein kleiner Tipp zum Vokabellernen: Schreibe dir neue Vokabeln immer auf kleine Karteikärtchen. Auf die Vorderseite kannst du das englische Wort schreiben und auf die Rückseite die deutsche Übersetzung. Besonderheiten, wie zum Beispiel die Pluralform mit **-ves**, gehören natürlich auch immer mit auf die Vokabelkärtchen.

•• Die verschiedenen Zimmer eines Hauses haben eigentlich ganz einfache Namen. Man kann daran schnell erkennen, was in diesem Zimmer getan wird. Versuch doch einmal dein Glück und ordne die Zimmer auf der rechten Seite den passenden Beschreibungen links zu!

1. You can take a bath	**a.** in the living room.
2. My parents' bed	**b.** in the dining room.
3. We keep our food	**c.** is in the bedroom.
4. We watch TV	**d.** in the children's room.
5. The children play and sleep	**e.** in the bathroom.
6. We have dinner	**f.** in the kitchen.
7. We prepare our meals	**g.** in the larder.

•• Bald wird Kim mit ihrer Familie in eine neue Wohnung ziehen. Die Zimmer sind schon aufgeteilt. Aber was gehört in welches Zimmer? Kims Vater grübelt schon die ganze Zeit. Hilf ihm doch dabei! In welches Zimmer würdest du die folgenden Gegenstände räumen? Ergänze die untenstehenden Sätze mit den jeweils passenden Möbelstücken.

1. The ______________ belongs into the living room.
2. We need the ______________ in the kitchen.
3. The children's ______________ belongs into the children's room.
4. All the ______________ belong into the children's room, too.
5. We want to have the ______________ in the living room.
6. The ______________ belongs into the dining room.
7. And we place all the ______________ round the table in the dining room.
8. My wife and I sleep in our ______________ in the bedroom.
9. The old ______________ looks great in the corner of the living room.
10. And we need a ______________ in every room.

sofa | stove | bunk bed | toys | TV set | table | chairs | armchair | lamp | double bed

Ein kleiner Tipp für die nächste Aufgabe: Vorsicht bei Verben! Es nützt nichts, wenn du Verben einfach nur auswendig lernst, du musst sie auch immer in die richtige Form bringen! Denke dabei vor allem and das **s** in der dritten Person Singular. Pssst, ich habe aber nichts gesagt...

•• Selbst nach dem Umzug hört die Arbeit nicht auf. Im Haushalt gibt es nämlich täglich viel zu erledigen. Weil aber jeder seine festen Aufgaben hat, geht das immer sehr schnell. Kim erzählt Marc in der Schule, wie die Aufgaben in ihrer Familie verteilt sind. Ergänze die untenstehenden Sätze mit Hilfe der Angaben in den Kreisen. Achte dabei auch immer auf die richtige Verbform!

Kim: lay the table · walk the dog · make the bed

Kim's mother: do the washing-up · clean the windows · do the washing

Delilah: water the flowers · tidy up · fold the washing

Kim's father: do the cooking · do the shopping · read the newspaper

1. I ____________________ before dinner.
2. After dinner I go outside and ____________________.
3. I ____________________ every morning.
4. My mother always ____________________ for all of us.
5. Sometimes she ____________________ in all of the rooms.
6. Every day after dinner she ____________________.
7. Delilah ____________________ our room everyday after dinner.
8. She also ____________________ and puts it into the wardrobe.
9. Then she ____________________ on the window sills.
10. After work my father ____________________ and then comes home.
11. Sometimes he helps my mother to ____________________.
12. In the evening we watch TV. But my father ____________________.

5 MEINE FAMILIE UND ICH

- Kannst du dich schon selbst vorstellen? Ergänze den folgenden Text mit Angaben zu deiner Person und kreuze dann in der Tabelle an, was du gerne magst.

Hello, my name is ________________. I come from ________________. This is a town in ________________. I'm ________ years old. I have got ________ brothers and ________ sisters. My mother's name is ________________ and my father is called ________________. And these are things I really like:

Hobbies *Hobbys*	**Favourite animals** *Lieblingstiere*	**Favourite programmes on TV** *Lieblingssendungen im Fernsehen*
☐ **swimming** *schwimmen*	☐ **dogs** *Hunde*	☐ ________________
☐ **computer games** *Computerspiele*	☐ **cats** *Katzen*	☐ ________________
☐ **singing** *singen*	☐ **rats** *Ratten*	☐ ________________
☐ **football** *Fußball*	☐ **lions** *Löwen*	☐ ________________
☐ **dancing** *tanzen*	☐ **horses** *Pferde*	☐ ________________
☐ ________________	☐ ________________	☐ ________________

BOXENSTOPP

Oft spricht man Familienmitglieder mit einer Koseform an. Einige davon hast du bestimmt schon einmal gehört, nicht wahr?

mother	**mum, mom, mummy, mommy**	*Mama*
father	**dad, daddy**	*Papa*
grandmother	**grandma, granny, gran**	*Oma*
grandfather	**granddad, granddaddy, grandpa**	*Opa*
aunt	**auntie**	*Tante*

In einer Anrede musst du diese Wörter groß schreiben! Man sagt zwar:
My **aunt** is called Jane. aber How are you, **Aunt** Jane?

•• Welche Puzzleteile passen zusammen? Ordne die richtigen Paare zu und ergänze die fehlenden englischen Ausdrücke.

mother Mutter

_______ Vater

grandfather

cousin

niece

father

uncle

son

husband

great grandmother

sister

brother Bruder

_______ Schwester

great grandfather Urgroßvater

_______ Urgroßmutter

aunt Tante

_______ Onkel

grandmother Großmutter

_______ Großvater

nephew Neffe

_______ Nichte

wife Ehefrau

_______ Ehemann

cousin Cousin

_______ Cousine

daughter Tochter

_______ Sohn

Für bestimmte Personengruppen gibt es Sammelbegriffe. Zum Beispiel sind **mother** und **father** beide **parents**. Oder **grandmother** und **grandfather** sind beide **grandparents**. Diese neuen Vokabeln kannst du gleich in der nächsten Übung ausprobieren!

••• Sieh dir den Stammbaum von Marcs Familie einmal genau an und ergänze anschließend den nachfolgenden Text mit den fehlenden Begriffen. Ein kleiner Tipp: Alle fehlenden Wörter sind dir in diesem Kapitel schon einmal begegnet!

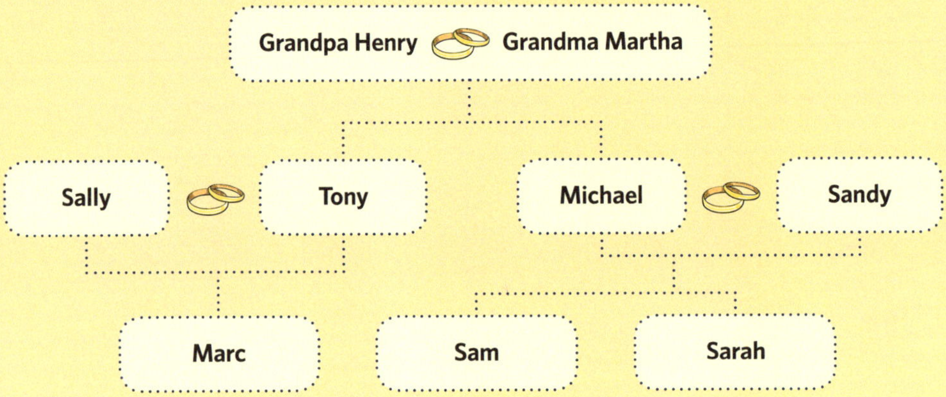

Tony is married to Sally. So they are (1) ______________ and (2) ______________. They have got a (3) ______________ whose name is Marc. They are his (4) ______________. Tony's (5) ______________, Michael, has got a (6) ______________, too. But Michael has also got a (7) ______________. She is Sam's (8) ______________ and Marc's (9) ______________. The (10) ______________ of Tony and Michael are called Henry and Martha. They are Sarah's, Sam's and Marc's (11) ______________. Marc is always excited when they all meet because (12) ______________ Sandy and (13) ______________ Michael bring a present for him. But Sally and Tony have got presents for their (14) ______________ Sarah and their (15) ______________ Sam, too.

Und noch eine etwas knifflige Frage zum Schluss. Marc hat eine Postkarte erhalten. Darauf steht nur die folgende merkwürdige Frage:

Who is that?

16. Your uncle has got a father, whose son's niece has got an aunt, whose son is called ______________.

Na, wer ist hier gemeint?

6 DATUM UND UHRZEIT

• Delilah und Kim haben sich einen neuen Kalender gekauft. Sie sind gerade dabei, alle wichtigen Termine einzutragen. Leider stimmt die Reihenfolge der Termine aber nicht mehr. Kannst du hier wieder für Ordnung sorgen, indem du die Termine der beiden durchnummerierst?

25th of December	**Christmas Day**	________
2nd of December	**Delilah's birthday**	________
26th of December	**Boxing Day**	________
1st of December	**School trip to London**	________
23rd of December	**Daddy's Birthday**	________

BOXENSTOPP

Wenn du ein Datum angeben möchtest, musst du **Ordnungszahlen (cardinal numbers)** verwenden. Du hast schon gesehen, dass man sie ganz einfach bilden kann: An die Zahlen ab 4 wird einfach ein **th** angehängt. Aber aufgepasst bei 1, 2 und 3!

the **first**	**1st**	*der/die/das erste*
the **second**	**2nd**	*der/die/das zweite*
the **third**	**3rd**	*der/die/das dritte*
the four**th**	**4th**	*der/die/das vierte*
the fif**th**	**5th**	*der/die/das fünfte*
the six**th**	**6th**	*der/die/das sechste*

Hast du ganz genau hingeschaut? Super, dann hast du bestimmt gesehen, dass sich bei **fifth** ein **f** eingeschlichen hat, richtig? Aus **five** wird also **fifth** und aus **twelve** wird **twelfth**!

•• Bei den folgenden Aufzählungen hat sich jeweils ein Fehler eingeschlichen. Welcher Begriff passt nicht dazu?

1. **morning, afternoon, evening, second**
2. **winter, spring, August, summer**
3. **Monday, Saturday, week, Wednesday**
4. **autumn, minute, hour, second**
5. **January, Tuesday, September, June, July**
6. **year, season, month, night**

•• In der folgenden Tabelle siehst du die wichtigsten Vokabeln zum Wortfeld **Datum und Jahreszeiten**. Kannst du die deutschen Übersetzungen ergänzen?

The day *Der Tag*	**The week** *Die Woche*	**The months** *Die Monate*	**The seasons** *Die Jahreszeiten*
morning **1.** ______	**Monday** **6.** ______	**January** **13.** ______	**spring** **25.** ______
noon **2.** ______	**Tuesday** **7.** ______	**February** **14.** ______	**summer** **26.** ______
afternoon **3.** ______	**Wednesday** **8.** ______	**March** **15.** ______	**autumn** **27.** ______
evening **4.** ______	**Thursday** **9.** ______	**April** **16.** ______	**winter** **28.** ______
night **5.** ______	**Friday** **10.** ______	**May** **17.** ______	
	Saturday **11.** ______	**June** **18.** ______	
	Sunday **12.** ______	**July** **19.** ______	
		August **20.** ______	
		September **21.** ______	
		October **22.** ______	
		November **23.** ______	
		December **24.** ______	

Hast du durchschaut, wie das mit den Wortfeldern funktioniert? Genau, wenn man mehrere Wörter unter einem Oberbegriff sortiert, erhält man ein Wortfeld. Auch du kannst dir Vokabeln besser merken, wenn du sie nach Wortfeldern ordnest. Dabei darfst du selbst entscheiden, wie du sie sortierst.

•• Kim hat heute noch vier Termine. Neben dem Chor und der Klavierstunde soll noch ein Abendessen mit Freunden stattfinden. Außerdem muss sie sich noch etwas Zeit für die Hausaufgaben nehmen. Ordne die Uhren den entsprechenden Terminen zu!

1. **2.** **3.** **4.**

a. Kim sings in the children's choir at six o'clock.
b. Kim goes to her piano lesson at half past three.
c. Kim does her homework at a quarter to five.
d. The whole family has supper with friends at a quarter past seven.

•• Es gibt noch eine weitere Möglichkeit, wie du die Uhrzeit ausdrücken kannst. Wenn ein Termin zwischen Mitternacht und 12:00 Uhr mittags liegt, schreibst du hinter die Uhrzeit das Kürzel **a.m.** Liegt der Termin aber in der anderen Hälfte des Tages, dann versiehst du die Uhrzeit mit einem **p.m.** Alles klar? Probier's gleich mal aus!

1. Kim and Delilah get up at 7:15 ________.

2. They have supper at 7:15 ________.

3. School starts at 9:00 ________.

4. They go to bed at 9:00 ________.

5. They play in the garden at 5:00 ________.

6. All the family is fast asleep at 3:00 ________.

7 ESSEN UND TRINKEN

• In Großbritannien sieht das Frühstück möglicherweise anders aus, als du es von zu Hause kennst. In der Wortschlange findest du 10 Nahrungsmittel. Ordne sie in die Tabelle auf der nächsten Seite ein! Was gehört unbedingt auf einen englischen Frühstückstisch?

eggsteahamsandbeansbonessausageselephanttoastcerealsshampoobuttermarmaladecoffeechips

English breakfast table
englischer Frühstückstisch

1. ____________________
2. ____________________
3. ____________________
4. ____________________
5. ____________________
6. ____________________
7. ____________________
8. ____________________
9. ____________________
10. ____________________

BOXENSTOPP

Hast du bemerkt, was bei der Pluralform **potatoes** passiert ist? Richtig, da ist nicht einfach nur ein **-s**, sondern ein **-es** angehängt worden. Du kannst dir also merken, dass die Mehrzahl von Wörtern, die auf **-o** enden, mit **-es** gebildet wird. Das ist außer bei **potatoes** und **tomatoes** auch bei **buffaloes** so, obwohl man die nicht zum Frühstück verdrückt!

Nur eine Mahlzeit reicht einem Sportler aber nicht aus! Deshalb verrate ich dir noch die anderen: Das *Mittagessen* wird als **lunch** bezeichnet und das *Abendessen* nennt man **supper**. **Dinner** heißt das Essen nur, wenn richtig gekocht wird. Das kann am Mittag oder am Abend sein.

•• Marc ist beim Schüleraustausch in Deutschland. Er hat für ein typisch englisches Essen eingekauft. Vergleiche seinen Einkaufszettel mit dem Kassenbon! Was gehört zusammen?

Marc's shopping list *Marcs Einkaufszettel*	**Receipt** *Kassenbon*
1. fillet of fish	**a.** Pommes Frites
2. chips	**b.** Brot
3. vinegar	**c.** Tunfisch
4. bread	**d.** Kopfsalat
5. cucumber	**e.** Essig
6. cheese	**f.** Käse
7. tuna	**g.** Fischfilet
8. lettuce	**h.** Gurke

•• Während Marc in Deutschland einkauft, wollen sich Kim und Delilah eine Pizza bestellen. Erkennst du, welche Beläge sie bestellt haben? Ergänze die untenstehenden Sätze mit den jeweils richtigen Begriffen.

Kim's pizza

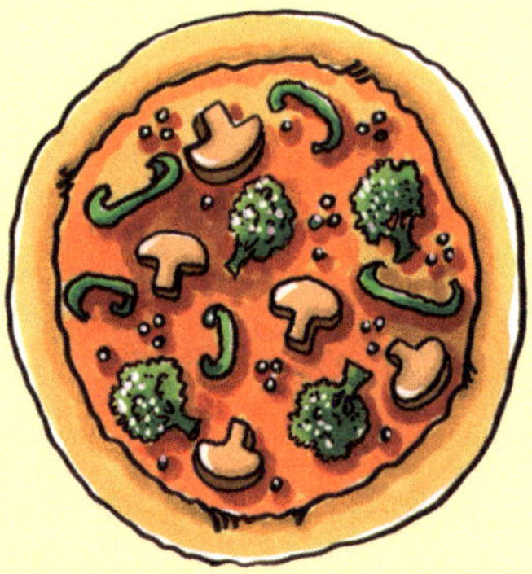

Delilah's pizza

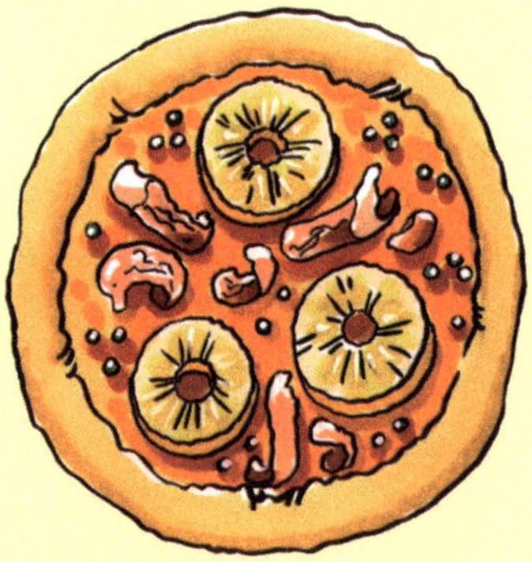

Pino's Pizza Delivery

Choose any of these toppings for your pizza:

ham	olives
salami	artichoke
chicken	paprika
mushrooms	banana
onion	pineapple
broccoli	egg
extra cheese	garlic

!!! call free !!!
24 25 26

1. Kim's pizza is with ________________, ________________ and ________________.

2. Delilah's pizza is with ________________ and ________________.

••• Während Marc in Deutschland ist, ist auch eine Austauschschülerin bei seinen Eltern. Ihr Name ist Lea. Auch sie muss einkaufen gehen. Vorher erklärt Marcs Mutter ihr, was sie alles besorgen soll. Kannst du ihr die deutschen Übersetzungen der hervorgehobenen Vokabeln verraten?

	Übersetzungen
1. **Peas** are those little, green balls.	______________
2. Rabbits love **carrots**.	______________
3. When I cut **onions** I must cry.	______________
4. Spaghetti and macaroni are called **pasta**.	______________
5. **Apples**? Come on, you know that word!	______________
6. And **pears** look a little bit like apples, but only a little bit.	______________
7. **Bananas** are yellow and curved.	______________
8. **Orange juice** is a drink made of oranges.	______________
9. Those little slices of potatoes are called **crisps**. They are in a bag.	______________
10. We need **tomatoes** for our spaghetti sauce.	______________
11. And we need **chicken** for our Asian dinner.	______________
12. **Pork** is the meat of a pig.	______________
13. **Beef** is the meat of a cow.	______________
14. And please bring **a bar of chocolate**! That's for you!	______________

Zu diesem Thema kannst du übrigens prima Wortfelder anlegen! Passende Überbegriffe sind zum Beispiel **vegetables** *(Gemüse)*, **fruit** *(Obst)*, **meat** *(Fleisch)*, **sweets** *(Süßigkeiten)* und **drinks** *(Getränke)*. Weißt du noch, wie das geht? Genau, ordne einfach alle Vokabeln dem passenden Oberbegriff zu. Besonders bequem geht das in einer Tabelle!

8 IM STRASSENVERKEHR

• Kennst du schon einige unterschiedliche Fortbewegungsmittel? Prima, dann kannst du hier bestimmt die fehlenden Buchstaben ergänzen!

1. b __ s	**3. tra __ n**	**5. pl __ n __**	**7. l __ r __ y**
2. v __ n	**4. b __ k __**	**6. c __ r**	**8. r __ ll __ r sk __ t __ s**

Als Sportskanone solltest du unbedingt wissen, dass **bike** die Abkürzung von **bicycle** ist. Dieses Wort kannst du also auch verwenden! Außerdem steckt da auch schon das Verb **to cycle** *(radeln)* drin.

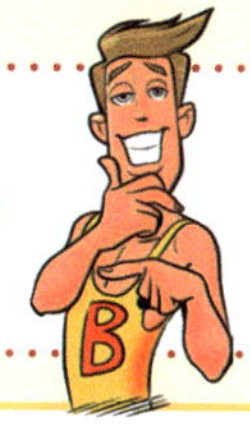

BOXENSTOPP

In den Straßen einer Stadt gibt es viel zu sehen. Wenn du dich umschaust, entdeckst du die verschiedensten Gebäude. Hier ist eine Übersicht von Wörtern, die du mit Sicherheit bei einem Ausflug in eine englische Stadt gebrauchen kannst:

station	*Bahnhof*	**pharmacy**	*Apotheke*
bus stop	*Bushaltestelle*	**town hall**	*Rathaus*
supermarket	*Supermarkt*	**church**	*Kirche*
corner shop	*kleiner Supermarkt*	**museum**	*Museum*
baker's (shop)	*Bäckerei*	**park**	*Park*
butcher's (shop)	*Metzgerei*	**petrol station**	*Tankstelle*
restaurant	*Restaurant*	**car park**	*(großer) Parkplatz*

•• Hier hat sich jeweils ein Verb der Fortbewegung versteckt. Findest du sie alle heraus? Wenn du ein Verb gefunden hast, kannst du es in die freie Zeile neben der Wortschlange eintragen.

1. **amundirecrundeamy** ______________________
2. **crufathikoodrivertage** ______________________
3. **cyclearnobodyssee** ______________________
4. **telimberawalkording** ______________________
5. **perridenthimpowiness** ______________________
6. **leempankingbango** ______________________

•• Ergänze nun die folgenden Sätze mit dem jeweils richtigen Verb aus der vorangegangenen Übung. Achte dabei auch immer auf die richtige Zeitform!

1. Kim gets on her bike and ______________ to school.
2. On her way home, she ______________ her bike, too.
3. Delilah's school is far away. She ______________ there by bus.
4. Their father has got a car. He ______________ to the office.
5. Their mother's way to work is not very long. She can ______________.
6. But when she is late she has to ______________.

••• Eine Kreuzung ist ein gefährlicher Ort. Wie du aber weißt, gibt es sichere Möglichkeiten, um über die Straße zu kommen. Kannst du den Abbildungen die richtigen Begriffe zuordnen?

zebra crossing | traffic lights | crossroads | underpass

1. ______ 2. ______ 3. ______ 4. ______

Aufgepasst: Falle nicht auf die Wörter **crossroads** oder **traffic lights** rein! Sie enden zwar auf **-s**, stehen aber im Singular!

••• Im folgenden Text sind einige Präpositionen verloren gegangen. Kannst du die jeweils richtige Präposition wieder ergänzen? Aber aufgepasst: Eine der angegebenen Präpositionen kommt zweimal vor!

on | off | by | in | around

Our school trip

Today we're going to Bath with our class. We go there (1) ______ bus. I can get (2) ______ the bus at the bus stop near our house. The bus leaves very early. So, I hope that I can sleep while we're (3) ______ the bus. When we arrive (4) ______ Bath, we get (5) ______ the bus and walk (6) __________ town.

9 AUS DER WELT DER TECHNIK

Die hier abgebildeten Geräte kennst du bestimmt schon. Wenn du die englischen Bezeichnungen der Geräte auch kennst, dann schaffst du auch das Kreuzworträtsel! Ergänze darin die fehlenden Ausdrücke. Damit es nicht ganz so schwierig ist, sind schon einige Felder ausgefüllt.

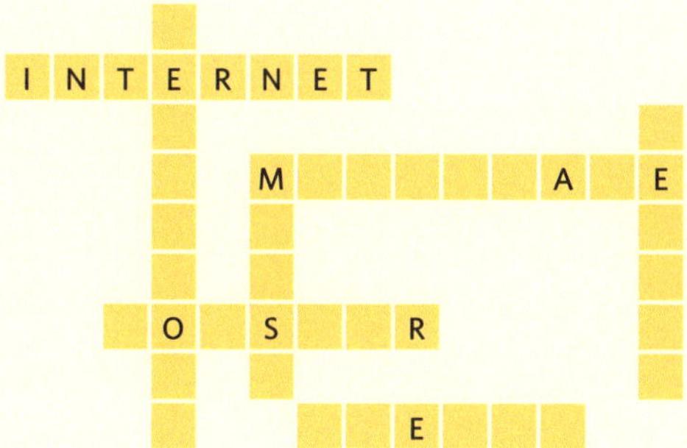

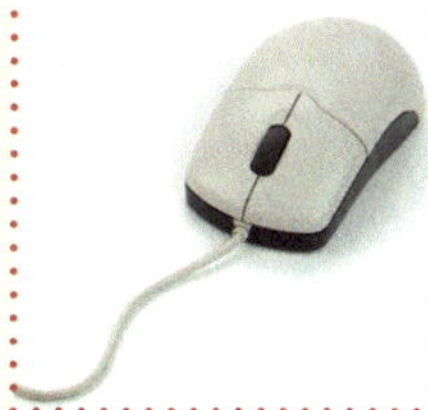

BOXENSTOPP

Dir ist bestimmt schon aufgefallen, dass wir im Deutschen viele englische Wörter verwenden. Gerade im Bereich der Technik ist das so. Das macht dir das Lernen einfach, weil du schon viele Begriffe aus dem Alltag kennst. Aber aufgepasst: Auf einige **false friends** *(falsche Freunde)* darfst du nicht reinfallen:

Das Wort **Handy** ist zwar ein englisches Wort, für ein Mobiltelefon benutzt man im Englischen aber andere Vokabeln: **mobile** oder **mobile phone** im Britischen Englisch und **cell phone** im Amerikanischen.

Einen Computerbildschirm nennt man im Deutschen auch **Monitor**. Das englische Wort **monitor** bedeutet jedoch etwas anderes. Wenn du über einen Computer- oder Fernsehbildschirm sprechen möchtest, musst du **screen** sagen.

Aufgepasst auch bei dem Wort **radio**. Damit bezeichnet man im Englischen nicht nur ein **Radio**, sondern auch ein **Funkgerät**.

Achtung, Sportsfreunde: Falsche Freunde lauern beinahe überall! Unbekannte Wörter im Englischen kannst du übrigens prima auf **www.pons.eu** nachschlagen. Dort findest du immer die richtige Bedeutung, auch **false friends** haben hier keine Chance!

•• Was für ein Durcheinander! Die Wörter sind in kleine Buchstabenketten zerfallen. Es haben sich immer zwei Wörter miteinander vermischt. Kannst du sie wieder richtig zusammensetzen?

1. **| ast | cof | mach | er | fee | ine | to |**

   You need a ______________ and a ______________ to make breakfast.

2. **| wash | fri | er | dge | dish |**

   There is a ______________ and a ______________ in the kitchen.

3. **| ing | ine | wash | ier | dr | mach |**

   A ______________ and a ______________ help to do the washing.

4. **| kers | reo | ea | sp | ste |**

   If you want to listen to music in the living room, you need a ______________ and ______________.

5. **| DVD | a | TV | yer | set | pl |**

   If you want to watch a film, you need a ______________ and a ______________.

6. **| ph | ay | mp3 | on | er | head | es | pl |**

   You can listen to music on the bus with an ______________ and ______________.

7. **| one | chi | eph | fax | ne | tel | ma |**

   A ______________ and a ______________ are for keeping in touch with other people.

Hast du schon einmal probiert, dir Sätze zu einem neuen Wort auszudenken? Schreibe dir immer einen ganzen Satz auf, in dem das neue Wort vorkommt. Du wirst sehen, dass du es dir dann besser merken kannst!

Hier siehst du einige wichtige Wendungen aus der Welt der Technik. Leider fehlt aber jeweils das Verb. Vervollständige die Ausdrücke mit den folgenden Verben und ergänze anschließend jeweils den Beispielsatz. Dann hast du's geschafft!

print · laugh · surf · write · read · sing · play · switch · walk · turn · call · fax · hold

1. to ________ **the internet** *im Internet surfen*
   Marc may ________________ after his homework is done.
2. to ________ **an e-mail** *eine E-Mail schreiben*
   Kim ________________ to her cousin in India.
3. to ________ **something out** *etwas ausdrucken*
   I did my homework on the computer. Now I have to ________________.
4. to ________ **a CD** *eine CD abspielen*
   Delilah and her friends want to dance. They ________________ with great music.
5. to ________ **down the stereo** *die Anlage leiser machen*
   Delilah's mother thinks that the music is too loud. She shouts, "________________!"
6. to ________ **up the stereo** *die Anlage lauter machen*
   When her mother leaves the house, Delilah ________________ again.
7. to ________ **somebody** *jemanden anrufen*
   Delilah goes to another room. She wants to ________________ from a quiet place.
8. to ________ **an order** *eine Bestellung faxen*
   You can order a pizza by telephone. But you can also ________________.
9. to ________ **something on** *etwas einschalten*
   "Come on, let's watch a film! ________________ the TV set!"
10. to ________ **something off** *etwas ausschalten*
    "It's time to sleep. ________________ the light, please!"

10 PRÄPOSITIONEN

- Im folgenden Text haben sich eine Menge Präpositionen versteckt. Markiere alle Präpositionen im Text und schlage anschließend im Anhang nach, ob du alle gefunden hast.

There are many houses upon the main street. Right at the corner there is a huge supermarket. Next to it you can see an old cafe. The town hall is across the street. But be careful because there are many cars on the street! In the town hall's yard you will find a beautiful fountain with a statue in front of it. Behind the town hall the children can play in a playground. When you look up, you can see the church in the distance. If you walk down the street, you will come to the station. Hurry, you must be there before the train leaves! You can relax later, after you found a seat inside the train.

BOXENSTOPP

Präpositionen tauchen ständig und überall auf. Sie geben uns Auskunft darüber, in welchem Verhältnis zwei Dinge oder Personen zu einander stehen. Also, ob zum Beispiel das rote Buch **neben** oder **auf** dem blauen Buch liegt. Oder zum Beispiel auch, ob Sam **vor** oder **nach** Marc ins Ziel gekommen ist. Wie du siehst, gibt es Präpositionen, die ein räumliches Verhältnis ausdrücken. Es gibt aber auch solche, die uns etwas über das Zeitverhältnis verraten. Außerdem kommen noch einige Präpositionen hinzu, die einen übertragenen Sinn haben. Ein Beispiel dazu:

In this chapter, we talk **about** prepositions.
In diesem Kapitel reden wir ***über*** Präpositionen.

Präpositionen lassen sich leider nicht einfach übersetzen, da sie oft mehrere Bedeutungen haben. Du musst sie also unbedingt im Zusammenhang mit bestimmten Vokabeln lernen! Es gibt auch eine Reihe von Verben, die in Verbindung mit einer Präposition eine andere Bedeutung bekommen, wie zum Beispiel **get up** *(aufstehen)* oder **give in** *(nachgeben)* und viele mehr. Findest du noch weitere Beispiele?

•• All diese Kästchen stehen in einem räumlichen Verhältnis zu einander. Das siehst du ja auf einen Blick! Aber wie drückt man das auf Englisch aus? Setze die Präpositionen in die entsprechenden Lücken ein!

below **between** **beside** **above**

1. This box is __________ box 2.

2. This box is __________ box 1 and box 3.

3. This box is __________ box 2.

4. This box is __________ box 3.

•• Wann musst du **into** verwenden, und wann heißt es **in**? Ergänze im folgenden Text das jeweils richtige Wort.

Kim opens the door and walks (1) __________ the room. Delilah is already (2) __________ the room. They write a letter to their cousin (3) __________ India. After they finished, they put the letter (4) __________ an envelope. Where are the stamps? Ah, they are (5) __________ the cupboard. Now they can go round the corner and put the letter (6) __________ the letterbox.

•• Marcs Austauschschülerin Lea hat noch einige Schwierigkeiten mit den Präpositionen. Das ist aber auch nicht ganz leicht! Du kannst ihr aber bestimmt trotzdem helfen! Sie hat räumliche und zeitliche Präpositionen verwechselt. Wie muss es richtig heißen?

1. ~~behind~~ midnight __________ midnight
2. ~~in front of~~ dinner __________ dinner
3. ~~after~~ the house __________ the house
4. ~~on~~ 4 o'clock __________ 4 o'clock
5. ~~before~~ the tree __________ the tree
6. ~~at~~ Wednesday __________ Wednesday

••• Lies dir die folgenden Sätze genau durch und überlege, welche Präpositionen fehlen. Kannst du alle Sätze vervollständigen? Prima, dann hast du's drauf!

1. Marc wants to visit his aunt. He wants to go there by bus. Now he is waiting for the bus ________ the bus stop.
2. Delilah's cat jumped onto the chair. She is very tired and so she is sleeping ________ the chair, now.
3. Sam and Marc are playing football. Sam kicks the ball very hard. Now, it is flying ________ the wall.
4. Sarah loves swimming and diving. She is not afraid of jumping ________ the water.
5. Tony's car is broken, and he must repair it. He is now lying ________ the car.
6. Where is Marc's dog? Have you seen her? Oh, she is sleeping ________ her basket.
7. Kim and Delilah want to go to the cinema ________ Friday.
8. Marc wants to play with his friends. But now they are having a maths lesson. So they play ________ school.
9. Kim is making a sandwich. She puts cheese and cucumber ________ two slices of bread.
10. It's raining outside. I must find my umbrella ________ I can go out in the rain.

Inhalt

Grammatik

Wortschatz

KLASSE 6

1 DIE SATZSTELLUNG IM ENGLISCHEN

- Bevor wir mit der Satzstellung im Englischen anfangen, schauen wir noch einmal nach, ob das mit den Satzteilen noch klappt. Folgende Satzteile sind für die Satzstellung wichtig:

Subjekt (S):	**Wer** oder **was**?
Objekt (O):	**Wen** oder **was**? (Akkusativobjekt)
	Wem? (Dativobjekt)
Verb (V):	Was **tut** das Subjekt?
Zeitangabe (Z):	**Wann** wird etwas getan?
Ortsangabe (OT):	**Wo** wird etwas getan?

Jetzt bist du dran: Versuche nun, die einzelnen Satzteile unten zu bestimmen. Trage dazu jeweils die entsprechenden Abkürzungen der Satzteile in die Klammern ein. Das Beispiel zeigt dir, wie es funktioniert.

1. Last week (**Z**) my sister (**S**) went (**V**) to Paris (**OT**).
2. My grandmother ( ) is knitting ( ).
3. My uncle ( ) married ( ) my aunt Patty ( ) 20 years ago ( ).
4. Tim ( ) bought ( ) me ( ) a flower ( ) yesterday ( ).
5. Yesterday ( ) my mother ( ) bought ( ) a new shirt ( ).
6. My mother ( ) bought ( ) a new shirt ( ) in the shop ( ) yesterday ( ).

BOXENSTOPP

Fällt dir bei der vorherigen Übung etwas auf? Achte einmal auf die Reihenfolge der Satzteile und ergänze dann die untenstehende Regel.

Anders als im Deutschen gibt es im Englischen eine **feste** Satzstruktur, die du **immer** beibehalten musst. Diese Satzstruktur sieht folgendermaßen aus:

(Zeit) ________ Verb (________) (Ort) (________)

Subjekt und Verb müssen in jedem Satz vorhanden sein. Wenn Objekte, Orts- und Zeitangaben im Satz gebraucht werden, werden sie besonders platziert: Zeitangaben können entweder ganz vorne oder ganz am Ende des Satzes stehen. Der Ort kommt immer vor der Zeitangabe.

Zeitangaben stehen fast nie in der Satzmitte! Eine Ausnahme bilden Zeitangaben aus einem Wort, die mit dem Simple Present gebraucht werden, wie z.B. **sometimes, usually, never, ever, always** oder **often**. Diese kannst du in der Satzmitte vor dem Vollverb platzieren.

•• Bringe die folgenden Satzteile in die jeweils richtige Reihenfolge.

1. never / some people / go / to church.

2. some magazines / Carol / is reading / in her room.

3. California Day / celebrate / the Americans / every year.

4. writes / Phillip / every day / her / a little message.

5. The Millers / go swimming / always / in summer.

•• Lies dir die folgenden Sätze durch und entscheide, ob sie richtig oder falsch sind.

	Richtig	Falsch
1. I sometimes listen to music in the evenings.	☐	☐
2. She went last summer to Venice.	☐	☐
3. Frances has always liked pancakes with ice cream.	☐	☐
4. Valerie goes everyday to school.	☐	☐

•• Wenn du jetzt noch die folgenden Sätze ins Englische übersetzen kannst, dann hast du die Satzstellung im Englischen drauf!

1. Mary geht jeden Dienstag ins Kino.

2. Lara und Sophie sind letzte Woche 13 Jahre alt geworden.

3. Millie liest gerade ein Buch in ihrem Zimmer.

4. Ich schaue niemals vor 6 Uhr abends fern.

2 DIE ZEITEN

2.1 Simple Present und Present Progressive

Simple Present	Present Progressive
Mr. Smith **works** here.	Please don't make so much noise. I **am trying** to read a book.
Lisa always **gets** up at 7 o'clock.	Where is Jennifer? – She **is speaking** to Susan on the phone.
Wayne never **tells** the truth.	Look! Frank **is coming** over.
Water **freezes** at zero degrees Celsius.	Sarah **is revising** for her exams at the moment.
Tom **plays** the piano.	

BOXENSTOPP

Schau dir die Beispiele oben genau an und vervollständige die Regel:

regelmäßige Ereignisse wissenschaftliche Fakten nie eintretende Ereignisse gerade ablaufende Ereignisse

Das Simple Present verwendet man für ____________________ und ____________________. Hierzu gehören auch Berufsbezeichnungen und Hobbys. Auch ____________________ werden mit dem Simple Present ausgedrückt. Das Present Progressive verwendet man dagegen für ____________________.

Los geht's! Setze die Verben in Klammern in der jeweils richtigen Zeit ein.

1. I'm sorry. I can't understand you. You ____________________ (to speak) too fast.
2. What's his job? – He ____________ (to work) in a restaurant. He is a waiter.
3. What ______ Sandra __________ (to do)? – She ____________________ (to repair) her bike.
4. Are you crying? – Yes, I always ______________ (to cry) when there is a happy ending.
5. Did you watch TV last night? – No, I never ______________ (to watch) TV.
6. The moon ____________________ (to circle) around the earth.

Das Simple Present ist mit der Infinitivform des Verbs identisch. Aber aufgepasst: Bei **he, she** und **it**, das **s** muss mit!

•• Lies dir die folgenden Sätze durch und entscheide, ob sie richtig oder falsch sind. Vergleiche deine Antworten mit dem Lösungsschlüssel.

	Richtig	Falsch
1. He sometimes goes to school alone.	☐	☐
2. What are you doing? – I read a book.	☐	☐
3. Water boil at 100 degrees Celsius.	☐	☐
4. Lara never finishes her homework before 9 o'clock in the evening.	☐	☐
5. These plants are dead. My mother never water them.	☐	☐

•• Übersetze nun die folgenden Sätze ins Englische.

1. Was machst du? Schreibst du eine E-Mail?

____

2. Frank spielt Fußball. Es ist sein Hobby.

____

3. Wo ist Michael? – Er führt seinen Hund spazieren. (**to take the dog for a walk**)

____

4. Susan und Manuel mögen Computerspiele.

____

5. Miriam fährt jeden Morgen mit dem Fahrrad zur Schule.

____

6. Die Sonne geht jeden Tag auf. (**to rise** = *aufgehen*)

____

2.2 Das Present Perfect

• **Sarah:** Have you ever been to Paris?

Simone: No I haven't. I would like to see the Eiffel Tower. Have you seen it yet?

Sarah: No I haven't. I have never been there, either. My friend Nora has been there twice. She has visited so many countries and has seen so many places already.

BOXENSTOPP

Das Present Perfect wird mit **have/has** + **Past Participle** gebildet und gehört zu den Gegenwartszeiten. Es beschreibt einen Zustand oder eine Situation, die in der Vergangenheit begonnen hat und bis jetzt andauert. Der Zeitraum ist also noch nicht abgeschlossen. Signalwörter für das Present Perfect sind **yet, not yet, already, so far, just, ever, never** sowie **for** und **since**.

I have never been to India. — *Ich war noch nie in Indien.*

→ Zeitraum hält noch an.

Miles has written 3 novels so far. — *Miles hat bis jetzt 3 Romane geschrieben.*

→ Zeitraum ist nicht abgeschlossen.

Eine andere wichtige Verwendung liegt vor, wenn das Ergebnis einer Handlung zu sehen ist:

Oh no! Where is my key? I think I've lost it. — *(Der Schlüssel ist im Moment nicht da.)*
Lucy! What have you done? – I have broken my arm! — *(Der Arm ist eingegipst.)*
Look! Mike has fallen off the ladder! — *(Mike liegt auf dem Boden vor der Leiter.)*

•• Versuche nun erst einmal, die richtigen Zeitformen in die Lücken einzutragen.

1. Mr. Turner ____________ (to be) ill since Christmas.
2. Look! I ____________ (to find) a pen on the floor.
3. What ____________ (you, to do)? – I ____________ (to break) my arm.
4. She ____________ (to live) here for 3 years.
5. I ____________ (never, to be) to America.
6. I ____________ (to know) Sally since I was 10 years old.
7. Tom ____________ (to play) tennis since he was a little boy.
8. The Smiths ____________ (to have) this dog for 8 years.
9. ____________ (you, ever, to see) a ghost?
10. You are too early. I ____________ (not yet, to finish) the cooking.
11. Does your uncle live in London? – Yes he ____________ (to live) there since 1981.

Since und **for** kann man im Deutschen mit *seit* übersetzen. Im Englischen macht man jedoch einen Unterschied im Gebrauch, den wir aus der deutschen Sprache nicht kennen. **Since** und **for** zu unterscheiden ist aber gar nicht so schwer, wenn du dir merkst, dass der **Punkt** auf dem **since** für einen Zeit**punkt** (**last week / month / year, yesterday, I was born, ...**) steht und **for** für einen **Zeitraum** (**2 days / weeks / years, a long time, ages, ...**).

•• Probieren wir doch gleich einmal aus, ob du den Unterschied verstanden hast. Ergänze **since** oder **for**.

I haven't seen her...

1. ... _________ last Christmas.	**6.** ... _________ 4 o'clock.
2. ... _________ a very long time.	**7.** ... _________ she moved away.
3. ... _________ she got married.	**8.** ... _________ we left school.
4. ... _________ April 4th, 1987.	**9.** ... _________ my birthday party.
5. ... _________ two weeks.	**10.** ... _________ ages. (= *ewig*)

•• Laura hat in 3 Tagen Geburtstag. Hier ist eine Liste mit Dingen, die sie schon erledigt hat ✔ und Dingen, die sie noch nicht erledigt hat ✘. Bilde Sätze im Present Perfect, in denen du beschreibst, was Laura schon oder noch nicht gemacht hat.

1. *Laura has invited friends from school.*

2. ______________________________

3. ______________________________

4. ______________________________

5. ______________________________

6. ______________________________

7. ______________________________

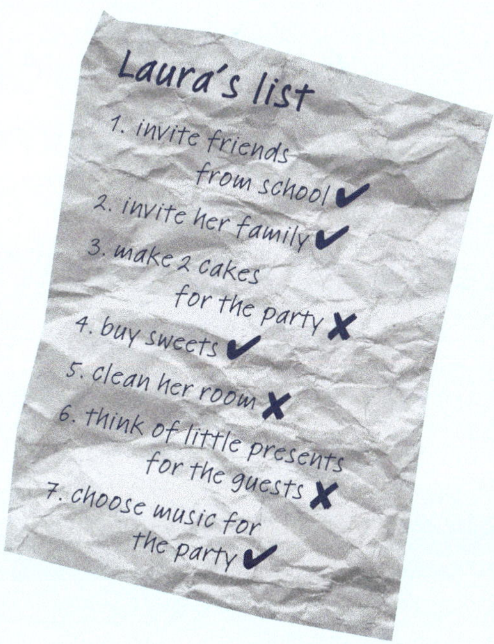

••• Jetzt wird es etwas kniffliger. Versuche, die folgenden Sätze ins Englische zu übertragen. Achte dabei auf die richtige Bildung der Zeit, den Unterschied zwischen **since** und **for**, und natürlich auf die Satzstellung.

1. Ich kenne Robert seit 8 Jahren.

____

2. Meine Mutter war noch nie in Australien.

____

3. Meine Mutter war noch nicht in Australien.

____

4. Was hast du denn gemacht? – Ich habe mir das Bein gebrochen.

____

5. Schau! Mike hat sein Bild fertiggestellt.

____

6. Wir wohnen hier schon ewig.

____

7. Die Connors haben dieses Auto schon seit 1991.

____

2.3 Das Simple Past

• Lies dir den Text über Daniel Defoe aufmerksam durch und markiere alle Verbformen.

Daniel Defoe

Daniel Defoe was an English author. He was born in London in the middle of the 17th century and died in April 1731. He married a very rich English woman whose name was Mary Tuffley. They had 8 children together. Only 6 of those children got older than 18. His most important novel was *Robinson Crusoe*. This novel made him very famous.

Ergeignis | Simple Past | Present Perfect

BOXENSTOPP

Das Simple Past beschreibt Ereignisse, die in der Vergangenheit geschehen sind. Wichtig hierbei ist, dass der **Zeitraum abgeschlossen** ist, in dem das Ereignis stattgefunden hat. Signalwörter für das Simple Past sind zum Beispiel **yesterday, last week, two days ago, last year, two hours ago**, etc. Auch nacheinander einsetzende (chronologische) Handlungen in der Vergangenheit werden im Simple Past ausgedrückt.

Regelmäßige Formen des Simple Past bildest du, indem du **-ed** an den Infinitiv des Verbs anhängst. Es gibt jedoch eine ganze Menge unregelmäßige Formen, die man nicht ableiten kann, sondern lernen muss.

Schreibe die passenden Formen des Simple Past hinter die Verben.

Infinitiv	Simple Past
1. to go	______
2. to walk	______
3. to talk	______
4. to see	______
5. to be	______
6. to do	______
7. to sing	______
8. to feel	______
9. to say	______
10. to drink	______

Es gibt eine Gruppe von Verben, deren Formen im Simple Past sich in der Aussprache sehr gleichen, aber unterschiedlich geschrieben werden – mit **-aught** oder mit **-ought**. Dazu ein kleiner Tipp: Wenn der Infinitiv ein **-a-** enthält, dann taucht das **-a-** im Simple Past und im Past Participle wieder auf. Ansonsten schreibst du **-ought**:

to teach – taught – taught   **to bring – brought – brought**
to catch – caught – caught   **to think – thought – thought**

What happens next? Ergänze die folgenden Sätze mit dem jeweils passenden Verb im Simple Past.

to strand *(stranden)* | **to find** | **to be** | **to leave** | **to try** | **to wreck** *(untergehen)* | **to teach** | **to count** | **to name** | **to convert** *(bekehren)* | **to teach**

1. Robinson Crusoe ______________ England in September 1659.

2. His ship ______________ in a storm and he ______________ on a lonely island.

3. He ______________ to escape from the island but he was not successful.

4. He ______________ alone for many years and ______________ the days by making marks into a piece of wood.

5. One day he ______________ another man on the island and ______________ him Friday.

6. He ______________ him English and ______________ him to Christianity.

7. Friday ______________ Robinson how to fish.

••• Jetzt wird's etwas schwieriger. Übersetze nun die nachfolgenden Sätze ins Englische. Achte dabei auch auf die Satzstellung!

1. Vor einer Minute war es dunkel.

____

2. Ich habe gestern zu meinem Geburtstag viele Geschenke bekommen.

____

3. Mary hat letzte Woche ihre Tante in New York besucht.

____

4. Daniel Defoe hat in seinem Leben viele Geschichten geschrieben.

____

5. Letztes Jahr sind wir nach England gefahren.

____

6. Wir haben vor 20 Minuten Mittag gegessen.

____

7. Gestern hatte ich keine Zeit.

____

8. Als er jung war, war er sehr klein.

____

2.4 Vergleich Present Perfect und Simple Past

• Vergleiche die beiden hervorgehobenen Sätze miteinander und finde heraus, worin der Unterschied zwischen dem Present Perfect und dem Simple Past besteht.

He was ill last week. → He is healthy now.
He has been ill since last week. → He is still ill.

BOXENSTOPP

Versuche nun, die Regel für die Verwendung dieser beiden Zeitformen zu vervollständigen.

Noch einmal zur Erinnerung: Das ____________________ beschreibt Handlungen, die in der Vergangenheit abgeschlossen sind. Das ____________________ beschreibt dagegen Handlungen, die noch Auswirkungen auf die Gegenwart haben, also noch nicht abgeschlossen sind. Auch das ____________________ einer Handlung kann im Present Perfect stehen.

Unterstreiche in den folgenden Sätzen die Signalwörter für das Simple Past rot und die Signalwörter für das Present Perfect grün.

1. Sarah had a party last weekend.
2. We haven't finished our homework yet.
3. Have you ever had an accident?
4. I've never liked red.
5. The Millers went to the USA last holiday.
6. You've already had two pizzas.
7. I went shopping with my friend yesterday.
8. I have known Silvia for many years.
9. They built this school in 1891.
10. The shops closed half an hour ago.

Achte beim Lernen der unregelmäßigen Verben im Englischen immer darauf, dass du die Grundform (Infinitiv) zusammen mit den Formen des Simple Past und des Past Participle lernst.

Trage die Signalwörter aus der vorigen Übung in die Tabelle ein.

Signalwörter für das Present Perfect	Signalwörter für das Simple Past

Übersetze die Signalwörter aus der vorangegangenen Übung ins Deutsche.

Übersetzung Signalwörter Present Perfect	Übersetzung Signalwörter Simple Past

•• Nachdem du die Signalwörter wiederholt hast, versuche nun mit deren Hilfe die richtigen Verbformen in die Lücken zu schreiben.

1. Laura ______________ (to buy) a newspaper yesterday.
2. ______________________ (you, ever, to watch) "Britain's Got Talent" on TV?
3. I ______________ (to be) a good swimmer since I was a little girl.
4. My sister ______________ (to be) ill since Christmas.
5. Conny ______________ (to wash) her hair half an hour ago.
6. We ______________ (to live) in this house for ages.
7. Tom ______________ (to learn) how to play golf in 2001.
8. ______________________________________ (you, ever, to see) an alien?
9. He ______________ (to do) a terrible job for the last four months.
10. Susan ______________ (to finish) her novel three weeks ago.
11. I can't come with you. I ______________ (not, to finish) the housework yet.
12. I don't know if I can still do it. I ______________ (not, to do) this for ages.

••• Und zum Schluss noch eine kleine Übersetzungsübung. Aber keine Angst: Wenn du dir die Beispielsätze und Übungen noch einmal durchliest, dann schaffst du das leicht. Los geht's!

1. Hast du jemals Golf gespielt?

____

2. John ist seit letztem Montag krank.

____

3. Ich war schon lange nicht mehr da.

____

4. Ich habe ihn gestern gesehen.

____

5. Ich kenne Claudia schon ewig.

____

6. Vor drei Wochen haben wir eine nette Frau in der U-Bahn getroffen.

____

7. Ich habe gerade zu Mittag gegessen.

____

2.5 Das Past Progressive

- **Police officer:** "The robbery took place at 10 o'clock last night. What were you doing at that time?"

  Young man: "I was watching TV."

BOXENSTOPP

Kannst du die Regel zum Past Progressive selbst vervollständigen?

wasn't / weren't **was / were** **to be** **Past Progressive**

Das ____________________ wird mit einer Form von ________________ im Simple Past (____________________) + **ing**-Form gebildet. Die Verneinung im Past Progressive wird mit ____________________ + **ing**-Form gebildet.

Man verwendet das Past Progressive im Englischen bei ...

a. zwei oder mehr Handlungen, die in der Vergangenheit gleichzeitig ablaufen.
b. länger andauernden Handlungen in der Vergangenheit, wenn eine kurze, punktuelle Handlung hinzukommt. Die punktuelle Handlung steht dann im Simple Past.
c. Rahmenhandlungen, die z.B. eine Szenerie in der Vergangenheit beschreiben.
d. Aussagen, die beschreiben, was man zu einem bestimmten Zeitpunkt in der Vergangenheit gemacht hat.

•• Lies dir die nachfolgenden Sätze genau durch und entscheide, in welche der oben genannten Kategorien (a - d) du die Sätze einordnen kannst.

1. What were you doing at 4 o'clock? - I was helping my brother in the garden. __
2. I was reading a book when the clock fell off the wall. __
3. It was a lovely morning. The sun was shining and the birds were singing. __
4. We were all having dinner when someone knocked on the door. __
5. Yesterday evening my father was working in the garage and I was having a party. __
6. My sister was making dinner when I arrived. __
7. We met at the airport. I was going to Paris and Sylvia was going to Barcelona. __
8. What were you doing at 11 o'clock yesterday? - I was having lunch. __
9. My aunt phoned me while I was having a bath. __
10. I was walking home when I met Jane. __

Im Deutschen gibt es eine Form, die dem Past Progressive entspricht. Sie existiert aber fast ausschließlich in der gesprochenen Sprache. Du solltest diese Form also nicht benutzen, wenn du einen Aufsatz oder einen Brief schreibst.

I was reading when the phone rang.
*Ich war gerade **am Lesen**, als das Telefon klingelte.*
I was reading and he was talking on the phone.
*Ich war **am Lesen** und er war **am Telefonieren**.*

•• Vervollständige die Sätze mit deinen eigenen Ideen. Im Anhang findest du Musterlösungen, die wahrscheinlich nicht deine Antwort wiedergeben, aber auf jeden Fall die richtige Zeitform, die du einsetzen musst.

1. When Martin phoned, we ____________________.

2. It was a wonderful day. The sun __________, the children __________.

3. What were you doing at 10 o'clock? – I ____________________.

4. Yesterday Susan __________ and Jim __________.

••• Zum Abschluss noch ein paar Übersetzungen. Überlege zuerst genau, um welche Kategorie es sich handelt und übersetze dann.

1. Als ich nach Hause kam, stand meine Mutter in der Küche, mein Bruder spielte Klavier, mein Vater las die Zeitung und meine Oma putzte das Haus.

____

____

2. Die Show fing an, als wir in den Raum hineingingen.

____

____

3. Was haben Sie um 7 Uhr gemacht? – Um 7 Uhr habe ich das Abendessen vorbereitet.

____

____

4. Es war eine wundervolle Party: Die Gäste tanzten, die Musik spielte und die Sonne schien.

____

____

2.6 Die Zukunft mit *going to*

BOXENSTOPP

Ergänze die folgende Regel zur Zukunft mit **going to** mit den angegebenen Begriffen.

Einfluss Vorhersagen Infinitiv geplant

Die Zukunft mit **going to** wird für zukünftige Ereignisse verwendet. Ganz besonders für solche Ereignisse, die ____________ sind und auf die man selbst ____________ hat. Auch für ____________ benutzt man die Zukunft mit **going to**, aber nur wenn es deutliche Anzeichen dafür gibt, dass ein Ereignis auch tatsächlich eintritt. Gebildet wird die Zukunft mit **going to** so:

Simple Present von **to be (am [not] / are [not] / is [not])** + **going to** + ____________

I **am [not] going to play** that game.	*Ich werde dieses Spiel [nicht] spielen.*
She **is [not] going to go** to the party tonight.	*Sie wird heute Abend [nicht] auf die Party gehen.*
We **are [not] going to watch** the new James Bond movie.	*Wir schauen uns [nicht] den neuen James Bond Film an.*

•• Übersetze Toms Ideen und Pläne für seine Geburtstagsparty ins Deutsche.

1. I'm going to invite all my friends from school.

____

2. My mother is going to make my favourite meal.

____

3. We are going to have so much fun.

____

•• Verstanden, wie es funktioniert? Dann wollen wir das gleich einmal probieren. Vervollständige die Formen der Zukunft mit **going to** in den nachfolgenden Sätzen mit der richtigen Form von **to be**. Das Beispiel zeigt dir, wie es funktioniert.

1.	(to) sit on that chair	**I**	*I am going to sit on that chair.*
2.	(to) fly to Brazil next summer	**we**	______________
3.	(to) meet the Queen in London	**they**	______________
4.	(to) rain	**it**	______________
5.	not (to) watch a movie tonight	**he**	______________
6.	(to) sell their car	**they**	______________
7.	(to) have fun	**we**	______________
8.	not (to) go to a concert	**she**	______________
9.	(to) be a nice day	**this**	______________
10.	not (to) buy you this thing	**I**	______________

Fragen in der Zukunft mit **going to** kannst du genauso leicht bilden. Ziehe einfach die Form von **to be** ganz nach vorne an den Satzanfang:

He **is** going to go to Spain in summer. → **Is** he going to go to Spain in summer?
It **is** going to rain. → **Is** it going to rain?

•• Benutze jetzt die folgenden Satzteile und bilde Fragen in der Zukunft mit **going to**.

1. you / bake / cookies / for your mother

____

2. he / go / to Paris / next summer

____

3. we / spend / the rest of the day / in this shopping centre

____

4. I / read / all those books / until next week

____

5. She / water / the plants / this afternoon

____

6. They / play / soccer

____

7. It / snow / soon

____

••• Jetzt bist du topfit für die letzte Übung. Übersetze die Sätze ins Englische. Achte wie immer auch auf die Satzstellung. Zeig mal, was du kannst!

1. Wir werden heute Abend Pizza machen.

____

2. Sally wird im Sommer ihre Tante in Mexiko besuchen.

____

3. Ich gehe nicht vor 9 Uhr zu Sally.

____

4. Mein Vater baut hinter dem Haus einen Swimmingpool.

____

2.7 Die Zukunft mit *will* und mit *going to*

- Markiere die Formen der Zukunft mit **will** in der folgenden Wettervorhersage.

The weather will be very nice tomorrow. There will be sunshine in the morning. In the evening, however, rain clouds will appear and there will be rain all over the country.

BOXENSTOPP

Die Zukunft mit **going to** und die Zukunft mit **will** beschreiben jeweils ein Ereignis in der Zukunft. Der Unterschied zwischen diesen beiden Zeiten besteht jedoch darin, dass die Zukunft mit **will** zum Ausdruck von **Vermutungen (I think, I hope, I'm sure)**, **festen Vorhersagen** (auch Wettervorhersagen) und **spontanen Äußerungen** verwendet wird. Gebildet wird die Zukunft mit **will** immer mit **will** + **Infinitiv** des jeweiligen Verbs.

•• Ergänze in den folgenden Sätzen jeweils das Verb in Klammern. Entscheide dabei, ob du die Zukunft mit **will** oder **going to** verwenden musst.

1. Oh, there is so much to do. - Don't worry. I ______________________ (to help) you.
2. My cat ran away. - Don't worry, darling. I'm sure you ______________________ (to find) it.
3. How about the picnic tomorrow? - Don't worry, I think the weather ______________________ (to hold).

Spontane Entscheidungen, die jetzt im Moment getroffen werden, stehen in der Regel in der Zukunft mit **will**. Wenn die Entscheidungen schon früher getroffen wurden, benutzt man die Zukunft mit **going to**. Vergleiche die beiden folgenden Beispiele:

There is someone on the phone for you. - Okay, **I'll** answer it.
→ Entscheidung fällt in diesem Moment

Steven called earlier. - Yes, I know. **I'm going to** phone him later.
→ Entscheidung fiel schon früher

•• Schau dir noch einmal die Erläuterungen zur Verwendung der Zukunft mit **going to** an. Lies dir dann die folgenden Aussagen durch und entscheide, mit welcher Absicht etwas gesagt wurde. Kreuze deine Entscheidung in der Tabelle an und finde anschließend die richtigen Überschriften für die helle und die dunkel unterlegte Spalte in der Tabelle.

1. My brother is going to go to Greece by plane.

2. Look at the sky! It is going to snow.

3. It will be very stormy tonight.

4. I'm so tired! – I'll do the washing up for you.

5. They all hope that I will get the Oscar for my new movie.

6. There will be rain all over the country in the afternoon.

7. We hope that he'll make it here in time.

8. We are going to have a barbecue with all our friends.

	______________			______________	
Satz	**spontane Entscheidung**	**Wettervorhersage**	**Vermutungen mit I'm sure, I think, I hope**	**Plan, Idee**	**Wettervorhersage mit deutlichen Anzeichen**
1.	☐	☐	☐	☐	☐
2.	☐	☐	☐	☐	☐
3.	☐	☐	☐	☐	☐
4.	☐	☐	☐	☐	☐
5.	☐	☐	☐	☐	☐
6.	☐	☐	☐	☐	☐
7.	☐	☐	☐	☐	☐
8.	☐	☐	☐	☐	☐

••• Fülle die Lücken aus.

1. (The postman rings the door bell.) I ____________________ (to get) it!

2. Have you seen the mail in the hallway? – Yes, I've seen it.

I ____________________ (to get) it after I've finished breakfast.

3. If you put water into the freezer, it ____________________ (to freeze).

4. I think this ____________________ (to be) great.

••• Übersetze im Folgenden die deutschen Aussagen ins Englische.

1. *Ich hoffe, dass ihr gewinnt.*

____

2. *Wir werden uns morgen alle das Fußballspiel ansehen.*

____

3. Don't worry about the keys. *Ich bin sicher, dass du sie wieder findest.*

____

4. Sorry, there is no more room for you in my car, Lucy. – *Kein Problem, ich nehme sie mit.*

____

3 *IF*-SÄTZE TYP I

• Welches Wort fehlt hier?

If I win the jackpot, I ____________ buy a new house.

BOXENSTOPP

Im Deutschen heißen **if**-Sätze **Bedingungssätze**, weil im **if**-Satz eine Bedingung steht, die entweder erfüllbar ist oder nicht. Es gibt insgesamt drei Arten von **if**-Sätzen. In Klasse 6 lernst du den ersten Typ kennen. Hier ist die Bedingung im **if**-Satz erfüllbar, das heißt es ist möglich oder wahrscheinlich, dass die Bedingung erfüllt wird.

Dabei steht im **if-Satz immer Simple Present** und im **Hauptsatz will / can / must (oder ein anderes Hilfsverb) + Infinitiv**. Im **verneinten** Hauptsatz stehen die entsprechenden Formen **won't / can't / needn't (oder ein anderes Hilfsverb) + Infinitiv**. **If** wird im Deutschen mit *wenn* oder *falls* übersetzt.

If you **help** me, I **will be** quicker.	*Wenn du mir hilfst, bin ich schneller.*
If it **rains** tomorrow, we **must stay** at home.	*Falls es morgen regnet, müssen wir zu Hause bleiben.*
We **can visit** you if we **have** enough time.	*Wir können dich besuchen, falls wir genug Zeit haben.*
He **won't earn** a lot of money if he works there.	*Er wird nicht viel Geld verdienen, wenn er dort arbeitet.*

•• Vervollständige nun die Satzbausteine auf der linken Seite sinnvoll mit einem Satzteil auf der rechten Seite.

1. If you go out with your friends tonight,
2. If I work there,
3. If you give me this book,
4. If it rains,
5. If you eat the whole pizza,
6. If you behave,
7. If he comes to the party,

a. you will get a stomach ache.
b. you must leave.
c. I will earn a lot of money.
d. you can come to my party.
e. I will give you ten pounds for it.
f. I can watch the football match on TV.
g. you must wear a raincoat.

Wenn der Hauptsatz vor dem **if**-Satz steht, dann darf kein Komma gesetzt werden. Steht der **if**-Satz jedoch vor dem Hauptsatz, dann **muss** zwischen den beiden ein Komma stehen.

•• Ergänze die folgenden Sätze mit der jeweils richtigen Form der Verben in Klammern. Setze Kommas, falls notwendig.

1. Your mother ______________ (to like) it if you ______________ (to buy) her roses.
2. If you ______________ (to eat) those mushrooms you ______________ (to die).
3. If I ______________ (to see) him I ______________ (to give) him something.
4. We ______________ (not, to go) home if the weather ______________ (to get) better.
5. I ______________ (not, to say) hello if I ______________ (to meet) her.
6. If you ______________ (to put) sugar into it, it ______________ (to taste) sweeter.
7. Sue ______________ (to buy) a house if she ______________ (to win) the lottery.

•• In jedem der folgenden Sätze ist mindestens ein Fehler versteckt. Schau genau hin und achte dabei auch auf Kommas. Den verbesserten Satz kannst du in die freie Zeile darunter schreiben.

1. If I see him I will greet him.

____

2. You win if you play.

____

3. If he speak English I can understand what he says.

____

4. If I lose it she is very angry.

____

5. You fix the vase with glue if you break it.

____

••• Gleich hast du es geschafft! Links sind Satzbruchstücke auf Englisch, die du mit Hilfe der deutschen Angaben vervollständigen kannst. Let's start!

1. If you mow the grass, you will get 10 euros. (→ € 10)
2. If you tell any more lies, ______________________ (→ *ich / böse)*
3. If you read in bad light, ______________________ (→ *du / Augen ruinieren)*
4. If you speak slowly, ______________________ (→ *ich / kann dich verstehen)*

••• Endspurt! Übersetze nun noch diese Sätze ins Englische. Achte dabei auch auf die Kommas!

1. Ich werde sehr böse sein, wenn dein Hund mich beißt.

____

2. Wenn wir jetzt wegfahren, sind wir um 4 Uhr da.

____

3. Wenn du viele Süßigkeiten isst, wirst du dick werden.

____

4. Du kannst Geld sparen, wenn du die Heizung abdrehst.

____

4 QUESTION TAGS

• Was fehlt hier? Vervollständige die Sätze mit den passenden **question tags**.

1. That was a great film, ______________? – Yes, it was really good.
2. You don't feel well, ______________? – No, I feel terrible.

BOXENSTOPP

Schau dir die beiden Beispiele oben genau an. Im Englischen gibt es so genannte **question tags** (Frageanhängsel), mit denen du die Zustimmung oder Bestätigung deiner Aussage einholen kannst. Hierbei gilt:

1. Ist das Verb im Aussagesatz ______________, dann ist das **question tag** verneint.
2. Ist das Verb im Aussagesatz ______________, dann ist das **question tag** bejaht.

Im Deutschen kann man **question tags** zum Beispiel mit *nicht wahr? / oder? / stimmt's?* oder *richtig?* übersetzen.

•• Versuche nun, die Aussagesätze in der linken Spalte mit den passenden **question tags** in der rechten Spalte sinnvoll zu kombinieren.

1. Karen is talking on the phone again,
2. Phillip and Tim are watching TV,
3. Susan isn't good at school,
4. We have had a good time,
5. You didn't believe him,
6. You two aren't listening to me,
7. Where is Tom? – He is playing the guitar,

a. haven't we?
b. aren't they?
c. are you?
d. isn't he?
e. isn't she?
f. is she?
g. did you?

Trage die Lösungen in die Tabelle ein.

1.	2.	3.	4.	5.	6.	7.

Bestimmt ist dir aufgefallen, dass die Verbformen in den Sätzen oben immer aus einem Hilfsverb (z.B. **have** oder **is**) und einem Vollverb (z.B. **watching** oder **listening**) zusammengesetzt sind. Wenn in einem Satz kein Hilfsverb zur Verfügung steht, dann musst du folgende **question tags** benutzen:

She likes apples, **doesn't she**? *Sie mag Äpfel, oder?*
We like apples, **don't we**? *Wir mögen Äpfel, nicht wahr?*

She liked apples, **didn't she**? *Sie mochte Äpfel, stimmt's?*
We liked apples, **didn't we**? *Wir mochten Äpfel, richtig?*

•• Versuche jetzt einmal, die **question tags** selbst einzusetzen und auch die neue Regel anzuwenden. Hier findest du die möglichen Antworten:

doesn't he? **doesn't she?** **doesn't she?** **didn't you?** **did you?** **wasn't she?** **isn't it?**

1. The weather is nice, ________________? – Yes, very nice.

2. Your granny likes tea, ________________? – Yes, green tea is her favourite.

3. Julia was on holiday, ________________? – No, she was not on holiday. She was in hospital.

4. You watched the talk show last night, ________________? – Yes, I did.

5. You didn't pass the test, ________________? – No, it was too difficult.

6. He always cries, ________________? – Yes, always.

7. Leticia studies very hard, ________________? – Yes, she is very good at school.

•• Kannst du die folgenden Sätze mit dem jeweils passenden **question tag** ergänzen?

1. **Lucy:** You have been to Berlin, ________________?
   Lara: Yes, I have. It's a very big city, ________________?
2. **Tim:** The movie was nice, ________________?
   Tony: Yes, it was great. It's late, ________________? Let's go home.
3. **Liz:** You saw Mr. and Mrs. Brown yesterday, ________________?
   Tom: Yes, I did. They look really old, ________________?

Fast geschafft! Das meiste zu den **question tags** hast du jetzt drauf. Hier gibt's noch einige Besonderheiten, bei denen du in der Schule richtig punkten kannst!

Das Frageanhängsel für Aufforderungen mit **let's** heißt **shall we**:

Let's go home, **shall we?** *Los, lasst uns nach Hause gehen!*

Für Befehle und Verbote benutzt du **will you**:

Be quiet, **will you?** *Wirst du wohl ruhig sein?*

Das verneinte Frageanhängsel für **I'm** lautet **aren't I**:

I'm late, **aren't I?** *Ich bin spät dran, oder?*

••• Mit diesen Regeln im Kopf geht auch der Rest ganz einfach. Ergänze das jeweils passende Frageanhängsel. Try it!

1. Let's have a party, ________________?
2. I am so great, ________________?
3. Don't shout in here, ________________?
4. Get up, ________________?
5. Let's make a move, ________________?
6. I am a student, ________________?
7. Listen to me, ________________?

5 ADJEKTIVE UND ADVERBIEN

- Größer oder kleiner? Vervollständige den folgenden Beispielsatz.

The elephant is ______________________ the mouse.

BOXENSTOPP

Adjektive und Adverbien können gesteigert werden. Es gibt insgesamt drei Steigerungsformen. Versuche, die drei Formen von **big** ins Deutsche zu übersetzen.

1. Der **Positiv**:
This house is **big**. *Dieses Haus ist ______________.*
This house is **as big as** that one over there. *Dieses Haus ist ____________________ das dort drüben.*

2. Der **Komparativ**:
This house is **bigger than** that one. *Dieses Haus ist _______________ das da.*

3. Der **Superlativ**:
This house is **the biggest**. *Dieses Haus ist _______________.*

Alle **einsilbigen**, sowie alle **zweisilbigen** Wörter auf **-y** werden im Komparativ auf **-er** und im Superlativ auf **-est** gesteigert:
fast → faster → the fastest *schnell → schneller → am schnellsten*

Aufgepasst: **-y** wird zu **-ie**:
easy → easier → the easiest *leicht → leichter → am leichtesten*

Alle **zwei- und mehrsilbigen** Wörter werden mit **more** im Komparativ und **most** im Superlativ gesteigert:
often → more often → the most often *oft → öfter → am öftesten*
expensive → more expensive → the most expensive *teuer → teurer → am teuersten*

Konsonanten am Ende des Wortes werden im Komparativ und im Superlativ oft verdoppelt:
thin → thinner → the thinnest *dünn → dünner → am dünnsten*
big → bigger → the biggest *groß → größer → am größten*

Außer wenn ...
... das Wort mit **2 Konsonanten endet**, z.B.: **long - longer - the longest**
... das Wort ein **w** oder ein **y am Ende** hat, z.B.: **new - newer - newest**
... am Wortende **zwei Vokale vor dem Konsonant** stehen, z.B.: **quiet - quieter - the quietest**

•• Ergänze die folgende Tabelle mit den Komparativ- und Superlativformen der angegebenen Adjektive und Adverbien:

Positiv	Komparativ	Superlativ
1. seriously		
2. high	higher	
3. boring		
4. important		
5. big		the biggest
6. peaceful		
7. cold		

•• Übersetze die folgenden Sätze ins Deutsche.

1. This car is more expensive than that one over there.

___

2. Mary's house is the biggest house in town.

___

3. Your room looks cleaner since you tidied it.

___

4. Hamburgers are as good as cheeseburgers.

___

5. A sofa is more comfortable than a chair.

___

Aufgepasst: Es gibt auch eine Reihe von unregelmäßigen Steigerungsformen, die du dir gut merken solltest:

good / well → better → the best

bad / badly → worse → the worst

far → further / farther → the farthest

little → less → the least

•• Beschreibe das Verhältnis der folgenden Dinge oder Lebewesen zueinander, indem du Sätze mit dem Komparativ bildest. Beginne deine Beschreibung immer mit dem zuerst genannten Ding oder Lebewesen.

1. Lena is 12 years / Phillip is 13 years (young)
Lena is younger than Phillip.

2. juice / water (taste good)

3. maths / English (complicated)

4. Mary / John (tall)

5. my grades / your grades (bad)

6. health / money (important)

7. Sydney / London (far away)

6 DAS *GERUND* ALS SUBJEKT UND OBJEKT

• Schau dir die Bilder an. Kannst du aufschreiben, was Sally, Tom und Steven gerne tun?

Sally (dance)

Tom (play football)

Steven (collect stamps)

1. Sally likes ______________________.
2. Tom likes ______________________.
3. Steven likes ______________________.

BOXENSTOPP

Das **gerund** ist eine **substantivische Verbform**, es verbindet also die Eigenschaften eines Substantivs mit denen eines Verbs. Es kann innerhalb eines Satzes verschiedene Positionen einnehmen. Man kann das **gerund** also z.B. als **Subjekt (Wer oder was?)** oder als **Objekt (Wen oder was?)** eines Satzes benutzen.

Subjekt: Swimming is healthy.
Objekt: I like swimming.

Setze ein:

be | -ing | verdoppelt | fällt weg | Satzanfang

Das **Gerund** wird aus dem Infinitiv eines Verbs + ____________ gebildet. Wenn das **Gerund** als Subjekt gebraucht wird, dann steht es meistens am ____________ und ihm folgt meistens eine Form von **(to)**____________. Vor einem **Gerund** steht im Englischen kein Artikel!
Achtung bei der Schreibung: Konsonanten werden am Wortende oft ____________ (**sit** → **sitting**), und ein **-e** am Verbende ____________ (**like** → **liking**).

•• Bestimme in den folgenden Sätzen jeweils, ob es sich beim **gerund** um ein Subjekt oder ein Objekt handelt. Kreuze an!

	Subjekt	Objekt
1. Playing the piano is one of my hobbies.	______	______
2. Peter hates **washing** his clothes.	______	______
3. I enjoy **reading**.	______	______
4. Watching movies is one of Larry's hobbies.	______	______

•• Bilde zu den folgenden Infinitiven jeweils das **gerund**:

1. play ____________	**6. sing** ____________
2. swim ____________	**7. love** ____________
3. be ____________	**8. go** ____________
4. sit ____________	**9. do** ____________
5. stop ____________	**10. ride** ____________

Als Objekt benutzt man das **gerund** häufig nach Verben, die eine Vorliebe oder Abneigung ausdrücken, wie z.B.:

to dislike	*nicht gerne tun*	Mary dislikes cleaning.	*Mary macht nicht gerne sauber.*
to enjoy	*genießen*	He enjoys playing cricket.	*Er genießt es Kricket zu spielen.*
to hate	*hassen*	I hate being late.	*Ich hasse es zu spät zu kommen.*
to love	*lieben*	We love singing.	*Wir lieben es zu singen.*
to like	*mögen*	They like going out.	*Sie mögen es auszugehen.*

•• Die folgenden Sätze sind durcheinander geraten. Bringe die Satzbruchstücke wieder in die richtige Reihenfolge und entscheide dabei jeweils, welches Verb als **gerund** benutzt werden muss.

1. read / books / hobby / is my

____

2. I / cycle / hate

____

3. we all / play / love / cards

____

•• Gleich hast du es geschafft! Übersetze die folgenden Sätze ins Englische und benutze dabei das **gerund**.

1. Ich hasse es, Briefe zu schreiben.

____

2. Schwimmen macht Spaß.

____

3. Marcy tanzt gerne.

____

4. Er genießt es, alleine fernzusehen.

____

____

7 POSSESSIVPRONOMEN UND POSSESSIVBEGLEITER

- Weißt du, welches Possessivpronomen und welchen Possessivbegleiter du hier einsetzen musst?

"Oh no, it's raining. I have forgotten ______ umbrella. "
"Here, take ______."

BOXENSTOPP

Possessiv bedeutet **besitzanzeigend**. Als Possessivbegleiter und Possessivpronomen werden also Wörter bezeichnet, die angeben, **wem** etwas gehört. **Possessivbegleiter** bestimmen wie Adjektive die Eigenschaft von Personen oder Dingen:

This is **my** car. *Dies ist mein Auto.*

Possessivbegleiter stehen **immer** bei dem Gegenstand oder der Person, die sie beschreiben; sie stehen **nie alleine**. **Possessivpronomen** ersetzen dagegen einen Gegenstand oder eine Person; sie stehen also **immer alleine**. Vergleiche die folgenden Sätze:

This is **my** car. → This is **mine**.
This is **her** cat. → This is **hers**.

Possessivbegleiter		Possessivpronomen	
my car	**mein** Auto	**mine**	**meins**
your car	**dein** Auto	**yours**	**deins**
his / her / its car	**sein / ihr / sein** Auto	**his / her / its**	**seins / ihres / seins**
our car	**unser** Auto	**ours**	**unseres**
your car	**euer** Auto	**yours**	**eures**
their car	**ihr** Auto	**theirs**	**ihres**

•• Hast du den Unterschied zwischen Begleitern und Pronomen verstanden? Finde heraus, ob es sich bei den hervorgehobenen Wörtern um Possessivbegleiter oder Possessivpronomen handelt. Schreibe deine Antworten hinter die einzelnen Sätze.

1. This is **our** cat. ______________________
2. **Their** uncle is very rich. ______________________
3. Caroline's house is bigger than **ours**. ______________________
4. I've bought this CD. It's not **yours**. ______________________
5. I've got something in **my** eye. ______________________
6. He has had it for years. It's **his**. ______________________
7. **Her** cat is very big. ______________________
8. Please give me **your** number. ______________________
9. Whose shoes are those? Are they **yours**? ______________________
10. Do you think he will bring **his** girlfriend along? ______________________

Wenn du wissen möchtest, wem etwas gehört, dann musst du folgende Fragen stellen:

Whose (dog) is this? *Wessen (Hund) ist das?*
Whose (dogs) are those? *Wessen (Hunde) sind das?*

•• Possessivbegleiter oder -pronomen? Ergänze in den folgenden Sätzen die jeweils richtige Form.

1. These are not __________ (my / mine) shoes. __________ (My / Mine) are black.
2. Sally gave me __________ (her / hers) umbrella. __________ (My / Mine) was at home.
3. __________ (Her / Hers) teacher is nicer than __________ (your / yours).
4. Can I use __________ (your / yours) phone? __________ (My / Mine) is broken.
5. Where are __________ (your / yours) parents? __________ (Her / Hers) are over there.
6. Is this __________ (my / mine) new bike? __________ (Your / Yours) looks much nicer.
7. Whose are these? __________ (My / Mine) or __________ (your / yours)?
8. She has finished __________ (her / hers) tea. Does she want to have __________ (my / mine) now?

••• Übersetze nun die folgenden Sätze ins Englische. Achte dabei wie immer auch auf die richtige Satzstellung.

1. Conny gab mir gestern mein Buch zurück.

____

2. Ist das euer Kind? - Nein, das ist meine Nichte.

____

3. Das ist meine Eiscreme. Du hast deine schon aufgegessen.

____

4. Wessen Fahrrad ist das? - Es ist meins.

____

5. Ist das dein Laptop oder ihrer? - Es ist ihrer.

____

8 PERSONALPRONOMEN

• Kannst du im folgenden Dialog die Personalpronomen vervollständigen?

you | we | I | me | you | I | it

"**I** know ________, don't ________? ________ are the guy that helped ________ with my bags. ________ talked for a while. Do **you** remember?"

"Yes, of course. ________ remember **you**. ________ was a pleasure to help **you**."

BOXENSTOPP

Personalpronomen hast du sicherlich schon im Deutschunterricht kennengelernt. Du weißt, dass es unterschiedliche Personalpronomen gibt, je nachdem für welchen Fall sie stehen. **Subjektpronomen** stehen für **Nominativobjekte**, nach denen man mit *Wer oder was?* fragen kann. **Objektpronomen** stehen für **Dativobjekte** *(Wem?)* und **Akkusativobjekte** *(Wen oder was?)*.

Hier siehst du alle Pronomen im Überblick:

Subjektpronomen	(Nominativ)	Objektpronomen	(Dativ / Akkusativ)
I	*ich*	**me**	*mir / mich*
you	*du*	**you**	*dir / dich*
he / she / it	*er / sie / es*	**him / her / it**	*ihm, ihr, ihm / ihn, sie, es*
we	*wir*	**us**	*uns / uns*
you	*ihr*	**you**	*euch / euch*
they	*sie*	**them**	*ihnen / sie*

•• Sieh dir die folgenden Beispielsätze genau an, und überlege, ob die hervorgehobenen Personalpronomen Subjekt- oder Objektpronomen sind. Kreuze deine Antworten in der Tabelle an.

	Subjektpronomen	Objektpronomen
1. My father is helping **me** with my bike.	☐	☐
2. I can see **her** in the garden.	☐	☐
3. Tom is not at home. **He** is working.	☐	☐
4. Mike is very strong. He can carry **me**.	☐	☐
5. **We** are not married.	☐	☐
6. Can you give that to **us**?	☐	☐
7. **They** are not very intelligent.	☐	☐
8. Who is this? I don't know **them**.	☐	☐
9. **We** have a big house in New York City.	☐	☐
10. I followed **them** to their flat.	☐	☐

Das Wort **Pronomen** kommt aus dem Lateinischen und bedeutet, dass man etwas für **(pro)** einen anderen Namen **(nomen)** einsetzt.

•• Versuche nun, die folgenden Sätze mit dem jeweils richtigen Personalpronomen zu ergänzen. Überlege immer zuerst, ob in die Lücke ein **Subjektpronomen** *(Wer oder was?)* oder ein **Objektpronomen** *(Wem? / Wen oder was?)* eingesetzt werden muss.

1. Let's sit down here. __________ have got sandwiches with __________.
2. Peter! Are __________ crazy?
3. Sally and Mike are getting married. __________ are very much in love.
4. Look, Tom! Sarah is over there. __________ has taken her dog along. Perhaps we can play with __________ (dog).
5. Tom wrote (mir) __________ an e-mail yesterday. __________ said that __________ would like to see __________.
6. Oh, these bags are so heavy! Can __________ help me carrying __________ to the station?
7. Look at the ducks over there. __________ are swimming in a line. Can you see __________?
8. We are the Millers. This is our son Charles. __________ is eleven years old. Our daughter's name is Sammy. Charles likes __________ very much. __________ often play together. It is nice watching __________.
9. Do you still have my computer game? Can __________ give __________ back to __________, please?
10. Look, there is Anna. What is __________ doing? Are those __________ kids? I've never seen __________ together.

••• Wenn du bis hierher gut zurecht gekommen bist, dann schaffst du diese Übung auch noch! Übersetze die folgenden Sätze ins Englische, und ersetze dabei die hervorgehobenen Substantive durch das jeweils richtige Personalpronomen. Das Beispiel zeigt dir, wie es geht. Let's go!

1. **Kathrin** fragt **ihre Eltern**. She asks them.
2. Er sieht **seinen Lehrer**. ____________________
3. Wir sehen uns. ____________________
4. **Mrs Smith** liebt **ihre Tochter**. ____________________
5. **Das Haus** ist leer. ____________________
6. **Mary und George** suchen **ihr Auto**. ____________________
7. Sie haben **meine Schwester und mich** gestern getroffen. ____________________
8. Timmy? Suchst du **deinen Bruder**? ____________________
9. Sucht **Timmy seine Geschwister**? ____________________

9 PRÄPOSITIONEN

• Sieh dir die folgenden Beispielsätze genau an und achte besonders auf die hervorgehobenen Ausdrücke:

The cat is **on** the sofa.	*Die Katze ist auf dem Sofa.*
The ball is **between** the box and the bin.	*Der Ball ist zwischen der Box und dem Mülleimer.*
Mary is sitting **in front of** her bed.	*Mary sitzt vor ihrem Bett.*

BOXENSTOPP

Präpositionen zeigen dir, in welchem Verhältnis ein Gegenstand zu einem anderen steht. Es gibt Präpositionen der Zeit, des Ortes und der Bewegung:

Zeit		Ort		Bewegung	
after	*nach*	**behind**	*hinter*	**into**	*hinein*
since	*seit*	**in front of**	*vor*	**off**	*runter*
until	*bis*	**between**	*zwischen*	**out of**	*raus*
from	*von*	**on**	*auf*	**against**	*gegen*
before	*vor*	**in**	*in*	**from**	*von*

Jahreszahlen werden mit **in** angegeben: **He was born in 1996.** *(Er ist 1996 geboren.)* Für **Fortbewegungsmittel** benutzt man **by: He goes to school by bus/bike/train/car.** *(Er fährt mit dem Bus/Fahrrad/Zug/Auto zur Schule.)*

•• Wo genau befinden sich die Dinge in Sarahs Zimmer? Schreibe einige Sätze auf.

in front of | on | in | next to | over | under

1. The bird is in the cage.
2. The cat is ______
3. The mouse is ______
4. The child is ______
5. The picture hangs ______
6. The dog sits ______

Achtung: *Nach Hause* heißt im Englischen **home** und wird **ohne Präposition** gebraucht. *Zu Hause* heißt **at home**. Vergleiche die beiden folgenden Beispiele:

I'm going home. *Ich gehe nach Hause.*
I'm at home. *Ich bin zu Hause.*

•• Ergänze das Kreuzworträtsel und die Beispielsätze mit der jeweils richtigen Präposition.

Senkrecht:

1. We meet ______________ (nach) the concert.
2. I must phone Alex ______________ (bevor) we leave.
3. Where is Missy? She is ______________ (hinter) the oven.
4. The plates are ______________ (auf) the table.

Waagerecht:

5. Lucy is sitting ______________ (zwischen) her sister Mary and her brother Alex.
6. What is Larry doing? – He is going ______________ (hinein) the shop right now.
7. Where are you? – I'm ______________ (zu Hause) home.

•• Schreibe die jeweils richtige Präposition in die Lücken.

by | in | between | into | at | in front of | from | until

1. We go to school ______________ bus every morning.
2. The bus stops ______________ the school building.
3. We all go ______________ the building.
4. We are ______________ our classroom ______________ 8 o'clock in the morning ______________ 2 o'clock in the afternoon.
5. I sit ______________ my best friends Missy and George.
6. At 3 o'clock I'm ______________ home again.

••• Gleich geschafft! Jetzt noch ein paar kurze Übersetzungen. Auf geht's! Achte beim Übersetzen auch auf die richtige Satzstellung.

1. Ich fahre **mit dem Fahrrad** zur Schule.

____

2. Unser Haus ist **vor** der Kirche.

____

3. Wir gehen **zwischen** 7 und 8 Uhr **nach Hause**.

____

10 RELATIVSÄTZE

- Schau dir die folgenden Beispielsätze genau an und versuche herauszufinden, wann **who, that** und **which** verwendet werden.

I have got a sister. She is married.
I have got a sister **who / that** is married.
Ich habe eine Schwester, die verheiratet ist.

These are the men. They told me the story.
These are the men **who / that** told me the story.
Das sind die Männer, die mir die Geschichte erzählten.

She has got a car. It is 20 years old.
She has got a car **which / that** is 20 years old.
Sie hat ein Auto, das 20 Jahre alt ist.

These are the shops. They are closed until March.
These are the shops **which / that** are closed until March.
Das sind die Geschäfte, die bis März geschlossen sind.

This is the man. His mother is 79 years old.
This is the man **whose** mother is 79 years old.
Das ist der Mann, dessen Mutter 79 Jahre alt ist.

BOXENSTOPP

Hast du etwas herausgefunden? Wie du an den Beispielen oben siehst, kann man mit einem Relativsatz zwei Sätze miteinander verbinden, indem man ein Relativpronomen benutzt. Hierbei gilt:

________________ wird nur für **Personen** *(Der Mann, der ...)* gebraucht und ________________ *(Die Uhr, die ...)* nur für **Gegenstände**. ________________ kann **für beide** Fälle verwendet werden. ________________ wird im Deutschen mit *wessen* oder *dessen/deren* übersetzt *(Die Frau, deren Mann ...)*. Alle Relativpronomen sind im Singular und Plural gleich.

•• Ergänze die folgenden Sätze mit dem jeweils passenden Relativpronomen. Aber aufgepasst: Manchmal gibt es mehrere Lösungsmöglichkeiten!

1. Mister Brown and Miss Wood were the teachers ________________ accompanied our class to London.
2. Michael Smith is the pupil ________________ aunt lives in Baltimore.
3. We saw a woman in the street ________________ had a funny haircut.
4. Miles is the man ________________ wife lived in Africa for a long time.
5. We have a house ________________ is on a hill.
6. A kiwi is a bird ________________ cannot fly.
7. Doesn't she have anybody ________________ can help her?

•• Verbinde immer zwei Sätze zu einem Satz, indem du ein Relativpronomen einsetzt.

1. Sally told us a story. I couldn't believe it.
   Sally told us a story which I couldn't believe.
2. Tim has got a dog. It is black.
   ____
3. Harry is a good boy. He can't tell a lie.
   ____
4. We have a nice flat. I like it.
   ____

Wenn das Relativpronomen Objekt des Satzes ist, kann es weggelassen werden. Man spricht dann von einem **contact clause**.

I was reading **a book**.
→ The book **(which / that)** I was reading was good.

We are listening to **a song**.
→ The song **(which / that)** we are listening to is okay.

•• Ergänze die folgenden Sätze mit dem jeweils richtigen Relativpronomen. In welchen Fällen kannst du das Relativpronomen auch weglassen? Trage hier **contact clause** ein.

1. What's the title of the book ________________ you bought yesterday? ☐
2. A teacher is a person ________________ helps you understand things better. ☐
3. The Smiths have a house ________________ has got 4 bathrooms. ☐
4. The film ________________ you gave me is not very good. ☐
5. I lost the ring ________________ you gave me for my birthday. ☐

•• Übersetze nun noch die folgenden drei Sätze ins Englische. Achte dabei wie immer auch auf die richtige Satzstellung.

1. Ich habe eine Tante, die auf einer Farm lebt.

___

2. Das ist der Mann, dessen Schwester 5 Kinder hat.

___

3. Die Frau, die ich gesehen habe, war allein.

___

11 *SOME* UND *ANY* IN AUSSAGEN UND FRAGESÄTZEN

• Sieh dir die folgenden Sätze genau an und achte dabei besonders auf die hervorgehobenen Ausdrücke. Was fällt dir bei der Verwendung von **some** und **any** auf?

My brother has got **some** nice toys.	My brother hasn't got **any** nice toys.
I have got **some** ideas.	I haven't got **any** ideas.
I can see **some** people over there.	I can't see **any** people over there.
Susan is making **some** cookies.	Susan is not making **any** cookies.
Have you got **any** butter?	Yes, I have got **some** butter. / No, I haven't got **any** butter.
Have you got **any** books?	Yes, I have got **some** books. / No, I haven't got **any** books.

BOXENSTOPP

Ergänze die untenstehende Regel mit den folgenden Begriffen:

some | bejahten | any | some | Verneinungen | any | *ein paar*

Man benutzt ______ oder ______ im Englischen, um eine unbestimmte Menge oder Anzahl auszudrücken. Übersetzt werden beide Ausdrücke ins Deutsche mit *etwas*, ______ oder *einige*. ______ benutzt man in ______ Sätzen. Bei Fragen und ______ wird dagegen meistens ______ verwendet. **Some** kann jedoch auch bei Fragen verwendet werden, wenn man eine **höfliche Bitte (Can I have some butter, please?)** oder ein **höfliches Angebot (Would you like some tea?)** formuliert.

•• Ergänze die folgenden Sätze jeweils mit **some** oder **any**.

1. Would you like to have ____________ coffee?
2. Can you remember ____________ line of this song?
3. I can give you ____________ films. I've got a huge collection.
4. I hope there will be ____________ snow on Christmas Day.
5. Can I have ____________ milk for my tea, please?
6. Are there ____________ people in this town who know how to drive a car?
7. There won't be ____________ sunshine all day.
8. Someone has to water your plants. Have you got ____________ neighbours you trust?
9. Would you like to meet ____________ of my friends?
10. There will be ____________ rain in the North of England.

Some und **any** werden im Deutschen manchmal gar nicht übersetzt:

Have you got **any** jam?	*Hast du Marmelade?*
Brian is getting **some** drinks for us.	*Brian holt uns Getränke.*

•• Bilde nun aus den vorgegebenen Satzteilen bejahte oder verneinte Sätze mit **some** oder **any**.

1. Sally / have not / friends. *Sally hasn't got any friends.*
2. I / cannot see / birds in the sky. ____________
3. You / like / sugar? ____________
4. I / can have / milk, please? ____________
5. We / have not / newspapers. ____________
6. You / know / people from Japan? ____________
7. My father / have / tools in the garage. ____________

•• Jetzt zum Endspurt! Versuche nun, die folgenden Sätze ins Englische zu übersetzen.

1. Hast du ein paar Tipps für mich?

____

2. Könntest du mir bitte etwas Salz geben?

____

3. Möchten Sie etwas Zucker?

____

4. Ich habe keine Haustiere.

____

5. Kannst du Butter kaufen?

____

12 MODALVERBEN

• Lies dir den Text, der auf Toms Anrufbeantworter gesprochen wurde, genau durch und versuche dann, die Modalverben richtig ins Deutsche zu übersetzen.

Hi Tom! It's me, John. I'm so sorry. I **cannot** come to your party tonight. I **must** help my sister with her homework tonight, because she **must** give a presentation on Australia. Maybe we **can** meet some other time. And Tom ... You **must not** call me back, because my parents **need not** know that I was planning to come to your party.

1. I cannot come to your party. ______________________________

2. I must help my sister. ______________________________

3. She must give a presentation. ______________________________

4. We can meet some other time. ______________________________

5. You must not call me back. ______________________________

6. My parents need not know that ... ______________________________

BOXENSTOPP

Mit Hilfe von Modalverben kann man **Erlaubnisse, Verbote, Verpflichtungen, Möglichkeiten** oder auch **Fähigkeiten** ausdrücken. Die Bedeutung eines Satzes ändert sich, je nachdem, welches Modalverb du benutzt. Im Text oben hast du bereits die Verwendung einiger Modalverben kennengelernt. Vergleiche nun folgende Beispiele:

She **can / cannot** sing.	*Sie kann / kann nicht singen.*
She **may / may not** sing.	*Sie darf / darf nicht singen.*
She **must / has to / does not have to** sing.	*Sie muss / muss nicht singen.*
She **must not** sing.	*Sie darf nicht singen.*
She **need not** sing.	*Sie braucht / muss nicht singen.*

Achtung: Die Verneinung von **must** ist **nicht mustn't**, sondern **doesn't / don't have to. Mustn't** übersetzt man mit *nicht dürfen.*

•• Übersetze die hervorgehobenen Fragen und Aussagen ins Deutsche.

1. May I have this DVD?

____

2. It's okay. **You need not say any more.**

____

3. My father is ill. **He must not go outside.**

____

4. Does your leg hurt much? **Can you stand up?**

____

5. You must not open this door. It's forbidden to open it.

____

6. The kiwi bird cannot fly. Its wings are too small.

____

7. The official part is over. **You need not stay here any longer.**

____

Modalverben haben immer nur eine Form. Auch bei **he, she** und **it** wird **kein -s** angehängt. Sieh dir dazu noch einmal die Beispiele mit **need not** oben an.

•• Ergänze die folgenden Sätze mit dem jeweils passenden Modalverb.

1. Can you turn off the light, please? I ______________ sleep when the light's on.
2. My aunt has visited many countries. She ______________ speak six languages.
3. No, not like this! You ______________ put this end here.
4. You ______________ help me. I can do that on my own.
5. No, Charlie. You ______________ go there. Father says it's forbidden.
6. ______________ I help you?

•• Ergänze die folgenden Sätze mit Hilfe der Vorgaben in Klammern und verwende jeweils das passende Modalverb. Das Beispiel zeigt dir, wie es funktioniert.

1. Stay away from the door! (not enter / the house) *You must not enter the house.*
2. I don't want to invite Petra. But I (invite / Sarah) ______________. She will be very angry if I don't invite her.
3. No, Tom. You (not come) ______________.There are enough people here to help me with the decoration.
4. What are we going to do tonight? – We (go) ______________ to the cinema, if you like.

13 ZEICHENSETZUNG

• Die Zeichensetzung im Englischen ist eigentlich gar nicht so schwierig. Trotzdem lohnt es sich, dir die **Zeichensetzung in der direkten Rede** und die **Kommaregeln** gut einzuprägen. Sieh dir die folgenden Sätze einmal genau an:

He said, "I don't like fish."
"If you don't like fish," she asked, "why don't you eat meat?"
"I don't like meat either," he replied.

Luca asked, "Is that all?"
"Yes, that's all! " Jane replied.

BOXENSTOPP

Kommas werden im Englischen zum Beispiel bei **Aufzählungen** verwendet:
He bought apples, pears and bananas. *Er kaufte Äpfel, Birnen und Bananen.*

Zwischen den letzten zwei Gliedern einer Aufzählung steht normalerweise **kein** Komma, es sei denn, sie sind sehr lang:
I spent the evening listening to records, talking to my sister on the phone, and watching the new James Bond movie on television.
Ich habe den Abend damit verbracht mir Platten anzuhören, mit meiner Schwester zu telefonieren und mir den neuen James Bond-Film im Fernsehen anzusehen.

Zwischen zwei Hauptsätzen steht meistens ein Komma, wenn sie mit **but, or, and** und **so** verbunden sind:
He decided to try the sausages, and she ordered a huge bowl of mashed potatoes.
Er entschied sich dazu die Würstchen zu probieren, und sie bestellte eine große Schale Kartoffelbrei.

Es sei denn, die beiden Sätze sind sehr kurz:
Jane had apple pie and Tom had fish. *Jane hatte Apfelkuchen und Tom hatte Fisch.*

Zwischen Hauptsatz und Nebensatz steht nur dann ein Komma, wenn der Nebensatz dem Hauptsatz vorausgeht. Vergleiche:
He will go home if he gets bored. *Er wird nach Hause gehen, wenn ihm langweilig wird.*
If he gets bored, he will go home. *Wenn ihm langweilig wird, wird er nach Hause gehen.*

•• Ergänze in den folgenden Sätzen Kommas, wo diese notwendig sind.

1. I will ask her what happened to her grandmother but I think she won't tell me.
2. Henry went shopping. He bought apples a loaf of bread a bottle of water and a toothbrush.
3. If you leave your cat out there it will die.
4. My mother was talking to my sister while I was upstairs.
5. I went to see my grandmother in Chicago and my wife visited her friends in Australia.
6. She had a lot of fun and he was bored.
7. If I see him I will tell him that you want to talk to him.
8. While you were away someone called on the phone.
9. She met an old man a lot of Japanese tourists with cameras and a small child that was looking for its mother.
10. Before she wrote this great novel no one knew who she was.

Nebensätze erkennst du daran, dass sie mit einer **Konjunktion** wie z.B. **when, while, if, though, as**, etc. eingeleitet werden.

•• Versuche nun, die folgenden Sätze mit Satzzeichen zu bestücken. Du kannst folgende Satzzeichen einfügen: **Anführungszeichen, Kommas, Punkte, Fragezeichen, Ausrufezeichen** und **Großbuchstaben** zu Beginn der direkten Rede. Los geht's!

1. Tom said come here

____

2. If you listen to what the teacher says my mother said you will get good grades

____

3. What's up asked Martin

____

4. I want to know Charles said who left the front door open

____

5. My aunt asked is there any mail for me today

____

•• Übersetze nun die folgenden Sätze ins Englische. Denke dabei vor allem an die richtige Zeichensetzung!

1. „Wer ist da?" fragte Maria.

____

2. „ Es ist ", sagte er, „ein Freund."

____

3. Verena fragte: „Wo bist du?"

____

1 ZAHLEN

- Hast du Lust auf eine Runde **Sudoku**? Fülle die leeren Kästchen auf. Jede Zahl darf in jeder Reihe und in jedem farbigen Feld nur einmal vorkommen. Viel Spaß!

one			four
	four	three	
	one	four	two
four	two		three

BOXENSTOPP

Hier ist eine Liste, mit der du die wichtigsten Grund- und Ordnungszahlen noch einmal wiederholen kannst. Schau dir die Liste gut an. Achte besonders auf die hervorgehobenen Ausdrücke. Diese sind nicht ganz regelmäßig in der Schreibung. Wenn du die Zahlen ausschreibst, vergiss nicht einen Bindestrich zwischen Zehnern und Einern (z.B. **twenty-seven, thirty-two, seventy-nine,** etc.) einzufügen.

Grundzahlen				Ordnungszahlen		
zero	*null*	**twenty**	*zwanzig*	**first**	1st	*der erste*
one	*eins*	twenty-one	*einundzwanzig*	**second**	2nd	*der zweite*
two	*zwei*	twenty-two	*zweiundzwanzig*	**third**	3rd	*der dritte*
three	*drei*	**thirty**	*dreißig*	fourth	4th	*der vierte*
four	*vier*	**forty**	*vierzig*	**fifth**	5th	*der fünfte*
five	*fünf*	**fifty**	*fünfzig*	sixth	6th	*der sechste*
six	*sechs*	sixty	*sechzig*	seventh	7th	*der siebte*
seven	*sieben*	seventy	*siebzig*	eighth	8th	*der achte*
eight	*acht*	eighty	*achtzig*	ninth	9th	*der neunte*
nine	*neun*	ninety	*neunzig*	last		*letzte/r/s*
ten	*zehn*	one hundred	*einhundert*	last but one		*vorletzte/r/s*

•• Schreibe die folgenden Zahlen auf Englisch aus.

1. 23 ____________________
2. 44 ____________________
3. 87 ____________________
4. 13 ____________________
5. 19 ____________________
6. 56 ____________________
7. 101 ____________________
8. 60 ____________________
9. 9 ____________________
10. 148 ____________________

Die Zahlen mit **-teen** (**thirteen, fourteen, fifteen,** etc.) sind leicht zu verwechseln mit den Zahlen, die auf **-ty** enden (**twenty, thirty, forty,** etc.). Den Unterschied zwischen diesen Zahlen kannst du besser behalten, wenn du dir merkst, dass ein **Teenager** jemand ist, der zwischen 13 und 19 Jahren alt ist. Diese Zahlen enden alle auf **-teen**.

•• Überlege bei den folgenden Zahlenreihen, welche Zahl logischerweise als nächstes kommen müsste. Schreibe die jeweils folgende Zahl aus.

1. seven - fourteen - twenty-one - twenty-eight → ____________________
2. two - four - eight - sixteen - thirty-two → ____________________
3. twenty-five - fifty - seventy-five → ____________________
4. eighty-eight - forty-four - twenty-two → ____________________
5. twenty - thirty - forty → ____________________
6. three - six - nine → ____________________
7. five - ten - fifteen - twenty → ____________________
8. three - nine - twenty-seven → ____________________

••• Schreibe in den folgenden Sätzen jeweils die richtige Zahl aus. Aber aufgepasst: Hier können Grund- und Ordnungszahlen gefragt sein.

1. A is the ______________________ letter in the alphabet.
2. Y is the ______________________ letter in the alphabet.
3. Seven times *(mal)* five makes *(ergibt)* ______________________.
4. Eighty-one divided by *(geteilt durch)* nine makes ______________________.
5. The one who finishes ______________________ wins the gold medal.
6. If you finish ______________________ you win the silver medal.
7. The one who finishes ______________________ wins the bronze medal.
8. If you finish ______________________ you lose the race *(Rennen)*.
9. Ten times four makes ______________________.
10. One hundred divided by four makes ______________________.

2 WORTBILDUNG

2.1 Präfixe im Englischen

• Schau dir die folgenden Beispielsätze an. Achte dabei besonders auf die hervorgehobenen Wörter und trage diese in die Tabelle ein.

1. He completely **misunderstood** the story.
2. Tim doesn't know much about music. He is very **unmusical**.
3. We can't use this. It has to be **non-metal**.
4. We don't meet every week. We only meet **biweekly**.
5. I have got a **prepaid** mobile phone.
6. Welcome to our **semi-annual** meeting.
7. It is very cold outside. You have to put some **antifreeze** in your car.
8. Look at the sky. It is **unclouded**.
9. We will go home if you **misbehave**.
10. "Girl" is a **monosyllabic** word.

1. ______________________	6. ______________________
2. ______________________	7. ______________________
3. ______________________	8. ______________________
4. ______________________	9. ______________________
5. ______________________	10. ______________________

BOXENSTOPP

Präfixe sind Wortteile, die am Wortanfang stehen und die Bedeutung eines Wortes verändern können. Einige hast du oben im Beispiel schon kennengelernt. Die wichtigsten Präfixe im Englischen sind:

Präfix	Deutsche Übersetzung	Beispiel	
anti-	*gegen / anti-*	antirust	*Rostschutzmittel*
bi-	*zwei-*	bipolar	*zweipolig (z.B. ein Magnet)*
counter-	*gegen-*	countermove	*Gegenzug (z.B. beim Schach)*
mono-	*ein- / einfach*	monosyllabic	*einsilbig*
mis-	*falsch / miss-*	misinterpret	*falsch interpretieren*
non-	*nicht / un-*	nonhuman	*nicht menschlich*
pre-	*vor-*	precondition	*Vorbedingung*
semi-	*halb-*	semicircle	*Halbkreis*
tri-	*drei-*	trisyllabic	*dreisilbig*
un-	*nicht / un-*	unclean	*unsauber*

•• Versuche jetzt mit Hilfe der Erklärungen die Wörter aus der Aufwärmübung ins Deutsche zu übersetzen.

1. ______________________

2. ______________________

3. ______________________

4. ______________________

5. ______________________

6. ______________________

7. ______________________

8. ______________________

9. ______________________

10. ______________________

Das Wort **Präfix** kommt aus dem Lateinischen und bedeutet in etwa *vorne festgemacht*.

•• In den folgenden Sätzen sind die Präfixe verloren gegangen. Kannst du sie richtig zuordnen?

mis- **bi-** **un-** **pre-** **counter-** **anti-** **non-** **semi-** **mono-** **tri-**

1. Eine	________	**colour**	ist eine Flagge mit drei Farben.
2. Wenn etwas	________	**liquid**	ist, dann ist es nur halbflüssig oder zähflüssig.
3.	________	**hear**	bedeutet: *etwas falsch verstehen.*
4. Wenn etwas	________	**finished**	ist, dann ist es nicht fertig oder unfertig.
5. Eine	________	**school**	besucht man, bevor man zur Schule geht.
6. Etwas ist	________	**sense**	, wenn es keinen Sinn hat.
7.	________	**clockwise**	bedeutet: *gegen den Uhrzeigersinn.*
8. Ein	________	**weight**	ist ein Gewicht, das ein anderes ausgleichen soll.
9. **Bottle** ist	________	**syllabic**	, es besteht also aus zwei Silben.
10. Wenn etwas	________	**tonous**	ist, dann ist es eintönig.

••• Versuche jetzt, die hervorgehobenen deutschen Ausdrücke ins Englische zu übersetzen. Schau dir am besten vorher die Präfixe noch einmal genau an. Los geht's!

1. Der Vorgang läuft **halbautomatisch**. ____________________
2. **Counterpart** ist ein **dreisilbiges** Wort. ____________________
3. Das ist **unglaublich**! ____________________
4. Das kann man **falsch interpretieren**. ____________________
5. Wir müssen das Essen **vorwärmen**. **(heat)** ____________________
6. Die Sitzungen sind **halbjährlich**. ____________________
7. Du musst **Frostschutz** nachfüllen. ____________________
8. Sie planen einen **Gegenschlag**. **(attack)** ____________________
9. Wir haben die Route falsch **berechnet**. **(calculate)** ____________________

2.2 Suffixe im Englischen

- Lies dir die folgenden Sätze genau durch und entscheide, ob die hervorgehobenen Wörter Nomen **(N)**, Adjektive **(A)** oder Verben **(V)** sind.

1. This t-shirt is machine **washable** ( ).
2. If you click this button, you will **activate** ( ) the machine.
3. It's freezing cold. I can't feel the **warmth** ( ) from the heating.
4. **Freedom** ( ) is precious *(wertvoll)*.
5. Don't be so **childish** ( ). You are too old for that.
6. Don't tell me any more of this story. It is too **frightening** ( ).
7. It is too bright in here. Can we **darken** ( ) the room a bit?
8. It is fascinating to watch the baby's **development** ( ).
9. This exercise is too hard. We have to **simplify** ( ) it.

BOXENSTOPP

Suffixe sind Endungen, die man an Wörter anhängen kann. Mit Hilfe der Suffixe kannst du aus Wörtern, die du schon kennst, jede Menge neue Wörter bilden. Es gibt feste Endungen für bestimmte Wortgruppen:

Nomen z.B. infin**ity** *(Unendlichkeit)*, kind**ness** *(Freundlichkeit)*, free**dom** *(Freiheit)*, warm**th** *(Wärme)*, ship**ment** *(Verschiffung)*, fascinat**ion** *(Faszination)*

Adjektive z.B. part**ial** *(teilweise)*, eat**able** *(essbar)*, child**ish** *(kindisch)*, harm**less** *(harmlos)*, interest**ing** *(interessant)*, forget**ful** *(vergesslich)*

Verben z.B. fantas**ize** *(fantasieren)*, black**en** *(schwärzen)*, just**ify** *(rechtfertigen)*, origin**ate** *(entstehen)*

Aber aufgepasst, Sportsfreunde: Welche Endung innerhalb einer Wortgruppe an welches Wort angehängt werden kann, ist nicht frei wählbar. Das muss man für jedes Wort lernen.

- - Trage die Wörter aus der Aufwärmübung (Sätze 1-9) in der jeweils richtigen Spalte ein und unterstreiche die Suffixe.

Nomen	Adjektive	Verben

Hier noch zwei kleine Tipps zur Rechtschreibung: Ein **e** am Wortende fällt weg, wenn ein Suffix angehängt wird: z.B. **possible - possibility** *(möglich - die Möglichkeit)*. Ein **y** fällt weg, wenn ein Suffix angehängt wird, das mit **i** beginnt: z.B. **fantasy - fantasize** *(Fantasie - fantasieren)*.

•• Übersetze die Wörter aus der vorigen Übung ins Deutsche.

Nomen	Adjektive	Verben

••• Wenn du jetzt noch die folgende Tabelle ausfüllen kannst, dann bist du ein Meister der Suffixe! In der ersten Spalte steht das Ausgangswort (Verb, Adjektiv oder Nomen), an welches das Suffix angehängt wurde, in der zweiten und vierten Spalte die jeweiligen deutschen Übersetzungen.

	Ausgangswort	Übersetzung	Ausgangswort + Suffix	Übersetzung
	develop	entwickeln	**development**	Entwicklung
1.			**lighten**	
2.			**symbolize**	
3.	free			
4.			**emotionless**	
5.		Orgel	**organist**	
6.			**kingdom**	
7.			**sicken**	
8.	bore	langweilen		
9.			**darkness**	
10.	feel			

2.3 Zusammengesetzte Wörter im Englischen

• Schau dir die folgenden Sätze genau an und unterstreiche darin alle zusammengesetzten Wörter.

1. Can you give me the toothbrush, please?
2. My granny gave me a goldfish for my birthday.
3. Do you like football? – No, I prefer baseball.
4. Have you seen my handbag? – I think I've seen it in the bathroom.
5. My father is a policeman.

BOXENSTOPP

Man kann im Englischen neue Wörter bilden, indem man zwei schon vorhandene Wörter einfach zusammenfügt. Diese Wörter nennt man **compounds**.

snow + man

snowman
Schneemann

flower + pot

flowerpot
Blumentopf

rain + bow

rainbow
Regenbogen

•• Trage hier die **compounds** aus der Aufwärmübung ein und schreibe die jeweils richtige deutsche Übersetzung daneben.

compound	Übersetzung	compound	Übersetzung

Bei **compounds**, die meistens aus zwei Einzelwörtern bestehen, wird der zweite Teil durch den ersten näher bestimmt. Ein **teapot** ist ein Gefäß für Tee, ein **flowerpot** ein Gefäß für Blumen. Beide Male wird das Wörtchen **pot** *(Gefäß)* verwendet, aber der erste Wortteil bestimmt näher, um welche Art von Gefäß es sich genau handelt.

•• Füge jeweils ein Wort aus der linken und ein Wort aus der mittleren Spalte zu sinnvollen **compounds** zusammen. Beginne jeweils mit dem erstgenannten Wort, das Beispiel zeigt dir, wie es geht!

Einzelwörter		compound
1. class	board	1. classroom
2. straw	man	2.
3. key	shine	3.
4. water	room	4.
5. sun	noon	5.
6. wind	ache	6.
7. fire	pot	7.
8. head	berry	8.
9. after	mill	9.
10. flower	fall	10.

••• Wenn du jetzt noch mit Hilfe der Hinweise die richtigen compounds findest, dann hast du verstanden, wie man Wörter zusammenfügt. Bist du bereit? Dann mal los…

board · grass · hopper · tea · tooth · house · pencil

sky · scraper · mother · ball · grand · butter

black · pot · case · hand · fly · boat · brush

1. A very high building. ____________
2. Something your teacher writes on at school. ____________
3. You drink tea out of it. ____________
4. A famous sport in Germany (not football). ____________
5. An insect with colourful wings. ____________
6. Your mother's mother is your… ____________
7. You put your rubber, ruler and pens into your… ____________
8. You clean your teeth with it. ____________
9. A small, green jumping insect. ____________
10. A big boat you can live on. ____________

3 IN DER SCHULE

- In der Wortschnecke haben sich 11 Schulfächer versteckt. Kannst du sie alle finden? Schreibe deine Lösungen auf und achte dabei auch auf die Groß- und Kleinschreibung.

1. ______________________
2. ______________________
3. ______________________
4. ______________________
5. ______________________
6. ______________________
7. ______________________
8. ______________________
9. ______________________
10. ______________________
11. ______________________

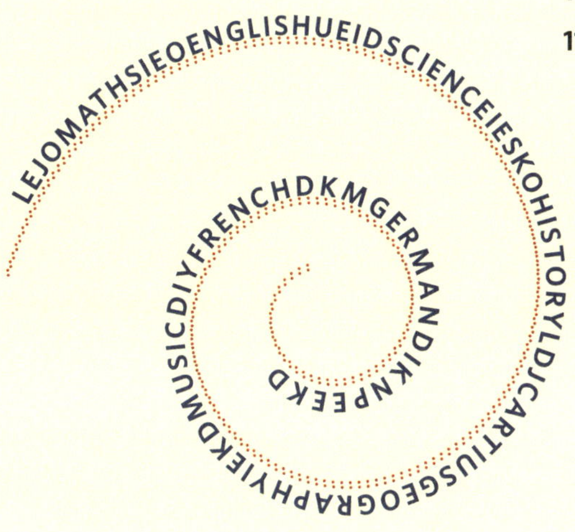

BOXENSTOPP

Achte bei den **sprachlichen Fächern** darauf, dass du die Großschreibung benutzt (**English, French, German, Spanish, Latin,** etc.). Abkürzungen wie **PE** für **physical education** *(Sport)* oder **RE** für **religious education** *(Religionslehre)* werden ebenfalls groß geschrieben. Hier noch einige Wörter, die du unbedingt kennen solltest:

headmaster (UK) **principal** (US)	*Direktor*	**assembly hall** (UK) **auditorium** (US)	*Aula*
secretary	*Sekretärin*	**library**	*Bibliothek*
caretaker (UK) **janitor** (US)	*Hausmeister*	**timetable** **schoolyard**	*Stundenplan* *Schulhof*

•• Hier kannst du deinen eigenen Stundenplan eintragen. Achte wieder auf Groß- und Kleinschreibung.

Uhrzeit	Monday	Tuesday	Wednesday	Thursday	Friday

Britische und amerikanische Schulen sind Ganztagesschulen. Die Kinder haben mittags eine längere Mittagspause (**lunch break**) und danach noch einige Stunden Unterricht. Hausaufgaben werden meistens direkt in der Schule gemacht. In den USA wiederholt sich der Stundenplan täglich, das heißt, wenn du in den USA zur Schule gehen würdest, dann hättest du jeden Tag zur gleichen Uhrzeit den gleichen Unterricht.

•• In diesem Gitternetz sind 15 Begriffe versteckt, die etwas mit der Schule zu tun haben. Kannst du sie alle finden?

Z	U	R	U	B	B	E	R	R	Z	G	B	M
B	S	C	H	O	O	L	B	U	S	L	B	P
L	S	E	K	B	P	W	Y	P	V	Y	O	E
A	Y	R	B	I	R	O	U	E	V	W	O	N
C	H	A	L	K	Z	Y	B	N	H	W	K	C
K	T	Z	D	E	S	K	J	T	V	B	E	I
B	T	U	D	B	E	R	H	K	C	T	R	L
O	E	K	P	K	E	G	L	U	E	J	U	C
A	A	L	U	D	G	E	R	Y	T	Z	L	A
R	C	U	P	F	K	E	W	L	C	N	E	S
D	H	T	I	M	E	T	A	B	L	E	R	E
Y	E	N	L	J	E	Y	R	T	K	U	Y	B
I	R	E	K	H	O	M	E	W	O	R	K	L

1. ______	6. ______	11. ______
2. ______	7. ______	12. ______
3. ______	8. ______	13. ______
4. ______	9. ______	14. ______
5. ______	10. ______	15. ______

•• Hier sind einige Sätze, die du wahrscheinlich schon öfter in der Schule gehört hast. Versuche, sie ins Deutsche oder eben ins Englische zu übersetzen.

English	German
1. ______	Setzt euch bitte hin.
2. Take the chalk (*Kreide*).	______.
3. ______?	Kannst du bitte das Fenster öffnen?
4. ______?	Wo ist dein Mäppchen?
5. Go to the headmaster's office.	______.
6. Can you close the door, please?	______?
7. If you know the answer, lift your arm.	______.
8. ______.	Herr Hill ist heute krank.

4 EUROPA

• Lies dir die folgenden Sätze genau durch. Unterstreiche darin die Ländernamen rot und die dazugehörigen Adjektive blau.

1. Cathérine is French. She lives in a small town in France.
2. Martin likes Italian food. He lived in Italy for some years.
3. Sarah's father is Greek, but she has never been to Greece herself.
4. Torben comes from Sweden. He has got a Swedish passport.
5. Susan learns Spanish. She wants to go to Spain next summer.
6. Switzerland is famous for watches. Swiss watches are popular all over the world.
7. If you go to Belgium, you have to try a Belgian waffle.

BOXENSTOPP

Manche Bezeichnungen (z.B. Städte- und Flussnamen) sind im Englischen anders als im Deutschen. Hier sind einige Bezeichnungen aus Deutschland, Österreich und der Schweiz, die du dir merken solltest.

Upper Austria	*Oberösterreich*	Lüneburg Heath	*Lüneburger Heide*
Lake Constance	*Bodensee*	Munich	*München*
Danube	*Donau*	Nuremberg	*Nürnberg*
Rhine	*Rhein*	Hanover	*Hannover*
The North Sea	*Nordsee*	Cologne	*Köln*
The Baltic Sea	*Ostsee*	Vienna	*Wien*
The Black Forest	*Schwarzwald*	Bavaria	*Bayern*
Bavarian Forest	*Bayerischer Wald*	Hesse	*Hessen*
Styria	*Steiermark*	Rhineland-Palatine	*Rheinland-Pfalz*
Carinthia	*Kärnten*	Franconia	*Franken*

Vergiss nicht, dass alle **Länder-, Städte- und Nationalitätenbezeichnungen** sowie **Namen** (auch Städte oder Flüsse) **immer groß geschrieben** werden. **Politische Bezeichnungen** wie **Federal Republic of Germany** *(Bundesrepublik Deutschland)* und **United Kingdom** *(Vereinigtes Königreich)* stehen immer **mit dem bestimmten Artikel the**:

I live in the Federal Republic of Germany. *Ich lebe in Deutschland.*

•• In der folgenden Liste sind einige Ländernamen Europas eingetragen. Allerdings fehlt jeweils entweder das Land oder das Adjektiv, mit dem man die dazugehörige Sprache oder die Leute bezeichnet, die in dem Land wohnen. Kannst du die fehlenden Wörter ergänzen?

Ländername	Adjektiv	Ländername	Adjektiv
1. Germany	____________	**8.** ____________	Belgian
2. ____________	Swiss	**9.** Austria	____________
3. ____________	Italian	**10.** England	____________
4. Spain	____________	**11.** ____________	Portuguese
5. France	____________	**12.** Denmark	____________
6. ____________	Norwegian	**13.** Sweden	____________
7. Greece	____________	**14.** ____________	Finnish

Wusstest du, dass es für **Ireland** *(Irland)* noch eine andere Bezeichnung gibt? Wegen den zahlreichen grünen Wiesen, die fast das gesamte Land bedecken, nennt man *Irland* auch **Emerald Island**, was soviel heißt wie *Smaragd-Insel* oder *grüne Insel*.

•• Ergänze im Folgenden jeweils das richtige Wort. Die einzelnen Sätze geben dir Hinweise auf ein Land (z.B. **Sweden**) oder eine Nationalität (z.B. **Swedish**). Wenn du das schaffst, dann hast du diese Lektion super verstanden!

1. Pizza is a famous ______________ dish *(Gericht)*.

2. ______________ is famous for kebabs and baklava.

3. You can find the Eiffel Tower in ______________.

4. Some people in ____________________ have beans on toast for breakfast.

5. Françoise, Jean, Claude and Catherine are ____________________ names.

6. The first marathon run took place in ______________.

7. Mozart was ______________. He was born in Salzburg.

8. Flamenco is a ______________ dance.

9. I have got a Yorkshire terrier. It's an ______________ dog.

10. ______________ is famous for its high-quality *(hochwertig)* watches.

5 IN DER STADT

- Schau dir die folgenden Sätze genau an und ergänze die Lücken in der deutschen Übersetzung. Die Vokabelangaben im Boxenstopp helfen dir dabei.

1. How do I get to the old part of town?
Wie komme ich zur ____________?

2. Go straight on until you get to the cinema.
Gehe ____________, bis du zum Kino kommst.

3. Turn right at the first set of traffic lights.
Biege an der ersten ____________ rechts ab.

4. At the roundabout, take the second exit.
Nimm im Kreisverkehr die zweite ____________.

BOXENSTOPP

Hier findest du einige Wendungen, die du sicher gut gebrauchen kannst, wenn du nach dem Weg fragen willst.

Turn left.	*Biege links ab.*	zebra crossing	*Zebrastreifen*
Turn right.	*Biege rechts ab.*	subway (UK) (pedestrian) underpass (US)	*(Fußgänger-) Unterführung*
Go straight on.	*Gehe geradeaus.*	pedestrian precinct (UK) pedestrian mall (US)	*Fußgängerzone*
bend	*Kurve*	old part of town	*Altstadt*
(set of) traffic lights	*Ampel*	It's on the left.	*Es befindet sich links.*
roundabout	*Kreisverkehr*	It's on the right.	*Es befindet sich rechts.*

•• **Wo** findet man **was** im Supermarkt?

In der Tabelle siehst du drei Abteilungen in einem Supermarkt. Weißt du, was man dort finden kann? Ordne die aufgeführten Produkte den einzelnen Abteilungen zu.

| **milk** | **jelly bears** | **pens** | **chocolate bars** | **glue** |
| **chewing gum** | **cheese** | **yogurt** | **envelopes** |

stationery *(Schreibwaren)*	**confectionery** *(Süßwaren)*	**dairy products** *(Milchprodukte)*

•• Lies dir die Hinweise auf der linken Seite durch und ordne sie dann den passenden Gebäuden rechts zu. Die richtigen Lösungen findest du wie immer im Anhang!

1. You can go there if you want to buy bread.
2. They look after your money in this building.
3. You can go there on Sundays and listen to a service.
4. He sells meat.
5. You can go there when you get robbed *(ausgeraubt)*.
6. They sell stamps and stationery.
7. If you you are ill, you have to go to this place.
8. If a car runs out of fuel *(Benzin)*, you can buy some there.
9. You can have a meal there.
10. They show the latest *(neuesten)* movies in this building.

a. post office
b. hospital
c. police station
d. church
e. bakery
f. butcher
g. restaurant
h. bank
i. cinema
j. petrol station

Aufgepasst beim Einkauf in der Stadt: Hosen (z.B. **jeans, shorts, underpants** *(Unterhosen)*, etc.) stehen im Englischen immer im Plural! Sieh dir hierzu auch das nachfolgende Verkaufsgespräch an.

••• Vervollständige nun noch das folgende Verkaufsgespräch mit den vorgegebenen Begriffen.

How much · Good morning · are · sale · change · take · looking · take · small · size · help you

Client: Good morning.

Shop assistant: (1) ________________, Madam. How can I (2) ________________?

Client: I'm (3) ________________ for a pair of trousers.

Shop assistant: Sure, Madam. What (4)____________ do you take?

Client: I (5) ____________ size 12.

Shop assistant: Here you are, Madam. What do you think?

Client: I think it's too (6) ____________. I need a bigger size.

Shop assistant: How about these ones here?

Client: These are perfect. I'll (7) ____________ them. (8) ____________ are they?

Shop assistant: They are on (9) ____________. Just £29.90, Madam.

Shop assistant: *(At the cash desk)* That's £ 29.90 then, Madam.

Client: Here you (10) ____________.

Shop assistant: Thank you very much. That's 10 pence (11) ____________ for you.

6 FUN TIME

• Lies dir die folgenden Sätze links einmal durch und versuche dann, die Vokabeln rechts daneben ins Deutsche zu übersetzen.

Red lorry, yellow lorry.	**1. lorry** = ________________
Red bulb, blue bulb.	**2. bulb** = ________________
Which wristwatches are Swiss wristwatches?	**3. wristwatch** = ________________
	4. swiss = ________________
A box of mixed biscuits, a mixed biscuit box.	**5. mixed** = ________________
	6. biscuits = ________________
Peter Piper picked a peck of pickled peppers,	**7. to pick** = ________________
A peck of pickled peppers Peter Piper picked.	**8. pickled** = ________________
If Peter Piper picked a peck of pickled peppers,	**9. peppers** = ________________
How many pickled peppers did Peter Piper pick?	

BOXENSTOPP

Bestimmt bist du beim Lesen der Sätze in der Aufwärmübung ein bisschen ins Stocken geraten, richtig? Es handelt sich hier um bekannte englische Zungenbrecher, so genannte **tongue twisters**. Diese sind deshalb so schwer auszusprechen, weil sie Wörter enthalten, die mit den gleichen Buchstaben beginnen und sich insgesamt sehr ähnlich anhören.

•• Sprich die **tongue twisters** aus der Aufwärmübung jeweils dreimal schnell hintereinander aus. Es ist gar nicht so leicht, sich dabei nicht zu versprechen, stimmt's? Wenn du das geschafft hast, kannst du versuchen, dein Buch zu schließen und die Zungenbrecher ohne Hilfe aufzusagen. Viel Spaß!

•• Den folgenden Kinderreim kennt im englischsprachigen Raum fast jeder. Lies ihn dir einmal durch und sprich nach. Versuche dann, den Reim ins Deutsche zu übersetzen. Deine Übersetzung muss sich nicht unbedingt reimen.

Humpty Dumpty sat on a wall, ____________________

Humpty Dumpty had a great fall, ____________________

All the King's horses and all the King's men, ____________________

Couldn't put Humpty together again. ____________________

Humpty Dumpty ist eine sehr bekannte Figur, genauer gesagt: ein Ei! Er stammt aus dem englischen Kinderreim **Mother Goose** *(Mutter Gans)*. Du kennst ihn vielleicht aber auch aus dem Märchen **Alice in Wonderland** *(Alice im Wunderland)* von Lewis Carroll.

●● Lies dir die folgenden Witze durch und versuche dann jeweils, die Vokabeln darunter ins Deutsche zu übersetzen. Wenn du sie dir gut merkst, kannst du die Witze in der Schule erzählen!

An elementary school teacher sends a message to all parents on the first day of school.

"If you promise not to believe everything your child says happens at school, I will promise not to believe everything your child says happens at home."

elementary school = ____________________

Two balloons are flying across the desert. One balloon says to the other, "Look out for the cactusssssssssssss!"

look out for = ____________________

The teacher says, "Mary, can you give me a sentence beginning with 'I', please."

Mary thinks for a second and then says, "I is..."

The teacher interrupts her and says, "No Mary, you cannot say 'I is...' – you must use 'I am...'."

Mary looks upset and says, "But Miss..."

The teacher shouts, "Give me a sentence that begins with 'I am', please."

Mary shrugs her shoulders and says, "I am the ninth letter of the alphabet."

interrupt = ____________________

upset = ____________________

shrug one's shoulders = ____________________

●●● Hast du Lust, zum Schluss noch ein paar **rebus puzzles** zu lösen? Das geht so: Ein **rebus puzzle** löst man, indem man die angegebenen Buchstaben, deren Anordnung und Darstellung miteinander verbindet und ein sinnvolles Wort, einen gebräuchlichen Ausdruck oder eine Redewendung im Englischen damit beschreibt. Hier musst du also „um die Ecke" denken! Das Beispiel zeigt dir, wie es funktioniert.

ARREST **YOU ARE**	*You are under arrest.*
talk	1. ____________________
MI1LLION	2. ____________________
XQQQME	3. ____________________
BIG BIG **ignore ignore**	4. ____________________

7 DAS WETTER

- Ergänze die Lücken im folgenden Text.

Wenn du beschreiben willst, wie das Wetter ist, dann musst du immer vier Dinge angegeben: die (1) ________________ (in °C oder °F), die **Bewölkung**, den **Niederschlag** und die (2) ______________________, aus welcher der Wind kommt.

Kannst du die fehlenden Himmelsrichtungen einfügen?

(3) ________

Northwest

(4) ________

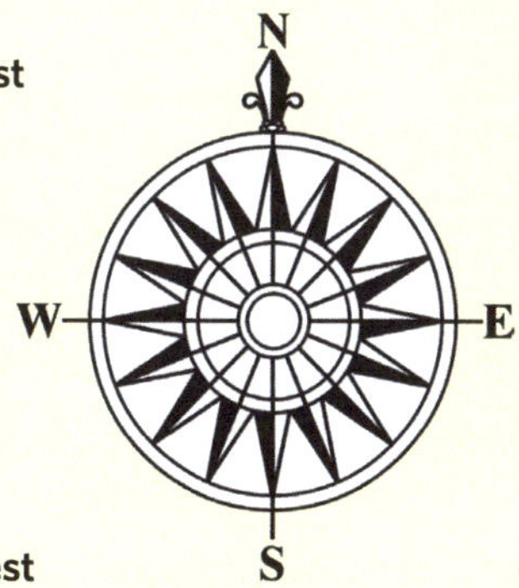

(6) ________

East

Southwest

(5) ________

South

BOXENSTOPP

Hier sind einige Wörter, die du gut gebrauchen kannst, wenn du übers Wetter sprechen möchtest:

weather forecast	*Wettervorhersage*	**sunny**	*sonnig*
low	*Tiefsttemperatur*	**cloudy**	*wolkig*
high	*Höchsttemperatur*	**rain**	*Regen*
heavy	*stark*	**snow**	*Schnee*
light	*leicht*	**sleet**	*Graupel*
partly	*teilweise*	**blizzard**	*Schneesturm*
mostly	*meist*	**sleet shower**	*Graupelschauer*
storm	*Sturm*	**shower**	*Schauer*
lightning	*Blitz*	**thunder**	*Donner*

●● In den folgenden zwei Wortschlangen sind insgesamt zwölf Wörter versteckt, die etwas mit dem Wetter zu tun haben. Findest du sie alle? Trage die Begriffe in der Tabelle unten ein.

Wortschlange 1	Wortschlange 2
1. ______	1. ______
2. ______	2. ______
3. ______	3. ______
4. ______	4. ______
5. ______	5. ______
6. ______	6. ______

In den USA benutzt man zur Angabe der Temperatur nicht **Grad Celsius (°C)**, sondern **Grad Fahrenheit (°F)**. Man findet diese Temperaturangaben auch noch in Großbritannien, aber Grad Celsius hat dort Grad Fahrenheit weitestgehend abgelöst. Hier findest du eine Umrechnungstabelle:

°C	°F	°C	°F	°C	°F	°C	°F
-15	5	0	32	+10	50	+25	77
-10	14	+1	33,8	+15	59	+30	86
-5	23	+5	41	+20	68	+35	95

•• Hier siehst du die Wettervorhersagen für vier Städte, die du bestimmt kennst. Trage einen Pfeil für die Windrichtung ein und ein Symbol (also eine Regenwolke, Sonne, etc.) für die Beschreibung der Wetterverhältnisse. Bei der Umrechnung der Angaben von Grad Fahrenheit zu Grad Celsius kannst du auch ungefähre Angaben machen, wenn die genaue Zahl nicht in der Umrechnungstabelle angegeben ist. Los geht's!

London

Wind: North	↓
Heavy rain	
Low: 14°F	**-10** °C
High: 27 °F	______ °C

Sheffield

Wind: South	
Light snow	
Low: 23°F	______ °C
High: 35 °F	______ °C

Los Angeles

Wind: Northwest	
Sunny	
Low: 68°F	______ °C
High: 90 °F	______ °C

Hong Kong

Wind: Southeast	
Thunder and lightning	
Low: 60°F	______ °C
High: 77°F	______ °C

••• Mit der folgenden Tabelle kannst du die Wetterverhältnisse an deinem Wohnort eine Woche lang beobachten. Fange am besten an einem Montag an. Trage für die Windrichtung einen Pfeil ein, beschreibe in der zweiten Zeile die Wetterverhältnisse (**sunny, cloudy, heavy rain,** etc.), zeichne dazu ein Symbol (Sonne, Regenwolke, etc.) und ergänze zum Schluss noch die Höchst- und Tiefsttemperaturen. Na, ist bei dir gutes Wetter?

	Monday	**Tuesday**	**Wednesday**	**Thursday**
Wind:				
Weather:				
Temperature: High	___°C / ___°F	___°C / ___°F	___°C / ___°F	___°C / ___°F
Low	___°C / ___°F	___°C / ___°F	___°C / ___°F	___°C / ___°F

	Friday	**Saturday**	**Sunday**
Wind:			
Weather:			
Temperature: High	___°C / ___°F	___°C / ___°F	___°C / ___°F
Low	___°C / ___°F	___°C / ___°F	___°C / ___°F

8 FAMILIE

- In der folgenden Wortschnecke sind 10 Begriffe versteckt, die etwas mit der Familie zu tun haben. Findest du sie alle? Schreibe die Wörter in die dafür vorgesehenen Zeilen auf der rechten Seite.

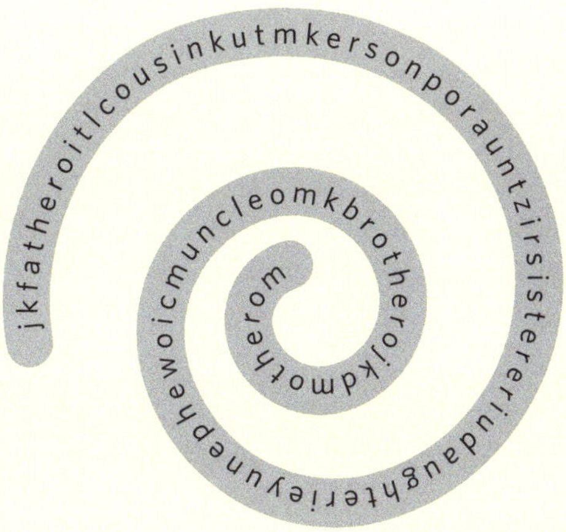

1. ______________________
2. ______________________
3. ______________________
4. ______________________
5. ______________________
6. ______________________
7. ______________________
8. ______________________
9. ______________________
10. ______________________

BOXENSTOPP

Bestimmt kennst du schon einige Wörter, die Familienmitglieder beschreiben. Hier sind noch einmal die wichtigsten Begriffe:

parents (mother / father)	*Eltern (Mutter / Vater)*
siblings (sister / brother)	*Geschwister (Schwester / Bruder)*
grandparents (grandmother / grandfather)	*Großeltern (Großmutter / Großvater)*
niece / nephew	*Nichte / Neffe*
cousin	*Cousine / Cousin*
aunt / uncle	*Tante / Onkel*
wife / husband	*Ehefrau / Ehemann*

Anstelle der deutschen Vorsilbe *Ur-* (wie z.B. in *Urgroßvater*) wird im Englischen das Adjektiv **great** verwendet:

great grandfather	*Urgroßvater / Urgroßmutter*
great-great grandfather	*Ururgroßvater / Ururgroßmutter*

•• Hier sind einige Buchstaben durcheinander geraten. Findest du heraus, um welches Familienmitglied es sich jeweils handelt?

1.	**treghadu**	______	**6.**	**nos**	______
2.	**wehpen**	______	**7.**	**suinco**	______
3.	**nuta**	______	**8.**	**thorem**	______
4.	**ecien**	______	**9.**	**tgrnafhdare**	______
5.	**rhtbore**	______	**10.**	**tissre**	______

Verwandtschaftswörter, die im Deutschen mit *Schwieger-* beginnen, werden im Englischen mit **in-law** übersetzt. Die *Schwiegermutter* heißt also **mother-in-law**, und **son-in-law** ist der *Schwiegersohn*. Ach ja, und der *Schwager* heißt auf Englisch **brother-in-law**.

••• Lies dir die folgenden Sätze durch und entscheide, ob sie richtig oder falsch sind.

	Richtig	Falsch
1. My sister's son is my cousin.	☐	☐
2. My mother's sister is my aunt.	☐	☐
3. My grandfather's father is my great grandfather.	☐	☐
4. The children of my father's brother are my nephews.	☐	☐
5. My mother's father is my uncle.	☐	☐
6. My husband's mother is my mother-in-law.	☐	☐

••• Zur Belohnung darfst du jetzt noch ein bisschen malen! Zeichne ein Bild von deiner Familie (Eltern, Geschwister, Großeltern) und benenne jedes Familienmitglied mit den Bezeichnungen, die du in diesem Kapitel geübt hast.

9 BERUFE

- Sieh dir die folgenden Beispielsätze genau an. Mit welcher Zeitform werden Berufsbezeichnungen im Englischen angegeben?

Jules: "What does you father do?"
Nick: "He is a shop assistant. And your father?"
Jules: "He works as a policeman. He arrests people. And what does your mother do?"
Nick: "She is a waitress."

Berufsbezeichnungen stehen im Englischen mit dem ____________________.

BOXENSTOPP

Bei den meisten Berufsbezeichnungen gibt es im Englischen für Männer und Frauen nur eine Form, z.B. **dentist** *(Zahnarzt / Zahnärztin)*. Nur bei manchen Berufsbezeichnungen unterscheidet man zwischen einer männlichen und einer weiblichen Form:

actor	*Schauspieler*	**actress**	*Schauspielerin*
waiter	*Kellner*	**waitress**	*Kellnerin*
policeman	*Polizist*	**policewoman**	*Polizistin*

•• In diesem Gitternetz sind 15 Berufsbezeichnungen versteckt. Kannst du sie alle finden? Trage die Begriffe in die Liste auf der nächsten Seite ein.

E	W	I	P	S	R	B	U	S	D	R	I	V	E	R
U	A	T	P	X	X	U	O	L	M	V	R	Y	M	U
H	I	Z	O	Y	C	L	E	A	N	E	R	L	Z	X
A	T	L	S	N	H	Z	D	M	U	L	S	R	F	G
I	R	B	T	M	E	H	C	R	R	H	J	K	S	R
R	E	S	M	K	F	B	B	T	S	K	C	X	N	M
D	S	C	A	R	U	V	J	D	E	N	T	I	S	T
R	S	H	N	Z	O	C	H	D	F	U	J	M	X	W
E	P	O	L	I	C	E	M	A	N	M	R	E	R	T
S	U	S	E	C	R	E	T	A	R	Y	I	J	F	E
S	R	E	Z	O	P	L	U	M	B	E	R	L	A	A
E	C	V	M	L	A	P	L	G	V	M	W	X	R	C
R	M	C	A	R	P	E	N	T	E	R	L	M	M	H
S	U	K	M	K	L	S	R	T	V	H	T	J	E	E
D	O	C	T	O	R	X	P	L	K	V	X	W	R	R

1. ______________ 6. ______________ 11. ______________
2. ______________ 7. ______________ 12. ______________
3. ______________ 8. ______________ 13. ______________
4. ______________ 9. ______________ 14. ______________
5. ______________ 10. ______________ 15. ______________

Aufgepasst, Sportsfreunde: Im Deutschen sagt man z.B. *Er ist Schreiner.* oder *Sie ist Ärztin.* Im Englischen wird jedoch immer der unbestimmte Artikel vor die Berufsbezeichnung gesetzt:
He is **a** carpenter. She is **a** doctor.

•• Übersetze die Berufsbezeichnungen ins Deutsche, die du im Gitternetz in der vorigen Übung gefunden hast.

1. ______________ 9. ______________
2. ______________ 10. ______________
3. ______________ 11. ______________
4. ______________ 12. ______________
5. ______________ 13. ______________
6. ______________ 14. ______________
7. ______________ 15. ______________
8. ______________

••• Ordne die Satzteile auf der rechten Seite den jeweils richtigen Satzanfängen links zu, dann kennst du dich mit Berufen bestens aus!

1. If you are a nurse,	**a.** plan houses.
2. A chef	**b.** you serve drinks and meals in restaurants.
3. A bus driver is someone who	**c.** you look after people in hospital.
4. Architects	**d.** stop fire.
5. A postman is someone who	**e.** drives a bus.
6. If you are a waiter,	**f.** you build houses, bridges, etc.
7. Fire fighters	**g.** brings you the mail.
8. Detectives	**h.** cuts your hair.
9. If you are a builder,	**i.** cooks in restaurants.
10. A hairdresser is someone who	**j.** solve crimes.

Inhalt

Grammatik

Wortschatz

KLASSE 7

1 DIE ZEITEN DER GEGENWART

- Simple Present oder Present Progressive? Setze die passenden Verbformen ein.

Eric usually (1) __________ (get up) at six o'clock. Then he (2) __________ (have) breakfast. He (3) __________ (like) cornflakes, and his sister Jenny also (4) __________ (like) them very much. At 7.30 both (5) __________ (leave) the house. Eric's school always (6) __________ (start) at 8 a.m. and lessons normally (7) __________ (finish) at 2 p.m. Later in the afternoon Eric (8) __________ (do) his homework, and after that he sometimes (9) __________ (surf) the internet. But on the weekend, the kids mostly (10) __________ (stay) in bed until 9 a.m. and they (11) __________ (not have) to do any homework!

It's 8.30 in the morning and Mum and Dad (12) __________ (eat) their breakfast. They (13) __________ (have) toast and eggs. Mum (14) __________ (read) the newspaper. Dad (15) __________ (listen) to the radio. And when Eric enters the kitchen, Dad (16) __________ (wonder): "Eric? What (17) __________ (do) here? You (18) __________ (be) late for school! And why (19) __________ Jenny __________ (come), too?" Mum and Dad (20) __________ (look) at each other. "What (21) __________ (go) on?" But the kids (22) __________ (laugh): "Don't worry, Dad. It's Saturday – we (23) __________ (not go) to school today!"

BOXENSTOPP

Kleine Auffrischung gefällig? Das ist nämlich gar nicht so schwer mit den Zeiten! Das Simple Present drückt aus, was **immer so ist** (Zustand) oder **regelmäßig** geschieht. Das Present Progressive drückt etwas aus, was **jetzt gerade** passiert. Du kannst die Zeiten auch ganz einfach an bestimmten Signalwörtern erkennen. Ordne die folgenden Signalwörter in die Tabelle ein:

sometimes   at the moment   often   every week   on Saturday   always
now   Listen!   still   Look!   usually   never   just   right now

Simple present	Present progressive

Vergiss nicht die richtige Verneinung für die beiden Zeitformen. Das Simple Present verneinst du mit dem Hilfsverb **don't** bzw. **doesn't**. Zum Verneinen des Present Progressive fügst du einfach **not** nach der entsprechenden Form von **to be** ein!

•• Du besuchst deinen Freund Eric in New York. Seine Mutter stellt dir einige Fragen. Was möchte sie alles wissen? Ergänze ihre Fragen an der jeweiligen Stelle.

1. Where exactly ______________ (to live) in Germany?
- I live in Hamburg.

2. When ______________ (to get up) in the morning?
- I mostly get up at 7 o'clock.

3. What ______________ (to like) for breakfast?
- I like orange juice and toast for breakfast.

4. ______________ (to have) a pet?
- Yes, I do. I have a dog called Shopper.

5. Who ______________ (to take care) of your dog at the moment?
- My parents are keeping an eye on him while I'm away.

6. How ______________ (to feel) being in New York ?
- I'm feeling fine, thanks.

•• Da du einen ganzen Tag mit Eric verbringst, weißt du anschließend ziemlich genau über seinen Tagesablauf Bescheid. Schreibe auf, was du mit ihm erlebst.

1. It's 7 a.m. Eric ______________ (to do) his homework. He sometimes __________ (to do) his homework before he goes to school.

2. It's 12 o'clock. Eric ______________ (to have) lunch. Sometimes he __________ (to have) three cheeseburgers for lunch!

3. It's 3 p.m. Eric ______________ (to play) the guitar. He always __________ (to practice) the guitar on Monday.

4. It's 4.30 p.m. Eric ______________ (to go) shopping with me. He usually ________ (to buy) nice things at the shopping mall.

5. Eric and I always ______________ (to have) a good time together. But school, lessons and shopping can be exhausting. It's now 11 p.m. and we ______________ (to go) to bed.

••• Im Einkaufszentrum hast du einen Mantel entdeckt, der dir gut gefällt. Notiere deine Unterhaltung mit dem Verkäufer. Die folgenden Angaben helfen dir dabei:

to wear | sales | to have a look at | to like | coat | to be sorry, but... | to not fit | usually | changing room | to look for something | size M | to try something on

Der Verkäufer begrüßt dich.

1. ______________________________

Du sagst, dass du nach einem neuen Mantel suchst.

2. ______________________________

Er fragt, welche Größe du normalerweise trägst.

3. ______________________________

Du sagst, dass deine deutsche Größe M ist.

4. ______________________________

Er legt dir einen schönen roten Mantel hin.

5. ______________________________

Du fragst nach dem Preis.

6. ______________________________

Er sagt, dass im Moment Schlussverkauf sei und nennt dir den Preis: $ 39,90.

7. ______________________________

Du fragst, wo du den Mantel anprobieren kannst.

8. ______________________________

Er zeigt dir, welche Umkleidekabine frei ist.

9. ______________________________

Du sagst, dass dir der Mantel gefällt, er dir aber nicht passt.

10. ______________________________

Er sagt, dass es leider der letzte Mantel sei.

11. ______________________________

Du bedauerst das und verabschiedest dich.

12. ______________________________

2 DIE ZEITEN DER ZUKUNFT

- Verbinde die folgenden Satzteile sinnvoll miteinander.

1. My older brother	're going to have to be quieter	soon.
2. I'm sure	he is going to shout	but that's still a secret.
3. Can you promise	you won't tell anybody	detention.
4. Look at Mr Mills,	he is going to give us	next lesson.
5. If we are too noisy	he'll have a party,	in June.
6. We	will be 18	about it?

BOXENSTOPP

Kurze Verschnaufpause! Die Zukunft mit **will** und die Zukunft mit **going to** kennst du ja schon. Aber wie war das noch gleich? Setze ein:

Absicht — Anzeichen — **keinen Einfluss** — **sicher** — Vermutungen

Man verwendet die Zukunft mit **will**, um Handlungen in der Zukunft auszudrücken, auf die man ______________________ hat und auch, um ______________ über die Zukunft anzustellen. Die Zukunft mit **going to** verwendet man dagegen, wenn man ______________ ist, dass etwas geschehen wird, weil es bereits erste ______________ dafür gibt, oder weil man die feste ______________ hat, etwas zu tun.

Im Englischen kannst du auch mit dem Present Progressive ausdrücken, dass jemand etwas für die Zukunft fest geplant hat. Um Verwechslungen mit der Gegenwart zu vermeiden, steht es dann meist mit Zeitbestimmungen der Zukunft wie **tomorrow, next week** etc. Das Simple Present verwendet man, wenn es sich um feste Termine in der Zukunft handelt. Vergleiche die folgenden Beispiele:

Tomorrow I'm visiting my friends in Dublin.
Morgen werde ich meine Freunde in Dublin besuchen.

My plane leaves at 8:45 and arrives in Dublin at 10:05.
Mein Flugzeug fliegt um 8:45 Uhr ab und landet um 10:05 Uhr.

•• Mit dem Future Perfect drückt man aus, dass eine bestimmte Handlung zu einem bestimmten Zeitpunkt in der Zukunft abgeschlossen sein wird. Verbinde die passenden Satzpaare miteinander und unterstreiche dann die neue Futurform.

1. Pam will get pocket money on Friday.
2. Nick will write an email to Tom.
3. Sally will borrow DVDs from the video shop.

a. She won't have watched them all by Monday.
b. She will have spent most of it by Sunday.
c. He will have got a reply by next week.

•• Nächste Woche ist Sportwoche in der Schule. Jeden Tag kann man eine neue Sportart ausprobieren. Schreibe auf, was genau an welchem Tag stattfindet. Benutze dafür das Present Progressive.

Monday: do skateboarding all day
Tuesday: have a judo competition
Wednesday: play tennis after lunch
Thursday: go swimming at the public pool
Friday: aerobics, start at 8:30 a.m.

1. On Monday ______
2. ______
3. ______
4. ______
5. ______

•• Um dir einen Überblick zu verschaffen, erstellst du dir einen Tagesplan. Notiere hier, welche Sportart du wann ausprobiert haben wirst. Achte dabei auf die richtige Zeitform!

1. By Monday ______
2. By Tuesday ______
3. By Wednesday ______
4. By Thursday ______
5. By Friday ______

••• In der übernächsten Woche steht leider ein Englischtest auf dem Programm. Kannst du die folgenden Sätze jetzt auch noch ins Englische übersetzen? Das ist schon ganz schön knifflig, was?

1. Am Wochenende werde ich viel lernen!

______

2. Meine Mutter wird mit mir bis dahin noch drei Mal geübt haben.

______

3. Bis Mittwoch werde ich mein Englischheft zwei Mal durchgelesen haben.

______

3 DIE ZEITEN DER VERGANGENHEIT

- Lies dir den Dialog zwischen Robert und Jane durch und vervollständige das Gespräch mit den Zeitformen des Simple Past und des Present Perfect. Achte auf die Verneinung.

Robert: Hey Jane, do you remember my friend Lukas? It (1) ______________ (to be) his birthday yesterday.

Jane: Of course! How old (2) _________ he _________ (to get)?

Robert: He (3) _________ (to turn) 15, but he (4) __________________ (not have) a birthday party yet because he (5) __________________ (not want) to party on a Monday.

Jane: I understand! But (6) _________ he _________ (to get) nice presents then?

Robert: Yes. His parents (7) _________ (to give) him a new mountain bike.

Jane: Wow! (8) _________ you ever _________ (to do) mountain biking?

Robert: Yes, I have. Lukas' family and I (9) _________ (to go) to France last year. That (10) _________ (to be) fun!

Jane: I (11) _________ never _________ (to do) mountain-biking in my life... Can I come next time?

Hier noch ein schlauer Merksatz für Englisch-Athleten: **Yesterday, ago** und **last** erfordern immer Simple Past!

BOXENSTOPP

Puh! Einmal kurz durchatmen, bevor's gleich weiter geht. Wie war das noch mal? Setze ein:

Present Perfect   Simple Past

Mit dem ______________________ drückt man aus, dass eine Handlung in der Vergangenheit **abgeschlossen** wurde und **vorbei** ist. Mit dem __________________ betont man, dass sich etwas in der Vergangenheit abgespielt hat, das **jetzt** (in der Gegenwart) **noch spürbar** ist. Bestimmte Zeitangaben (z.B. **already, never, just, (not) yet**) zeigen, dass es sich um einen **Zeitraum** handelt, der von der Vergangenheit bis in die Gegenwart reicht.

•• Wenn man betonen möchte, dass sich ein Ereignis **vor** einem anderen Ereignis in der Vergangenheit abgespielt hat, verwendet man das Past Perfect. Hier sind jedoch einige Buchstaben durcheinander geraten. Kannst du die Worte entschlüsseln?

1. Lukas had prepared lots of snacks **R O B E F E** __________ his birthday party started.

2. H E W N __________ all of his guests had arrived, they all sang him a song.

3. E R F T A __________ Lukas had thanked them for singing, they had a great party together.

•• Lies dir die folgenden Sätze durch. Kreuze dann an, in welcher Reihenfolge die Ereignisse stattgefunden haben.

1. Lukas did his homework. Then he invited his friends.
- ☐ After Lukas had invited his friends he did his homework.
- ☐ After Lukas had done his homework he invited his friends.

2. I finished my book. Then I went to the party.
- ☐ I had already finished my book when I went to the party.
- ☐ I went to the party before I had finished my book.

3. I phoned Maria at about six. She came to the party at eight.
- ☐ I phoned Maria, but she had already left for the party.
- ☐ After I had phoned Maria she came to the party.

•• Bevor die Party losging, hatte Lukas noch viele Dinge zu erledigen. Setze die richtige Zeitform des Verbs ein (Simple Past oder Past Perfect).

1. The atmosphere __________________ (be) really nice. Lukas __________________ (decorate) the garden with lots of balloons and flowers.

2. Lots of people __________________ (come) to the party, because Lukas __________________ (send) invitation cards to all of his friends.

3. Lukas __________________ (go) shopping the day before the party, so there __________________ (be) enough sweets and snacks.

4. Lukas' mother __________________ (bake) a big cake, which ______________ (taste) very good.

5. Lukas' father __________________ (put out) chairs and tables, so everyone __________________ (can) sit down.

••• Warum ist Lukas' Cousine Lucy nicht zur Party erschienen? Bilde Sätze und verwende dabei das Past Perfect. Mit den Präpositionen **after, before** oder **when** kannst du die Sätze miteinander verbinden.

1. 6 p.m.: Lucy arrives at the bus stop - 5:50 p.m.: the bus leaves

____

2. 6:15 p.m.: next bus arrives - Lucy gets on the bus

____

3. 6:20 p.m.: buy ticket - 6:25 p.m.: Lucy takes the wrong bus

____

4 MODALE HILFSVERBEN

• Die folgenden modalen Hilfsverben und ihre Verneinung kennst du schon. Verbinde die Sätze auf der linken Seite mit der jeweils passenden Verneinung rechts.

1. In Germany, pupils **can** wear jeans to school.
2. **May** I use my mobile phone at school?
3. I **must** do my English homework.

a. I **needn't** do my homework. Mine is already done.
b. That's great! In British schools they **can't**...
c. No, you **mustn't**. Leave it at home!

Aufgepasst und nicht verwechseln: Die Verneinung von **must** ist **needn't,** und **may** wird mit **mustn't** verneint!

BOXENSTOPP

Schon ganz aus der Puste? Hier gibt's eine kleine Erfrischung! Da die modalen Hilfsverben meist nur im Präsens verwendet werden, benutzt man für die anderen Zeitformen die Ersatzformen. Ergänze die Regel und setze ein:

notwendig ist | in der Lage ist / fähig ist | darf | nicht notwendig ist

1. Mit **can** kann man ausdrücken, dass jemand ____________________, etwas zu tun. Die Ersatzform lautet **be able to**.
2. Mit **can / may** kann man ausdrücken, dass jemand etwas tun ____________________. Die Ersatzform lautet **be allowed to**.
3. Mit **must** kann man ausdrücken, dass etwas ____________________. Die Ersatzform lautet **have to**. Mit **needn't** kann man ausdrücken, dass etwas ____________________. Die Ersatzform lautet **not have to**.

•• Schau dir die folgenden Sätze an und unterstreiche jeweils die korrekte Ersatzform des hervorgehobenen Hilfsverbs.

1. Our school has a cafeteria. That means that we **can** (are able to / are allowed to / have to) have lunch at school.
2. We **may** (are able to / are allowed to / have to) take our mobiles to school, but we **mustn't** (aren't able to / aren't allowed to / may not) use them.
3. We never **must** (are able to / are allowed to / have to) go to school on Saturdays, and we **needn't** (aren't able to / aren't allowed to / don't have to) go to school in the afternoon.
4. We always get homework, but we **can** (are able to / are allowed to / have to) do it at school, if there's time.
5. School starts at 8 a.m., and we **mustn't** (aren't able to / aren't allowed to / may not) come in late.

Um die Ersatzformen der Modalverben in allen Zeiten verwenden zu können, solltest du die Formen von **be** und **have** beherrschen. Denn nur **be** und **have** müssen dabei in die entsprechende Zeit versetzt werden. Der Rest der Ersatzform bleibt unverändert.

••• Alles nur Fantasie? Oder welche Regeln herrschen in der Schule der Zukunft? Beschreibe, wie Lehrer und Schüler in der Zukunft zusammen arbeiten könnten. Hier sind natürlich unterschiedliche Lösungen möglich, einige davon findest du im Anhang!

Teachers	can	do	comics
Pupils	may	eat	TV
	must	play	ice-cream
	needn't	read	school uniforms
	mustn't	talk	e-mails
		use	homework
		wear	mobile phones
		write	SMS messages
		watch	...?
		...?	

Teachers must wear school uniforms.

____

____

____

____

____

5 VOM AKTIV INS PASSIV

• Lies dir die beiden Beispielsätze durch und beantworte dann die folgenden Fragen.

Aktiv: The teacher chose Eric as the best student.

Passiv: Eric was chosen as the best student by the teacher.

1. Welches ist das Subjekt des Aktivsatzes? ☐ the teacher ☐ Eric

2. Welches ist das Subjekt des Passivsatzes? ☐ the teacher ☐ Eric

Aktivsätze betonen, **wer** etwas tut. Passivsätze betonen, **was** getan wird oder wem etwas widerfährt. Hier steht die Handlung im Vordergrund und nicht derjenige, der etwas tut!

BOXENSTOPP

Aufgepasst! Wird ein Aktivsatz in einen Passivsatz umgewandelt, dann ist Folgendes zu beachten:

1. Das Objekt des Aktivsatzes wird zum Subjekt des Passivsatzes.
2. Die passiven Zeitformen werden mit einer Form von **to be** und dem Past Participle gebildet.
3. Das Aktivverb wird zum Passivverb, aber die Zeit bleibt in beiden Sätzen gleich. Im Passivsatz verändert sich nur die Form von **to be** je nach Zeit.
4. Möchte man betonen, von wem etwas getan wird, dann kann man den Verursacher der Handlung mit Hilfe der Präposition **by** am Satzende anfügen.

•• **Is** oder **are**? Setze die Zubereitung für ein leckeres Sandwich mit **peanut butter** und **jelly** ins Passiv.

1. Spread peanut butter on one slice of bread.

____

2. Spread jelly or jam on the other slice of bread.

____

3. Use slightly less jelly than peanut butter.

____

4. Put the two pieces of bread together.

____

5. Cut the sandwich in half for easier eating.

____

Kannst du jetzt auch die folgende Tabelle mit Hilfe der Regel vervollständigen?

	Aktivsatz	Passivsatz
Simple Present	I love sandwiches.	6. ______
Simple Past	I loved sandwiches.	7. ______
Present Perfect	I have loved sandwiches.	8. ______
Past Perfect	I had loved sandwiches.	9. ______
Zukunft mit **will**	I will love sandwiches.	10. ______

•• Du bist mit deiner Familie in einem Restaurant und es geschehen so einige Dinge. Aber niemand will es gewesen sein. Wer gibt hier wem die Schuld? Bilde Sätze im Passiv und füge den Urheber der jeweiligen Handlung mit **by** an.

1. Jon: "Stella and Jonas drank up my juice!"

My juice was drunk up by Stella and Jonas.

2. Bill: "Someone took my money!"

3. Mona: "Philip ordered the same meal!"

4. Emma: "The dog ate my hamburger!"

5. Lisa: "My parents spilled coffee all over the table!"

6. Dylan: "The waiter didn't bring the bill!"

•• In einem Restaurant arbeiten viele Leute. Einige Buchstaben sind durcheinander geraten. Finde zuerst die Berufe und bilde dann Passivsätze. Was wird von wem erledigt?

okoc
erawti
wtirases
arb ekper

mix the drinks
welcome the guests
prepare the meals
wash the dishes
set the table

1. The meals are prepared

2. The guests

3.

4.

5.

Viele englische Sätze können mit zwei Objekten verwendet werden. Beide Objekte des Aktivsatzes können dann zum Subjekt des Passivsatzes werden.

••• Markiere die Objekte des Aktivsatzes (Personen grün, Sachen rot) und verwandle dann die Sätze in jeweils zwei Passivsätze mit unterschiedlichem Subjekt.

1. The waiter showed the bill to my mother.

a. (Person) ____________________

b. (Sache) ____________________

2. My dad gave the bar keeper a tip.

a. (Person) ____________________

b. (Sache) ____________________

3. The waitress brought coffee to all of us.

a. (Person) ____________________

b. (Sache) ____________________

6 DAS GERUND

• Stell dir vor, du gewinnst im Lotto. Was würdest du tun? Notiere deine Ideen und benutze dabei das **gerund**.

1. I can imagine (to buy) ____________________

2. I would enjoy (to travel) ____________________

3. I would prefer (to have) ____________________

4. I wouldn't mind (to own) ____________________

Das **gerund** ist eine grammatikalische Form, die es so im Deutschen nicht gibt. Im Englischen steht das **gerund** nach bestimmten Verben. Da es dafür keine festen Regeln gibt, lernst du diese Verben am besten auswendig!

BOXENSTOPP

Wie bitte, jetzt erstmal ausruhen? No way! Es geht gleich weiter! Im folgenden Wortgitter sind weitere 8 Verben versteckt, auf die automatisch das **gerund** folgt. Finde sie und übertrage sie anschließend neben die deutsche Übersetzung in die Tabelle.

S	B	L	U	A	V	O	I	D	Q	D
X	F	I	N	I	S	H	P	P	W	U
D	Q	K	T	T	A	A	O	R	S	H
W	U	E	K	J	N	T	P	A	A	I
T	C	I	V	M	B	E	I	C	Y	K
M	X	T	I	O	E	P	C	T	G	R
I	W	T	F	H	T	U	N	I	H	R
S	U	G	G	E	S	T	L	C	N	T
S	D	E	R	Y	R	G	H	E	L	O
L	O	O	K	F	O	R	W	A	R	D

______________	*vermeiden*
______________	*mögen*
______________	*hassen*
______________	*vermissen*
______________	*beenden*
______________	*vorschlagen*
______________	*üben*
______________	*sich auf etwas freuen*

•• Das **gerund** kann sowohl Subjekt als auch Objekt eines Satzes sein. Verbinde die Sätze sinnvoll miteinander und unterstreiche dann das **gerund** als Subjekt rot und als Objekt blau.

1. Winning the next tennis match
2. I like
3. Winning just one tournament

a. playing tennis a lot .
b. is my biggest dream!
c. once a year isn't enough for me.

Auch nach bestimmten Präpositionen folgt übrigens meist das **gerund**! Die solltest du dir auch merken!

•• Finde die Präpositionen in der Wortschlange, die das **gerund** einleiten und übertrage sie neben der deutschen Übersetzung in die Tabelle.

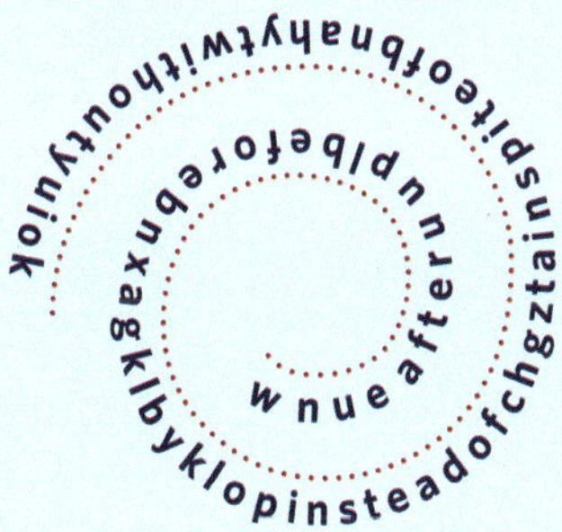

______________	*obwohl*
______________	*durch, wenn, indem*
______________	*ohne*
______________	*bevor, vor*
______________	*nach, nachdem*
______________	*(an)statt*

•• Bilde aus den folgenden zwei Sätzen immer jeweils einen Satz, indem du eine Präposition aus der letzten Übung und ein **gerund** verwendest.

1. I will call you. But I must go home now.

____

2. Please have a drink. Don't leave the party yet.

____

3. John always tells jokes. He never laughs.

____

4. You should always tell the truth. Don't lie!

____

5. Take the train! You won't get into a traffic jam then.

____

••• In dieser Einladung sind einige Endungen verschwunden. Ergänze sie, wenn nötig. Aber achte auch auf die Schreibweise!

Dear player,

Remember (1) __________ the tennis match on Saturday!

Play (2) __________ tennis in a competition is fun.

And we always need (3) __________ motivated players

in our tournament! Win (4) __________ this Saturday's match

could bring you to a training camp in the US.

So why don't you invite (5) __________ your friends, too?

The matches this weekend need to have (6) __________ lots

of support to become (7) __________ a really big event.

We look forward to see (8) __________ you

at the tennis court!

7 PRONOMEN ALS OBJEKT

- Ergänze die folgenden Sätze mit den jeweils richtigen Possessivbegleitern. Diese findest du in der Wortschlange!

1. Jimmy is in __________ classroom.
2. Ann and Mary like __________ sister. She is seven years old.
3. Mandy, is this __________ pen?
4. I have got many books in __________ room.
5. We sing songs in __________ music lesson.
6. We have got a little cat. __________ name is Jasper.
7. Bob has got a sister. __________ name is Mary.
8. Girls, can you hand me __________ books, please?

Mit den Possessivbegleitern kannst du ausdrücken, wem etwas gehört oder zu wem etwas gehört. Aber Vorsicht bei **your**: Je nach Zusammenhang kann es *dein*, *euer* oder *Ihr* heißen! Die Possessivpronomen verwendest du, wenn das Nomen bereits bekannt ist, du es aber im Satz nicht wiederholen möchtest.

BOXENSTOPP

Genau wie Personalpronomen stehen auch Possessivpronomen für ein Substantiv (pro Nomen = für ein Nomen). Possessivpronomen können alleine stehen, verändern sich nicht und treten besonders häufig mit dem Verb **to be** auf. Schreibe die Possessivpronomen und die Possessivbegleiter an der richtigen Stelle in die Tabelle.

Personalpronomen	Possessivbegleiter	Possessivpronomen
I	**my**	**mine**
you		
he		
she		
it		
we		
you		
they		

•• Unterstreiche die Possessivbegleiter rot und die Possessivpronomen grün.

1. Hi. My name is Jimmy.
2. Look at those CDs. They are all ours.
3. And these books? – They belong to Mum and Dad. They are theirs.
4. This is Ann's and Mary's sister. Her name is Mona.
5. Mandy, what's your tutor's name again?
6. We've got a new cat. Its colour is black.
7. This is Brad's flat. Its rooms are rather small.
8. I like singing. And our music classroom is very nice.
9. What about these shoes? – They are mine!
10. Bob's sister is eleven years old. His best friend is eleven, too.
11. Whose books are these? Are they yours?
12. These are their books. They're fantastic!
13. Whose lunch box is this? Is it his?
14. Is this your friend? I know him, too.
15. Whose exciting book is this? – It's hers.
16. Don't eat these biscuits. They are not yours.

•• Hier ist einiges durcheinander geraten und keiner weiß mehr, was wem gehört. Verbinde die Aussagen passend miteinander.

1. Here are Mike's CDs.
2. Maya and Tom, put your school bags away.
3. There are two lunchboxes in my bag...
4. Please take Julia's shoes outside.
5. Look at these five cute little birds.
6. Please return the Millers' keys.

a. The blue one is mine!
b. Sorry, but they're not theirs, their Dad's.
c. But they're not hers.
d. Oh yes. Aren't they cute? Are they yours?
e. They're not his, they're Leo's!
f. But they're not ours.

Du kennst ja bereits die Personalpronomen in der Subjektform (**I, you, he/ she, ...**) Sie geben an, **wer** oder **was** etwas tut. Diese Pronomen gibt es auch in der Objektform! Sie geben dann an, auf **wen** oder **was** sich eine Handlung bezieht.

•• Setze das richtige Personalpronomen als Objekt ein: **them, him, her, it**

1. Peter is Paula's boyfriend. He loves ___________.

2. Paula is Peter's girlfriend. She loves ___________.

3. Peter and Paula don't like Caroline and John. They don't like ___________.

4. Here's a book. Read ___________.

•• Auch hier tauchen die Personalpronomen als Objektform auf. Nur wie übersetzt man sie richtig? Aber immer schön wachsam sein - manchmal gibt es mehr als eine Möglichkeit!

1. I can tell **you** the way to the next supermarket.

____

2. We can't find **you** in that picture.

____

3. Here's a ball. Why don't you play with **it**?

____

4. Jerry is here. Let's talk to **him** now.

____

5. My dad? Yes, let's ask **him**.

____

8 DIE REFLEXIVPRONOMEN

• Unterstreiche in jedem der folgenden Beispielsätze das Subjekt und das dazugehörige Reflexivpronomen.

1. My name is Joanna. I'm a clever girl. I taught myself how to read when I was 4 years old.
2. This is Peter. He's a football player, but unfortunately he hurt himself in the match on Saturday.
3. This is Anne. She is a nice girl. But she only thinks of herself. I don't like that!
4. Look at my cat. It's cleaning itself.
5. "You can help yourselves to whatever I put on the table for you!" says John, the cook.
6. When I go out with my friends we usually enjoy ourselves very much.
7. These are Pat and Billy. They enjoy themselves most when both of them are together.

Mit den Reflexivpronomen kannst du ausdrücken, dass jemand etwas **für sich selbst** oder **auf sich bezogen** tut (reflexiver Gebrauch). Reflexivpronomen sind Objekt im Satz und beziehen sich zurück auf das Subjekt. Allerdings kommen die Reflexivpronomen im Englischen sehr viel seltener vor als im Deutschen. Viele Verben, die im Deutschen mit *sich* gebildet werden, übersetzt man ins Englische mit nicht-reflexiven Verben.

BOXENSTOPP

Ein kleiner Zwischenstopp mit Übersetzungsauftrag. Übersetze die beiden folgenden Sätze und vervollständige dann die Regel.

1. Tom and Perry are looking at themselves in the mirror.

____

2. Tom and Perry are looking at each other.

____

Setze ein: gegenseitig einander zwischen

Wenn du ausdrücken möchtest, dass etwas ____________ mehreren Personen wechselseitig geschieht, so musst du **each other** verwenden. Im Deutschen kann **each other** mit *sich*, ____________ oder ____________ wiedergegeben werden.

•• Richtig oder falsch? Kreuze an. Im Anhang findest du die Lösungen!

	Richtig	Falsch
1. The girls helped each other with the cooking.	☐	☐
2. Mary and Jane hugged.	☐	☐
3. My friends are never shouting at themselves.	☐	☐
4. Phil and Alex haven't met each other in a long time.	☐	☐
5. Grit and Bella haven't seen each other for some time.	☐	☐

•• Im folgenden Wortgitter sind 14 Verben versteckt, die im Englischen nicht reflexiv gebraucht werden. Finde sie und übertrage sie anschließend hinter der entsprechenden deutschen Übersetzung in die Tabelle.

B	J	X	Y	C	H	A	N	G	E	U	G	G	H
G	E	T	L	O	S	T	H	O	L	Y	X	K	U
Q	T	S	I	T	D	O	W	N	Y	C	C	B	R
R	M	F	G	R	E	L	A	X	H	I	A	H	R
S	O	M	J	G	C	W	S	V	T	G	L	A	Y
F	V	H	X	Q	I	V	M	E	E	T	T	P	Q
F	E	E	L	O	D	S	P	L	I	T	U	P	O
G	X	V	U	G	E	T	D	R	E	S	S	E	D
R	M	I	E	A	M	T	G	U	O	P	E	N	Y
R	E	M	E	M	B	E	R	N	N	M	B	Y	Q

Deutsch	Englisch
sich (ver)ändern	(to) change
sich anziehen	
sich beeilen	
sich bewegen	
sich entscheiden	
sich entspannen	
sich ereignen	
sich erinnern	
sich fühlen	
sich öffnen	
sich (hin)setzen	
sich treffen	
sich trennen	
sich verirren	

•• Setze in dieser Übung entweder ein Reflexivpronomen oder **each other** ein. Aber Vorsicht, manchmal muss die Lücke auch leer bleiben.

1. Sarah and Betty, your faces are dirty. Look at ____________.

2. My brother and I bought ____________ ten new CDs.

3. My mum and I don't go to the hairdresser's. We do our hair ____________.

4. How did you learn French? – Well, I taught ____________. But my mum and her friend didn't, they taught ____________.

5. The people in my family see ____________ very often.

6. My brother and I were looking after ____________ when my parents went on holiday.

7. Nick and his friends meet ____________ at school every day.

8. I tried to see where the cat was – but it didn't move ____________.

9 ADJEKTIV UND ADVERB

- Finde im folgenden Wortgewimmel alle Adjektive und markiere sie blau. Die Adverbien kannst du grün markieren.

angry rarely exactly hungry internationally sadly crazy happy loudly
positively slowly carefully holy friendly fully dirty bloody chilly easy dry

Markiere nun in den folgenden Sätzen die jeweils richtige Stelle, an der das Adverb eingesetzt werden muss.

1. Most people go to bed at half past ten. **generally**
2. Mike's mother spoke to him. **angrily**
3. Anne has decided to quit basketball. **definitely**
4. Susan liked the end of the movie. **particularly**
5. Nina began to sing. **suddenly**
6. Megan ate the burger. **hungrily**

Sicher erinnerst du dich, dass **Adjektive** ein Nomen näher bestimmen (sie geben an, **wie** eine Person oder Sache ist). **Adverbien** hingegen beziehen sich auf das Verb des Satzes (sie geben an, **wie** jemand etwas **tut** oder **wie** etwas **geschieht**).

BOXENSTOPP

Es gibt eine Reihe von Verben, die keine Tätigkeit, sondern einen Zustand, eine Eigenschaft oder eine Sinneswahrnehmung beschreiben. Auf diese Verben folgt immer ein **Adjektiv**!

Kannst du die folgenden Verben den beiden Spalten der Tabelle richtig zuordnen?

look stay taste seem feel sound be smell

Verben, die eine **Sinneswahrnehmung** beschreiben	Verben, die einen **Zustand** oder eine **Eigenschaft** beschreiben

•• Scott und seine Freunde sind auf Campingtour. Fehlt hier ein Adjektiv oder ein Adverb? Setze die jeweils richtige Form ein.

1. When Scott did his camping expedition, he didn't ________ (real) like it.
2. The weather was ________ (terrible) and he felt ________ (cold) most of the time.
3. During the day the weather was better and Scott and his friends ________ (happy) walked up the hills.
4. The last hill was very ________ (steep) and it was very ________ (hard) for them to reach the top.
5. The girls and boys also had to cook on their own and the food tasted ________ (good) most of the time.
6. When they started to walk, Scott couldn't walk very ________ (fast).
7. Unfortunately, he also got some blisters and they had to climb ________ (slow).
8. When they came back from their trip, Scott felt ________ (happy) to ________ (final) be back home.

•• Scotts Freunde entdecken auf der Tour, was Scott alles kann und was er nicht so gut kann. Schreibe auf.

1. (nicht schnell laufen): Scott can ________
2. (nicht leise Gitarre spielen): ________
3. (schön singen): ________
4. (gut Geschichten erzählen): ________
5. (nicht gut kochen): ________
6. (laut lachen): ________

•• Adjektiv oder Adverb? Übersetze ins Englische.

1. Scott ist ein guter Freund von mir.

____

2. Leider konnte er auf unserer Tour nicht lange wandern.

____

3. „Könnt ihr bitte langsam gehen?", sagte er. „Ich habe Blasen."

____

4. Er musste ganz vorsichtig gehen.

____

5. Als wir auf ihn warteten, lächelte er glücklich.

____

10 ADJEKTIVE ALS NOMEN

- Ergänze die passenden Adjektive im Satz.

sad   good   bad   nervous   young

1. In my favourite book the ______________ always win over the ______________.

2. "Nightmare" is not a film for the ______________!

3. The playground in the schoolyard isn't only for the ______________.

4. Tell a joke to the ______________ and they will laugh.

BOXENSTOPP

Aufgepasst, Sportsfreunde! Im Englischen können manche Adjektive, die bestimmte körperliche oder soziale Merkmale beschreiben (zum Beispiel *arm, reich, jung, alt, …*), als Nomen verwendet werden. Dies ist anders als im Deutschen und es gelten dafür auch bestimmte Regeln! Vergleiche zunächst einmal die beiden folgenden Sätze und übersetze sie ins Deutsche.

a. The blind very often have a good sense of hearing.

____

b. Margaret helped the blind man across the street.

____

Kannst du nun schon eine Regel daraus ableiten? Ergänze die Lücken mithilfe dieser Wortvorgaben:

bestimmten Artikel   **Nomen**   **Gruppe**   einzelnen Personen

1. Wenn man von einer ganzen ______________ von Menschen spricht, kann das Adjektiv als Nomen verwendet werden. Es steht dann mit dem ______________.

2. Wenn man von ______________ spricht, muss das **Adjektiv** durch ein ______________ (z.B. **woman, girl, man, boy, people, …**) ergänzt werden. Anders als im Deutschen kann das Adjektiv hier also nicht alleine stehen.

•• Wie lautet die Übersetzung der folgenden Sätze? Ergänze **girl, person, man** (2x) und **blind, sick, little, famous**.

1. *Die Kleine hat ihre Eltern verloren.* – The __________ __________ has lost her parents.

2. *Der Kranke wurde ins Krankenhaus gebracht.* – The __________ __________ was taken to hospital.

3. *Der Blinde hat keinen Blindenhund.* – The __________ __________ doesn't have a guide dog.

4. *Ich habe einen Berühmten gesehen.* – I saw a __________ __________.

•• Hier sind einige Werbeanzeigen durcheinander geraten. Verbinde sie so miteinander, dass sie wieder einen Sinn ergeben.

1. Smile! Invite Jimmy the clown to your party	**a.** for the young.
2. Wheelchairs welcome: Our new shopping centre	**b.** not only for the rich!
3. Kid's corner: Friday night swimming class	**c.** with the famous.
4. Reasonable prices: Fashion wear	**d.** and the sad will laugh.
5. Talking celebrity: Sunday morning debate	**e.** is also suitable for the disabled.

•• Wer kann was und was interessiert hier wen? Beende die Sätze mit den passenden Adjektiven aus der Box.

weak   strong   sick   rich   famous

1. Reporters in Hollywood like to interview ____________________.

2. Doctors must always help ____________________.

3. In nature only ____________________ survive.

4. Some people are always jealous of ____________________.

5. Big boys sometimes make fun of ____________________.

Bestimmt ist dir schon aufgefallen, dass das Adjektiv als Nomen kein **-s** im Plural hat. Als Subjekt des Satzes verlangt es jedoch ein Verb im Plural:

Only the rich **are** able to afford expensive cars.

Und vergiss nicht, den bestimmten Artikel zu setzen, wenn du eine bestimmte Gruppe von Menschen beschreibst!

••• Übersetze nun noch die folgenden Sätze ins Englische, dann hast du die Adjektive als Nomen drauf!

1. Die Alte trank eine Tasse Tee.

____

2. Ein Blinder wartete an der Bushaltestelle.

____

3. Wir können eine Menge von den Alten lernen.

____

4. Der Kleine zeichnete ein Bild.

____

11 DIE ARTIKEL

• Lies dir die folgenden Texte durch und entscheide, ob der bestimmte Artikel **the** oder der unbestimmte Artikel **a(n)** stehen muss oder nicht. Streiche den Artikel durch, wenn er überflüssig ist.

Goal is a very popular magazine with the young and sporty in the UK. In it you will find many articles about the different football clubs in Britain. And there is usually an interview with a star from the world of the sport. In the last month's edition there was an article about the football world cup of the year 1966 in England. The time goes by so quickly. The last world cup took place in 2010.

Jim has got a pair of new football trainers. He had bought them for a match on Saturday, but then he couldn't play. Why? Well, his older brother is a football coach at Jim's club. He is five years older than Jim, he has a car and he usually drives to the matches by a car. He then takes Jim's bag with him because it's a heavy bag. But on a Saturday he left home early after a breakfast and Jim couldn't give him his bag with the shoes in it. That's why Jim couldn't play on that day. He was an athlete without trainers.

BOXENSTOPP

Wie in jeder Sportart gelten auch für den Gebrauch des Artikels im Englischen besondere Regeln. Setze ein:

bestimmte – **of** – Dingen – bestimmte – **a / an** – Berufsbezeichnungen – **the** – unbestimmte

1. Der ____________ Artikel ________ zeigt an, dass etwas näher bestimmt ist. Nomen können z.B. durch einen Relativsatz oder eine Ergänzung mit ________ näher bestimmt werden. Der ____________ Artikel steht nicht, wenn von Personen und ____________ ganz allgemein gesprochen wird.

2. Der ____________ Artikel ________ wird im Englischen meistens genauso verwendet wie im Deutschen. Nur in wenigen Fällen unterscheidet sich der Gebrauch, so z.B. bei ____________ und feststehenden Wendungen.

Nomen wie zum Beispiel **love**, **fun** oder **luck** sind abstrakte Begriffe. Wenn sie im allgemeinen Sinn verwendet werden, stehen sie ohne Artikel. In der Regel gibt es hier keine Pluralform.

•• Im Folgenden hat jemand einige Redewendungen falsch aufgeschrieben. Wie heißen sie richtig?

1. on the TV: ____________
2. to have headache: ____________
3. at the work: ____________
4. the most people: ____________
5. to be in the hurry: ____________
6. on a radio: ____________
7. to play a guitar: ____________
8. on telephone: ____________

•• Schau dir die Tabelle an und schreibe auf, was du über die Personen erfährst.

person	job	goes to work
Bill	taxi driver	taxi
Uncle Joe	teacher	bike
Mandy	manager	car
Monica	shop assistant	train
Lewis	doctor	bus

1. Bill is a taxi driver. He goes to work by taxi.
2. ______
3. ______
4. ______
5. ______

••• Schau dir die folgenden Zeitungsüberschriften an und überlege, ob ein Artikel (bestimmt oder unbestimmt) gesetzt werden muss.

1. SURPRISE: Lucky lottery winners on ______ TV.
2. TEACHERS PROTEST: Under these circumstances pupils can't learn at ______ school.
3. DANGEROUS: Eating lemons may lead to having ______ headache.
4. ON THE NEWS: People who play ______ music are happier.
5. STAR TALK: More interviews with ______ famous five.

12 DIREKTE UND INDIREKTE REDE

• Lies dir die Aussagen der Kinder durch und unterstreiche darin die Verbformen.

Helen: "Our class trip starts on Friday."

Chris: "We'll fly to Dublin just one day after my birthday."

Mary Ann: "I don't want to visit any museums!"

Benny: "I want to visit St. Patrick's Cathedral."

BOXENSTOPP

Hey, Sportskanone! Sicher erinnerst du dich noch, oder? Die **direkte Rede** ist ein direktes Zitat und steht deshalb in Anführungszeichen. Wenn du jedoch wiedergeben möchtest, was jemand gesagt hat, benutzt du die **indirekte Rede**. Dabei verändert sich die Zeitform des Verbs. Lies noch einmal die Aussagen aus der Aufwärmübung und setze die passenden Wörter in die Lücken.

didn't | started | would | wanted

1. Helen said that **their** class trip ______________ on Friday.
2. Chris said that **they** ______________ fly to Dublin just one day after **his** birthday.
3. Mary Ann said that **she** ______________ want to visit any museums.
4. Benny said **he** ______________ to visit St. Patrick's Cathedral.

Aufgepasst: Nicht nur die Zeitformen, sondern auch die Personalpronomen und Possessivbegleiter des Satzes ändern sich in der indirekten Rede!

•• Was alles auf der Klassenfahrt passiert, liest du im nächsten Abschnitt. Sieh dir die Aussagen der Kinder an und entscheide, welches Pronomen das richtige ist. Die Buchstaben der richtigen Lösung ergeben den Namen ihres Hotels.

	my	their	his	them	her	our
1. Tom said that __________ money got stolen.	A	V	T	J	U	O
2. Jane said she didn't find __________ way back to the hotel.	C	A	A	T	R	L
3. Phil and Josh said they went shopping with __________ Irish friends.	R	I	H	Y	W	U
4. Mona said Mr Hill had booked __________ a nice hotel.	A	G	B	N	I	E
5. George said __________ bus driver was mean.	S	I	F	T	R	E
6. Fred said he didn't write __________ family a post card.	O	I	T	U	Z	R
7. Jenna said __________ class trip was fun.	H	Y	N	J	K	D

Lösung:

1.	2.	3.	4.	5.	6.	7.

•• Lies dir die Beispielsätze auf der linken Seite durch und unterstreiche jeweils die Verbform. Setze dann die Verben in der indirekten Rede auf der rechten Seite ein. Wenn das klappt, dann hast du's verstanden – super!

	The kids **told** their parents that they ...
1. We take a class trip to Dublin this year.	... ________ a class trip to Dublin that year.
2. We're planning everything for the trip on our own.	... ____________ everything for the trip on their own.
3. We've already booked our tickets.	... ________ already ________ their tickets.
4. We prepared the trip with a guide book and by using the internet.	... ____________ the trip with a guide book and by using the internet.
5. We hadn't imagined that Dublin was such a beautiful place.	... ____________ that Dublin was such a beautiful place.
6. We will get back to Dublin some day.	... ____________ back to Dublin some day.
7. We can always visit the friends we made again.	... ________ always ________ the friends they made there again.

••• Du weißt jetzt, dass bei der indirekten Rede eine Verschiebung der Zeiten auftritt, wenn das einleitende Verb in der Vergangenheit steht (z.B. **said** oder **told**). Bestimme die Zeitformen aus der vorigen Übung und übertrage sie dann in die beiden Spalten.

Direkte Rede	Indirekte Rede
1. Simple Present	
2.	
3.	
4.	
5.	
6.	
7.	

13 INDIREKTE FRAGEN

- Verbinde die direkte Frage links mit der jeweils passenden indirekten Frage auf der rechten Seite.

1. When did you go to bed last night?
2. Who did you dream of?
3. Did you go to bed later than midnight?
4. What did you do before you went to bed?
5. Why didn't you sleep in this morning?

a. My dad asked me **what** I had done before I went to bed.
b. He wanted to know **why** I hadn't slept in this morning.
c. He also wanted to know **when** I had gone to bed last night.
d. He asked me **who** I had dreamed of.
e. He asked me **if** I had gone to bed later than midnight.

Steht in der direkten Rede ein Fragewort (**what, when, who**), wird es in der indirekten Rede beibehalten. **Do**, **does** oder **did** werden in der indirekten Frage jedoch **nicht** verwendet.

BOXENSTOPP

Bei indirekten Fragen gelten dieselben Regeln in der Zeitenfolge, die du schon aus dem indirekten Aussagesatz kennst. Auch die Wortstellung in indirekten Fragesätzen bleibt dieselbe wie im Aussagesatz. Zum Vergleich:

"Did **you sleep well?**" Mum asked me if **I had slept well**.

Und nun noch einmal volle Konzentration. Gibt es in der direkten Rede kein Fragewort, dann wird der Nebensatz in der indirekten Rede mit __________ oder **whether** eingeleitet (im Deutschen: ..., *ob* ...).

•• Übersetze die indirekten Fragen aus der Aufwärmübung ins Deutsche.

1. ______________________________
2. ______________________________
3. ______________________________
4. ______________________________
5. ______________________________

Bei der **indirekten Frage** benutzt man als einleitendes Verb **ask** oder **want to know**. Bei **Befehlen** hingegen benutzt man als einleitendes Verb oft **tell**. Weitere gebräuchliche Formen für Befehle sind **ask** und **advise**.

•• Ergänze die Verben **warned, asked, told, advised**. Aber aufgepasst, manchmal gibt es mehr als eine mögliche Lösung.

1. George ____________________ Mike to return the books to the library.
2. Jill's mother ____________________ her to take a hot bath because she was so wet.
3. The coach ____________________ his team to practice more.
4. The dentist ____________________ the patient to keep still.
5. The police officer ____________________ us not to cross the road here.

Sicher ist es dir längst aufgefallen: Aufforderungssätze werden in der indirekten Rede meist als Infinitivkonstruktionen mit **to** oder **not to** wiedergegeben.

•• Nun forme die Aufforderungen aus der vorangegangenen Übung in die direkte Rede um.

1. ____________________
2. ____________________
3. ____________________
4. ____________________
5. ____________________

••• Ergänze nun noch die Sätze mit den vorgegebenen Satzteilen, dann hast du wieder ein ganzes Stück geschafft!

advise / get here earlier | warn / not lose it | ask / get classic CD | remind / pack it

1. Here you are. The new Disco Girls CD.
   – Didn't you listen to me? I ____________________
2. You probably don't want to hear this, but I just can't find my wallet..."
   – Oh no! I ____________________
3. I'm afraid I didn't take my bathing suit with me.
   – Are you sure? I remember that I ____________________
4. Look at those people in front of the cinema...!
   – Well, dear, I ____________________

14 RELATIVSÄTZE MIT *WHICH, THAT, WHO* UND *WHOSE*

- Vergleiche die folgenden Relativsätze miteinander und kreuze dann bei den Aussagen unten an, was auf den Relativsatz zutrifft und was nicht.

1. It's someone **who** coaches a rugby team.

2. It's the person **that** controls the football matches.

3. It's a sport **which** is rather popular in the USA.

4. It's a thing **that** you use for playing tennis.

5. It's a person **whose** job is to prevent the players to score in football.

	Richtig	Falsch
a. Who im Relativsatz bezieht sich nur auf Personen.	☐	☐
b. Which kann sich auf Dinge und auf Personen beziehen.	☐	☐
c. That kann sich auf Dinge und auf Personen beziehen.	☐	☐
d. Whose hat immer ein Nomen nach sich stehen.	☐	☐
e. Whose hat im Singular und Plural nur eine Form.	☐	☐
f. Whose drückt Besitz oder Zugehörigkeit aus (*dessen / deren*)	☐	☐
g. Who, **which** und **that** werden nur für den Singular verwendet.	☐	☐

BOXENSTOPP

Zum Durchatmen und wach werden: Notwendige Relativsätze bestimmen das Wort näher, auf das sie sich beziehen. Ohne den Relativsatz wäre der Hauptsatz unklar.

Lies dir noch einmal die Definitionen aus der Aufwärmübung durch. Was wird hier beschrieben? Die folgenden fünf Wörter helfen dir auf die Sprünge: **goalkeeper, baseball, coach, racket, referee**

1: ______________ **4:** ______________

2: ______________ **5:** ______________

3: ______________

Wenn das Relativpronomen **Objekt** des Relativsatzes ist, wird es häufig weggelassen. Solche Relativsätze nennt man **contact clauses**, da sie direkt an das Bezugswort angehängt werden. Vergleiche:

1. The man **that** plays football on TV is very successful.

2. The man **(that)** you can see on TV is a famous English football player.

Vorsicht, nicht zu schnell: Anders als im Deutschen steht zwischen dem Hauptsatz und dem notwendigen Relativsatz **kein** Komma!

•• Vervollständige die folgenden Sätze, indem du das richtige Relativpronomen einsetzt. Manche Relativpronomen kannst du mehr als einmal verwenden.

which who that whose

1. Ice skating is a sport ______________ you can only do in winter.
2. Athletes ______________ can run fast are always good at track & field.
3. Lots of people ______________ don't do sports still enjoy watching it on TV.
4. Top athletes work with personal trainers ______________ task is to coach them.
5. This is the famous man ______________ homerun will always be remembered in baseball.
6. The Super Bowl is a football event on TV ______________ Americans enjoy every year.

•• Finde die beiden Sätze aus der vorangegangenen Übung, in denen das Relativpronomen auch weggelassen werden kann und notiere sie hier in verkürzter Form.

1. ______________________________
2. ______________________________

••• Bilde jeweils aus zwei Hauptsätzen einen Hauptsatz mit dazugehörigem Relativsatz.

1. The coach is happy. His team won the championship.
The coach, whose team won the championship, is happy.
2. The striker scored a goal. It was a brilliant goal!
____
3. The team is fighting to win. Its captain can't play today.
____
4. This woman here is our coach. She coaches us twice a week.
____
5. Rugby is a rough sport. It is rather popular in Britain, Australia and France.
____

15 TEMPORALSÄTZE

- Finde die acht Konjunktionen im Wortgitter, die eine zeitliche Bestimmung einleiten.

A	**S**	G	H	J	C	F	Q	W	A	E	R	T
M	A	D	E	V	J	N	N	B	B	T	Z	H
T	R	T	U	U	Z	J	A	G	E	Z	G	S
G	G	X	D	U	A	E	R	H	F	U	R	I
C	W	H	E	N	R	F	Y	V	O	T	E	N
Y	H	Y	I	T	E	C	X	F	R	R	A	C
K	I	C	U	I	F	A	F	T	E	R	S	E
V	L	D	H	L	D	E	D	D	F	B	C	D
C	E	P	E	D	A	W	E	S	O	S	N	G
R	J	E	A	S	S	O	O	N	A	S	M	J

BOXENSTOPP

Bevor du weiterspurtest, hier eine kleine Zwischenübung. Wie übersetzt man die Konjunktionen richtig ins Deutsche? Übertrage die englischen Wörter aus dem Wortgitter in die folgende Übersicht und ergänze die deutsche Übersetzung.

während | wenn / als | nachdem | bis | seit(dem) | ~~als~~ | jedes Mal, wenn | bevor

1. **as** ________ *als* ________
2. ________ ________
3. ________ ________
4. ________ ________
5. ________ ________
6. ________ ________
7. ________ ________
8. ________ ________

Und weiter geht's! Wie verwendet man die Konjunktionen **as**, **while** und **when** richtig? Ergänze die folgende Regel.

Man verwendet ________ und ________ im Sinne von *als* für einen Vorgang, der sich abspielte, während etwas anderes passierte. Dabei verwendet man ________ meist für gleichzeitige, länger andauernde Vorgänge. ________ verwendet man ebenfalls im Sinne von *als*, allerdings um hervorzuheben, dass etwas in einem bestimmten Zeitraum geschah.

•• Hier darfst du korrigieren. Streiche diejenigen Konjunktionen durch, die man hier **nicht** verwenden kann.

1. Bye, Marta! Please ring me **as / when** you get home.
2. The garden is wet this morning, it must have rained **during / while** the night.
3. Would you look after the cat **while / when** I'm on holidays?
4. Why don't you go shopping **while / as** you are waiting for your bike to be repaired?
5. I watched **as / when** the policemen examined the crime scene.
6. The phone rang **when / while** I was getting into the tub.

•• Bilde Temporalsätze mit **when** und den Satzbausteinen, die vorgegeben sind.

1. nice / her / when / guests / had prepared / a / just / dinner / she / arrived

____

2. broke / football / I / my / I / leg / played / when

____

3. the / turn off / to / bed / when / lights / please / you / go

____

••• Was ist hier richtig? Ergänze die folgenden Sätze mit der jeweils richtigen Konjunktion.

1. I'll cook you dinner ________ I come home.	**when**	**while**	**as**
2. I'll e-mail you ________ I arrive.	**since**	**until**	**when**
3. She won't speak to her boyfriend ________ he apologizes.	**until**	**while**	**as**
4. Every night ________ I go to bed, I brush my teeth.	**as**	**when**	**before**
5. Don't forget to pack your suitcase ________ you go to the airport.	**before**	**when**	**as**
6. I want to graduate from school ________ possible.	**since**	**while**	**as soon as**

16 *IF*-SÄTZE

- Lies dir die folgenden **if**-Sätze aufmerksam durch. Unterstreiche die unterschiedlichen Zeitformen im **if**-Satz und im Hauptsatz und übertrage sie anschließend in die Tabelle.

1. If you set the table, I'll do the washing up.

2. If I asked you to help me with the laundry, would you help me?

3. If you finish your homework early tonight, you may watch your favourite TV show.

4. If you had tidied up your room, you would have found the keys earlier.

5. You would become more fluent in English if you spent more time in England.

6. If you had worn your rain coat, you wouldn't have got so wet.

Satz	Verbform im **if**-Satz	Verbform im Hauptsatz
1.	Simple Present	Zukunft mit will
2.		
3.		
4.		
5.		
6.		

BOXENSTOPP

Moment, wie ist das mit den sportlichen Regeln der **if**-Sätze? Genau, der **if**-Satz beschreibt eine Bedingung und der Hauptsatz drückt aus, was passieren wird oder passieren könnte. Kennst du den Unterschied zwischen den drei Typen von Bedingungssätzen? Setze ein:

would | unwahrscheinliche | **Simple Present** | realistisch | Zukunft mit **will** | **Simple Past** | erfüllbar | **Past Perfect**

Im Bedingungssatz **Typ 1** hält der Sprecher die Bedingung für ____________. Im **if**-Satz steht das ____________, im Hauptsatz steht meist die ____________ oder ein modales Hilfsverb (**can, must, may**, etc.).

Im **if**-Satz **Typ 2** steht das ____________. Es drückt jedoch nicht aus, dass die Handlung in der Vergangenheit stattgefunden hat, sondern es beschreibt eine ____________ Handlung. Im Hauptsatz steht das **conditional** (____________ + **Infinitiv**).

Beim Bedingungssatz **Typ 3** weiß der Sprecher, dass die Bedingung nicht ____________ ist, weil es sich um eine Situation handelt, die in der Vergangenheit liegt und bereits vorbei ist. Im **if**-Satz steht das ____________, im Hauptsatz das **Conditional Perfect** (**would** + **have** + **past participle**).

Vorsicht! Hier musst du aufpassen: **'d** kann die Kurzform von **had** oder **would** sein. Oft macht erst der Satzzusammenhang klar, um welche Form es hier geht.

•• **Had** oder **would**? Um welche Form handelt es sich denn hier? Schreibe die Kurzform in den Sätzen aus.

1. If he'd studied for the test, he'd have passed it.

____

2. She'd have understood you if you'd spoken English.

____

3. I'd have written you a postcard if I'd had your address.

____

4. If you'd listened to the radio, you'd have heard the news.

____

5. If you'd dropped the vase, it'd have broken.

____

••• Setze jeweils zwei Verben in der richtigen Zeitform ein. Achte dabei besonders auf die richtige Verneinung.

1. We ______________ (swim) in the sea last summer if there ______________ (not be) so many sharks there.

2. If she ______________ (take) the bus, she ______________ (not arrive) on time.

3. I ______________ (not go) to school by bus if I ______________ (have) a driving licence.

4. We ______________ (be) stupid if we ______________ (not tell) him the truth. Let's talk to him!

5. If I ______________ (be) you, I ______________ (not go) to school today – you're ill!

6. If my dad ______________ (not lose) the keys, he ______________ (open) the door.

1 HÖFLICHKEITSFORMEN

So, Sportsfreund. Eine neue sportliche Etappe wartet auf dich. Damit du diese erfolgreich meisterst, hier noch ein paar Tipps: Zum Lernen neuer Vokabeln brauchst du vor allem Ruhe. Suche dir einen Arbeitsplatz, an dem du möglichst ungestört und regelmäßig arbeiten kannst. Außerdem solltest du noch herausfinden, wie du neue Wörter am leichtesten lernst: Durch Lesen, Hören, Schreiben oder Aufzeichnen? Diese Methode kannst du dann gezielt zum Vokabellernen einsetzen. Also: Auf die Plätze, fertig, los!

- Im folgenden Wortgitter sind 8 Begriffe versteckt, mit denen man seine **Hilfe anbietet** oder **sich entschuldigt**. Findest du sie alle? Aber Achtung: Du solltest von oben nach unten, von rechts nach links und umgekehrt lesen! Die Lösung findest du wie immer im Anhang.

J	B	H	B	N	K	O	L	V	K	Y	Q
E	C	W	E	Y	A	T	S	O	R	R	Y
E	E	D	S	M	I	A	N	D	P	H	E
Z	T	X	A	A	Q	C	V	N	B	N	O
I	W	E	E	C	E	F	S	E	D	U	R
G	D	E	L	F	X	Y	S	V	C	T	U
O	D	A	P	U	A	E	H	E	L	P	Z
L	Q	V	I	H	J	J	B	R	G	R	C
O	W	E	R	A	C	E	W	M	C	U	B
P	O	L	I	T	E	O	R	I	U	A	F
A	A	S	F	O	T	H	A	N	K	S	T
P	E	W	S	U	V	U	I	D	Q	A	R

BOXENSTOPP

Wenn man sich mit Leuten unterhält, dann sollte man auch darauf achten, den richtigen Umgangston zu treffen. Achte also darauf, wie du dich ausdrückst. Hier siehst du einige Ausdrücke, die dir helfen, dich in Gesprächssituationen höflich auszudrücken.

Das sagt du, wenn du jemandem helfen willst:

Can I help you?	*Kann ich dir / Ihnen helfen?*
Shall I ...?	*Soll ich...?*

So kannst du antworten, wenn dir jemand seine Hilfe anbietet:

That's very kind of you.	*Das ist sehr freundlich von dir / Ihnen.*
You've been a great help.	*Du bist / Sie sind eine große Hilfe.*

Und so kannst du dich entschuldigen:

I apologize ...	*Ich entschuldige mich (für)...*
I'm terribly / very sorry...	*Es tut mir schrecklich / sehr leid...*
I didn't mean to ...	*Ich wollte doch nicht...*

Wenn sich jemand bei dir entschuldigt, kannst du Folgendes antworten:

Never mind. / No problem.	*Keine Ursache.*
Don't worry.	*Mach dir keine Sorgen / Gedanken.*

•• Und nun versuche doch einmal, die folgenden Sätze etwas höflicher zu formulieren. Dann hört es sich doch gleich viel netter an, oder?

1. What do you want to know?

___

2. There isn't any dessert left for you.

___

3. Open the window!

___

4. It's good that you carry that heavy bag for me.

___

•• In den folgenden Sätzen sind die Buchstaben etwas durcheinander geraten. Wie muss es richtig heißen? Ordne die Sätze auf der rechten Seite richtig zu.

1. Sey, fo rousec.	**a.** No problem.
2. Knath oyu, satt'h ecin.	**b.** That's very kind of you.
3. Duloc uyo lphe em, laepse?	**c.** You're welcome.
4. Satt'h revy dink fo you.	**d.** Yes, of course.
5. On lrembop.	**e.** Thank you, that's nice.
6. Oyu'er lewmeco.	**f.** Could you help me, please?

••• Im Folgenden liest du 5 Ausschnitte aus unterschiedlichen Gesprächssituationen. Überlege, welche Antwort jeweils passend wäre und kreuze die richtige an.

1. I'm sorry, but I can't find your keys...!

☐ **a.** I'll never lend you my keys again.
☐ **b.** Well, I'm not surprised you lost them.
☐ **c.** Never mind. Let's look for them together.

2. Excuse me, Sir. Can I ask you something?

☐ **a.** What, madam?
☐ **b.** Of course, madam. How can I help you?
☐ **c.** What do you want?

3. Wait for me, please. I can't walk any faster.

☐ **a.** No, hurry up!
☐ **b.** No problem. We aren't in a hurry.
☐ **c.** You're welcome.

4. Would you help me with my homework, please?

☐ **a.** I only help nice people.
☐ **b.** Not right now.
☐ **c.** I'd be glad to help, but I don't have time now.

5. Let me help you set the table.

☐ **a.** No way. That's my job.
☐ **b.** Oh, thanks. That's very kind of you.
☐ **c.** OK. Do that.

2 SIGHTSEEING IN LONDON

- Hast du Lust auf eine kleine Reise nach London? Überlege einmal, was du schon alles über London weißt, und kreuze die jeweils richtige Antwort an. Aber aufgepasst: Manchmal ist auch mehr als eine Lösung möglich!

1. London is in the ... of Great Britain.

- ☐ **a.** south-east
- ☐ **b.** south-west
- ☐ **c.** north-west

2. London is the capital of

- ☐ **a.** Ireland.
- ☐ **b.** Great Britain.
- ☐ **c.** England.

3. Tower Bridge

- ☐ **a.** is across the River Thames.
- ☐ **b.** can't open for ships.
- ☐ **c.** is new and very modern.

4. The Tower of London

- ☐ **a.** is a clock tower.
- ☐ **b.** was a prison.
- ☐ **c.** is a museum.

5. In London, you can visit sights by

- ☐ **a.** red taxis.
- ☐ **b.** double-decker buses.
- ☐ **c.** the Tube.

6. Tourists go shopping

- ☐ **a.** at street markets.
- ☐ **b.** in pubs.
- ☐ **c.** in theatres.

BOXENSTOPP

Meistens weiß man doch mehr als man zunächst meint, stimmt's? Jetzt stell dir einmal vor, du bist in London und willst eine Woche dort bleiben. Sicher möchtest du dir viele Dinge ansehen und viele Orte besichtigen. Dabei wirst du natürlich auf viele Menschen treffen, die dir Informationen zu ihrer Stadt geben können. Finde in der folgenden Wortschlange 5 Gesprächssituationen, die dir begegnen können und schreibe sie auf.

1. ______________________________
2. ______________________________
3. ______________________________
4. ______________________________
5. ______________________________

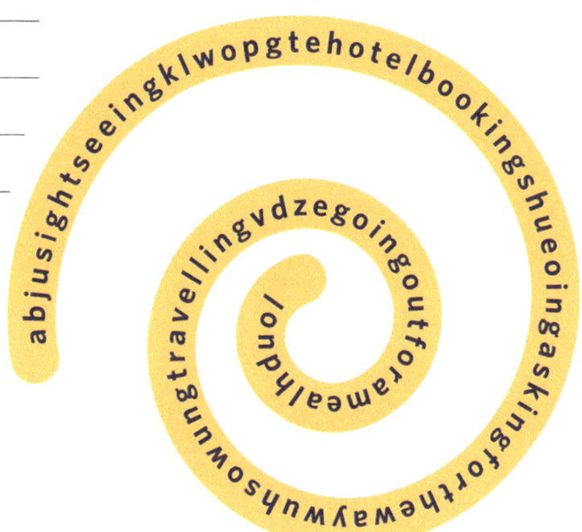

Das alles sind Gesprächssituationen, die natürlich bei jedem Besuch in so ziemlich jeder Stadt im Ausland auf dich warten. Daher solltest du dich sprachlich fit fühlen in diesen Situationen. Also, ran an die Übungen!

•• Kannst du das Kreuzworträtsel lösen? Die folgenden Sätze helfen dir dabei.

Across

1. When you're in London, Shakespeare's Globe Theatre is a ____________. You just have to go there!

2. Let's go to the National Gallery and ____________ the exhibition there.

3. Excuse me, could you ____________ a picture of me in front of Buckingham Palace?

4. If you need tourist information on London, go get this ____________. It's full of useful information on places to visit.

5. How much is a ____________ for the show tonight?

6. London has got a ____________, too. You can sit in the water's edge café there and enjoy a nice meal along the river Thames.

Down

7. It's easiest to travel by Tube in London. A one day ____________ costs £ 7,20.

8. Watch out, there's usually quite a crowd in that tea shop. You have to wait in the ____________ for your scones and tea.

•• Kannst du die folgenden Sätze umformulieren, indem du die hervorgehobenen Begriffe durch die Vorgaben in der Box ersetzt? Versuche es doch einfach mal mal. Einen Begriff kannst du zweimal verwenden.

open | **the museum** | **enter** | **could** | **far** | **Mondays** | **supermarket**

1. **May** I take pictures in this museum?

2. Where's the next **bus station**?

3. How **old** is **Christ Church**?

4. How much does it cost to **go there**?

5. What time does the museum **close** on the weekend?

6. Is the **zoo** open on **a Saturday**?

••• Wenn du jetzt noch die folgenden Sätze ins Deutsche übersetzen kannst, dann bist du fit für einen Ausflug nach London! Also, los geht's!

1. I would like to visit the British Museum because it is more interesting than the London Eye.

2. Although the entrance fee is very expensive, Madame Tussauds is really worth a visit.

3. The Sherlock Holmes museum is less expensive than the Tower of London.

4. Have you ever been to Camden Town?

3 HOTEL GEBUCHT?

- Mr Higgins möchte telefonisch ein Hotelzimmer buchen. Leider ist nicht immer klar verständlich, was der Herr an der Rezeption sagt. Kannst du die Lücken im Gespräch mit den folgenden Wörtern an der jeweils passenden Stelle füllen?

| **nights** | **double** | **help** | **booking** | **bathroom** | **dates** | **rooms** | **need** | **breakfast** |

Receptionist: Good morning and thank you for calling the Dominican Hotel. How may I (1) ______________ you?

Mr Higgins: Good morning, Sir. I'd like to make a reservation, please.

Receptionist: Most certainly. Could I have the (2) ______________, please?

Mr Higgins: Yes, it's from the twentieth to the twenty-fifth of November this year.

Receptionist: So that's five (3) ______________ in all... Yes, we do have rooms available then. How many (4) ______________ do you need?

Mr Higgins: We need one single room and a double room. Are the rooms en-suite?

Receptionist: Yes, of course. All of our rooms have their own (5) ______________ and shower.

Mr Higgins: That's good to know. And how much will the rooms cost?

Receptionist: The single room including (6) ______________ is £ 60 per night and the (7) ______________ room is £ 95 per night.

Mr Higgins: Good, I'd like to book then.

Receptionist: In that case, I'd (8) ______________ your name and address, please.

Mr Higgins: Of course. My name is Mr Higgins and the address is 4, Lloyd Street in Birmingham.

Receptionist: OK. I've got that. I'll fax you a confirmation of your (9) ______________ and send you a brochure of our hotel.

Mr Higgins: Thank you very much!

Receptionist: You're very welcome. Thank you for calling the Dominican. Goodbye!

BOXENSTOPP

Großartig! Jetzt ist auch ganz klar, worum es im Telefonat ging. Hier sind noch einmal die wichtigsten Vokabeln im Überblick, die man für eine Hotelbuchung gut gebrauchen kann:

to make a reservation	*reservieren*
single room	*Einzelzimmer*
available	*verfügbar*
bathroom	*Badezimmer*
to cost	*kosten*
per person / per night	*pro Person und Nacht*
to book	*buchen*
confirmation	*Bestätigung*

•• Lies dir die folgenden Beschreibungen genau durch. Was wird hier beschrieben? Schreibe das jeweilige Lösungswort auf, einige Buchstaben sind bereits vorgegeben.

1. If you want to book a room for two people in a hotel, you can ask for a ...

d __ __ b __ __ r __ __ m

2. Breakfast and other meals in hotel are usually served in the ...

__ __ n i __ g r o __ __

3. If you like to order a drink in your room, you can call the ...

r o __ m __ __ r v __ c __

4. A room with its own toilet facilities is called ...

e n - s __ __ t __

•• Deine Eltern möchten nach Edinburgh reisen und du sollst Ihnen in der Stadt für drei Nächte ein Hotelzimmer buchen. Deshalb schreibst du eine E-Mail an verschiedene Hotels und Pensionen, die du im Internet finden konntest und erkundigst dich nach Preisen und freien Zimmern. Deine Mutter hat für dich ein paar Angaben zusammengestellt, die du schon stichwortartig ins Englische übersetzt hast. Verfasse mit Hilfe dieser Notizen eine E-Mail nach Schottland. Auf der nächsten Seite geht's los!

Dear Sir or Madam,

____

____

____

____

____

____

____

____

____

____

____

____

Yours faithfully,

____

- book double room
- my parents
- bed and breakfast
- 3 nights (1–4 August)
- arrive at 5 p.m. by car
- leave after breakfast (August 4)
- en-suite facilities?
- costs per night?

4 WEGBESCHREIBUNGEN

- Wenn man zu Besuch in einer fremden Stadt ist, dann weiß man oft nicht, wie man an bestimmte Orte kommt, stimmt's? Am besten fragt man sich also einfach durch. Sieh dir einmal die Abbildung genau an und ergänze dann die Wegbeschreibung auf der nächsten Seite mit den fehlenden Wörtern.

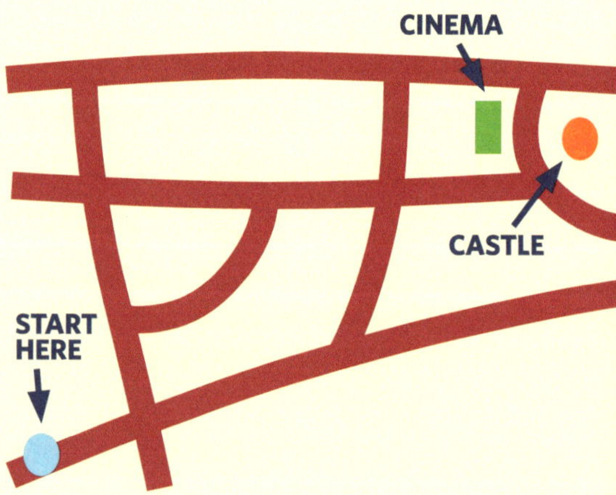

continue | next | opposite | end | left | straight on | excuse | right | turn | get | left | second

1. "____________ me, how do I ________ to the cinema?"
2. Go ______________.
3. Turn ____________ at the corner.
4. Then take the ____________ road on your ____________.
5. ____________ to the ____________ of the road.
6. ____________ left there.
7. The cinema is on your ____________, ____________ the castle.

BOXENSTOPP

Na, bist du gut am Ziel angekommen? Um auf Nummer sicher zu gehen, kannst du hier noch einmal überprüfen, ob du die Richtungsangaben schon drauf hast!

1. **o __ the l __ __ t**	*auf der linken Seite*
2. **o __ the __ i __ __ __**	*auf der rechten Seite*
3. **s __ r __ __ __ __ t __ n**	*geradeaus*
4. **o __ __ o __ __ t __**	*gegenüber von*
5. **__ e __ r**	*in der Nähe von*
6. **__ __ x __ t __**	*neben*
7. **b __ t __ __ __ n**	*zwischen*
8. **__ __ the e __ __ (__ f)**	*am Ende (von)*
9. **o __ / __ t the c __ __ __ __ r**	*an der Ecke*
10. **__ __ hin __**	*hinter*
11. **__ n f __ __ __ t of**	*vor*
12. **(just) __ r __ __ nd the c __ __ n __ __**	*(gleich) um die Ecke*

Hey, das klappt ja wie am Schnürchen! Um dir die Vokabeln besser merken zu können, schau dich doch mal in deinem Zimmer um und stelle dir die Vokabeln im Satzzusammenhang vor. So kannst du sie dir viel besser merken. Du kannst dann zum Beispiel Sätze bilden wie **My desk is opposite the window.** etc.

•• Kennst du dich aus im Straßenverkehr? Ordne die englischen Ausdrücke in der linken Spalte jeweils einer der Aussagen in der mittleren Spalte zu. Kannst du die Begriffe danach auch noch ins Deutsche übersetzen?

		Übersetzung
1. traffic lights	**a.** "Watch out in front of you, there's a pedestrian crossing the road."	______________
2. intersection	**b.** "There's a car ahead and it may pull out before you!"	______________
3. roundabout	**c.** "Why didn't you stop here? You've just driven through a red light!"	______________
4. zebra crossing	**d.** "You've taken the wrong turn. Cars may only go in one direction here."	______________
5. right of way	**e.** "Wait. Montgomery Street and Lincoln Avenue cross here – we're there!"	______________
6. one-way street	**f.** "Look. The two roads aren't crossing here any longer but form a circle and then go on."	______________

••• Stell dir vor, ein Tourist fragt dich in deiner Stadt nach dem Weg zum Freibad. Da du dich gut auskennst, kannst du natürlich weiterhelfen. Gib eine Wegbeschreibung mit Hilfe der vorgegebenen Anhaltspunkte. Und sei möglichst präzise in deinen Angaben, denn schließlich soll der Tourist sein Ziel ja auch erreichen, stimmt's?

Tourist: Excuse me. I'd like to go swimming, but I'm not familiar with the area here. Could you please tell me the way to the next swimming pool?

You:

1. go / straight on **2. turn right / second traffic lights** **3. cross / intersection** **4. go on / roundabout** **5. turn left / behind petrol station** **6. stop / end of the road** **7. parking lot / in front of you** **8. arrive / swimming pool**

1. ______________________________
2. ______________________________
3. ______________________________
4. ______________________________
5. ______________________________
6. ______________________________
7. ______________________________
8. ______________________________

5 ÖFFENTLICHE VERKEHRSMITTEL

- Schau dir an, wohin die unterschiedlichen Leute reisen und überlege dann, wie sie am besten dort hinkommen. Verbinde zuerst die Sätze mit dem passenden Verkehrsmittel und schreibe danach auf, wie die Leute an ihr Ziel kommen.

1. Tom is a truck driver. He has to go to Spain.
2. Jack and Lisa want to go shopping. The shopping mall isn't nearby.
3. Miguel is from Mexico. He wants to visit his family in Acapulco.
4. Mr and Mrs Jones are on their honeymoon. They are taking a boat tour down the Nile.
5. Clarisse doesn't have a car. She needs to see the doctor.
6. Mary-Ann is visiting Canada and the USA. She's travelling on a greyhound.
7. Robin has missed the bus. He doesn't want to be late for school.
8. Martin is taking Puppy for a walk. They are in Hyde Park.
9. Grandpa and grandma can't drive. They want to visit Vienna in spring.

a. by bus
b. by coach
c. by train
d. by bike
e. by car
f. by ferry
g. by plane
h. by lorry
i. on foot

1. *Tom is going to Spain by lorry.*
2. Jack and Lisa are going ______
3. Miguel ______
4. Mr and Mrs Jones ______
5. Clarisse ______
6. Mary-Ann ______
7. Robin ______
8. Martin ______
9. Grandpa and grandma ______

BOXENSTOPP

Wenn du zum Beispiel in London unterwegs bist, dann hast du mehrere Möglichkeiten zu reisen. Hier siehst du einige Wörter, die mit dem Reisen zu tun haben. Kannst du die Begriffe den vier Kategorien unten zuordnen?

information desk · ticket counter · station · bus stop · double-decker · luggage check-in · track · lost and found · platform · black cab · driver · schedule · taxi rank

plane	train	bus	taxi

•• Hier ist die Satzstellung etwas durcheinander geraten. Aber du kannst die folgenden Fragesätze bestimmt wieder in die richtige Reihenfolge bringen, stimmt's?

1. this / go / Does / New York / train / to / ?

2. flight / How / is / Denver / the / to / long / ?

3. does / When / the / to / leave / bus / Seattle / ?

4. arrive / Philadelphia / When / we / do / in / ?

5. catch / can / Where / I / taxi / a / ?

•• Und hier spielen plötzlich die Buchstaben ganz verrückt. In den folgenden Sätzen kann man nur noch die Städtenamen entziffern. Kannst du die Sätze richtig aufschreiben?

1. Wehre si het citket erontcu, elpase?

____

2. Ohw cumh era tow stcekti ot Boston, eslepa?

____

3. A rntreu tekcit ot New Orleans, eaples.

____

•• Du stehst am Ticketschalter und bist endlich an der Reihe, um dir und deiner Schwester Zugtickets für einen Ausflug von Cambridge nach London zu kaufen. Die Frau am Schalter spricht dich an. Wenn du den folgenden Dialog ergänzen kannst, dann bist du fit für die Reise!

Ticket clerk: "Next, please. How can I help you?"

You: (1) ______________________________

Ticket clerk: "Alright. Is that for today?"

You: (2) ______________________________

Ticket clerk: "What time of day would you like to travel?"

You: (3) ______________________________

Ticket clerk: "And how do you wish to travel? First class or second class?"

You: (4) ______________________________

Ticket clerk: "Two return tickets, first class to London. That's £40 then, please."

You: (5) ______________________________

Ticket clerk: "You can either pay cash or by credit card."

You: (6) ______________________________

Ticket clerk: "If you want to book a seat, that'll cost you £2 extra each."

You: (7) ______________________________

Ticket clerk: "That's £44 for you then."

You: (8) ______________________________

Ticket clerk: "Thank you, have a good trip! Next, please!"

6 IM RESTAURANT

- Wer is(s)t wo am liebsten? Kannst du die unterschiedlichen Restaurantbesucher auf der rechten Seite den jeweiligen Restaurants links zuordnen?

1. hamburger restaurant	**a. wealthy people**
2. seafood restaurant	**b. travellers on trains or planes**
3. deli restaurant	**c. truck drivers**
4. motorway restaurant	**d. lovers of fish and mussels**
5. on-board restaurant	**e. little children with their parents**
6. self-service restaurant	**f. visitors of cafeterias**

BOXENSTOPP

Wie du siehst, gibt es also viele unterschiedliche Arten von Restaurants. Und falls du schon einmal in Großbritannien, den USA oder einem anderen englischsprachigen Land gewesen bist, dann ist dir vielleicht aufgefallen, dass es viele unterschiedliche Bezeichnungen für Gaststätten gibt. Hier ein paar Beispiele:

bar	*Bar*
pub	*Kneipe*
canteen	*Mensa, Kantine*
eatery	*Restaurant; Esslokal*
tavern	*Gasthaus, Gasthof* (AE)
inn	*Gasthaus* (BE)
diner	*Restaurant* (meist am Rande einer großen Straße gelegen)

•• Du bist zu Gast in **Bunky's Seafood Grill** und hörst, wie sich deine Tischnachbarn mit dem Kellner unterhalten. Leider verstehst du aber nicht alles sofort richtig. Lies dir die folgende Unterhaltung durch und kreuze jeweils das richtige Wort an.

Guest: A (1) □ **table** □ **place** □ **party** for two, please.
Waiter: Smoker or non-smoker?
Guest: Non-smoker, please.
Waiter: Here you go. Would you like to see the (2) □ **card** □ **menu** □ **list**?
Guest: Yes, please. We are very (3) □ **full** □ **thirsty** □ **hungry**.
Waiter: Just let me know when you're ready to (4) □ **wait** □ **order** □ **serve**.
Guest: We'd like (5) □ **fish and chips** □ **cheeseburger and fries** □ **chicken sandwich and crisps**, please.
Waiter: Would you like any (6) □ **drinks** □ **water** □ **soda**?
Guest: Yes, an orange juice, a coke and some water, please.
Waiter: And would you also like a (7) □ **desert** □ **dessert** □ **table**?
Guest: No, thank you. Could we just have the (8) □ **bill** □ **receipt** □ **invoice**, please?

•• Jetzt kannst du selbst einmal einen Blick auf die verlockende Speisekarte werfen. Entscheide dich, ob du ein Frühstück, Mittagessen oder Abendessen bestellen möchtest und schreibe einen Dialog zwischen dir und dem Kellner.

Our Menu

Breakfast		***Lunch***		***Dinner***	
Bowl of cereal	*$ 1,95*	*Spicy pumpkin, chilli and coconut soup*	*$ 3,95*	*Marinated warm chicken salad*	*$ 10,95*
Egg sandwich	*$ 2,95*	*Roast tomato and basil soup*	*$ 3,95*	*Seafood pasta*	*$ 12,95*
Bagel with cream, cheese and jam	*$ 3,99*	*West country goat's cheese salad*	*$ 4,65*	*Rib eye steak with french fries and salad*	*$ 16,95*
Pancakes	*$ 3,99*	*Honey roast chicken sandwich*	*$ 6,95*	*Cheeseburger with french fries*	*$ 11,95*

Waiter: ______________________________

____

You: ______________________________

____

Waiter: ______________________________

____

You: ______________________________

____

Waiter: ______________________________

____

You: ______________________________

____

Waiter: ______________________________

____

You: ______________________________

____

7 SMALL TALK

- Kannst du die folgenden Puzzleteile richtig zuordnen? Es passen immer jeweils zwei Teile zusammen, eine gesprochene Kurzform und die dazugehörige ausgeschriebene Langform.

3. can't
b. going to
1. wanna
d. isn't
f. cannot
4. dunno
a. have got to
5. ain't
e. want to
2. gonna
6. gotta
c. don't know

Ist es nicht schön, sich ganz einfach mit Leuten unterhalten zu können, die man trifft? In Gesprächen benutzt man oft Wörter und Ausdrücke, die man in geschriebenen Texten so nicht finden würde. Achte mal darauf, wenn du demnächst unterwegs bist!

BOXENSTOPP

Wenn du dich mit Leuten unterhältst, dann ist es nicht nur wichtig zu verstehen, was jemand sagt und wie etwas gesagt wird. Es ist auch schön, wenn man seinen Gesprächspartnern zeigen kann, dass man sie versteht und ihnen aufmerksam zuhört. Dabei können eine Reihe von besonderen Ausdrücken und bestimmten Füllwörtern sehr hilfreich sein. Kannst du die folgenden Ausdrücke an der jeweils richtigen Stelle ergänzen? Damit es etwas einfacher wird, ist der Anfangsbuchstabe jeweils vorgegeben.

Max: Hi, Rachel. Is this seat taken?

Rachel: Oh, hi Max. Have a seat, please. But, I'm waiting for someone...

Max: (1) **I**__________ You're always busy. Aren't you? You're very popular.

Rachel: (2) **R**__________ What makes you think so? Is it only because I'm mostly with someone?

Max: (3) **E**__________ Oh, look. There's Finn coming!

Rachel: (4) **Y**__________ I have been waiting for him to get here.

Max: (5) **O**__________ I don't believe you. Finn is the least popular boy at school. Why would you wait for him?

Rachel: (6) **R**__________ Max. He might not be popular with you. But I still like him. Now, would you get up and leave us alone, please?

Really?

I see.

Oh no!

Right,

Exactly.

Yes, I know.

•• Gesprochene Sätze sind oft viel länger, als sie eigentlich sein müssten. Sieh dir einmal den folgenden Satz an und umkreise darin alle Wörter, die man auch weglassen könnte. Anschließend kannst du den Satz noch einmal ohne Füllwörter aufschreiben.

____

____

____

•• Hier siehst du fünf weitere Füllwörter (**fillers**), mit denen englische Muttersprachler ihre Sätze oft ausschmücken. Kannst du das auch? Schmücke die folgenden drei Sätze mit Füllwörtern aus und schreibe deine umgangssprachlichen Varianten auf.

I mean | really | you know | actually | or something

1. Yesterday I was at the movies and liked the film.

___

2. I didn't go to the swimming pool on Thursday because I lost my ticket.

___

3. We had to wait until they were all gone and it was dark when we got home.

___

••• Stell dir vor, jemand erzählt dir etwas Bestimmtes. Wie würdest du deinem Gesprächspartner oder deiner Gesprächspartnerin zeigen, dass du am Gesprächsverlauf interessiert und beteiligt bist? Finde jeweils eine passende Antwort zu den folgenden Sätzen, in denen die folgenden Füllwörter anzeigen, dass du dich in die jeweilige Situation hineinversetzt.

Right! | Exactly. | Oh no! | Really? | Definitely!

1. I always win when I'm in a match.

___

2. Your shirt surely was expensive, wasn't it?

___

3. My bike was stolen.

___

4. I wish it was summer and the sun would be shining.

___

5. We'll arrive at London airport about 50 minutes later than expected.

___

Vergiss nicht: Um deine Sprachkenntnisse zu verbessern, solltest du jede Gelegenheit nutzen, tatsächlich Englisch zu sprechen. Hab keine Angst vor Fehlern, man wird dich trotzdem verstehen! Und wenn dir mal etwas nicht einfällt, kannst du es sicher mit Hilfe anderer Wörter und Wendungen umschreiben!

8 FAMILIENLEBEN

- Bist du bereit für ein kleines Familienquiz? Los geht's: Finde heraus, welches Familienmitglied sich hinter der jeweiligen Beschreibung verbirgt.

1. The husband of your aunt? ______________________________

2. A person's father and mother? ______________________________

3. Your grandparents' parents? ______________________________

4. The daughter of your sister? ______________________________

5. A person's male child? ______________________________

6. The father of your father? ______________________________

7. The child of your uncle? ______________________________

8. The brother of your sister? ______________________________

BOXENSTOPP

Sieh dir noch einmal die Lösungen aus der Aufwärmübung an und ergänze anschließend die folgende Tabelle mit dem jeweils richtigen englischen Wort. Hier noch ein paar Vokabeln, die dir auf die Sprünge helfen. Es sind aber nicht alle Übersetzungen vorgegeben. Schaffst du den Rest auch alleine?

| grandson | aunt | husband | granddaughter | daughter | grandparents |
| nephew | siblings | couple | niece | grandchild | great-grandfather |

Enkel		*Enkelin*		*Enkelkind*	
Großvater	**grandfather**	*Großmutter*		*Großeltern*	
Urgroßvater		*Urgroßmutter*	**great-grandmother**	*Urgroßeltern*	
Vater	**father**	*Mutter*		*Eltern*	**parents**
Sohn		*Tochter*		*Kinder*	
Bruder		*Schwester*	**sister**	*Geschwister*	

Ehemann		*Ehefrau*	**wife**	*Eheleute*	
Onkel		*Tante*		*Verwandte*	**relatives**
Neffe		*Nichte*			
Cousin	**cousin**	*Cousine*			

•• Hier siehst du den Stammbaum der Familie Royal. Kannst du beschreiben, in welchem Verhältnis die Familienmitglieder zueinander stehen? Versuche, über jede der unten genannten Personen drei Aussagen zu machen.

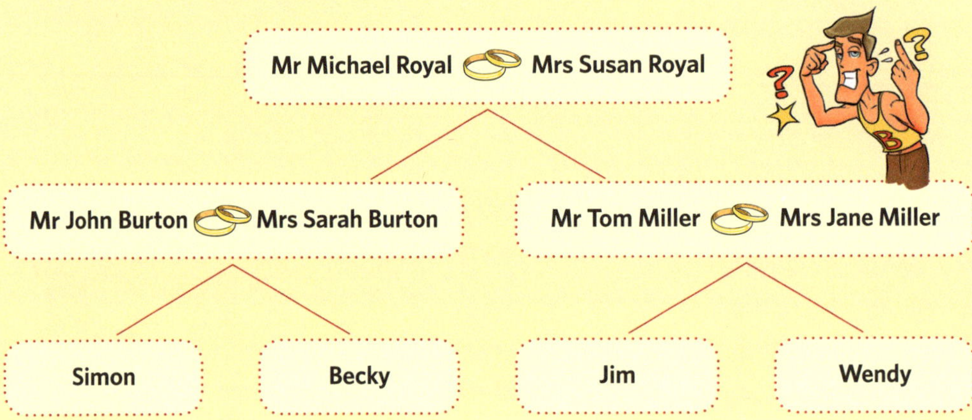

1. Sarah Burton is the daughter of ______________________________

____

____

2. Michael Royal is ______________________________

____

____

3. Wendy Miller ______________________________

____

____

••• Stell dir vor, du nimmst an einem Schüleraustausch in die USA teil. Bevor es losgeht, bekommst du eine E-Mail von deiner Gastschwester. Schau mal, was sie dir schreibt:

Hi,

my name is Catherine Jameson from Reno, Idaho. I'm thirteen years old and my family will be your host during your stay in the US. I'd like to introduce the different members of my family to you before you get here. You are going to live with me, my brothers and sisters and my mum. My parents aren't together any more. They were divorced when I was ten years old. My mum's name is Jane, she's 34 years old. And then there's my younger brother Fred, who is 6 years old, and my sisters Jeannie and Julie. They are nine-year old twins. My dad has got a new wife. Her name is Angela and they have just had a baby, little Jessica. She's very cute. We're a nice family and we look forward to meeting you in summer! Please write back to us and tell us about you and your family.

Beantworte Catherines E-Mail und schreibe ihr über deine Familie. Wer gehört alles dazu? Wie alt sind deine Geschwister? Wo leben deine Großeltern? Bestimmt fallen dir selbst noch viele Dinge ein, die du gerne erzählen möchtest!

9 DIE WELT DES SPORTS

- Kennst du dich gut aus in der Welt des Sports? Dann kann's losgehen: Ordne den Begriffen links das jeweils passende Gegenstück auf der rechten Seite zu.

1. champion	**a. referee**
2. contest	**b. crew**
3. team	**c. winner**
4. umpire	**d. practice**
5. training	**e. keeper**
6. goalie	**f. competition**

BOXENSTOPP

Es gibt eine ganze Menge unterschiedlicher Sportarten. Aber wo werden sie betrieben und was braucht man dazu? Kannst du die folgende Tabelle mit dem jeweils richtigen Ort und der zur Sportart passenden Ausrüstung ergänzen?

Ort

track | stadium | field | court | arena | pitch | gym | pool

Ausrüstung

helmet | racket | running shoes | bat | goggles | music | goal | basket

Sportart	Ort	Ausrüstung
aerobics		
baseball		
basketball		
football		
rugby		
swimming		
tennis		
track and field / athletics		

•• Drinnen oder draußen? Finde zunächst alle Sportarten in der Wortschlange und ordne sie richtig in die Tabelle ein. Du weißt bestimmt, welche Sportarten drinnen und welche draußen stattfinden, oder?

cyclingsquashskiingbadmintontennisclimbingfootballtabletennisswimminggolfcri cketbaseballwindsurfingrugbyjudovolleyballridingbasketballrunninggymnastics

indoor activities	outdoor activities

•• Im folgenden Text erfährst du, welche unterschiedlichen Sportarten die Mitglieder der Familie Jones mögen und ausüben. Vervollständige die Sätze mit den Vorgaben aus der Box, dann bist du fit beim Thema Sport!

| real | play | favourite | really | best | play | good | play | go | do |

My (1) ______________ sport is basketball, and I also like to (2) ______________ football. But I don't (3) ______________ swimming very often.

My Dad likes golf (4) ______________. He would also like to (5) ______________ tennis more often, but he hasn't got the time.

My Mum is (6) ______________ at dancing. She practices once a week. She doesn't (7) ______________ ice-skating, but she would love to learn it.

My sister is a (8) ______________ hockey fan. She loves to (9) ______________ hockey twice a week. We (10) ______________ like to watch boxing on TV.

10 DIE WELT DER MEDIEN

• Kennst du dich aus beim Thema Fernsehen? Kreuze jeweils die richtige Lösung an.

1. The time of day when most people are watching television is known as ______________.
☐ **a.** prime time
☐ **b.** popular time
☐ **c.** best time

2. A ______________ is a daily TV show based on all sorts of relationships.
☐ **a.** documentary
☐ **b.** soap opera
☐ **c.** sit-com

3. "I don't like that stupid show. Could you switch to another ______________, please?"
☐ **a.** host
☐ **b.** channel
☐ **c.** transmission

4. „Those were today's headlines. And now it's Ally Tileman with her weather ______________."
☐ **a.** forecast
☐ **b.** broadcast
☐ **c.** presentation

5. "There are ______________ news that there has been a crash-landing at Heathrow airport."
☐ **a.** sensation
☐ **b.** arriving
☐ **c.** breaking

BOXENSTOPP

Auch die englischsprachigen Kids lieben es, per SMS zu kommunizieren. Sie haben hierfür eine spezielle SMS-Sprache erfunden, um möglichst platzsparend mehr Informationen in einer Nachricht unterbringen zu können. Hier findest du eine Übersicht über einige der geläufigsten Abkürzungen:

Buchstaben können ganze Wörter ersetzen:	Zahlen- und Buchstabenkombinationen:
B = be	**gr8** =great
C = see	**l8r** = later
R = are	**sk8** = skate
U = you	**2moro** = tomorrow
Y = why	**b4** = before
	4ever = forever

Zahlen können für Wörter eingesetzt werden:

8 = ate

4 = for

2 = to / too

Buchstabenkombinationen:

WB = write back	**DF** = Dear friend
NP = no problem	**CM** = call me
WKD = weekend	**MSG** = message
BC = because	**JAM** = just a minute
HF = have fun	**THX** = thanks
GB = Goodbye	**FYI** = for your information
UR = you are	**PLS** = please
HAND = have a nice day	**RUOK** = are you ok?
IDK = I don't know	**TLK** = talk
ILU = I love you	

•• Kannst du die folgenden SMS-Nachrichten verstehen? Übersetze sie zweimal, zuerst ins Englische, und anschließend ins Deutsche.

Text message	Englische Übersetzung	Deutsche Übersetzung
GR8 2 CU. TLK 2 U 2MORO. Mick	**1.**	**a.**
THX FYI. I CALL U L8R. Nina	**2.**	**b.**
DF, RUOK? Tim	**3.**	**c.**
IDK, MY SISTER IS HERE. I CY L8R. Mel	**4.**	**d.**
GR8 2 HEAR. ILU 4EVER. Sandra	**5.**	**e.**
NP. HAND. CM 2MORO. Sam	**6.**	**f.**
CU IN SCHOOL. GB. Will	**7.**	**g.**
Y CAN'T U COME? WB. Steve	**8.**	**h.**

• Hier siehst du fünf Begriffe, die etwas mit dem Telefonieren zu tun haben. Ordne jedem Begriff das passende Verb zu und überlege dir anschließend zu jedem Begriffspaar einen Beispielsatz.

a. to leave a message | ~~**b. to pick up**~~ | **c. to hang up** | **d. to text** | **e. to dial**

1. receiver **b. to pick up**

Example: *Before you can talk on the phone, you need to pick up the receiver.*

2. mobile phone

Example: ______________________________

3. answering machine

Example: ______________________________

4. a busy line

Example: ______________________________

5. telephone number

Example: ______________________________

Wiederholen und Üben in den Klassen 8 – 10

Nachdem du in den Klassen 5 bis 7 die Grundlagen der Grammatik gelernt und dir schon einen beachtlichen Wortschatz zugelegt hast, wird in der Schule ab der 8. Klasse wiederholt und vertieft.

Daher ändert sich auch der Aufbau dieses Buches ab hier ein wenig.

In den Bereichen **Grammatik** findest du zunächst zu jedem Grammatikthema einen ausführlichen Nachschlageteil. Im Anschluss daran kannst du im Übungsteil wieder in drei unterschiedlichen Schwierigkeitsstufen üben.

Auf S. 284 findest du zudem noch eine praktische Gesamtübersicht über die Zeiten im Englischen mit allen wichtigen Regeln und Signalwörtern. Hier kannst du jederzeit auf einen Blick schnell nachschlagen.

In den Bereichen zum **Wortschatz** begegnest du unter anderem typischen Fallen im Englischen, sogenannten Falschen Freunden und schwierigen Fällen. Hier lernst du, wie du Fehler vermeiden kannst. Außerdem wiederholst du noch einmal die wichtigsten Unterschiede zwischen amerikanischem und britischem Englisch.

Der Bereich **Referate halten** hält für dich das wichtigste Handwerkszeug bereit, das du brauchst, um ein perfektes Referat zu halten. Hier bekommst du neben fertigen Sprachbausteinen, viele Tipps zur Planung, Vorbereitung und Durchführung eines Referates.
Die Sprachbausteine kannst du auch als Audio-Datei unter **www.pons.de/referate-englisch** downloaden. So kannst du alles nachhören, mitsprechen und deine Aussprache perfektionieren.

Also dann – off you go!

KLASSE 8–10

Inhalt

Grammatik

Wortschatz

KLASSE 8

1 IF-SÄTZE

Wenn ich diese Schuhe heute Abend anziehe, kann ich garantiert nicht tanzen. Wenn ich ein anderes Paar Schuhe tragen würde, würde ich mich viel besser fühlen. Wenn ich statt den hohen Schuhen Turnschuhe gekauft hätte, hätte ich nicht so viel Geld ausgegeben.

SPRACHTIPP

Es spielt keine Rolle, ob der if-Satz vorne oder hinten im Bedingungssatz steht. Steht der if-Satz vorne, wird er mit einem Komma vom Hauptsatz getrennt.

if-Sätze (if-clauses) sind Nebensätze, die durch das Wort **if** (= wenn, falls) eingeleitet werden. Sie stellen Bedingungen für eine andere Handlung, die im Hauptsatz steht. Solche Satzgefüge heißen daher auch Bedingungssätze (conditional sentences).

Arten von if-Sätzen

if-Sätze mit allgemeingültiger Bedingung

if-Satz	Hauptsatz
if + simple present	**simple present**

if – *wenn, falls*

when – *wenn (zeitlich)*

Mit dieser Art **if-Satz** werden allgemeingültige Aussagen oder Tatsachen ausgedrückt. Es geht nicht darum, für wie wahrscheinlich der Sachverhalt gehalten wird. Man kann → **if** oder **when** verwenden.

If/When you **add** fresh herbs to the salad, it **tastes** delicious.
You **don't drown if/when** you **bathe** in the dead sea.

!

Lass dich von den deutschen Wenn-/Falls-Sätzen nicht in die Irre führen! In englischen if-Sätzen steht kein will oder would! Will und would stehen nur im Hauptsatz!

if-Sätze mit erfüllbarer Bedingung (Typ I)

if-Satz	Hauptsatz
if + simple present	**will -future**
(auch: if + present perfect)	(auch: Imperativ oder can, may, must, needn't)

Die **if-Sätze** vom **Typ I** beschreiben eine Bedingung, die mit sehr hoher Wahrscheinlichkeit eintritt. Die Bedingung ist wirklich erfüllbar

Wird **will** durch ein **Modalverb** oder einen **Imperativ** ersetzt, ändert sich die **Bedeutung** der Sätze entsprechend.

I'll be very sad if you don't come over the weekend.
If we save some money, we'll be able to go to the USA next year.
If you see Mia tonight, tell her to phone me.

if-Sätze mit schwer erfüllbarer Bedingung (Typ II)

if-Satz	Hauptsatz
if + simple past	**conditional (would/could/might + Infinitiv)**

Die **if-Sätze** vom **Typ II** beschreiben eine Bedingung, die unwahrscheinlich ist. Man geht davon aus, dass der Sachverhalt im if-Satz eher nicht eintritt. Das past tense im if-Satz entspricht dabei einem deutschen Konjunktiv.

Ersetzt man **would** durch ein **Modalverb in der Vergangenheitsform**, ändert sich die **Bedeutung** der Sätze entsprechend.

If we went to Paris for the weekend, we would go by train. *... würden wir ... fahren*
If I were a millionaire, I could spend a lot of money. *... könnte ich ... ausgeben.*
Mum might get angry if you didn't call her. *... würde vielleicht ärgerlich werden ...*

if-Sätze mit unerfüllbarer Bedingung (Typ III)

if-Satz	Hauptsatz
if + past perfect	**conditional perfect (would/could/might + have + past participle)**

Die **if-Sätze** vom **Typ III** beschreiben eine unerfüllbare Bedingung. Das Ereignis hat in der Vergangenheit bereits stattgefunden. Es ist nicht mehr zu ändern. Nur gedanklich lassen sich Alternativen durchspielen (was wäre passiert, wenn ... hätte/wäre). Das past perfect im if-Satz entspricht dabei einem deutschen Konjunktiv. Ersetzt man **would** durch ein Modalverb in der Vergangenheitsform, ändert sich die **Bedeutung** der Sätze entsprechend.

SPRACHTIPP

Beim simple past von **be** in der 1. und 3. Person Singular heißt es:

If I were you, ...
Wenn ich du wäre/ich an deiner Stelle ...

If he were here, ...
Wenn er hier wäre, ...

SPRACHTIPP

if-Sätze Typ III können auch wie folgt aufgebaut sein:

if + simple past/ conditional perfect

If you **didn't drive** so well, you **would have had** an accident.

if + past perfect/ conditional

If you **had left** earlier, you **would be** on time now.

SPRACHTIPP

In formeller Sprache benutzt man auch **Had I + past participle** statt **If I had + past participle:**

Had I heard (= If I had heard ...) of his accident, I would have visited him.

Siehe auch **Alternativen für if** und den Sprachtipp zu **should in if-Sätzen**.

If Bob **hadn't spent** so much money on his new car, he **wouldn't have been** so angry after the crash.	*... wäre er nicht so ärgerlich gewesen.*
If she **had talked** about her problems, we **could have helped** her.	*... hätten wir ihr helfen können.*
If you **had told** Mike about the party, he **might have asked** Jess right away.	*... hätte es sein können, dass er Jess sofort fragt.*

Weitere Varianten von Bedingungssätzen

if oder when

1 Will you help me in the garden when you get back?

2 If I'm back before sunset, I will help you.

1. *Hilfst du mir im Garten, wenn du zurückkommst?*
2. *Falls ich vor Sonnenuntergang zurück bin, helfe ich dir.*

! Auch für when-Sätze gilt: steht im when-Satz **simple present**, folgt im Hauptsatz **will-future**. Kein **will/won't** im when-Satz! Kein Komma vor **when!**

if = *wenn* (falls)	**when** = *wenn* (auf jeden Fall; zeitlicher Bezug)
If I go to the museum, I'll bring you a poster.	**When I go to the museum, I'll bring you a poster.**
Der Sachverhalt ist noch **nicht sicher**. Es kann noch etwas dazwischenkommen. Aber wenn ich gehe, dann bringe ich ein Poster mit.	Der Sachverhalt ist **sicher**. Ich gehe auf jeden Fall und bringe dann ein Poster mit. Mit **when** stellt man immer einen zeitlichen Bezug her.

Alternativen für if

Bedingungssätze können auch mit anderen Wörtern und Ausdrücken als mit **if** beginnen. Das sind meist:

as long as	**As long as Mum doesn't feel any pain, she won't go to the doctor.**
in case	**I'll take a raincoat in case it rains.**
unless	**Unless you give me a ring, I won't know where Susan's party is taking place. (= If you don't give me a ring, ...)**
even if	**Even if the computer works now, I don't want to work on it.**

as long as – *solange*
in case – *für den Fall, dass*
unless = if not – *falls nicht*
even if – *auch wenn, sogar wenn*

should in if-Sätzen

if-Satz	Hauptsatz
if + should + Infinitiv	**Imperativ/will-future/conditional**

Mit Hilfe von should (‚sollte') im if-Satz kann man ein **denkbares Ereignis** und seine Konsequenz ausdrücken.

If you should need help, just call me.
If I should be late, Mike will call you.
If there should be a traffic jam, we would hear it on the car radio.

SPRACHTIPP

In sehr formeller Sprache (z. B. in Geschäftsbriefen) ersetzt man **if** manchmal durch eine andere **Wortstellung:**

Should the fault persist, we will gladly replace the machine. (= If the fault should persist/persists, ...)

Sollte der Fehler bestehen bleiben, werden wir gern die Maschine ersetzen.

Wunschsätze und Aufforderungen

will/would in if-Sätzen

Eine wichtige Regel im Zusammenhang mit Bedingungssätzen ist:
Kein will oder would im if-Satz!

Es gibt jedoch ein paar Ausnahmen, mit deren Hilfe **besondere Höflichkeit** ausgedrückt wird:

- Aufforderung im if-Satz

If you would only stop smoking I would be much happier.	*Wenn du doch bloß mit dem Rauchen aufhören würdest, wäre ich viel glücklicher.*

- Bitte oder Wunsch im if-Satz

If you would just fill in this form here ... Thank you.	*Wenn Sie bitte dieses Formular hier ausfüllen würden ... Danke.*
If you would just like to take this table over there ...	*Wenn Sie bitteschön diesen Tisch hier drüben nehmen würden ...*

Wunschsätze mit past tense oder past perfect

schwer erfüllbarer Wunsch:	**I wish/If only/I'd rather/It's (high) time + simple past**
unerfüllbarer Wunsch:	**I wish/If only/I'd rather + past perfect simple**

Wunschsätze mit ähnlicher Struktur wie der der Bedingungssätze Typ II und Typ III kann man **mit bestimmten Wendungen** formulieren. Sie drücken aus, dass ein Wunsch entweder nur schwer oder gar nicht mehr erfüllt werden kann, da er sich auf ein Ereignis in der Vergangenheit bezieht. Das past tense bzw. das past perfect entspricht dann – wie bei den if-Sätzen Typ II und III – deutschen Konjunktivformen.

I wish I were/was in Hawaii.	**It's time you found a new job.**
If only I had phoned you earlier.	**I'd rather she hadn't gone by plane.**

LERNTIPP

Wendungen für Wunschsätze:

I wish –
ich wünschte

if only –
wenn ... nur
(+ **Konjunktiv**)

I'd rather –
es wäre mir lieber

it's (high) time –
es ist (höchste) Zeit, dass ...

★ **1.** Wähle aus den vorgegebenen Verben aus und setze sie jeweils in der richtigen Zeit ein. Beachte, dass es sich um allgemeingültige Aussagen handelt.

ask get burn not have do be stay need

1. If young people ________________ advice, they most often ________________ their best friends first.

2. If children ________________ a lot of sports, they ________________ any weight problems.

3. You ________________ your skin if you ________________ in the bright sun for too long.

4. Some people ____________ seasick if the sea ____________ too rough.

★★ **2.** Setze die Verben in die richtige Zeit. In einigen Fällen kannst du die Verben durch passende Modalverben ergänzen.

can may

roll – *Brötchen*

1. If it rains, we (play) ____________________ games inside.

2. You (catch) ____________________ the train if you hurry up.

3. I (travel) ____________________ around the world if I win a million euros.

4. If you (come) ____________________ tomorrow, I'll cancel my aerobics.

5. If you give me his number, I (call) ____________________ him right away.

6. I (go and get) ____________________ some rolls if you set the table.

★★ **3.** Setze die Verben in die richtige Zeit.

row – *Reihe*

1. If the restaurant at the corner didn't offer any vegetarian meals, we (have to eat) ____________________ our lunch elsewhere.

2. If you (book) ____________________ your tickets early enough, you would be able to get some for the front row.

3. I (do) ____________________ all my shopping at the weekend if the shops were open.

4. If my son read the newspaper regularly, he (know) ____________________ more about politics.

5. Jake (not be at work) ____________________ in time if Tina didn't wake him up every morning.

6. If Great Britain (be) ____________________ a sunnier country, we would spend our holidays there more often.

** **4.** Setze die Verben in die richtige Zeit.

1. If Mike hadn't come home by ten o'clock,
I **(call)** ________________ the police.

2. I **(not know)** ________________ about the fight at school if Patrick hadn't told me about it.

3. If you had listened to Lisa more carefully,
you **(understand)** ________________ her much better.

4. Karen **(live)** ________________ in Tokyo if her mum had taken that job in Japan last year.

5. My brother **(pay for)** ________________ the new car for Mum if she had asked for support.

6. My friends wouldn't have bought a dog for me
if I **(not wish for)** ________________ one.

support – *Unterstützung*

wish for – *sich (etw.) wünschen*

*** **5.** Hier findest du **Bedingungssätze** vom **Typ I, Typ II** und **Typ III**.
Setze die richtige Zeit ein.

1. If we go to France, we **(spend)** ________________ a few days in Paris, too.

2. I think more people **(go)** ________________ by train if the tickets were cheaper.

3. If we **(not take)** ________________ the short cut, we would have got completely wet.

short cut – *Abkürzung*

4. If I were you, I **(not ask)** ________________ Thomas again.

5. What would you do if you **(have)** ________________ a lot of money?

6. Your back will hurt if you **(not do)** ________________ your exercises.

7. I **(not have)** ________________ the same earrings as Patricia if I had bought the pink ones.

8. Chris, if you don't work harder, you **(not pass)** ________________ your exam.

9. I **(love)** ________________ to come to your party if it hadn't been Grandma's 80th birthday last Saturday.

*** **6.** Lies die folgenden drei Sätze. Entscheide zuerst, welchem Typ die Sätze zuzuordnen sind. Übertrage sie dann ins Englische.

silly things – *dumme Sachen*

pretty angry – *ziemlich sauer*

1. *Wenn sie dumme Sachen über mich erzählen würde, wäre ich ziemlich sauer.*
2. *Wenn sie dumme Sachen über mich erzählt, werde ich sauer sein.*
3. *Wenn sie dumme Sachen über mich erzählt hätte, wäre ich ziemlich sauer gewesen.*

erfüllbare Bedingung

schwer erfüllbare Bedingung

unerfüllbare Bedingung

SPRACHTIPP

Denke an die unterschiedlichen Arten der Bedingungssätze und ihre Zeitenfolge und lass dich nicht von den Zeiten im Deutschen in die Irre führen!

*** **7.** Übertrage die Bedingungssätze ins Englische.

ask for – *bitten um*

get – *besorgen*

be afraid of flying – *Angst vorm Fliegen haben*

more often – *öfter*

1. *Wenn ich deinen Ring finde, rufe ich dich an.*
2. *Wenn du Tom um 3.500 € bätest, was würde er sagen?*
3. *Ich komme mit dir, wenn du einen Moment wartest.*
4. *Wenn du willst, besorge ich dir einen Job in dieser Firma.*
5. *Wenn ich Angst vorm Fliegen hätte, hätte ich ein großes Problem mit meinem Job.*
6. *Wenn ich mehr Zeit gehabt hätte, wäre ich öfter joggen gegangen.*

2 GERUNDIUM UND INFINITIV

Rudern macht Spaß. Ich mag das Rudern wirklich. Ich hoffe auch, Muskeln aufzubauen.

Das Gerundium

Ein Substantiv kann ein Gegenstand, eine Person, ein Tier oder ein abstrakter Begriff sein. Aber auch Tätigkeiten kann man mit einem Substantiv ausdrücken. Im Englischen benutzt man dafür das **Gerundium (gerund)**. Es entspricht einem substantivierten Verb im Deutschen (‚laufen' → ‚das Laufen').

Bildung des Gerundium

Das **Gerundium** wird (wie das present participle) aus dem **Infinitiv des Verbs + -ing** gebildet und heißt deshalb auch **ing-Form**. Beim Gerundium sind die **Regeln zur Schreibweise** identisch mit denen des **present participle**, das für die progressive-Zeitformen benutzt wird.

reading running smiling lying

Will man ein Gerundium **verneinen**, stellt man ‚not' davor:

I like walking but not running.	*... nicht zu rennen.*

Die **Passivform** des Gerundium wird folgendermaßen gebildet:

being + past participle des Verbs

She was angry about being left at home.	*... gelassen zu werden.*

!

Das **gerund** darf man nicht mit dem **present progressive** verwechseln:

gerund:
verb + -ing

present progressive:
be + verb + -ing.

SPRACHTIPP

Das **gerund** hat auch **Perfektformen im Aktiv:**

having + past participle des Verbs

I remember having closed the windows.

... und im **Passiv:**

having been + past participle des Verbs

I remember having been asked for help.

Gebrauch des Gerundium

Das Gerundium als Subjekt

Das Gerundium kann wie andere Substantive Subjekt (wer oder was?) eines Satzes sein. Dabei kann es auch mit einem weiteren Substantiv oder mit anderen Wörtern einen Verbund bilden.

Dancing is my hobby.	*Tanzen ist mein Hobby.*
Writing postcards is boring.	*Das Schreiben von Postkarten ist langweilig.*
Rock climbing can be fun.	*Das Klettern in Felsen kann Spaß machen.*
Discussing different points of view is often tiring.	*Das Diskutieren verschiedener Ansichten ist oft ermüdend.*

Das Gerundium als Objekt

Das Gerundium kann auch Objekt (wen oder was?) eines Satzes sein. Dabei steht es meistens nach Verben, die eine Vorliebe (z. B. like, love, enjoy) oder eine Abneigung (z. B. verneintes like, dislike, hate) ausdrücken.

I love **writing letters.**	*Ich liebe es, Briefe zu schreiben.*
We hate **arguing.**	*Wir hassen Streit.*
Do you enjoy **cooking at the weekend?**	*Genießt du das Kochen am Wochenende?*
Mr Spencer is interested in **repairing computers.**	*Mr Spencer interessiert sich für das Reparieren von Computern.*
Dad is thinking about **buying a new camper.**	*Vater denkt an den Kauf eines neuen Wohnmobils.*

Für die Übertragung des Gerundiums ins Deutsche gibt es mehrere Möglichkeiten:

I love **writing letters.**	*Ich liebe das Briefeschreiben.* *Ich liebe das Schreiben von Briefen.* *Ich liebe es, Briefe zu schreiben.*
We hate **arguing.**	*Wir hassen Streit.* *Wir hassen das Streiten.* *Wir hassen es, zu streiten.*

Weitere Satzfunktionen des Gerundium

Außerdem kann das Gerundium im Satz auftreten als

- adverbiale Bestimmung (Gerundium nach Präpositionen wie **in spite of, for, before, after, on**). Solche Konstruktionen entsprechen Nebensätzen. Sie können daher durch Komma abgetrennt auch vorne im Satz stehen.
- Attribut zu einem Substantiv,
- Ergänzung des Subjekts nach einer Form von **be**.

adverb. Bestimmung	**She won't get in without showing her ID card.**
Attribut	**I don't see a possibility of accepting that essay.**
Subjekt-Ergänzung	**My favourite sport is dancing.**

Das Gerundium nach bestimmten Verben und Wendungen

Ein Gerundium steht meist nach Verben, die eine **Vorliebe** oder eine **Abneigung** ausdrücken und nach verschiedenen anderen Verben und Ausdrücken. Am besten lernt man diese Verben und Wendungen auswendig. Hier die wichtigsten in einer Übersicht:

be afraid of	I'm afraid of **bungee jumping.**
be interested in	Are you interested in **jazz dancing**?
be tired of	I'm tired of **waiting** for you all the time.
be/get used to	I'm used to **going** to bed early.
be good/bad at	She's quite good at **skiing.**
can't help	I can't help **thinking** of you.
do the	Let me do the **talking.**
go	We never go **shopping** in the morning.
go on	Go on **explaining** the problem, please.
finish	Have you finished **preparing** your speech ?
enjoy	My friend enjoys **sleeping** late on Sundays.
can't stand	I can't stand **driving** at night.
miss	I miss **walking** at the seaside.
practise	Do you practise **playing** the piano regularly?
suggest	Maja suggested **going** to the Bee Bar tonight.
talk about/of	They talked about **sailing** the whole evening.
think about/of	We're thinking about **moving** to Spain.
worry about	Mum always worries about **cooking** lunch or dinner.
look forward to	I look forward to **seeing** you soon.
Thank you for ...	Thank you for **inviting** me.
How/What about ...?	How/What about **going** to the cinema?
Would you mind ...?	Would you mind **closing** the window?
(don't) mind	I don't mind **closing** the window.
It's worth ...	It's worth **talking** about the issue.
It's no use ...	It's no use **telling** him the whole story.
It's no good ...	It's no good **ignoring** the problem.
without	You can't wear this jacket without **asking** her.
instead of	Instead of **watching TV** all the time you should study.
by	You can learn a lot by **reading** alone.
apart from	Apart from **cleaning** the bathroom, we must hoover the floor.
as well as	My dog always looks for mice as well as **chasing** cats.

!

be used to + gerund – *es gewohnt sein, etw. zu tun*

get used to + gerund – *sich daran gewöhnen, etw. zu tun*

aber Infinitiv nach:

used to (do sth.) - (etw.) früher/immer (getan haben).

LERNTIPP

Das Gerundium steht auch nach:

be ashamed of
be proud of
be keen on
be famous for
be crazy about
dream of
succeed in
insist on
rely on
dislike
avoid
complain about

LERNTIPP

Das gerund steht auch nach einigen Substantiven + Präposition:

(the) idea of
(be) in danger of
(a) chance of
(have) difficulty in
(a) way of

Solche Ausdrücke klingen oft etwas formeller.

be tired of sth. – *es satt haben, etw. zu tun*

speech – *Rede*

it's worth – *es ist es wert*

it's no use – *es hat keinen Sinn*

it's no good – *es nützt nichts*

Es gibt einige Verben, die sowohl ein Gerundium als auch den Infinitiv nach sich ziehen können. Die **Bedeutung** des Satzes **ändert sich** dadurch **nicht**. Im Wesentlichen sind das:

love	**like**	**hate**	**begin**	**prefer**	**continue**	**intend**	**start**

! In höflichen Fragen und Bitten mit **like** kann nur der Infinitiv stehen:

Would you like **to go** swimming with me?/I'd like **to watch** that new movie

My husband prefers working on his computer.
I prefer to work in the garden.
The neighbour's dog Rex always starts barking when I go by.
But he never starts to bark when the postman comes.

Achtung: **need** gehört auch in diese Gruppe. Nach **need** entspricht das Gerundium jedoch einem **passiven Infinitiv**!

need	**The hedge needs trimming/to be trimmed.**

hedge – *Hecke*
trim – *in Form bringen*
to be trimmed – *in Form gebracht (zu) werden*

Das Gerundium mit eigenem Sinnsubjekt

Zwischen Verb und Gerundium kann auch ein **Substantiv** oder **Pronomen** erscheinen. Die Gerundium-Konstruktion **bezieht sich** dann auf dieses Wort als deren eigenes **Sinnsubjekt**. Beachte, dass die Pronomen normalerweise in der **Objektform** verwendet werden. Manchmal können auch Possessivbegleiter oder Substantive mit s-Genitiv stehen.

Mike suggested Sarah (Sarah's) writing crime stories.	*Mike schlug vor, dass Sarah Krimigeschichten schreiben sollte.*
Jeannie is afraid of her little sister (her little sister's) getting in trouble.	*Jeannie befürchtet, dass ihre kleine Schwester in Schwierigkeiten gerät.*
Do you mind me (my) watching TV?	*Macht es dir etwas aus, dass ich fernsehe?*

SPRACHTIPP
Solche Konstruktionen kann man oft mit Hilfe eines **dass-Satzes** ins Deutsche übertragen.

Gerundium oder Infinitiv?

1 Matt, do you remember scuba-diving in the Red Sea last year?

2 Yes, it was great. I meant to go on another diving holiday but Lisa forgot to ask her boss for leave in time.

1. *Matt, erinnerst du dich ans Tauchen im Roten Meer letztes Jahr?*
2. *Ja, das war toll. Ich wollte einen weiteren Tauchurlaub machen, aber Lisa hat vergessen, rechtzeitig bei ihrem Chef Urlaub zu beantragen.*

Einige Verben können sowohl ein Gerundium als auch einen Infinitiv nach sich ziehen, ändern aber dadurch ihre **Bedeutung**. Die wichtigsten sind:

	Gerundium	Infinitiv
stop	aufhören, etwas zu tun	anhalten, um etwas zu tun
	She stopped smoking.	**She stopped to smoke a cigarette.**
forget	vergessen, dass man etwas getan hat	vergessen, etwas zu tun
	I forgot inviting Caren.	**Oh no, I forgot to invite Rita.**
remember	sich daran erinnern, dass man etwas getan hat	sich erinnern/daran denken, dass man etwas tun muss
	I remember telling her the whole story.	**Remember to tell her the whole story.**
regret	bedauern, dass man etwas getan hat	bedauern, etwas tun zu müssen
	Sam regrets buying the expensive watch.	**We regret to inform you that the train is delayed.**
mean	bedeuten, etw. zur Folge haben	etwas tun wollen, fest vorhaben
	Better results mean working harder every day.	**I mean to see the exhibition next Sunday.**
try	Das Gerundium beschreibt eine Alternative.	Der Infinitiv beschreibt eine Bemühung.
	Try walking more often.	**I tried to walk every day but I was too busy.**

LERNTIPP

Ob ein **gerund** oder ein Infinitiv nach einem Verb folgt, lässt sich nicht aus der deutschen Übersetzung ableiten. Die Wendungen muss man einfach lernen!

give sb. a ring – *jdn. anrufen*

be likely to forget – *wahrscheinlich vergessen*

dentist's appointment – *Zahnarzttermin*

Der Infinitiv nach bestimmten Verben

Nach bestimmten Verben steht stets **der Infinitiv**.

agree	**be afraid**	**be likely**	**be prepared**
be sorry	**decide**	**hope**	**learn**
offer	**plan**	**promise**	**refuse**
would like			

Please, give me a ring. I'm likely to forget the dentist's appointment.
Some people are afraid to lose their jobs.
We would like to spend our holidays in Denmark.

SPRACHTIPP

Übersetzt man Verb + Infinitiv ins Deutsche, wird (wie beim Verb + gerund) auch oft ‚zu' eingeschoben, z. B.:

agree to write something – *zustimmen, etwas zu schreiben*

hope to arrive on time – *hoffen, pünktlich anzukommen.*

Gebrauch des Infinitivs

Die Infinitivkonstruktion wird auch vor allem gebraucht für Sätze wie:

Ich möchte/will/erwarte, dass ...

Ähnlich wie beim Gerundium kann auch hier ein **Objekt** als **Sinnsubjekt** der Infinitivkonstruktion zwischen Verb und Infinitiv eingeschoben werden.

Nach **like** – *mögen* kann auch das gerund stehen, jedoch nicht in höflichen Fragen und Bitten mit would!

I want you to listen.	unbedingt wollen/verlangen, dass jemand anders etwas tut
I expect her to be punctual.	erwarten, dass jemand anders etwas tut
I'd like you to meet my friend.	wollen/wünschen, dass jemand anders etwas tut

Besonderheiten
zu Bildung und Gebrauch des Infinitivs

Aufgepasst bei **verneinten Sätzen**: Der verneinte Infinitiv wird mit einem vorangestellten ‚not' gebildet. Verneint man das einleitende Verb, ändert sich die Bedeutung des Satzes:

He promised *Er versprach,*	**He didn't promise** *Er versprach nicht,*
... to talk about this matter. *... über die Sache zu sprechen.* (Er wird darüber sprechen.)	**... to talk about this matter.** *... über die Sache zu sprechen.* (Er behält sich vor, **nicht** darüber zu sprechen.)
... not to talk about this matter. *... nicht über die Sache zu sprechen.* (Er wird schweigen.)	**... not to talk about this matter.** *... nicht über die Sache zu sprechen.* (doppelte Verneinung: Er behält sich vor, darüber zu sprechen.)

Die Passivform des Infinitivs lautet: **to be + past participle**. Sie wird verwendet, wenn im vergleichbaren Satz ohne Infinitiv das Passiv stehen würde. Sie steht auch nach **be** und **remain**, wenn die Ausdrücke passive Bedeutung haben (z. B. it is to be expected, it remains to be seen).

it is to be expected – *es ist zu erwarten*

it remains to be seen – *es bleibt abzuwarten*

She expects to be offered the job.	*Sie erwartet, dass ihr der Job angeboten wird.*

⋆ **1. Gerundium** als Subjekt oder als Objekt? Bilde aus den Vorgaben einen Satz bzw. eine Frage und übersetze dann.

1. watching TV | our children | on | enjoy | Saturday evenings

2. own money? | do you | earning | your | miss

3. very useful | can be | foreign language | learning | a

learn - *(er)lernen*

4. is | hobby | playing golf | in Germany | an expensive

BE: gɒlf
AE: gɑːlf

⋆ **2.** Übertrage ins Englische. Benutze ein **Gerundium**.

1. *Segeln macht Spaß.*

2. *Links fahren ist nicht schwer.*

3. *Fußballspielen ist das größte Hobby unseres Sohnes.*

4. *Ich interessiere mich für das Erlernen einer Fremdsprache.*

5. *Mein Chef zieht es vor, morgens Tee zu trinken.*

6. *Ich liebe es, sonntags Fernsehen zu gucken.*

____

7. *Ich habe vor zwei Wochen mit dem Joggen angefangen.*

____

3. Gerundium oder Infinitiv? Setze das richtige Wort in die Lücke.

1. I like (chat) ____________ on the Internet.
2. Are you afraid of (travel) ____________ on your own?
3. Robert promised (take) ____________ his new girlfriend home.
4. Did you enjoy (talk to) ____________ your mother after such a long time in the United States?
5. My sister is only interested in (buy) ____________ expensive clothes.
6. Elena stopped (eat) ____________ fast food last May.
7. I'm not afraid (speak) ____________ in front of a lot of people.
8. Everybody stopped (laugh) ____________ when the boss came in.
9. Would you mind (catch) ____________ that spider over there?
10. We hope (see) ____________ you again next summer.

4. Was passt zusammen? Es gibt mehrere Möglichkeiten. Trage alle Möglichkeiten in den Kasten ein.

enjoy
decided
don't miss
hope
promised
love
be afraid of
don't like
offered
hate

I	*enjoy, don't like, love, hate, don't miss*	**listening to classic music.**
I		**flying.**
I		**to come earlier next time.**
I		**to book the Westminster Hotel in London.**

I		**to argue with my best friends.**
I		**smoking in trains.**
I		**living in the city.**
I		**eating in Italian restaurants.**

*** **5.** Gerundium und Infinitiv bei einem Verb? Bei bestimmten Verben ist beides möglich. Die Bedeutung ändert sich. Übertrage die Bedeutungsunterschiede ins Deutsche.

1. Julie stopped playing the piano when she was eighteen.

Julie stopped to play the piano because she hadn't practised that day.

2. The secretary forgot cancelling the booking.

cancel – *rückgängig machen, stornieren, absagen*

The secretary forgot to cancel the booking.

3. A beautiful garden means working in it nearly every day.

But I don't really mean to criticize you for your garden.

4. Do you remember talking to Helen about her life insurance?

life insurance – *Lebensversicherung*

Remember to talk to Helen about her life insurance.

3 DAS CONDITIONAL

1. *Schau dir mal das Wetter an! Wir hätten einen anderen Tag zum Einkaufen aussuchen können. Ich wäre sowieso gerne zu Hause geblieben.*
2. *Ja, ich weiß. Aber wenn wir immer das tun würden, was du willst, würden wir jeden Tag zu Hause bleiben.*

Das conditional

Bildung

Das **conditional** wird für alle Personen gebildet mit

would + Infinitiv

Person	Langform	Kurzform	Infinitiv
alle Personen	**would**	**'d**	**go (laugh, agree,**
	would not	**wouldn't**	**wake up, ...)**

Auch die Modalverbformen **could**, **should**, und **might** sind conditional-Formen. Sie werden nach demselben Muster wie **would** benutzt:

could/should/might + Infinitiv

Gebrauch des conditional

Das conditional wird verwendet:

- für Vorschläge und Ansichten oder für Handlungen bzw. Ereignisse, die eintreten können oder auch nicht.

Toni: "Look, which T-shirt shall I take?" — Lucy: "I'd take that one."

- in If-Sätzen Typ II. Dabei steht im If-Satz (=Nebensatz) das **simple past** und im dazugehörenden Hauptsatz das **conditional**. Es spielt keine Rolle, ob der Hauptsatz vorne oder hinten steht.

We **could go** to the new exhibition if we had enough time.
If my alarm clock didn't ring at 7 o'clock, I **wouldn't get up** in time.

- in höflichen Fragen und Bitten.

Would you **like** a cup of tea?	*Hättest du/Hätten Sie gern eine Tasse Tee?*
Would you **close** the door, please?	*Würdest du/Würden Sie bitte die Tür schließen?*

LERNTIPP

Für das conditional gibt es keine Signalwörter, es wird aber häufig in → **If-Sätzen** (S. 215) verwendet.

Übersetzungstipps

Das **conditional** wird im Deutschen korrekt mit dem Konjunktiv wiedergegeben.

Tina **would be** disappointed.	*Tina wäre enttäuscht (ugs.: Tina würde enttäuscht sein.)*
She **wouldn't be** happy.	*Sie wäre nicht glücklich. (ugs.: Sie würde nicht glücklich sein.)*
Sam **would talk** to her.	*Sam spräche mit ihr. (ugs.: Sam würde mit ihr sprechen.)*
He **wouldn't tell** lies.	*Er erzählte keine Lügen. (ugs.: Er würde keine Lügen erzählen.)*

SPRACHTIPP

Häufige Wendungen sind:

I'd rather (+ Verb ...) – *Ich würde lieber ...*

I'd like to (+ Verb ...) – *Ich möchte gerne ...*

Das conditional perfect

Bildung

Das **conditional perfect** wird für alle Personen gebildet mit

would + have + past participle

Person	Langform	Kurzform	Infinitiv
alle Personen	**would have**	**'d have**	**gone (laughed,**
	would not have	**wouldn't have**	**agreed, ...)**

Gebrauch des conditional perfect

Das conditional perfect wird verwendet für:

- gedachte, nicht mehr realisierbare Handlungen, Ereignisse und Ansichten in der Vergangenheit, die in Wirklichkeit nicht stattgefunden haben und auch nicht mehr stattfinden können.

I'd have apologized for that.

LERNTIPP

Für das conditional perfect gibt es keine Signalwörter, es wird aber häufig in **If-Sätzen** verwendet.

- If-Sätze Typ III. Dabei steht im If-Satz (=Nebensatz) das **past perfect** und im dazugehörenden Hauptsatz das conditional perfect. Es spielt keine Rolle, ob der Hauptsatz vorne oder hinten steht.

If you had told him the truth, he wouldn't have had such a bad conscience.
He'd have seen the traffic lights if he had looked properly.

bad conscience - *schlechtes Gewissen*

traffic lights - *Ampel*

Übersetzungstipps

Das conditional perfect wird im Deutschen dem Konjunktiv wiedergegeben:

Would you have told me the truth?	*Hättest du mir die Wahrheit gesagt?*
I would have spoken to Dad at first.	*Ich hätte zuerst mit Dad gesprochen.*
Justin would have been too afraid to do that.	*Justin wäre zu ängstlich gewesen, das zu tun.*

Achtung!
Would und **had** haben die gleiche Kurzform. Nur an der jeweils **folgenden Verbform** lässt sich erkennen, um welches der beiden Wörter es sich handelt. Vergleiche die folgenden drei Sätze und ihre unterschiedlichen Bedeutungen:

I'd pay for the tickets.	**I would pay ...** conditional	*Ich würde ... bezahlen.*
I'd paid for the tickets.	**I had paid ...** past perfect	*Ich hatte ... bezahlt.*
I'd have paid for the tickets.	**I would have paid ...** conditional perfect	*Ich hätte ... bezahlt.*

SPRACHTIPP

Conditional und conditional perfect benutzt man auch in der **indirekten Rede**. Sie stehen dann für das will-future bzw. das future perfect der direkten Rede.

Unterschied zwischen conditional und conditional perfect

conditional	conditional perfect
I would answer the e-mail at once.	**I would have answered the e-mail at once.**
Ich würde die E-Mail sofort beantworten.	*Ich hätte die E-Mail sofort beantwortet.*
Die E-Mail ist noch nicht beantwortet. Man kann noch reagieren. Ein Vorschlag wird gemacht.	Aber jetzt ist es zu spät. Man spricht also über etwas, was gar nicht stattgefunden hat und nicht mehr zu ändern ist.

1. Übertrage folgende Sätze ins Deutsche.

1. We could ask Valerie. She would know what to do.

____

2. Let's go on Sunday. On Sunday there wouldn't be much traffic.

____

3. Would you buy these musical tickets for 40 pounds?

____

4. Grandma wouldn't have managed to walk to the doctor. I took her.

____

5. They would have won £ 3,000,000 if they had hit the jackpot.

____

manage to do sth. – es schaffen, etw. zu tun

take – hier: bringen

2. Übertrage die Sätze ins Englische und benutze dabei die vorgegebenen Verben.

1. *Ich würde mit dir eine Wohnung teilen.*

____

2. *Tom würde gerne mit Lena zusammen nach Australien reisen.*

____

3. *Wir hätten das Rennen nicht gewonnen, wenn es geregnet hätte.*

____

4. *Ich hätte nicht gedacht, dass du schon 30 bist!*

____

5. *Wir würden lieber hier wegziehen.*

____

6. *Thomas hätte dich nicht gefragt.*

____

BE: **flat** – *Wohnung*

AE: **apartment** – *Wohnung*

think
share
move away
like
ask
win

move away – *wegziehen*

4 DIE INDIREKTE REDE

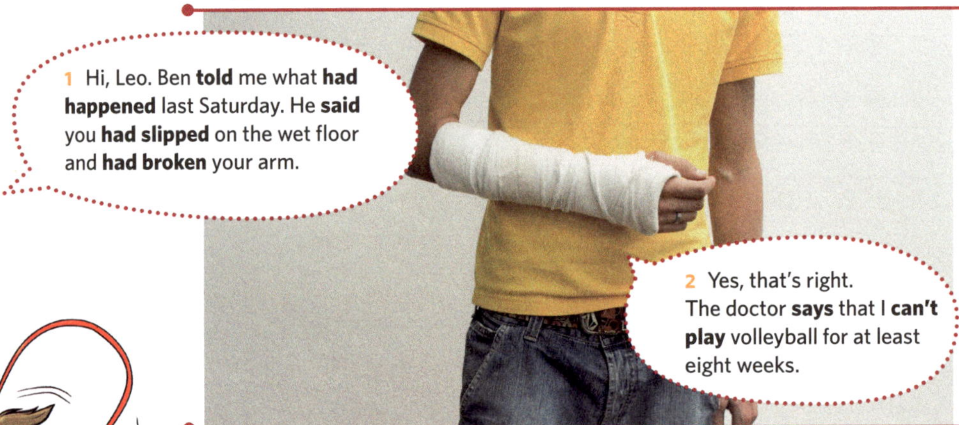

1. Hallo, Leo. Ben hat mir erzählt, was letzten Samstag passiert ist. Er sagte, du bist auf dem nassen Boden ausgerutscht und hast dir den Arm gebrochen.
2. Ja, das stimmt. Der Arzt sagt, dass ich mindestens acht Wochen lang kein Volleyball spielen kann.

Die indirekte Rede (indirect or reported speech) wird gebraucht, wenn man erzählen will, was jemand anders oder man selbst gesagt hat.

Bildung der indirekten Rede

- Ausgangspunkt für Sätze in der indirekten Rede sind immer Sätze in der **direkten Rede** (direct speech):

„Mary has booked a trip to New Zealand."

- Diese können in die indirekte Rede gesetzt werden. Aussagen in der indirekten Rede bestehen aus einem **Einleitungssatz**, der ein Verb des Mitteilens enthält (**say, tell**, usw.) und einem **Folgesatz**, der mit **that** eingeleitet wird. Vor diesem Folgesatz steht **kein Komma**.
- Die Konjunktion **that** kann auch entfallen.

Hi, Mary. I heard (that) you had booked a trip to New Zealand.	*Ich habe gehört, dass du eine Reise nach Neuseeland gebucht hast.*

LERNTIPP

Häufig verwendete einleitende Verben:

say (to sb.), hear, tell (sb.), learn, declare, explain, mention, complain, agree, answer, repeat, suggest, write.
Beachte:

She told me that ...

She said (to me) that ...

- Wird **zeitlich versetzt** berichtet, steht der Einleitungssatz im **past tense**. Die **Zeiten** aus der direkten Rede werden im Folgesatz eine Stufe in die Vergangenheit **verschoben**.
- Wird **sofort** berichtet, steht der Einleitungssatz im **present tense**. Die **Zeiten** aus der direkten Rede **bleiben** im Folgesatz **stehen**.
- **Pronomen**, **Zeit-** und **Ortsangaben** müssen an den **Standpunkt** des Sprechers in der indirekten Rede **angepasst** werden.

Indirekte Rede mit Zeitverschiebung

Aussagen, die zeitlich deutlich der Vergangenheit angehören, werden in der Regel mit einem einleitenden Verb im **simple past** gebildet. Der Folgesatz wird in der Regel gegenüber der direkten Rede nach folgendem Muster um **eine Zeitstufe zurück**gesetzt:

Verwendete Zeit in der direkten Rede	Verwendete Zeit in der indirekten Rede
simple present	**simple past**
present progressive	**past progressive**
simple past	**past perfect simple**
present perfect simple	**past perfect simple**
present perfect progressive	**past perfect progressive**
past perfect	**past perfect (unverändert)**
will-future	**conditional (would + Infinitiv)**
conditional	**conditional (unverändert)**
conditional perfect	**conditional perfect (unverändert)**
going to-future	**was/were going to + Infinitiv**
can	**could**
may	**might**
must	**had to**
will	**would**
shall	**should**

Beispiele für die Zeitverschiebung:

Direkte Rede	Indirekte Rede
simple present **Oliver: "I'm glad to see you."**	simple past **Oliver said (that) he was glad to see me.**
simple past **Sarah: "We didn't go out on Saturday."**	past perfect **Sarah told me (that) they hadn't gone out on Saturday.**

present perfect **Bob: "I've finished the puzzle."**	past perfect **Bob said (that) he had finished the puzzle.**
past perfect **Liz: "I had been in India for four months before I visited the Taj Mahal.**	past perfect **Liz declared (that) she had been in India for four months before she visited the Taj Mahal.**
will-future **Greg: "I'll talk to Jim later."**	conditional **Greg mentioned (that) he would talk to Jim later.**
conditional perfect **Tom: "I would have come to Lee's party if I had been back in time."**	conditional perfect **Tom said (that) he would have come to Lee's party if he had been back in time.**
Modalverben present tense **Susie: "I can translate this article."**	Modalverben past tense **Susie said (that) she could translate that article.**
Modalverben past tense **Laura and Jake: "We might spend a week at the seaside."**	Modalverben past tense **They said (that) they might spend a week at the seaside.**

Veränderungen des Standpunkts in der indirekten Rede

In den Folgesätzen der indirekten Rede sind oft Veränderungen nötig, um **Pronomen, Zeit- und Ortsangaben** an den **Standpunkt des Berichterstatters** in der indirekten Rede anzupassen. Diese Änderungen hängen stark vom Zusammenhang ab, man kann sie daher nicht konkret in Regeln fassen. Hier aber einige Beispiele:

1. Personenbezogene Veränderungen, z. B.:

Direkte Rede	Indirekte Rede
Robert: "I can help Rebecca."	**Luisa: "Robert says(that) he can help her."**
	Rebecca: "Robert says (that) he can help me."

2. Änderungen von Zeit- und Ortsangaben werden nötig, wenn der in direkter Rede erwähnte Zeitraum oder Zeitpunkt für den Berichterstatter schon vergangen ist bzw. wenn der Berichterstatter sich nicht selbst am erwähnten Ort befindet.

Beispiele:

Direkte Rede	Indirekte Rede (Standpunkt Berichterstatter)
today	**that day**
tonight	**that night**
yesterday	**the day before**
tomorrow	**the next day, the following day**
this week (month, year ...)	**that week (month, year ...)**
next month (year ...)	**the next/the following month (year ...)**
last Saturday (month ...)	**the Saturday (month ...) before**
here	**there**
in this house (city ...)	**in that house (city ... /Name d. Stadt etc.)**

Beachte auch, dass man so mit der Beschreibung von Zeit und Ort unterschiedliche Bedeutungen wiedergeben kann:

Direkte Rede	Indirekte Rede
"I really like it here."	**I told Jim that I really liked it there.** (Ich bin inzwischen nicht mehr dort. > mit Zeitverschiebung)
	I told Jim that I really like it here. (Ich bin immer noch am selben Ort. > ohne Zeitverschiebung)

!

Steht das einleitende Verb im simple past, erfolgt im Folgesatz trotzdem keine Zeitverschiebung, wenn

1. Ort bzw. Zeit für Sprecher und Berichterstatter gleich sind
2. bei Tatsachen, Naturgesetzen und Gewohnheiten (s.u.)

Indirekte Rede ohne Zeitverschiebung

Gibt man durch indirekte Rede etwas **sofort** weiter, also zeitnah am Geschehenen, dann verwendet man im **Einleitungssatz** das **simple present**. Im Folgesatz steht die gleiche Zeit wie in der direkten Rede.

Direkte Rede	Indirekte Rede
Henry: „I don't know the address."	**Henry says (that) he doesn't know the address.**
Nina: "Our guests are here."	**Nina says (that) our guests are here.**

SPRACHTIPP

Für die Übersetzung ins Deutsche verwendet man dann den Konjunktiv:

Henry sagt, dass er die Adresse nicht wisse.

Nina sagt, dass unsere Gäste da seien.

Indirekte Rede bei Tatsachen, Naturgesetzen, Gewohnheiten

Bei unabänderlichen Tatsachen, Aussagen von allgemeingültiger Bedeutung und Gewohnheiten findet in der indirekten Rede **keine Zeitverschiebung** statt, auch wenn das einleitende Verb im simple past steht, denn zu dem Zeitpunkt der indirekten Rede gelten die Tatsachen und Gewohnheiten weiterhin.

Direkte Rede	Indirekte Rede
Teresa: „London **is** an exciting city." (allgemeingültig)	Teresa said (that) London **is** an exciting city.
Steven: "We always **go** for a long walk at the weekend." (Gewohnheit)	Steven said (that) they always **go** for a long walk at the weekend.
Dad: "The sun **rises** in the east." (Naturgesetz, unabänderl. Tatsache)	Dad told me (that) the sun **rises** in the east.

Fragen in der indirekten Rede

Entscheidend bei der Wiedergabe von Fragen in der indirekten Rede ist, ob die Frage in der direkten Rede mit oder ohne Fragewort gestellt wurde.

- Fragen **ohne Fragewort** werden mit **if** oder **whether** eingeleitet.

Direkte Rede	Indirekte Rede
"Are you married?"	He asked me **whether I was/I'm** married.
"Did you meet Linda?"	He asked me **if I had met** Linda.

SPRACHTIPP

Häufig verwendete einleitende Verben sind **ask sb., want to know, wonder.**

- Fragen mit Fragewort greifen in der direkten Rede das **Fragewort** wieder auf. Es steht **direkt nach dem einleitenden Verb**. Danach folgen Subjekt und Prädikat wie in einem **Aussagesatz**.

Direkte Rede	Indirekte Rede
„**Why did you leave** so early?"	She wondered **why I had left** so early.

SPRACHTIPP

In indirekten Fragesätzen werden modale Hilfsverben oft weggelassen. Der Folgesatz besteht dann nur aus Fragewort + Infinitiv (mit to).

Where can I put my hat?

I asked

- **where to put** my hat.
- where I could put my hat.

Aufforderungen in der indirekten Rede

Um Aufforderungen, Warnungen und Ratschläge in der indirekten Rede wiederzugeben, verwendet man nach dem einleitenden Verb meist den **Infinitiv (mit to) + Personalpronomen (als Objekt)**. Zur Verneinung stellt man **not** vor den Infinitiv.
Es ist aber auch möglich, einen **that-Satz mit should (not)** zu verwenden. Häufige einleitende Verben sind **tell sb., ask sb., warn sb., advise sb.**

Direkte Rede	Indirekte Rede
"Please, come an hour earlier."	Nick **asked me to come** an hour earlier.
"Listen carefully."	I **told you to** listen carefully.
"Don't talk about Tom."	Lia **advised us not to talk** about Tom. Lia said **that we shouldn't talk** about Tom.

SPRACHTIPP

Ausrufe, Begrüßungen und andere Satzfragmente ergänzt man oder umschreibt sie in der indirekten Rede. **Question tags** werden nicht übernommen.

"Hi, Mike. Let's have lunch together, **shall we**?" — I said hi to Mike and **suggested** to have lunch together.

★ **1.** Vervollständige die Sätze in der **indirekten Rede**.

1. They renovated the office very quickly.

Frank said (that) they ___

2. I can organize the next meeting.

Chris said (that) he ___

3. Mum had definitely closed the door.

Dad said (that) Mum ___

4. I've visited many European countries.

He said (that) he ___

5. It'll rain tomorrow.

Scott said (that) it ___

6. We've been living in Hamburg for five years.

Christina said (that) they ___

7. We've already talked about that problem several times.

My boss said (that) we ___

8. There was no snow in Germany last year.

Mrs Meyer said (that) there ___

9. We're going to sell our house.

The Hansons said (that) they ___

★★ **2.** Allgemeingültig, Gewohnheit oder nicht? Entscheide, ob in der **indirekten Rede** eine Zeitverschiebung nötig ist oder nicht.

1. My children always walk to school.

Mrs Pringle said (that) ___

2. I never work at weekends.

I told you (that) ___

3. Aboriginals live in Australia.

Our geography teacher said (that) ___

4. I'll prepare the dinner.

Christopher said (that) ___

5. Each village in Great Britain has at least one pub.

Bridget said (that) ___

6. Ireland has got beautiful beaches.
   Michael said (that) ____
7. I've read so many fantastic books.
   Stefanie said (that) ____

*** **3.** Dein Freund (deine Freundin) stellt Dir eine Menge Fragen. Du teilst diese Fragen am nächsten Tag deiner Freundin (deinem Freund) mit. Was sagst du? Setze die Fragen in die indirekte Rede.

1 Have you got time to go out?
2 Can you repair my alarm clock?
3 How long will you need for that?
4 Do you want me to pick you up?
5 Why aren't you listening?
6 Have I upset you?
7 I'm sorry.
I didn't mean to pressure you.

! Denke an die Veränderungen bei der Wiedergabe von Informationen in der indirekten Rede!

1. Adam/Eve asked me if/whether I ____
2. Adam/Eve wondered ____
3. Adam/Eve wanted to know ____
4. Adam/Eve asked me ____
5. Adam/Eve wondered ____
6. Adam/Eve asked carefully ____
7. In the end he/she told me (that) ____
   and (that) ____

*** **4.** Gib die Aufforderungen in der indirekten Rede wieder.

1 Kim asked me
2 Luke advised me
3 Tom asked me
4 Sheila told me
5 Ben warned me

1. Go home.
____
2. Open the window.
____
3. Don't wait for me.
____
4. Don't miss the new film.
____
5. Don't forget your umbrella.
____

5 DER ARTIKEL

Ich nehme das Tagesessen und eine Flasche Wasser, bitte.

Der bestimmte Artikel

Im Englischen haben alle Substantive nur einen bestimmten Artikel: **the**.

Gebrauch des bestimmten Artikels

Der bestimmte Artikel (the definite article) **the** wird für alle weiblichen und männlichen Lebewesen (**the** man, **the** woman) und für alle Gegenstände, Tiere und abstrakten Dinge (**the** table, **the** dog, **the** trouble) benutzt.

Der bestimmte Artikel bleibt in allen Fällen (Nominativ, Genitiv, Dativ und Akkusativ) gleich. Das gilt sowohl für den Singular als auch für den Plural (**the** girls, **the** flowers, **the** questions).

Man verwendet den bestimmten Artikel vor Substantiven, die im Text näher bestimmt oder erklärt werden. Vor nicht näher bestimmten Substantiven (z. B. in allgemeinen Aussagen) steht kein bestimmter Artikel.

mit bestimmtem Artikel	ohne bestimmten Artikel
Abstrakte Begriffe, Stoffe	
Substantiv + of-Genitiv oder Relativsatz oder Ortsangabe	Substantiv mit allgemeiner Bedeutung
The picture of your wedding is nice. I liked **the food** Julie cooked yesterday.	**Italian food** is very popular in Germany.

Most im Sinn von ‚die Mehrzahl' erscheint ohne Artikel:

Most dogs are not very well-behaved. – *Die meisten Hunde benehmen sich nicht sehr gut.*

The milk from that farm is very creamy.	**Milk** is good for your bones and teeth.
Institutionen, Verkehrsmittel	
bestimmtes Gebäude/Fahrzeug	Zweck einer Institution; Verkehrsanbindung
The university in the city centre was built around 1870.	Sam goes back to **university** in October.
The train to London is late again.	Sam always goes by **train**.
Wochentage, Monate, Mahlzeiten	
bestimmte(r) Tag/Monat/Mahlzeit	wiederkehrende Ereignisse
Do you remember **the Thursday** when your car broke down?	The summer holidays start on **Thursday.**
The January of 1976 was very cold.	**January** is normally the coldest month of the year.
The Sunday lunch at Julie's was great.	As a student, I usually had **lunch** at the cafeteria.
Familiennamen (Plural)	**Vornamen, Verwandtschaft (Sg.)**
The Scotts have moved into the house on the corner.	**Grandpa and Mary** like to play chess together.
Namen mit of-Genitiv	**Straßen, Parks, Gebäude**
The Isle of Man is famous for the Manx cat.	The Queen goes to **Balmoral Castle** for her summer holidays.
The Crown Jewels can be seen at **the Tower (of London).**	**Central Park** is crowded on weekends.
Meere, Flüsse	**Seen**
The River Thames runs through London.	**Loch Ness** is maybe the most popular Scottish lake.
The North Sea and **the English Channel** can be much rougher than **the Baltic Sea.**	
Länder (Plural), Gebirge	**Länder (Singular), einzelne Berge**
The Rocky Mountains are situated in the west of **the United States.**	**Mount Everest** is the highest mountain in the world.

Manx – *(von) der Insel Man*

SPRACHTIPP

Ländernamen im **Singular** stehen **ohne** Artikel.

Mit Artikel stehen Ländernamen

- im **Plural**, oft Inselstaaten (the Philippines)
- mit **of** im Namen (the Democratic Republic of the Congo)
- mit **Republic** oder **Kingdom** im Namen (the Dominican Republic, the United Kingdom)

Besonderheiten bei der Aussprache

the [ðə]	vor allen Wörtern, die mit einem **gesprochenen Konsonanten** beginnen	**the book, the picture, the children, the university, the uniform, the hospital**
the [ðiː]	vor allen Wörtern, die mit einem **gesprochenen Vokal** beginnen	**the example, the apple, the orange, the information, the underground, the hour**

Aufgepasst bei den Buchstaben u und h:

Es heißt: the university [ðə‿ˈjuːnɪˈvɜːsəti], the unit [ˈðə‿ˈjuːnɪt],
aber: the upper class [ðiː‿ˈʌpə ˌklɑːs], the ultimate [ðiː‿ˈʌltɪmət]

Es heißt: the hour [ˌðiː‿ˈaʊə], the honour [ˌðiː‿ˈɒnə]
aber: the house [ˌðə‿ˈhaʊs], the hospital [ˌðə‿ˈhɒspɪtl]

:ə

Soll der bestimmte Artikel besonders betont werden, wird er stets [ðiː] gesprochen:

Julie's birthday party will be **the** [ðiː] party of the year.

Besonderheiten bei der Stellung

Der bestimmte Artikel steht in der Regel **vor Adjektiv + Substantiv**.

the green car, the comfortable sofa

Im Zusammenhang mit den Wörtern **half, both, twice, double, all** wird der bestimmte Artikel jedoch nachgestellt:

I haven't read half the book yet.	*... das halbe Buch ...*
Both the recipes sound good.	*Beide Rezepte ...*
She made twice the number of muffins.	*... die doppelte Anzahl Muffins...*
We need double the amount of napkins on the table.	*... die doppelte Menge Servietten ...*
You used all the writing paper without replacing it!	*... das ganze Briefpapier ...*

Der unbestimmte Artikel

Gebrauch des unbestimmten Artikels

Der unbestimmte Artikel (the indefinite article) heißt im Englischen **a** oder **an.**

Spricht man über **Berufsbezeichnungen**, die **Nationalität** oder **Religionszugehörigkeit**, verwendet man den unbestimmten Artikel:

Mr Jones is a dentist.	*Herr Jones ist Zahnarzt.*
His wife Donna is an Italian.	*Seine Frau Donna ist Italienerin.*
Donna is a Catholic, and her husband is a Protestant.	*Donna ist Katholikin, und ihr Mann ist Protestant.*

SPRACHTIPP

Zusammen mit Zeit- und Maßeinheiten bedeutet der unbestimmte Artikel auch **je** oder **pro**:

She throws a party three times **a year.**
... dreimal im/pro Jahr.

The tomatoes are 30p **a pound** or £1 **a packet.**
... 30p pro Pfund oder £1 pro Packung.

Spricht man über Titel, die nur von einer Person (z. B. in einem bestimmten Land oder einer Stadt) geführt werden können, wird der unbestimmte Artikel nicht verwendet:

Elizabeth II has been Queen for many years.	*... ist ... Königin.*
Rudy Giuliani was mayor of New York several times.	*... war ... Bürgermeister*

an vor gesprochenem Vokal ermöglicht ein fließendes Lesen. Verbinde die Wörter beim Lesen!

an idea [ən‿aɪˈdɪə]

Besonderheiten bei der Aussprache

a [ə]
vor allen Wörtern, die mit einem gesprochenen Konsonanten beginnen:

a conference	*eine Konferenz*
a European company	*eine europäische Firma*
a uniform	*eine Uniform*
a house	*ein Haus*

an [ən]
vor allen Wörtern, die mit einem gesprochenen Vokal beginnen:

an international conference	*eine internationale Konferenz*
an exercise	*eine Übung*
an uncle	*ein Onkel*
an hour	*eine Stunde*

Der unbestimmte Artikel wird außerdem nachgestellt bei **too + Adjektiv:**

Chess is **too** difficult **a** game for a six-year-old.
... ein zu schwieriges Spiel ...

Besonderheiten bei der Stellung

Der unbestimmte Artikel steht in der Regel vor Adjektiv + Substantiv.

a blue car, an uncomfortable chair

Im Zusammenhang mit den Wörtern **half, such, quite, rather, what** wird der unbestimmte Artikel jedoch nachgestellt:

Can you help me for half an hour?	*... eine halbe Stunde ...*
There is such a mess in the kitchen, I have to clean up first.	*... eine solche Unordnung ...*
You have quite a lot of homework to do.	*... eine ziemliche Menge Hausaufgaben ...*
Their visit was rather a surprise for us.	*... eine ziemliche Überraschung ...*
What a pleasure to meet you!	*Was für eine Freude ...*

★ **1.** Lies laut. Welches **the** passt nicht in die jeweils waagerechte Reihe?

the house	the building	the office	the hospital	the hotel
the daughter	the grandma	the woman	the lady	the aunt
the eyes	the feet	the legs	the knees	the fingers
the uniform	the shoe	the shirt	the earring	the coat
the husband	the humour	the hobby	the hour	the heart

LERNTIPP

Sprich den Text laut, damit du hörst, welche Vokale auch wie Vokale gesprochen werden und welche nicht.

★ **2.** Übersetze jeweils das **the** im Satz.

1. Excuse me, where is the entrance? ________

2. Sorry, I don't know. But you can ask the woman over there. ________

3. OK. Excuse me, I'm looking for the entrance. Where is it? ________

4. The entrance is opposite the car park. ________ , ________

5. Can I help you with the luggage? ________

6. Oh, yes please. The bags are quite heavy. ________

★ **3.** Setze **a** oder **an** ein.

1. ____ university ____ old university

2. ____ American ____ young American

3. ____ vegetarian ____ pure vegetarian

4. ____ apple ____ green apple

5. ____ interview ____ stupid interview

6. ____ address ____ wrong address

7. ____ headache ____ terrible headache

LERNTIPP

Immer das unmittelbar folgende Wort ist entscheidend für die Wahl zwischen **a** und **an**.

★★ **4.** Ordne die folgenden Begriffe in die Tabelle ein.

a	an

interesting film
early flight
orange juice
useful book
young uncle
angry man
old church
safe underground
ugly house
English flag
fantastic office
high building
brilliant idea
clever agent

★★ **5.** Setze **the** oder **a/an** oder nichts ein.

Dear Sandy, we are on __ holiday in __ France this Christmas! Luckily, there is enough snow in __ French Alps so we are all taking __ skiing course. Our ski instructor __ Marc is __ Frenchman. In __ summer he works as __ sailing instructor at __ Mediterranean Sea. Last year, he even worked at __ Super Sail School at __ Lake Windermere! Therefore Marc speaks __ English quite well. __ Smiths are here, too, but they don't like __ skiing. They go hiking and visit __ famous sights. Josh plans a trip to __ Mont Blanc. It seems there is __ bus right from __ hotel to __ foot of __ mountain. It runs every day from __ October to __ April, except on __ Mondays. __ Christmas holidays will soon be over – see you back at __ school then! — Yours, Bella

stand in a queue – *anstehen, Schlange stehen*

★★★ **6.** Bringe die Bruchstücke der Sätze wieder in die richtige Reihenfolge. Es gibt manchmal auch mehrere Möglichkeiten.

1. half | went | last summer | students | the | of our class | to Madame Tussaud's

____

2. the | in advance | people | all | had booked | in our bus | tickets

____

3. for | an | everybody else | half | stood in a queue | hour

____

4. James Bond actor | already | to see | what | the | surprise | new | a | there

____

5. a | quite | of him | a lot of | photo | took | people

____

6. they | spent | everybody | amount | of money | the | twice | had planned

____

7. photos | were | both | the | very popular | and | the | souvenirs

____

6 SOME UND ANY

1. Hast du Schokolade?
2. Nein, ich habe keine. Aber ich habe Kekse, was hältst du davon?

Allgemeines

Some und **any** drücken eine unbestimmte Menge oder Anzahl von etwas aus, z. B. einige, ein paar. Man verwendet sie vor Stoffnamen, anderen nicht zählbaren Substantiven und Substantiven im Plural. **Some** und **any** werden dabei im Deutschen oft nicht übersetzt.

Gebrauch von some und any

- In bejahten Aussagesätzen und bei Fragen, auf die man eine positive Antwort erwartet (z. B. höfliche Angebote oder Bitten, etc.), wird grundsätzlich **some** verwendet.

Let's bake some muffins.	*Lass/t uns Muffins backen.*
Would you like some more tea?	*Hättest du/hätten Sie gern noch etwas Tee ?*

- In Fragen und verneinten Aussagesätzen wird grundsätzlich **any** verwendet.

Have we got any baking chocolate?	*Haben wir Blockschokolade?*
No, we haven't got any chocolate.	*Nein, wir haben (überhaupt) keine Schokolade.*
I've never got any chocolate.	*Ich habe niemals Schokolade.*

:ə

some vor Substantiv spricht man unbetont:

some bread [səm]

entfällt das Substantiv, spricht man es betont:

some [sʌm]

!

Any (nicht some!) folgt auf Wörter mit verneinender Bedeutung: not, never, rarely, scarcely/hardly *(kaum)*

baking chocolate – *Blockschokolade*

- Ist das Substantiv schon bekannt, können **some** oder **any** allein stehen.

I've never got any.	*Ich habe niemals welche.*

Some und any und ihre Zusammensetzungen

Die gleichen Regeln wie für **some** und **any** gelten auch für ihre **Zusammensetzungen** (compounds). Es gibt folgende Bedeutungen:

SPRACHTIPP

Somebody und anybody sind in der Umgangssprache geläufiger als someone und anyone!

somebody/someone **anybody/anyone**	*(irgend)jemand*
something **anything**	*(irgend)etwas*
somewhere **anywhere**	*irgendwo*
not anybody/anyone	*niemand*
not anything	*(überhaupt) nichts*
not anywhere	*nirgendwo, nirgends*

Gebrauch der Zusammensetzungen mit some und any

- In bejahten Aussagesätzen und bei höflichen Fragen oder Angeboten werden grundsätzlich Zusammensetzungen mit **some** verwendet.
- In Fragen und verneinten Aussagesätzen werden grundsätzlich Zusammensetzungen mit **any** verwendet.

Have you seen anybody/anyone? — No, I haven't seen anybody/anyone.
Is there anything you want to tell me? — No, I can't think of anything.
Have you seen my glasses anywhere? — Sorry, I haven't seen them anywhere.

Ausnahme:
Any und seine Zusammensetzungen in bejahten Aussagesätzen

- **Any** bzw. **not any** benutzt man in bejahten Aussagesätzen, wenn es die Bedeutung **jede/r/s (beliebige)** bzw. **überhaupt kein/e/en** hat. Meist sind das Aufforderungen und Sätze mit **can, may** und **will**.

You can choose any ring you like.	*jeden (beliebigen)*
I didn't get any sleep last night.	*(überhaupt) kein/e/en*
I'll follow you anywhere.	*überall(hin)*

- Nach Zusammensetzungen mit **some** oder **any** kann das Wort **else** oder ein **Adjektiv** stehen.

Have you got something else?	*Hast du/haben Sie noch etwas anderes?*
There wasn't anyone famous there.	*Es war niemand Berühmtes da.*

Weitere Mengenwörter

Much und little, many und few

Much und **many** drücken eine unbestimmte Menge oder Anzahl von etwas aus. Man verwendet sie meist in verneinten Aussagesätzen und in Fragen.

- **Much** wird für Substantive verwendet, die im **Singular** stehen und **nicht zählbar** sind (z. B. Stoffbezeichnungen).

We cannot get much information.	*... viele Informationen ...*

- **(Ein) wenig** von **nicht zählbaren** Dingen heißt **a little** bzw. **little**:

Do you need a little help?	*Brauchst du/brauchen Sie ein wenig Hilfe?*
Little has been done so far.	*Bisher ist wenig unternommen worden.*

- **Many** wird für Substantive verwendet, die im **Plural** stehen und **zählbar** sind.

Sarah hasn't got many friends.	*Sarah hat nicht viele Freunde.*

- Für **wenige** zählbare Dinge verwendet man **few** bzw. für **einige/ein paar** steht **a few**:

Only few people in the team disagreed.	*Nur wenige Leute ...*
A few club members were angry.	*Einige Klubmitglieder ...*

SPRACHTIPP

In bejahten Aussagesätzen wird statt **much** und **many** umgangssprachlich meistens **a lot of, lots of** oder **plenty of** verwendet.

LERNTIPP

Beachte die Steigerungsformen von **much, little, many** und **few**:

much, more, (the) most

little, less, (the) least

many, more, (the) most

few, fewer, (the) fewest

ugs. sagt man **not much** (statt little) und **not many** (statt few)

Every, each und all

Jede/r/s bzw. **alle(s)** heißen im Englischen je nach Bedeutung:

every	*jede/r/s* (von einer Gruppe als Ganzes)
each	*jede/r/s* (Einzelne von einer Gruppe)
all	*alle/alles* (aus einer Menge ohne Einschränkung), verallgemeinernd; nur vor Pluralformen und nicht zählbaren Substantiven sowie Zeitbezeichnungen (I slept all night.)
all the	*alle/alles* (aus einer eingeschränkten Menge); vor Demonstrativ- und Possessivbegleitern (all this trouble, all her money)

Every child loves dogs.	*Jedes Kind ...*
Tony knows every girl in town.	*... jedes Mädchen in der Stadt.*
vgl. dazu: ... each girl ...	*... jedes einzelne Mädchen ...*
We interviewed each member of the club.	*... jedes einzelne Klubmitglied.*
I like all children.	*... alle Kinder.*
All the children in our house love dogs.	*Alle Kinder in der Nachbarschaft ...*

SPRACHTIPP

Genauso werden auch die Zusammensetzungen von every verwendet:

everybody/everyone - *jede/r, alle*

everything - *alles* (ohne Ausnahme)

everywhere - *überall* (an allen Orten)

!

Each kann wie every für jede/n/s aus einer Gruppe stehen, betont dabei aber den Einzelnen besonders.

Both, either, neither

both	(alle) beide
either	jede/r/s von beiden
neither	keine/r/s von beiden

Both boys look the same.	*Beide Jungs ...*
Both of them were at the party.	*Beide ...*
Either boy was nice.	*Jeder Junge (von beiden) ...*
Neither of them stayed long.	*Keiner (von beiden) ...*

No und seine Zusammensetzungen

No vor einem Substantiv bedeutet **kein/e**. Will man ein Substantiv nicht wiederholen, verwendet man **none**. Auch mit **no** können einige Zusammensetzungen gebildet werden:

no	kein/e	**I've got no idea.**
none (= no one)	keine/r von	**None of us asked him for help.**
nobody	niemand	**Nobody knew who he was.**
nothing	nichts	**I said nothing.**
nowhere	nirgends, nirgendwo	**Where are you going? — Nowhere special.**

SPRACHTIPP

Nowhere steht meist in der Konstruktion (there) is/was nowhere to be ...

He was nowhere to be seen. - *... nirgends zu sehen.*

There's nowhere I'd rather be. - *Nirgendwo wäre ich lieber.*

* **1.** Setze **some** oder **any** ein.

1. It's always good to take ______ water with you.

2. Have you got ______ problems with your homework?

3. Kim went to the supermarket on her own but she wasn't allowed to buy ______ sweets.

4. When I went to Australia I didn't see ______ kangaroos.

5. But I saw ______ koala bears.

6. Tina doesn't want to lend me ______ money.

7. But I need ______ money for the bus.

* **2.** Übertrage die folgenden Begriffe ins Deutsche.

1. everywhere in Germany ______

2. nothing special ______

3. Anything new? ______

4. some problems ______

5. Any suggestions? ______

6. in the middle of nowhere ______

7. No idea. ______

8. Everything's OK. ______

9. all day ______

10. all the time ______

** **3.** Fülle die Lücken mit dem jeweils passenden **Mengenwort** oder einer Zusammensetzung.

Come on, Cliff, let's go out tonight. Let's book a table ______ *(irgendwo)*. — OK. What about Harp's Restaurant? — Do they serve ______ *(irgendwelche)* vegetarian food? — Yes, of course, they do. You can have ______ *(alles)* there. Or do you want ______ *(irgendetwas)* special? — No, I'll be happy with ______ *(etwas)* vegetables. — We could phone ______ *(einige)* friends. Maybe Thomas and Nina. — Good idea. Is there ______ *(sonst jemand)* else? — ______ *(jemand)* from the tennis club perhaps.

★★ **4.** Schreibe die folgenden Aussagesätze verneint.

1. I've got some interesting hobbies.

2. We can do something.

3. You should tell somebody the truth.

★★★ **5.** Übersetze ins Deutsche.

1. I haven't asked anybody for help.

2. No news is good news.

3. We didn't know anything about the disaster.

LERNTIPP

Abgeschlossene Handlungen werden mit dem **simple past** ausgedrückt.

★★★ **6.** Übersetze ins Englische.

1. *Hast du gestern Abend irgendetwas gehört?*

2. *Ich habe ein paar Fotos gemacht. Man kann nur sehr wenig darauf sehen.*

3. *Warum hast du es nicht allen erzählt?*

4. *Alle Nachbarn sind neugierig.*

take a photo – *ein Foto machen*

you – hier: *man*

curious – *neugierig*

1 AMERICAN ENGLISH & BRITISH ENGLISH

Es gibt Leute, die sagen, dass die Briten und Amerikaner so unterschiedlich sind wie ihre Sprache. Das ist sicherlich etwas übertrieben, aber dennoch gibt es eine Reihe von Unterschieden zwischen den beiden Sprachvarianten, was den **Wortschatz**, die **Rechtschreibung** oder etwa die **Aussprache** angeht.

Unterschiede im Wortschatz

American English (AmE)	Deutsch	British English (BrE)
baggage	*Gepäck*	**luggage**
basement	*Keller*	**cellar**
busy	*besetzt (Tel.)*	**engaged**
can	*Dose*	**tin** (Essen), **can** (Getränk)
cellphone	*Handy*	**mobile phone**
check	*Rechnung (im Restaurant)*	**bill**
elevator	*Aufzug*	**lift**
eraser	*Radiergummi*	**rubber**
fall	*Herbst*	**autumn**
faucet	*Wasserhahn*	**tap**
first floor	*Erdgeschoss*	**ground floor**
french fries	*Pommes*	**chips**
garbage can	*Mülleimer*	**dustbin**
gas	*Benzin*	**petrol**
movie theater	*Kino*	**cinema**
pants	*Hose*	**trousers**
rest room	*öffentliche Toilette*	**public toilet**
sidewalk	*Bürgersteig*	**pavement**
subway	*U-Bahn*	**underground**
truck	*LKW*	**lorry**

1. Wo befindest du dich, wenn dir die folgenden Sätze begegnen? In den USA oder in Großbritannien?

AmE BrE	a. The rest rooms are in the basement.
AmE BrE	b. Did you remember to get petrol on the way home?
AmE BrE	c. The sidewalk in front of the movie theater is under construction.
AmE BrE	d. All passengers of flight 831 can pick up their luggage at belt 3.
AmE BrE	e. In 50% of all subway stations the elevator is out of order.
AmE BrE	f. Would you like some ketchup with your chips?
AmE BrE	g. That pair of trousers is ugly, love!
AmE BrE	h. The public toilet is on the ground floor, but the tap is broken.

BOXENSTOPP

Die regionalen Unterschiede im Englischen werden am deutlichsten, wenn du den Wortschatz genau lernst. Außerdem musst du bedenken, dass auch die englische Sprache sich immer wandeln kann. Was vor einigen Jahren noch Standard war, kann irgendwann überholt sein. Es gibt zum Beispiel Wörter, die im britischen Englisch früher als „falsches Englisch" angesehen wurden, heute jedoch völlig akzeptabel sind. So ist das Adjektiv **trashy** in Großbritannien durchaus geläufig, auch wenn man das amerikanische Wort **trash** noch nicht anstelle von **rubbish** verwendet.

Rechtschreibung

Unterschiedliche Schreibweisen im amerikanischen und britischen Englisch kommen relativ häufig vor. Die wichtigsten Unterschiede und Beispiele haben wir hier für dich aufgelistet.

Endungen

Die Endung **-our** wird im amerikanischen Englisch oft zu **-or** verkürzt:

BrE	**behaviour** (*Verhalten*), **colour** (*Farbe*), **favourite** (*Lieblings-*), **humour** (*Humor*), **labour** (*Arbeit*)
AmE	**behavior**, **color**, **favorite**, **humor**, **labor**

Die Endung **-re** wird im amerikanischen Englisch oft zu **-er**:

BrE	**centre** (*Zentrum*), **litre** (*Liter*), **manœuvre** (*Manöver*), **metre** (*Meter*), **theatre** (*Theater*)
AmE	**center**, **liter**, **maneuver**, **meter**, **theater**

Im britischen Englisch ist die Endung **-nce** geläufiger, im amerikanischen Englisch die Endung **-nse**:

BrE	**defence** (*Verteidigung*), **licence** (*Lizenz*, *(Führer)schein*), **offence** (*Straftat*, *Beleidigung*), **pretence** (*erfundene Geschichte*)
AmE	**defense**, **license**, **offense**, **pretense**

Weitere Unterschiede in der Schreibung

Die hier aufgelisteten Unterschiede muss man lernen. Es gibt nur wenige Regelmäßigkeiten:

American English	Deutsch	British English
aluminum	*Aluminium*	**aluminium**
analyze	*analysieren*	**analyse**
catalog	*Katalog*	**catalogue**
check	*Scheck*	**cheque**
jewelry	*Schmuck*	**jewellery**
traveler	*Reisender*	**traveller**
practice	*üben*	**practise**
program	*Programm, Sendung*	**programme**
realize	*realisieren, erkennen*	**realise**

2. Der Brite Robin Hood trifft auf Batman, den amerikanischen Superhelden. Die beiden unterhalten sich über ihre Arbeit, Ziele und Träume. Leider fehlen Ihnen manchmal die Worte. Kannst du sie ergänzen?

Batman: Hey Rob, what's up? That's a nice piece of silver ___________ (*Schmuck*) round your neck!

Robin Hood: Nah, that's nothing. I nicked it at the Sheriff of Nottingham's banquet the other day. Thought it was quite posh, but then I ___________ (*realisieren* - Past tense) that it's nothing but polished ___________ (*Aluminium*). But how are you? Taking your Batmobile out for a ride to the city ___________ (*Mitte*)?

Batman: No, I'm going to the training ___________ (*Zentrum*). I have to ___________ (*trainieren*) my ___________ techniques (*Verteidigungstechniken*). The risky ___________ (*Manöver* - Plural) are getting harder and harder.

Robin Hood: Yes, none of us are getting any younger, are we? My fellow ___________ (*Reisende* - Plural) are on strike. They think it's an ___________ (*Beleidigung*) that the Sheriff only deals with ___________ (*Schecks* - Plural) nowadays!

BOXENSTOPP

Man kann nicht sagen, dass nur eine Variante des Englischen richtig ist und die andere falsch. Aber sicherlich ist es guter Stil, die beiden Varianten nicht zu vermischen.

Entscheidest du dich also zum Beispiel dazu, amerikanisches Englisch zu schreiben, dann verwendest du die Endungen ______________ wo im Britischen **-our**, **-nce** und **-re** stehen.

Sammle weitere Beispiele für unterschiedliche Schreibweisen im amerikanischen und britischen Englisch:

____

____

Grammatik

Have oder have got?

Genau wie das Verb **be** kann auch **have** sowohl als Vollverb als auch als Hilfsverb verwendet werden.

Im Sinne von ***besitzen***, ***bei sich haben*** kann man **have** oder auch **have got** benutzen:

I have a headache.	*Ich habe Kopfschmerzen.*
I have got a pain killer.	*Ich habe ein Schmerzmittel.*

Im Amerikanischen wird die Konstruktion mit **have got** oft als umgangssprachlich betrachtet und eher in informellen Situationen verwendet.

Konstruktionen, in denen ein Hilfsverb benötigt wird, sind mit **have** besonders problematisch. Zwei verschiedene Strategien sind dabei möglich:

Have als Vollverb

Diese Konstruktion ist die gängige Variante im amerikanischen Englisch:

They don't have a bicycle. *Sie haben kein Fahrrad.*
Do you have a car? *Hast du ein Auto?*

Have wird durch have got ersetzt

Dies ist die moderne Lösung in Großbritannien. Wie schon erwähnt, entspricht diese Variante im Amerikanischen eher dem lockeren Sprachgebrauch:

They haven't got a bicycle. *Sie haben kein Fahrrad.*
Have you got a car? *Hast du ein Auto?*

Got oder gotten?

Achtung: Das ist keine Glaubensfrage! **Gotten** ist eine alte britische Partizip-Perfekt-Form von **get**, die im amerikanischen Englisch bewahrt wurde!

BOXENSTOPP

Den Fall „**Have** oder **have got**?" kannst du nur abschließen, indem du dich für eine Variante entscheidest. Was wählst du?

☐ Variante 1: ______________________________

☐ Variante 2: ______________________________

Got ist die Partizip-Perfekt-Form von **get** im ___________________________.

Gotten verwendet man als Partizip-Perfekt-Form im ____________________.

Datums- und Zeitangaben, Zahlen

Bei der numerischen Angabe eines Datums verwenden Amerikaner die Reihenfolge **Monat - Tag - Jahr**. Daher schreibt man das Datum 24. Dezember 2010 nicht 24/12/2010, sondern **12/24/2010**.

Das kann manchmal recht verwirrend sein, wenn die Datumsangabe zum Tag kleiner als 13 ist: 12/09/09. Um Missverständnisse zu vermeiden, kann man auch den Monatsnamen ausschreiben: **December 9, 2009**. Briten würden hier eher **9 December 2009** schreiben. In jedem Fall sollte man im amerikanischen Englisch keine Punkte verwenden, da dies als befremdlich wahrgenommen wird: ~~12.09.09.~~

Bei den **Uhrzeiten** wird die 24-Stunden-Zählung in den USA fast nur vom Militär verwendet. Daher ist es eleganter, diese zu vermeiden und stattdessen die 12-Stunden-Zählung mit **a.m.** (*morgens*) und **p.m.** (*nachmittags / abends*) zu verwenden.

Eine Null bei einer **Telefonnummer** wird in den USA meistens als **zero** gesprochen, während viele Briten sie wie den Buchstaben „o“, also [əʊ], aussprechen.

Darüber hinaus gibt es einige kleine formale Unterschiede bei der Benennung der Zahlen:

Zahl	American English	British English
233	**two hundred thirty-three**	**two hundred and thirty-three**
2400	**twenty-four hundred** (oder **two thousand four hundred**)	**two thousand four hundred**

Aussprache

Die Aussprache des r

Im amerikanischen Englisch wird jedes geschriebene **r** auch ausgesprochen, während im Britischen das **r** nur direkt vor einem Vokallaut ausgesprochen wird, nicht aber vor einem Konsonanten bzw. vor einer Pause.

	AmE	BrE
very (*sehr*)	['veri]	['veri]
father (*Vater*)	['fɑːðər]	['fɑːðə]
turn (*wenden*)	[tɜːrn]	[tɜːn]

AmE [uː] vs. BrE [juː]

	AmE	BrE
new (*neu*)	[nuː]	[njuː]
stupid (*dumm*)	['stuːpɪd]	['stjuːpɪd]
tune (*Melodie*)	[tuːn]	[tjuːn]

AmE [æ] vs. BrE [ɑː]

Bei vielen Wörtern, die ein **a** vor [f], [v], [s] oder [z] enthalten, verwendet das amerikanische Englisch ein kurzes [æ] statt einem längeren, dunkleren [ɑː].

	AmE	BrE
bath (*Bad*)	[bæθ]	[bɑːθ]
last (*letzte(r/s)*)	[læst]	[lɑːst]
after (*nach*)	['æftər]	['ɑːftə]

BOXENSTOPP

Hörübungen machen den Meister! Versuche so viele Originaltexte zu hören wie möglich. Schau dir dazu DVDs in der Originalsprache an oder höre zum Beispiel englisches Radio. Im Internet gibt es unendliche Möglichkeiten, ganz verschiedene Varianten des Englischen zu hören. Auf der Website **www.pons.de** findest du immer interessante Audios im PONScast!

2 LEICHT VERWECHSELBARE WÖRTER

Aufgepasst: Im Englischen gibt es eine Reihe von Wörtern und Ausdrücken, die zwar dieselbe Aussprache haben, aber ganz unterschiedlich geschrieben werden und auch sehr unterschiedliche Bedeutungen haben!

Affect oder effect?

affect	*wirken auf, betreffen*
effect	*Effekt, Auswirkung*

Brake oder break?

brake	*Bremse, bremsen*
break	*Pause, Bruch, brechen*

Desert oder dessert?

desert	*Wüste, verlassen*
dessert	*Nachtisch, Dessert*

Its oder it's?

its	*sein* (besitzanzeigendes Fürwort, sachlich)
it's (it is)	*es ist*

Their, there oder they're?

their	*ihr* (besitzanzeigendes Fürwort, 3. Person Plural)
there	*da*
they're (= they are)	*sie sind*

Who's oder whose?

who's (= who is)	*wer ist, der / die ist*
whose	*wessen / dessen / derer* usw. (Fragewort bzw. besitzanzeigendes Relativpronomen)

1. Ergänze die Sätze mit **affect, effect, break, brake** oder **dessert**:

a. The ________________ of being alone is that you often feel bad.

b. In what way does this ________________ your health?

c. We've been working for such a long time now. Let's take a ____________.

d. Would you like a delicious ______________?

e. You'll have to _____________, there's a speed limit!

2. Ergänze in den folgenden Sätzen die Ausdrücke **its** oder **it's**:

a. Have you noticed how this cat protects _________ kittens?

b. Look, _________ not so difficult to clean your room now, is it?

3. Ergänze: **who's** oder **whose**?

a. _____________ books are these?

b. _____________ that guy over there? Do you know him?

BOXENSTOPP

Im Englischen gibt es eine Reihe von Wörtern und Ausdrücken, die in der Aussprache zwar gleich _____________, aber eine völlig andere _____________ haben und auch ganz anders _____________ werden. Damit man diese Begriffe nicht verwechselt, prägt man sich die Unterschiede am besten gut ein, zum Beispiel zwischen **affect** und **effect**,

____

____.

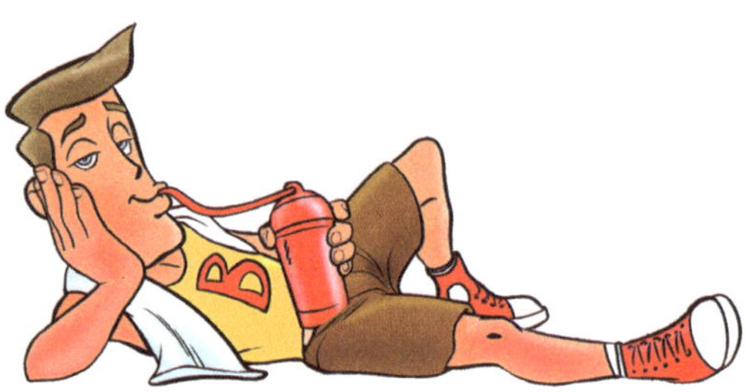

Inhalt

Grammatik

Wortschatz

KLASSE 9

Zeit	Bildung	Person	Bsp. (regelmäß. Verb)
simple present (= present tense simple) / einfache Gegenwart	Grundform Grundform + -(e)s	I/you/we/they he/she/it	talk talks
present (tense) **progressive** / Verlaufsform Gegenwart	am/are/is + Grundform + -ing	I you/we/they he/she/it	am talking are talking is talking
simple past (= past tense simple) / einfache Vergangenheit	Grundform + -ed (regelmäß. Verben); 2. Form (unregelm. Verben)	I/you/he/she/it we/they	talked
past (tense) **progressive** / Verlaufsform Vergangenheit	was/were + Grundform + -ing	I/he/she/it you/we/they	was talking were talking
present perfect simple / einfache vollendete Gegenwart	have/has + Grundform + -ed (regelm.); have/has + 3. Form (unregelm. V)	I/you/we/they he/she/it	have talked has talked
present perfect progressive / Verlaufsform vollendete Gegenwart	have/has + been + Grundform + -ing	I/you/we/they he/she/it	have been talking has been talking
past perfect simple / einfache Vorvergangenheit	had + Grundform + -ed (regelm. V.); had + 3. Form (unregelm. V.)	I/you/he/she/it/ we/they	had talked
past perfect progressive / Verlaufsform Vorvergangenheit	had + been + Grundform + -ing	I/you/he/she/it/ we/they	had been talking
will-future (= future I simple) / einfache Zukunft I	will + Grundform	I/you/he/she/it/ we/they	will talk
will-future (future I) **progressive** / Verlaufsform Zukunft I	will + be + Grundform + -ing	I/you/he/she/it/ we/they	will be talking
going-to-future (= future I simple) / Zukunft I	am/are/is + going to + Grundform	I you/we/they he/she/it	am going to talk are going to talk is going to talk
future perfect (= future II) simple / einfache Zukunft II	will have + Grundform + -ed (regelm.); will have + 3. Form (unregelm. V.)	I/you/he/she/it/ we/they	will have talked
future perfect (= future II) **progressive** / Verlaufsform Zukunft II	will have been + Grundform + -ing	I/you/he/she/it/ we/they	will have been talking
conditional I simple / einfaches Konditional I	would + Grundform	I/you/he/she/it/ we/they	would talk
conditional (I) **progressive** / Verlaufsform Konditional I	would be + Grundform + -ing	I/you/he/she/it/ we/they	would be talking
conditional perfect (= cond. II) simple / einfaches Konditional II	would have + Grundform + -ed (regelm.); would have + 3. Form (unregelm. V.)	I/you/he/she/it/ we/they	would have talked
conditional perfect (= cond. II) **progressive** / Verlaufsform Konditional II	would have been + Grundform + -ing	I/you/he/she/it/ we/they	would have been talking

Bsp. (un-regelm. Verb)	Anwendung	Signalwörter
go **goes**	regelmäßige/dauerhafte/aufeinander folgende Vorgänge, Fahrpläne etc., allgemein gültige Aussagen	always, often, sometimes, rarely, never, usually, normally, every day
am going **are going** **is going**	noch nicht abgeschlossene, z. Zt. ablaufende Vorgänge (auch über längere Zeit/ mit Unterbrechung), zukünftige Vorgänge (Verabredungen, feste Pläne)	at the moment, just (now), (right) now, next … , Look!, Listen!; this week/season
went	einmalige/wiederholte/aufeinander folgende Vorgänge, vollständig in der Vergangenheit	ago, yesterday, in (past year), last Monday/year, when-Fragen
was going **were going**	Gleichzeitigkeit oder Ablauf eines Vorgangs zu einem (bestimmten) vergangenen Zeitpunkt	when, while
have gone **has gone**	Beginn eines Vorgangs in der Vergangenheit, Dauer bis (kurz vor od.) in die **Gegenwart** od. **Auswirkung** darauf	since, for, already, just, until/up to now, so far, never, (not) yet, ever, this year etc.
have been going **has been going**	betont, dass ein Vorgang, der in der Vergangenheit begonnen hat, noch in der **Gegenwart** andauert (**Ablauf**)	since, for, how long, the whole morning/day etc., all day/year etc.
had gone	Ende eines Vorgangs zu oder Beginn vor vergangenem Zeitpunkt (ggf. Dauer bis dahin od. länger)	(since, for)
had been going	Beginn eines Vorgangs vor einem vergangenen Zeitpunkt und Dauer bis zu diesem oder bis kurz davor	
will go	nicht beeinflussbare Vorgänge in der Zukunft, Vermutungen, spontane Entschlüsse, if-Satz Typ I	(the day after) tomorrow, next … , in (future year/… days/years)
will be going	Ablauf von Vorgängen zu einem zukünftigen Zeitpunkt, sichere Annahmen über zukünftige Ereignisse	(the day after) tomorrow, next … , in (future year/… days/years)
am going to go **is going to go** **are going to go**	Absichten/Vorhaben; logische Schlussfolgerungen	
will have gone	zu einem zukünftigen Zeitpunkt abgeschlossene Vorgänge und Handlungen	in … (days/years …/ future year), by … (future date/then), next … (future date), when …
will have been going	zu einem zukünftigen Zeitpunkt abgeschlossene Vorgänge, hebt dabei die Fortdauer des Vorgangs hervor	
would go	allg. für Konjunktiv (würde tun), if-Satz Typ II, indirekte Rede, typ. Verhalten (Vergangenheit)	
would be going	siehe conditional (I) simple, hebt dabei die Fortdauer des Vorgangs hervor	
would have gone	allgemein für Konjunktiv in der Vergangenheit (hätte), if-Satz Typ III, indirekte Rede	
would have been going	siehe conditional perfect simple, hebt dabei die Fortdauer des Vorgangs hervor	

1 DIE GEGENWART

From Monday to Friday I always **get up** at 7 o'clock. I **go** to the bathroom, **wash** and **get** dressed. Then I **have breakfast**. At 8 o'clock I usually **leave** the house and **take** the bus into town. School never **starts** before 8:45. My friend Tom never **gets up** before 7.30 and he often **misses** the bus.

Von Montag bis Freitag stehe ich immer um 7 Uhr auf. Ich gehe ins Bad, wasche mich und ziehe mich an. Dann frühstücke ich. Um 8 Uhr gehe ich gewöhnlich aus dem Haus und fahre mit dem Bus in die Stadt. Die Schule beginnt nie vor 8 Uhr 45. Mein Freund Tom steht nie vor halb acht auf und verpasst oft den Bus.

Die englische Gegenwartszeit, das **present tense**, hat wie jede andere Zeitform im Englischen eine **simple form** (einfache Form) und eine **progressive form** (Verlaufsform). Diese Form wird manchmal auch als continuous form bezeichnet.

Jedes Verb kann in der **simple form** auftreten. Die **progressive form** kann man dagegen nur mit Verben bilden, mit denen man aufgrund ihrer Bedeutung einen **Ablauf** ausdrücken kann. Das sind Tätigkeits- und Vorgangsverben.

Das simple present

Bildung

Das **simple present** ist bei den Personen **I, you** (Singular und Plural), **we**, **they** identisch mit dem Infinitiv des Verbs.
In **bejahten** Aussagesätzen wird bei der 3. Person Singular **(he, she, it)** ein **-s** an den Infinitiv des Verbs angehängt.

Verneinte Aussagesätze mit Vollverben brauchen die Unterstützung des Hilfsverbs **do**: Je nach Person wird **don't** oder **doesn't** dem Infinitiv vorangestellt. Beachte: In der 3. Person wird dann an das Vollverb **kein -s** angehängt!
Das **do** bzw. **does** wird nicht übersetzt.

!
He, she, it – das **-s** muss mit!

I, you, we, they	**understand**	**don't understand**
he, she, it	**understands**	**doesn't understand**

!

Besonderheiten
in Schreibung und Aussprache in der 3. Person Singular:

Endet ein Verb auf einem **stimmlosen** Laut, spricht man das Endungs-s [s], nach **stimmhaften** Lauten [z].

walk — walks [ks]
rain — rains [nz]

Endet ein Verb auf **-s** oder einem **anderen Zischlaut**, wird daran **-es** angehängt, gesprochen [ɪz]. Wichtig: Dabei entfällt ein vorher evtl. vorhandenes stummes End-e (z. B. bei ‚freeze').

kiss — kisses **wish — wishes**
watch — watches **freeze — freezes**

Endet ein Verb auf **Konsonant + -y**, wird das **-y** durch **-ies** ersetzt.

try — tries **fly — flies**

Bei **go** und **do** wird ein **-es** angehängt. Beachte die **unregelmäßige Aussprache** von **does** und **says**.

go [gəʊ] — **goes** [gəʊz] **do** [du:] — **does** [dʌz] **say** [seɪ] — **says** [sez]

LERNTIPP

Der Vokal e [ɪ] wird hier stets zwischen zwei Zischlauten eingeschoben, um die Aussprache zu erleichtern.

Gebrauch des simple present

Das simple present wird gebraucht für:

- Handlungen und Ereignisse, die **regelmäßig oder aus Gewohnheit** geschehen.

We spend the Easter break in Italy every year.
We always go there by car because mom doesn't want to fly.

- Erzählungen oder Beschreibungen von mehreren (gewohnheitsmäßigen) **aufeinander folgenden Handlungen oder Ereignissen** (z. B. auch Inhaltsangaben, Live-Sportberichte etc.). Das simple present verwendet man auch, wenn man über Texte (Bücher, Kurzgeschichten, Gedichte) schreibt oder spricht.

My brother Mike always walks to work. Then he gets a cup of coffee and reads his e-mails. After that he usually has a meeting with his team.

- Abfahrzeiten, Fahrpläne und sonstige, nicht vom Sprecher beeinflussbare **feststehende Ereignisse** in der Zukunft.

The plane arrives at 15.45. **The concert starts at 8 p.m. tonight.**

- **Allgemeingültige Aussagen** (z. B. Fähigkeiten, Eigenschaften, Naturgesetze).

The sun often shines in California. **Ice melts at one degree.**

!

Wortstellung in Aussagesätzen im simple present

Die **Signalwörter** für das simple present sind Adverbien oder adverbiale Bestimmungen. Ihre Stellung im Satz erfolgt nach bestimmten Regeln:

- **Adverbien der Häufigkeit** bestehen nur aus einem Wort und stehen meist vor dem Vollverb bzw. nach dem ersten Hilfsverb in der so genannten **Binnenstellung**. Ausnahme: bei **be** werden sie **immer nachgestellt**.

My sister often invites her friends over for a coffee. They always chat so much. Her friends are never boring.

to chat – *quasseln, quatschen*

- **Adverbiale Bestimmungen der Zeit** bestehen oft aus mehr als einem Wort und stehen meistens am **Satzende**, zur besonderen Betonung auch am Satzanfang.

I play the guitar every day. Once a year we give a concert at school.

Das present progressive

1 You're wearing a pretty pullover today, Sarah.

2 Thank you, Lucy. I like it very much myself.

1. Du hast heute einen hübschen Pullover an, Sarah.
2. Danke, Lucy. Ich mag ihn selbst sehr gern.

Bildung

Das **present progressive** besteht immer aus mindestens zwei Wörtern: eine **Form von be im simple present + present participle**

Die **Formen von be** (am, are, is) hängen von der jeweiligen **Person** im Singular oder im Plural ab.

LERNTIPP

Alle progressive-Zeitformen werden mit einer Form von **be + present participle** gebildet!

Das **present participle** wird durch das **Anhängen von -ing an das** jeweilige **Verb** gebildet. Es wird deshalb auch als **ing-Form** bezeichnet.

Person	Langform	Kurzform
I	**am (not) working.**	**'m (not) working.**
He/she/it	**is (not) working.**	**'s (not) working.** verneint auch: **... isn't working.**
We/you/they	**are (not) working.**	**'re (not) working.** verneint auch: **... aren't working.**

Beachte: Die Kurzformen werden bevorzugt, wenn das Subjekt ein Personalpronomen ist. Bei Namen oder Bezeichnungen verwendet man immer die Langform bzw. die Form mit verkürztem **not**.

Besonderheiten
in der Schreibweise des present participle:

Nach **kurzem Vokal** wird der **Endkonsonant verdoppelt**.

sit — sitting **swim — swimming** **run — running** **travel — travelling**

Ein **stummes -e** am Ende des Verbs **entfällt** vor dem -ing.

smile — smiling **argue — arguing**

Aus **-ie** am Ende des Verbs **wird -y**.

lie — lying **tie — tying**

SPRACHTIPP

AE: travel - traveling

to tie - *binden, knoten*

Gebrauch des present progressive

Das present progressive wird gebraucht für:

- Handlungen, die jetzt in diesem Augenblick stattfinden (und noch nicht abgeschlossen sind).

Look, Mrs Johnson is just leaving the house.

- Handlungen, die über einen gewissen Zeitraum hinweg andauern können, aber vorübergehend sind; sie können auch während des Sprechens unterbrochen sein.

Everybody is collecting money for the victims of the earthquake these days.

LERNTIPP

Die Verwendung der progressive form zusammen mit Wörtern wie ‚always' drückt Ärger aus:

You're always walking in with your dirty shoes on. – *Immer kommst du mit deinen dreckigen Schuhen herein!*

victim - *Opfer*

earthquake - *Erdbeben*

- Handlungen, die in der Zukunft liegen und schon (vom Sprecher) geplant oder fest beschlossen sind.

My parents are celebrating their 25th wedding anniversary next Sunday.

Ausnahmen:
Einige Verben bilden **keine progressive-Formen**. Das sind

- Verben der **Sinneswahrnehmung**, z. B.
see, hear, feel, notice, taste, smell

- Verben, die **Gefühle**, **Meinungen** oder **Wissen** ausdrücken, z. B.
like, love, hate, prefer, want, wish, hope, think, believe, know, imagine, forget, understand, cost, weigh

- **Zustandsverben** und Verben, die **Besitz** oder **Zugehörigkeit** ausdrücken, z. B.
be, have, belong, possess

- die Verben
seem, mean, look, sound

Achtung: Manche dieser Verben können zwar eine progressive-Form bilden, ändern damit aber ihre Bedeutung. Sie beschreiben dann eine (momentane) **Tätigkeit**.

I think you're right.	**What are you thinking?**
I guess you like that.	**Come on, you're only guessing.**
These oranges taste sweet.	**Mary is tasting the dessert.**

Unterschiedliche Bedeutung von present progressive und simple present

An zwei Beispielen wird gezeigt, dass je nach Sprechabsicht beide Zeitformen korrekt sind. Entscheidend ist, was man ausdrücken möchte.

vorübergehender Job	**I'm working in an office.**
fester Job, keine Absicht zu wechseln	**I work in an office.**
auf der Durchreise, provisorische Bleibe	**I'm living in Stuttgart.**
fester, ständiger Wohnsitz	**I live in Stuttgart.**

Übungen zum simple present

★ **1.** Vervollständige den Text, indem du die Verben korrekt einsetzt.

Thomas ___________ as a postman. He ___________ his job. He ___________ very early every morning and ___________ the bus to the main post office. Thomas and his colleagues ___________ their huge amounts of letters and ___________ them into their cars. Then Thomas ___________ to the outskirts of his town. He ___________ in his district around 10 o'clock. Thomas ___________ his car at the carpark and ___________ the letters into his big bag. Then he ___________ from house to house and ___________ having a job outside the city centre. It usually ___________ him four to five hours until no letters ___________ left in his bag. He ___________ his job in the early afternoon.

leave, collect, get up, finish, walk, work, be, put, enjoy, drive, like, take, start, take, put

outskirts – *Außenbezirke*

★★ **2.** Was machen deine Freunde und du in eurer Freizeit und was nicht?
Bilde bejahte und verneinte Sätze im **simple present**.

	Robin	Sarah	Nick and Sam	Alice	I	Justin
+	play football	cook large meals	go fishing	love shopping	________ ________ ________	surf the Internet
-	play every weekend	like the washing up	eat the fish	spend much money	________ ________ ________	go into chat rooms

1. *Robin plays football but he doesn't play every weekend.*
2. ______________________________
3. ______________________________
4. ______________________________
5. ______________________________
6. ______________________________

3. Wähle aus den Wörtern 5 Signalwörter für das simple present aus und notiere sie mit ihrer jeweiligen Übersetzung.

often | now | always | just | at the moment | usually | sometimes
never | these days | this week

Englisch	Deutsch
1. ______	______
2. ______	______
3. ______	______
4. ______	______
5. ______	______

4. Übertrage die folgenden Sätze ins Englische.

1. *Judy steht jeden Morgen um 6.30 Uhr auf.*

______

2. *Sie frühstückt gewöhnlich zuhause.*

______

3. *Manchmal kauft sie sich ein Sandwich beim Bäcker nebenan.*

______

4. *Judy nimmt immer die U-Bahn zur Schule.*

______

5. *Die Schule ist oft um 16 Uhr aus* (=out).

______

6. *Nach der Schule trifft sie manchmal eine Freundin.*

______

7. *Abends macht Judy normalerweise ihre Hausaufgaben in ihrem Zimmer.*

______

______

8. *Sie geht jeden Abend um 22 Uhr ins Bett.*

______

***5. Hier sind ein paar Beispiele im simple present. Weißt du, wie die deutsche Entsprechung heißt?

1. The early bird catches the worm.

____

2. A new broom sweeps clean.

broom - *Besen*

____

3. He's like a bull in a china shop.

____

4. You can't teach an old dog new tricks.

____

5. You can bet your life on that.

____

6. All's well that ends well.

____

7. The exception proves the rule.

____

8. A friend in need is a friend indeed.

____

9. Money talks.

____

10. No news is good news.

____

11. It takes two to tango.

____

12. Tomorrow is another day.

____

13. Where there's a will, there's a way.

____

Übungen zum present progressive

are drinking
are standing
is laughing
is talking to
is saying
is dancing
is telling
is wearing

★ **6.** Stell dir vor, du kommst gerade auf eine Party und sollst (z. B. am Handy) beschreiben, was in diesem Moment geschieht. Ordne dazu die Vorgaben in die richtigen Sätze ein.

1. Joe ______________ his new girlfriend.

2. Both ______________ a coke at the bar.

3. Five boys ______________ around Tina.

4. Nick ______________ a funny joke and Nicole ______________ about it.

5. The music is brilliant but nobody ______________ .

6. There's Rebecca. She ______________ hello to everybody.

7. She ______________ a brilliant outfit.

★ **7.** Es ist 10 Uhr morgens. Viele Leute sind mit unterschiedlichen Arbeiten beschäftigt. Was tun sie gerade?

kindergarten teacher – *Erzieher(in), Kindergärtner(in)*

shoe-laces – *Schuhbänder*

1. The hairdresser next door **(cut)** ______________ hair.

2. Four teachers at the local high school **(teach)** ______________ French.

3. Doctors at the hospital **(operate)** ______________ on ill people.

4. Policemen **(control)** ______________ the traffic.

5. A pilot **(fly)** ______________ his helicopter.

6. Two shop assistants **(sell)** ______________ mobile phones.

7. A kindergarten teacher **(tie)** ______________ a little girl's shoe-laces.

8. A taxi driver **(drive)** ______________ to the station.

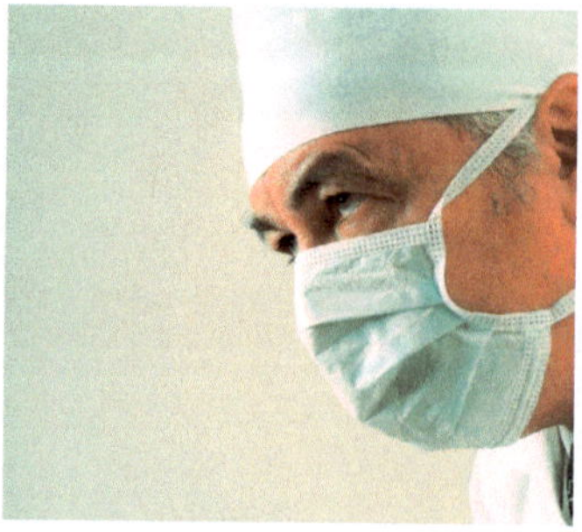

★ 8. Welche Verben können normalerweise in der progressive-Form verwendet werden und welche nicht? Ordne sie in die richtigen Spalten ein.

simple + progressive form	**nur simple form**
___	___
___	___
___	___
___	___
___	___
___	___
___	___
___	___
___	___
___	___

understand
run
hate
talk
watch
see
want
carry
read
imagine
like
work
tell
smell
know
notice
try
think
make
get

★★ 9. Setze bejahte oder verneinte **present progressive**-Formen ein. Benutze die Kurzformen, wenn möglich.

It's Monday afternoon. What a day! The sun (not shine) ________ ____________ . It (rain) ____________ cats and dogs. Mr Spencer (sit) ____________ in his office. He (not talk) ____________ on the phone. He (write) ____________ a report. His secretary (write) ____________ an e-mail. But not everybody (work) ____________ . A young girl in a building across the street (daydream) ____________ . She (not do) ____________ her homework although she has a lot to do. And Mr and Mrs Frazer from next door (go) ____________ for a walk in the park. They (not wear) ____________ their rain coats. But they (have) ____________ an umbrella each. Their dog, Colin, (enjoy) ____________ the walk. He (chase) ____________ a rabbit.

although – *obwohl*

chase – *jagen*

*** **10.** Übersetze das folgende Telefongespräch ins Englische. Benutze dabei das **present progressive**.

John: *Hallo Martin. Wie geht's? Was macht ihr gerade?*

____

Martin: *Hi, John. Also, Sandra arbeitet am Computer und ich bereite mich für die Mathe-Prüfung morgen vor. Und was machst du?*

____

____

John: *Ich liege auf meinem Bett und schaue gerade fern. Können wir morgen früh zusammen mit dem Fahrrad zur Schule fahren?*

____

____

Martin: *Ja, gute Idee. Lass uns um 8 Uhr am Bahnhof losfahren.*

____

John: *OK. Bis dann. Ich wünsch dir viel Erfolg für dein Mathe-Lernen. Tschüs.*

____

Martin: *Danke, bis morgen. Tschüs.*

____

*** **11.** **Present progressive** oder **simple present**? Setze die richtigen Zeitformen ein und beachte dabei die Wortstellung.

1. Luke (always, get up) ______________ at six o'clock in the morning but today he (get up) ______________ later.

2. This time Jenny (write) ______________ her christmas cards on the computer although she (usually, create) ______________ ______________ handwritten cards.

3. Mr Lanson (sometimes, work) ______________ at home on Sundays. Today he (work) ______________ at his office.

4. I (look for) ______________ a new job because I (need) ______________ more money.

2 DIE VERGANGENHEIT

1. Was für ein toller Ort. Hast du deinen letzten Urlaub auch hier verbracht?
2. Nein, ich war mit ein paar Freunden in Schweden. Das war fantastisch, aber mir war die ganze Zeit kalt. Deshalb wollte ich dieses Jahr nicht wieder in den Norden fahren.

Das simple past

Bildung

Beim **simple past** gibt es **nur eine Verbform** für alle Personen.

Bildung des simple past **bei regelmäßigen Verben**:

Infinitiv (Grundform des Verbs) **+ -ed**, z. B. walk + ed = walk**ed**

> ! Die einzige Ausnahme bildet das Verb **be**.

Besonderheiten
bei der Bildung und Schreibweise der **regelmäßigen** simple past-Formen:

Endet ein Verb auf **kurzen Vokal + Konsonant**, wird der **Endkonsonant verdoppelt**.

stop — stopped **cancel — cancelled**

Bei Verben, die mit einem **stummen -e** enden, wird nur ein **-d** angehängt.

phone — phoned **prepare — prepared**

Endet ein Verb auf **Konsonant + y**, wird das **y** durch **-ied** ersetzt.

try — tried **marry — married**

> !
> prefer — preferred
> transfer — transferred
> enden auf langem Vokal + Konsonant und verdoppeln trotzdem den Endkonsonanten!
> Ausnahmen AE:
> cancel — canceled
> travel — traveled

Aussprache der regelmäßigen simple past-Formen

Nach Vokalen und stimmhaften Konsonanten wird ein weiches [d] gesprochen.

stayed [steɪd] **loved** [lʌvd]

Nach stimmlosen Konsonanten wird ein hartes [t] gesprochen.

asked [ɑːskt] **touched** [tʌtʃt]

Endet ein Verb im Infinitiv auf d oder t, wird ein [ɪd] gesprochen.

visited [vɪzɪtɪd] **landed** [lændɪd]

Bildung des simple past **bei unregelmäßigen Verben:**

Für die Bildung des simple past bei unregelmäßigen Verben gibt es keine Regel - man muss sie einfach lernen. Beispiele:

Infinitiv	simple past	Infinitiv	simple past
go	**went**	**make**	**made**
think	**thought**	**read** [riːd]	**read** [red]
see	**saw**	**speak**	**spoke**

Bejahte Aussagesätze im **simple past** werden, genau wie im simple present, **ohne Hilfsverb** gebildet.

Nach **did** oder **didn't** folgt der Infinitiv, nicht die simple past-Form!

Verneinte Aussagesätze brauchen die Unterstützung des Hilfsverbs **do**, hier in seiner **simple past-Form**: Für alle Personen wird **didn't** (bzw. **did not**) dem Infinitiv des Vollverbs vorangestellt. Das **did** wird nicht übersetzt.

Person	regelmäßiges Verb	unregelmäßiges Verb
alle Personen	**worked**	**went**
	did not (didn't) work	**did not (didn't) go**

Gebrauch des simple past

Das simple past wird gebraucht für:

- Handlungen und Ereignisse, die als **abgeschlossen** gelten und definitiv der Vergangenheit angehören.

When our parents were young they lived a completely different life.

- Das Erzählen von Geschichten oder Berichten in der Vergangenheit (aufeinander folgende Handlungen).

The traffic lights turned red but the BMW speeded up and raced across the crossroad.

- Aussagen, die von Zeitangaben in der Vergangenheit begleitet werden.

I didn't talk to Sarah yesterday. But I spoke ten minutes ago.

- Fragen mit **when** und Antworten darauf.

When did you go out with Sarah? — Oh, that was two weeks ago.

Achtung beim Übersetzen ins Deutsche oder aus dem Deutschen! Im Englischen kann für vergangene, abgeschlossene Handlungen und Ereignisse immer nur das **simple past** stehen! Vergleiche:

I didn't work last week.	**I went home.**
Ich habe letzte Woche nicht gearbeitet.	*Ich bin nach Hause gegangen.*
Ich arbeitete letzte Woche nicht.	*Ich ging nach Hause.*

Besonderheit:
Das simple past von be

Be ist das einzige Verb, das zwei Formen für das simple past hat.

I, he, she, it was — **you** (Sg. und Pl.)**, we, they were**

Be kann bei Verwendung als Vollverb bejahte und verneinte Aussagesätze sowie Fragen im simple past selbst bilden. In Kurzantworten wird **was** oder **were** aus der Frage wieder aufgegriffen.

Frage	Kurzantwort	lange Antwort/Erläuterung
Were you out last night?	**Yes, I was.**	**(Yes,) I was at the new disco in town.**
Was your Tom with you?	**Yes, he was.**	**He wasn't alone. He brought two friends.**
Were you back home in time?	**No, we weren't.**	**(No,) We were two hours late.**

Das past progressive

Bildung

Das **past progressive** besteht immer aus mindestens zwei Wörtern:

eine **Form von be** im **simple past + present participle**.

Die **Formen von be** (was, were) hängen von der jeweiligen **Person** im Singular oder im Plural ab.
Das **present participle** wird durch **Anhängen von -ing** an den Infinitiv des jeweiligen **Verbs** gebildet und heißt daher auch **ing-Form**.

LERNTIPP
Alle progressive-Zeitformen werden mit einer Form von be + present participle gebildet und beschreiben eine andauernde Handlung.

Person	Langform	Kurzform (nur verneint!)	
I/He/She/It	was (not)	wasn't	working.
You/We/You/They	were (not)	weren't	working.

Gebrauch des past progressive

Das past progressive wird gebraucht für:

- Situationen in der Vergangenheit, in denen ein **kurzes Ereignis in eine bereits andauernde Handlung** oder Begebenheit **eintrat**. Das bereits **ablaufende** Ereignis steht im **past progressive**. Das **neu eintretende** Ereignis steht im **simple past**.

While Liz and Sue were discussing the latest fashion, Mia went to the post office.
When she came back, the two of them were still talking about the same topic.

- Handlungen und Ereignisse in der Vergangenheit, die über einen längeren Zeitraum **gleichzeitig abliefen**. Haupt- **und** Nebensatz stehen dann im **past progressive**.

While the fans were clapping their hands, the popstar was singing the last song.
Mr Smith was presenting the new maths problem and everybody was listening.

LERNTIPP
Signalwörter für das past progressive sind
while - *während* (+ past progressive)
when - *als* (+ simple past)

- Zur **Betonung der Dauer** einer Handlung oder eines Ereignisses in der Vergangenheit.

I was answering e-mails all afternoon.

While und when

Um bereits ablaufende Handlungen in der Vergangenheit von neu eintretenden zu unterscheiden, sind die Konjunktionen **while** und **when** nützlich.

Sie leiten beide einen Nebensatz ein. Davor oder danach steht ein Hauptsatz, wobei es keine Rolle spielt, welcher Satzteil zuerst genannt wird. Dabei gelten folgende Regeln:

- Steht ein While- oder When-Satz vorne, wird er **mit einem Komma** vom Hauptsatz abgetrennt.

While + past progressive **While we were waiting for the bus,**	Hauptsatz + simple past **it started to rain.**
When + simple past **When I came home,**	Hauptsatz + past progressive **dad was reading and mom and Lisa were watching TV.**

- Steht der Hauptsatz zuerst, folgt **kein Komma**!

It started to rain	**while we were waiting for the bus.**
Mom and Lisa were watching TV	**when I came home.**

Achtung! **While** und **when** können auch bei der Schilderung von Ereignissen in der **Gegenwart** stehen. Die Kommaregeln gelten auch hier:

While + present progressive drückt Gleichzeitigkeit in der Gegenwart aus, z. B. bei Vorschlägen.

While I'm laying the table,	**you're washing the salad.**

Steht **when + present simple** ändert sich die Bedeutung von **when** in **wenn**, **sobald**. Im Hauptsatz steht das **future**.

When Thomas comes,	**I'll cook spaghetti.**

Das present perfect simple

Bildung

Das **present perfect simple** besteht immer aus mindestens zwei Wörtern:

eine **Form von have** im **simple present + past participle**.

Die **Formen von have** (has, have) hängen von der jeweiligen **Person** im Singular oder im Plural ab.

Das **past participle** wird bei den regelmäßigen Verben gebildet wie die simple past-Form: **Infinitiv** (Grundform des Verbs) **+ -ed**.

!

Das deutsche Perfekt wird manchmal mit **haben** und manchmal mit **sein** gebildet. Im Englischen werden alle perfect-Formen mit einer **Form von have** (+ 3. Form des Verbs) gebildet!

Person	Langform	Kurzform
I	**have (not) worked.**	**'ve (not) worked/haven't worked.**
You	**have (not) worked.**	**'ve (not) worked/haven't worked.**
He/She/It	**has (not) worked.**	**'s (not) worked/hasn't worked.**
We/You/They	**have (not) worked.**	**'ve (not) worked/haven't worked.**

Im Deutschen entspricht das **past participle** dem **Partizip Perfekt**:

worked – *gearbeitet* **played** – *gespielt* **answered** – *geantwortet* usw.

Besonderheiten bei der Schreibweise der regelmäßigen past participle-Formen:

Das past participle stimmt bei allen regelmäßigen Verben mit der simple past-Form überein. Auch die Regeln für besondere Schreibweisen und für die Aussprache sind identisch.

Unregelmäßige past participle-Formen

Bei den unregelmäßigen Verben ist neben der simple past-Form auch die past participle-Form unregelmäßig. Man muss sie auswendig lernen. Einige Beispiele sind:

LERNTIPP

Am besten lernst du immer gleich alle drei Formen eines Verbs!

Infinitiv	simple past-Form	past participle-Form
go	**went**	**gone**
make	**made**	**made**
drive	**drove**	**driven**
see	**saw**	**seen**

Gebrauch des present perfect simple

Das present perfect simple wird gebraucht für:

- Handlungen und Ereignisse, die sich **in der Vergangenheit** abspielen **und** noch **in der Gegenwart von Bedeutung** sind. Dabei steht das **Ergebnis** der Handlungen im Vordergrund. Der Zeitpunkt des Geschehens ist nicht wichtig. Es kann sich also auch um etwas handeln,
  - das gerade erst (‚just') abgeschlossen wurde,
  - das noch nicht/nie (‚not … yet', ‚never') passiert ist,
  - nach dem man fragt, ob es bis jetzt schon (‚yet') oder überhaupt jemals (‚ever') geschehen ist.

I've repaired your computer. It should work now.
The dogs **have** just **eaten.** Now they're sleepy.
Have you **written** your essay yet? I **have** already **finished** it.
Have you ever **been** on a French campsite? - No, I've never **been** to France.

For und since

Zeitangaben im present perfect werden mit **for** oder **since** gemacht. Zusammen mit solchen Angaben zur Zeitdauer können auch Verben, die keine progressive-Formen bilden, ausdrücken, dass ein Zustand in der Vergangenheit begann und bis in die Gegenwart andauert. Bei der Übersetzung ins Deutsche verwendet man dann die Gegenwart mit ‚schon'.

For beschreibt einen Zeit**raum**, den eine Handlung andauert und der von der Vergangenheit bis in die Gegenwart reicht. Im Deutschen sagt man auch: jahrelang, zwei Stunden lang usw. **Beachte** aber, dass Zeitangaben mit **for** auch in anderen Zeitformen auftreten können.

I haven't seen Lucy for days.	*Ich habe Lucy seit Tagen nicht gesehen.*
He has known her for years.	*Er kennt sie (schon) seit Jahren.*

!

for - *seit*
(+ Angabe eines Zeit**raums**)

since - *seit*
(+ Angabe eines Zeit**punkts**)

Since nennt den genauen Zeit**punkt**, seit dem ein bestimmtes Ereignis stattfindet oder auch nicht stattfindet.

I haven't seen Lucy since last Tuesday.	*Ich habe Lucy seit letzten Dienstag nicht gesehen.*
He has known her since 2004.	*Er kennt sie (schon) seit 2004.*

for steht vor Zeiträumen wie **half an hour, two days, several, weeks, years, ages, etc**	**since** steht vor Zeitangaben wie **1 o'clock, 8th April, last Wednesday, 2001, ... I was a child, etc**

for ages - *seit Ewigkeiten, ewig lange*

yet - *schon*

not yet - *noch nicht*

Unterschied zwischen present perfect und simple past

Das **present perfect** darf nicht mit dem **simple past**, der abgeschlossenen Vergangenheit, verwechselt werden! Vergleiche:

- Nicht der Zeitpunkt einer Handlung, sondern die **Handlung selbst** wird in den **Vordergrund** gestellt: **present perfect**

Have you spoken to Vanessa yet ?	*Hast du schon mit Vanessa gesprochen?*

!

Im Deutschen wird das Perfekt auch für abgeschlossene Handlungen benutzt. Das Wort ‚haben' kann irreführend sein! Achte auf Signalwörter und überlege, ob die Handlung wirklich abgeschlossen ist oder nicht.

- Die Kurzantwort richtet sich noch nach der Frage. Der folgende Satz beinhaltet eine **abgeschlossene Handlung in der Vergangenheit** (mit **Signalwort**): **simple past**

Yes, I have. I phoned her yesterday.	*Ja, hab' ich. Ich habe sie gestern angerufen.*

- Die Frage **bezieht sich** (auch ohne Signalwort) auf das Telefonat, eine **abgeschlossene Handlung in der Vergangenheit**: **simple past**

And what did she say?	*Und was hat sie gesagt?*

- Die **Handlung** steht **im Vordergrund**. Sie hat in der **Vergangenheit begonnen** und **reicht bis in die Gegenwart**: **present perfect**

She hasn't prepared the photo album yet.	*Sie hat das Fotoalbum noch nicht vorbereitet.*

Das present perfect progressive

Bildung

Das **present perfect progressive** besteht immer aus mindestens drei Wörtern:

eine **Form von be** im **present perfect + present participle**

Die **Formen von be** (has been, have been) hängen von der jeweiligen **Person** im Singular oder im Plural ab.
Das **present participle** wird durch das **Anhängen von -ing** an den **Infinitiv** gebildet und heißt daher auch **ing-Form**.

Person	Langform	Kurzform	present participle
I/You/We/You/They	**have been**	**'ve been**	**working.**
	have not been	haven't been	
He/She/It	**has been**	**'s been**	
	has not been	hasn't been	

Beachte auch, dass bestimmte Verben keine progressive-Form bilden können.

Gebrauch des present perfect progressive

Das present perfect progressive wird gebraucht:

- für Handlungen und Ereignisse, die **in der Vergangenheit beginnen, bis in die Gegenwart ununterbrochen andauern und weiterhin andauern können** (oft mit Zeitangaben wie **all day**, **all morning**). Im Gegensatz zum **present perfect simple** führen sie **nicht** zu einem Ergebnis in der Gegenwart. Der **Ablauf** der Handlungen wird betont; sie finden meist noch **weiterhin** statt.

I've been working on the computer all day.

SPRACHTIPP

Ins Deutsche übersetzt man das present perfect progressive meist mit dem Präsens und dem Wort ‚schon'.

- zur **Betonung der Dauer einer ununterbrochenen Handlung**. Die Zeitangaben erfolgen am Ende des Satzes mit **for** + Zeit**raum** oder mit **since** + Zeit**punkt**.

We've been living in Hamburg for ten years.
Alyssa **has been playing** the violin since she was four years old.

LERNTIPP

Es gibt keine besonderen Signalwörter für das present perfect progressive. Es wird aber oft mit **for** und **since** verwendet.

- mit Verben wie **wait, sit, stand, rain, snow, shine**. Solche Verben treten üblicherweise im Zusammenhang mit längeren Vorgängen auf.

I've been waiting for ages!
It's warm. The sun**'s been shining**.

Unterschied zwischen present perfect progressive und present progressive

Die progressive-Formen des **present tense** und des **present perfect** dürfen nicht verwechselt werden. Vergleiche:

present perfect progressive:

He's (=He has) been working all day.	*Er arbeitet schon den ganzen Tag (und arbeitet immer noch).*

present progressive:

He's (= He is) working.	*Er arbeitet gerade.* (Hier wird betont, was er gerade tut. Was er zuvor getan hat, spielt keine Rolle.)

Das past perfect simple

!

Im Englischen bildet man present perfect und past perfect stets mit einer**Form von have** (+ past participle).

Bildung

Das **past perfect simple** wird für alle Personen im Singular und Plural folgendermaßen gebildet:

have im **simple past + past participle**

Person	Langform	Kurzform	past participle
alle Personen	**had (not)**	**'d/ hadn't**	**worked, gone, etc.**

!

had und would haben die gleiche Kurzform:

I'd = I had oder **I would**! Das gilt für alle Personen.

Gebrauch des past perfect simple

Berichtet man über Ereignisse in der Vergangenheit, benutzt man in der Regel das **simple past**. Das **past perfect** bezeichnet man auch als Vorvergangenheit. Man übersetzt es mit dem deutschen Plusquamperfekt. Es gibt keine besonderen Signalwörter für das **past perfect simple**, es steht aber häufig mit Wörtern wie **after** und **before**.

Das **past perfect simple** wird für Ereignisse in der Vergangenheit benutzt, deren Vorzeitigkeit ausgedrückt werden soll, d. h. es handelt sich um:

- Handlungen und Ereignisse, die in der Vergangenheit noch **vor einem anderen Ereignis in der Vergangenheit** stattfanden.

LERNTIPP

Im Deutschen wird das Plusquamperfekt (wie das Perfekt) manchmal mit **haben**, manchmal mit **sein** gebildet. Das past perfect im Englischen wird immer mit had gebildet!

Das **past perfect** steht oft in einem Satzgefüge von Haupt- und Nebensatz **in Kombination mit dem simple past**.
Beide Satzteile geben **abgeschlossene** Handlungen wieder.

After I had taken a bath I felt much better.	*Nachdem ich ein Bad genommen hatte, fühlte ich mich viel besser.*

- Auch mit Hauptsätzen können zwei Handlungen in der Vergangenheit in ein zeitliches Verhältnis gesetzt werden. Das **past perfect** zeigt an, welche Handlung noch **vor einer anderen** in der Vergangenheit stattfand.

to tighten – *(fest an-) ziehen*

handbrake – *Handbremse*

The car rolled slowly into the fence. The driver had forgotten to tighten the handbrake.	*Das Auto rollte langsam gegen den Zaun. Der Fahrer hatte vergessen, die Handbremse anzuziehen.*

Unterschied zwischen past perfect und simple past

Oft kann man den gleichen Sachverhalt mit unterschiedlichen Satzmustern ausdrücken. Je nach Sprechabsicht muss man verschiedene Zeitformen benutzen. Vergleiche:

Im **simple past** werden abgeschlossene Handlungen in der Vergangenheit ausgedrückt. Man benutzt es, wenn man von **aufeinander folgenden Vorgängen in der Vergangenheit** berichtet.

We arrived at the airport in time. First of all a safety guard checked our tickets, then he wanted to have a look at our luggage. Everything was OK.

Hier wird nacheinander erzählt, in der Reihenfolge, in der die Ereignisse stattgefunden haben.

Mit dem **past perfect** werden auch abgeschlossene Handlungen und Ereignisse ausgedrückt. Es **betont** aber, dass diese **zeitlich vor anderen Handlungen in der Vergangenheit** stattgefunden haben.

We arrived at the airport in time. After a safety guard had checked our tickets he wanted to have a look at our luggage. Everything was OK.

Hier wird ausgedrückt, dass das Kontrollieren der Tickets vor dem Anschauen des Gepäcks stattfand.

Das past perfect progressive

Bildung

Das **past perfect progressive** wird für alle Personen im Singular und im Plural folgendermaßen gebildet:

be im **past perfect + present participle**.

Das **present participle** wird durch das **Anhängen von -ing** an den **Infinitiv** des jeweiligen Verbs gebildet und heißt daher auch **ing-Form**.

Person	Langform	Kurzform	present participle
alle Personen	**had (not) been**	**'d (hadn't) been**	**working**

Beachte auch, dass bestimmte Verben keine progressive-Form bilden können.

LERNTIPP

Alle progressive-Zeitformen werden mit einer Form von **be + present participle** gebildet und beschreiben eine **andauernde** Handlung.

Gebrauch des past perfect progressive

Das **past perfect progressive** wird (wie das past perfect simple) im Deutschen mit dem Plusquamperfekt übersetzt. Dabei verdeutlicht das deutsche Wort ‚schon' die Situationen, in denen im Englischen die progressive form verwendet wird. Es gibt keine bestimmten **Signalwörter** für das **past perfect progressive**. Es kann jedoch wie das present perfect und das present perfect progressive Sätze mit **for** und **since** bilden.

LERNTIPP

Dabei wird oft (z. B. mit **for** oder **since**) eine Angabe über die Länge der andauernden Handlung gemacht bis zu dem Zeitpunkt, an dem eine neue Handlung einsetzte.

Das past perfect progressive wird verwendet,

- wenn man eine **länger andauernde Handlung**, die **vor einer anderen Handlung in der Vergangenheit** stattgefunden hat, beschreiben möchte. Die neu eingetretene Handlung wird häufig durch **when-Sätze im simple past** geschildert.

I had been working on the computer for four hours when we had a power cut.	*Ich hatte schon vier Stunden am Computer gearbeitet, als der Strom ausfiel.*

Unterschied zwischen past perfect progressive und simple

Das **past perfect progressive** betont die **Dauer** einer Handlung in der Vergangenheit.

AE: neighbor

Our neighbour who had been repairing our computer for more than two hours didn't accept any money.

Der Nachbar hatte sehr lange, nämlich mehr als zwei Stunden am Computer gearbeitet.

Beim past perfect simple ist nicht die Dauer, sondern das **Ergebnis** wichtig.

to mention - *erwähnen*

Simon knew much about Australia because he had already been there.
But he hadn't heard of the famous group "Down Under" until I mentioned them.

Simon war zwar schon in Australien gewesen, hatte aber von der Gruppe „Down Under" bisher noch nichts gehört.

Unterschied zwischen past perfect progressive und past progressive

Das **past perfect progressive** betont die **Dauer** einer Handlung, die **vor** einer anderen Handlung in der Vergangenheit stattfand. Die zweite Handlung steht im **simple past**:

Lucy told me that the man who had been sitting in his car opposite the house all night was a detective.

Das **past progressive** beschreibt eine länger andauernde Handlung in der Vergangenheit **während der** ein neues Ereignis eintrat. Die neu eingetretene Handlung steht im **simple past**:

While we were staying in New York, the weather changed and we had a lot snow for the rest of the trip.

Es kann aber auch mehrere gleichzeitig ablaufende Handlungen in der Vergangenheit beschreiben:

While mom was preparing dinner, I was helping dad with the garden work.

Übungen zum simple past

★ **1.** Hier sind 20 unregelmäßige Verbformen im simple past versteckt, waagerecht (9) und senkrecht (11). Schreibe sie auf und setze den entsprechenden Infinitiv des Verbs daneben.

said – say

s	a	i	d	w	a	s	b	s
t	u	w	e	n	t	a	u	t
o	l	o	m	h	e	w	i	o
o	w	r	i	a	k	d	l	o
d	r	e	a	d	c	t	t	k
t	o	l	d	r	a	h	e	a
a	t	s	w	a	m	r	a	n
p	e	n	c	n	e	e	l	d
s	o	l	d	k	d	w	o	n

★ **2.** Fülle die Satzlücken mit der richtigen Verbform im **simple past** aus.

When I **(be)** ________ a child life **(be)** ________ quite different. We **(live)** ________ in a small house in the country and we **(have)** ________ a big garden. We **(spend)** ________ most of the time outside. My father **(go)** ________ to work every morning and Mum **(stay)** ________ at home. She **(have to)** ________ look after us. We **(be)** ________ three boys and a girl. When Dad **(come)** ________ home he **(take)** ________ a shower first and then he **(play)** ________ with us. That **(be)** ________ always great fun. Our parents **(insist on)** ________ having dinner together. We **(like)** ________ that. My mother **(cook)** ________ wonderful meals and my father often **(tell)** ________ funny stories. After that Mum **(put)** ________ us to bed and everybody **(listen)** ________ to her brilliant good night stories. Those **(be)** ________ great times.

insist on – *bestehen auf*

3. Vervollständige die Sätze, indem du bejahte und verneinte Sätze im **simple past** bildest.

1. I (come) ______________ home late last night
   but I (not wake up) ______________ the dog.
2. She (not answer) ______________ the phone
   but she (hear) ______________ it ringing five minutes ago.
3. Tony (invite) ______________ all his relatives to stay over the weekend
   for his birthday. They all (agree) ______________ to come for the party
   but they (not want) ______________ to stay overnight.
4. We (move) ______________ into our new house last summer.
   So we (not have) ______________ enough money to go on holiday last year.

4. Wähle die richtige Reihenfolge und bilde eine Frage.

1. you | your driver's licence | last week | get | did | ?
   ____
2. that house | did | in Florida | buy | your parents | ?
   ____
3. computer course | did | the | do | your mum | ?
   ____
4. she | that funny teacher | tell you | did | about | ?
   ____
5. successful | was | in his | Henry | Maths test | ?
   ____
6. you | gave detective story | like | did | the | Mary | her | ?
   ____
7. prepare | your friends | did | for you | a surprise party | ?
   ____

*** **5.** Eine Sprache lässt sich nicht wörtlich in eine andere übertragen. In den folgenden Aussagen sind im Englischen andere Verben als im Deutschen nötig. Ordne die korrekte Übersetzung zu und unterstreiche die verschiedenen Verben beider Sprachen.

I thought it was brilliant. | What was the weather like? | I loved the view. | Where did you go? | What did you do there? | What did you think about the hotel? | Where did you stay? | We stayed in a hotel.

1. *Wo wart ihr?* ______________________
2. *Was habt ihr dort gemacht?* ______________________
3. *Wo habt ihr gewohnt?* ______________________
4. *Wir waren in einem Hotel.* ______________________
5. *Wie fandest du das Hotel?* ______________________
6. *Ich fand es hervorragend.* ______________________
7. *Mir gefiel die Aussicht sehr.* ______________________
8. *Wie war das Wetter?* ______________________

LERNTIPP

Abgeschlossene Handlungen werden mit dem **simple past** ausgedrückt.

*** **6.** Übertrage ins Englische.

1. *Bist du im Reisebüro gewesen? Ja.*

____

2. *War Jennifer auch da? Nein.*

____

3. *Hast du mit ihr gesprochen? Ja.*

____

!

Kurzantworten im Englischen bestehen aus mehr als einem Wort!

Übungen zum past progressive

was *oder* were

snoring
lying telling
sleeping
striking
burning
reading running

★ **7.** Fülle die Lücken mit der passenden Verbform aus dem Kasten. Entscheide Dich für das jeweils richtige Hilfsverb: **was** oder **were**.

When I came home last night, ...

1. ... Grandad ______________________ in front of the TV.

2. ... our dog Jessie ______________________ next to him.

3. ... the cowboys on TV ______________________ silly jokes in the saloon.

4. ... Mum ______________________ a detective story in bed.

5. ... the lights in the hall ______________________ .

6. ... Jason's English test ______________________ on the table.

7. ... the washing machine ______________________ in the cellar.

8. ... Grandma's clock ______________________ 1 o'clock. Time to go to bed.

SPRACHTIPP

Um nach einer Folge zu fragen, müsste es heißen: What did you do when the telephone rang?

★ **8.** Beantworte die Fragen mit den gegebenen Informationen. Womit war(en) die Person(en) gerade beschäftigt, als etwas Neues eintrat?

1. What were you doing when the telephone rang at midnight?

____

2. What was Rita doing when Mrs Smith spilled coffee over her desk?

____

3. What were the people doing when the bus didn't come?

____

4. What was Lucy doing when you called her?

____

5. What were the dinner guests doing when the live music started?

____

6. What was Gina's husband doing when she visited him at his office?

____

7. What were all those young people doing when the police arrived?

____

A sleep
B answer an e-mail
C grumble about public transport
D listen to her new CD
E eat their dessert
F work on his computer
G demonstrate for human rights

9. Übertrage ins Englische, was sich zum Zeitpunkt ihres Eintretens abspielte.

When Mrs Evans entered the classroom, ...

1. *(tanzte Lukas auf dem Tisch)*

____

2. *(warf Tim den Schwamm auf Nico)*

____

sponge – *Schwamm*
throw at – *werfen auf*

3. *(spielten vier Jungen Karten)*

____

4. *(stand Simone auf einem Stuhl neben ihnen)*

____

5. *(malten drei Mädchen Bilder an die Tafel)*

____

draw – *malen*

6. *(lehnten sich Nina und Patrick aus dem Fenster)*

____

lean – *(sich) lehnen*

7. *(kämpften Toby und Kim auf dem Fußboden)*

____

floor – *Fußboden*

8. *(schrie Susan ihre Freundin an)*

____

shout at sb. – *jdn. anschreien*

10. Lies deine Sätze aus Übung 9 noch einmal und beschreibe nun zwei gleichzeitig ablaufende Ereignisse in einem Satz. Beginne deine Sätze mit while.

1. und **2.**: While Lukas ______________ on the table, Tim ______________ the sponge at Nico.

3. und **4.**: ______________________________

____

5. und **6.**: ______________________________

____

7. und **8.**: ______________________________

____

*** **11.** Lies den Text und bearbeite die folgenden zwei Fragen.

Welche Sätze drücken zwei gleichzeitig andauernde Handlungen in der Vergangenheit aus? Unterstreiche sie farbig.

Welche Sätze beschreiben eine längere Handlung in der Vergangenheit, in die ein neues Ereignis eintritt? Unterstreiche sie in einer anderen Farbe.

delay – *Verspätung*

vacant – *frei, unbesetzt*

sigh – *Seufzer*

bunch of keys – *Schlüsselbund*

Yesterday Jeannie had to go to work by train because her husband needed the car. When she arrived at the station, lots of people were already waiting on the platform. The train was late. Some people were nervously walking up and down while others were talking about the delay. Fortunately Jeannie found a vacant seat on a bench. While she was reading her morning paper, the woman next to her opened her bag. The woman was making a lot of noise while she was searching for something. Finally she stopped with a deep sigh. "Is everything OK?" Jeannie asked her. "Yes, thanks," she replied with a smile. "I was just thinking about my new flat when I thought I had left the keys at home. But I hadn't." "Lucky you", Jeannie said as the woman waved a bunch of keys in her hand.

*** **12.** Übersetze die while- und when-Sätze aus Übung 11.

1. ______________________________

____

2. ______________________________

____

3. ______________________________

____

4. ______________________________

____

5. ______________________________

____

6. ______________________________

____

Übungen zum present perfect simple

⋆ **13.** Ergänze die fehlenden Formen.

	Infinitiv	**simple past-Form**	**past participle**
1.	break	______	______
2.	answer	______	______
3.	send	______	______
4.	see	______	______
5.	______	cost	______
6.	______	bought	______
7.	______	spoke	______
8.	______	watched	______
9.	______	______	done
10.	______	______	made
11.	______	______	invited
12.	______	______	caught

⋆ **14.** Fülle die simple past-Form und die past participle-Form mit den fehlenden Vokalen.

1. teach - t __ __ ght - t __ __ ght
2. pay - p __ __ d - p __ __ d
3. think - th __ __ ght - th __ __ ght
4. begin - beg __ n - beg __ n
5. read - r __ __ d - r __ __ d
6. bring - br __ __ ght - br __ __ ght
7. get - g __ t - g __ t
8. fi ght - f __ __ ght - f __ __ ght

⋆ **15.** Beantworte die Fragen. Bitte verwende Kurzantworten.

1. Have you finished the report? Yes, ______
2. Have you seen Teresa? No, ______
3. Has Ben passed his exam yet? Yes, ______
4. Have you ever been to Moscow? Yes, ______
5. Has your team decided on the new concept? No, ______
6. Have they talked about that matter before? Yes, ______

16. Setze die Verben im **present perfect** ein.

BE: ['mærəθn]
AE: ['merəθɑːn]

1. I **(win)** ____________________ two marathons this year.
2. My father **(restore)** ____________________ our antique wardrobe.
3. We **(not see)** ____________________ our friends from Bruxelles for a long time.
4. I **(not hear)** ____________________ from Julie since July.
5. Thank God. Lucy **(do)** ____________________ all the ironing.
6. We hope Tina **(not fail)** ____________________ her driving test.
7. My parents **(not be)** ____________________ out of Germany so far.
8. They **(be)** ____________________ at the North Sea and in the Black Forest.

17. Unterstreiche die Signalwörter für das present perfect und übertrage die Sätze ins Deutsche.

1. Have you read the latest detective story by Elizabeth George yet?

   ____

2. No, I haven't read it yet.

   ____

3. What have you written so far?

   ____

4. I've just finished the first two paragraphs.

   ____

5. Have you ever watched elephants in the wild in Africa?

   ____

6. No, I've never been to Africa at all.

   ____

7. But I've already seen some in a safari park in France.

   ____

*** **18.** Die Eltern fahren übers Wochenende zu einer Tagung und lassen Ihre zwei Kinder und den Hund mit einer Liste von Aufträgen zu Hause. Am Sonntagabend sehen sie nach, was davon erledigt wurde und was nicht.

List for the weekend:

1 go out with the dog ✓
2 put the rubbish in the bin –
3 buy some apples, yoghurt and two pizzas ✓
4 do your homework ✓
5 tidy up your rooms –
6 hoover the ground floor ✓
7 lock the front door ✓
8 go to bed before midnight –

BE: **rubbish** – *Müll*
AE: **garbage** – *Müll*
BE: **(dust)bin** – *Mülleimer*
AE: **garbage (can)** – *Mülleimer*
BE: **hoover** – *staubsaugen*
AE + BE: **vacuum** – *staubsaugen*

1. *They have gone out with the dog.* ______
2. *They haven't* ______
3. ______
4. ______
5. ______
6. ______
7. ______
8. ______

*** **19.** Fülle die Lücken mit der richtigen Verbform. Die Signalwörter helfen dir.

1. Lisa, ______ to Kim yet ?
Yes, I ______ to her yesterday.
2. Mum, ______ your pills?
Yes, I ______ them this morning.
3. Steve, ______ with the dog?
No, I ______ it yet.
4. Darling, ______ the new carpet?
No, I ______ . I ______ in the livingroom so far.
5. Sarah, ______ your sister already ______ the new catalogue? Yes, she ______ . She ______ it last Friday.

1 speak
2 take
3 go out, do
4 notice, not be
5 order

Übungen zum present perfect progressive

⋆ **20.** Vervollständige die **present perfect progressive**-Formen.

1. I ______________________ working all day.
2. You ______________________ working all day.
3. David ______________________ working all day.
4. Victoria ______________________ working all day.
5. The computer ______________________ working all day.
6. We ______________________ working all day.
7. You ______________________ working all day.
8. They ______________________ working all day.

⋆⋆ **21.** Kreuze bei den folgenden Sätzen an, ob es sich um einen Zeitraum oder einen Zeitpunkt handelt. Setze dann entsprechend **for** oder **since** in die Lücken ein.

autograph – *Autogramm*

	Zeitraum	Zeitpunkt
1. Mr Hunt has been waiting for his wife ____________ half past four.	☐	☐
2. The postman has been delivering the letters ____________ the early morning.	☐	☐
3. Two men have been repairing the pavement ____________ last Tuesday.	☐	☐
4. Victor and his friends have been jogging round the sports field ____________ half an hour.	☐	☐
5. Melissa has been watching TV ____________ 8 o'clock.	☐	☐
6. Our children have been collecting autographs ____________ five years.	☐	☐
7. Mrs Colin has been correcting the tests ____________ two hours.	☐	☐

22. Übertrage die Sätze aus Übung 21 ins Deutsche.

1. *Herr Hunt* ___
2. *Der Briefträger* ___
3. *Zwei Männer* ___
4. *Victor und seine Freunde* ___
___
5. *Melissa* ___
6. *Unsere Kinder* ___
7. *Frau Colin* ___

SPRACHTIPP

Present perfect progressive wird mit dem deutschen Präsens (+ schon) übersetzt!

23. Ordne die bejahten und verneinten Prädikate den Zeitformen zu.

present progressive	**simple past**
___	wished
___	___
___	___
present perfect simple	**present perfect progressive**
___	___
___	___
___	___

has written
wished
have printed
haven't been teaching
hasn't read
are repairing
am travelling
has been living
didn't want
understood
isn't driving
have been waiting

24. Übertrage die folgenden Sätze ins Englische. Hier brauchst du present perfect simple und progressive sowie das simple present.

1. *Wir wohnen in dieser Wohnung schon seit 15 Jahren.*
___
2. *Ich habe sie gerade renoviert. Jetzt sieht sie wieder wie neu aus.*
___
___
3. *Ich lerne seit 1980 Englisch und ich weiß immer noch nicht alles.*
___
___

renovate – *renovieren*
look like – *aussehen wie*

Übungen zum past perfect simple

★ **25.** Unterstreiche im Text die past perfect-Formen.

Last year we had asked our neighbours to look after the house and the garden while we were staying in Italy for a fortnight. When we came back two weeks later we couldn't believe what we saw. The letterbox was bursting because they hadn't emptied it. The lawn in the garden was brown because they hadn't watered it. And all the lovely plants in the garden! What a shame. We were so surprised because our neighbours had always made such a positive impression on us. After the first shock we went over to them. But they weren't at home. In the evening we received a phone call from the neighbours' son. And then we understood: Mr Hill and Mrs Hill had had an accident and were both still in hospital. We weren't annoyed any longer and visited them. They were pleased to see us and very sorry at the same time but that wasn't important anymore. They're wonderful neighbours.

a fortnight - *14 Tage*

be annoyed - *verärgert sein*

be pleased - *erfreut sein*

★★ **26.** Übersetze die **past-perfect**-Sätze aus Übung 25.

1. ______________________________

____

2. ______________________________

3. ______________________________

4. ______________________________

____

5. ______________________________

____

★★ **27.** Entscheide, welche Handlung vor einer anderen stattfand und setze **simple past** oder **past perfect simple** ein.

cable - *Kabel*

1. I (start) ______________ the computer again after I (check) ______________ the cables.

2. Suddenly I (remember) ______________ what she (tell) ______________ me the day before.

3. Martin proudly (present) ____________________ the picture that he (draw) ____________________ at school.

4. Mrs Cain (suggest) ____________________ two books which she (read) ____________________ in her holidays.

suggest – *vorschlagen*

5. After I (miss) ____________________ the bus I (have to wait) ____________________ half an hour for the next one.

6. The guests (go home) ____________________ already when Mike (notice) ____________________ that Samira (leave) ____________________ her handbag on the sofa.

7. Some politicians (not keep) ____________________ what they (promise) ____________________ on the last party conference.

8. By the time the police (arrive) ____________________ at the scene of the accident the paramedics (already treat) ____________________ the injured person.

*** **28.** Übertrage ins Englische.

1. *Bevor Marian im Büro anfing zu arbeiten, hatte sie die Kinder schon zur Schule gebracht.*

____

____

2. *Sie erzählte mir nicht, dass ihr Freund sie verlassen hatte.*

____

3. *Nachdem wir unseren Flug gebucht hatten, kauften wir einen Reiseführer.*

____

4. *Er erzählte mir, wie er seinen Arm gebrochen hatte.*

____

5. *Gestern konnte Ted nicht ins Haus, weil er seine Schlüssel in der Schule liegen gelassen hatte.*

nicht ins Haus können – *can't get into the house*

____

____

Übungen zum past perfect progressive

★ **29.** Setze das passende Verb im **past perfect progressive** ein.

1 work
2 read
3 live
4 work
5 follow

suspect - *Verdächtige/r*
arrest - *verhaften*

1. Mr Frazer was tired because he ______________________ hard all day.
2. Barbara ______________________ the papers for an hour when she realized that she had missed the news on TV.
3. Before I moved to Germany I ______________________ in France quite happily.
4. Andrew and Mark ______________________ on the new project for two weeks already when it was stopped because of lack of money.
5. The police ______________________ the suspect for two weeks before they arrested him.

★★★ **30.** Nach einem Brand in einem Mehrfamilienhaus wurden die Anwohner gefragt, womit sie beschäftigt waren und ob ihnen im Vorfeld irgendetwas aufgefallen war. Übertrage ins Englische. Hier brauchst du **past perfect simple** und **progressive** sowie **simple past**.

fire brigade - *Feuerwehr*
knock - *klopfen*
beforehand - *vorher*

1. *Mr Turner hatte die ganze Zeit Fernsehen geguckt.*

____

2. *Mrs Cook hatte das Feuer gerochen und die Feuerwehr gerufen.*

____

3. *Mrs Joyce sagte, dass irgendjemand vorher an ihre Tür geklopft hatte.*

____

4. *Sie hatte die Tür aber nicht geöffnet.*

____

5. *Mr und Mrs Stilton hatten zu Abend gegessen.*

____

have a headache - *Kopfschmerzen haben*
notice - *bemerken*

6. *Einige Leute sagten, dass sie Kopfschmerzen gehabt hatten.*

____

7. *Andere sagten, dass sie nichts bemerkt hatten.*

____

3 DIE ZUKUNFT

1. Wenn wir unsere Abschlussprüfung machen, werden wir 18 sein.
2. Und wenn ich 18 bin, gehe ich für ein halbes Jahr nach Australien.
3. Ich werde ein Jahr in USA verbringen. Wenn ich genug Geld habe, würde ich gerne so viel wie möglich herumreisen.
4. Nimmst du irgendjemanden mit? 5. Ich weiß noch nicht.

Im Englischen gibt es mehrere Möglichkeiten, zukünftige Handlungen und Ereignisse auszudrücken:
Man kann je nach Sprechabsicht das **will-future**, das **going-to future**, das **future progressive** oder das **future perfect** benutzen. Außerdem kann man auch das **present simple** und das **present progressive** verwenden. Die wichtigsten Unterscheidungsmerkmale dieser Zeitformen für den richtigen Gebrauch fasst der Überblick auf S. 284 zusammen.

Das will-future

Bildung

Das **will-future** wird für alle Personen im Singular und Plural folgendermaßen gebildet:

will + Infinitiv des Verbs.

Verneinte Aussagesätze werden oft in der Kurzform benutzt und lauten:

won't + Infinitiv des Verbs.

Person	Langform	Kurzform	Infinitiv
alle Personen	**will**	**'ll**	**understand (play,**
	will not	**won't**	**sleep, find, go ...)**

Im Deutschen verwenden wir oft auch das Präsens für Zukünftiges. Beim Übersetzen ins Englische ist das aber nicht entscheidend! Es kommt bei der Auswahl der richtigen Zeitform nur auf die Sprechabsicht (Vorhersage, Vermutung, etc.) an!

LERNTIPP

Signalwörter für das will-future sind im Beispiel unterstrichen - grundsätzlich sind das alle Zeitangaben in der Zukunft. Gesammelt findest du sie in der → **Zeitenübersicht**, S. 284.

Gebrauch des will-future

Das will-future wird für folgende Handlungen und Ereignisse verwendet:

- **Vorhersagen**, die von **äußeren Umständen** abhängen, z. B. Wetter.

Look at the clouds. It'll rain soon.	*Sieh dir die Wolken an. Es wird bald regnen.*

- **Vermutungen** über die Zukunft, die mit **perhaps, maybe, probably, I hope, I think, I'm sure, I'm afraid** verbunden sind.

Poor Liz is ill. Perhaps she'll be back in the office on Monday.	*Die arme Liz ist krank. Vielleicht ist sie am Montag wieder im Büro/wird sie ... sein.*
I'm sure you'll make it.	*Ich bin sicher, dass du das schaffst/schaffen wirst.*

- **spontane Entscheidungen**

There's no mineral water in the fridge. — Wait a minute. I'll get you some.	*Im Kühlschrank ist kein Mineralwasser. — Warte, ich hole dir welches/ich werde dir welches holen.*

- in **If-Sätzen** vom Typ I

I'll be very sad if you don't come over the weekend.

Das going-to future

Bildung

Das **going to-future** wird folgendermaßen gebildet:

eine **Form von be im present simple + going to + Infinitiv** des Verbs

Person	Langform	Kurzform		Infinitiv
I	'm	am	going to	leave
	'm not	am not		
He/She/It	's	is		
	's not/isn't	is not		
You/We/You/They	're	are		
	're not/aren't	are not		

Achtung!
Mit dem Verb **go** funktioniert die Bildung genauso:

Infinitiv	going to-future
go swimming	**I'm/He's/We're going to go swimming.**
go for a walk	**I'm/He's/We're going to go for a walk.**

Auch die Bildung von Fragen funktioniert wie bei allen Fragen mit Hilfsverben: Das erste Hilfsverb (also **am, is** oder **are**) wird mit dem Subjekt des Satzes vertauscht. Zur Bildung von **Kurzantworten** verwendet man das erste Hilfsverb aus der Frage

Is he going to go swimming? **Yes, he is./No, he's not.**

Gebrauch des going to-future

Das going to-future wird mit folgender Sprechabsicht verwendet:

- **Plan oder Idee** für eine zukünftige Handlung oder ein Ereignis (meist in der nahen Zukunft, sonst mit Zeitangabe, z. B. **in a few years** etc.).

I'm going to relax this weekend.
What are you going to do?
Well, I'm definitely not going to be at home.

- **Vorhersage** über ein eintretendes Ereignis, wenn es **deutliche Anzeichen** für das tatsächliche Eintreten gibt.

Hurry up, Jason. You're going to be late.
What a nice day today. The garden party is going to be great.

Das future progressive

Bildung

Das **future progressive** wird für alle Personen im Singular und im Plural folgendermaßen gebildet:

will + be + present participle

Das **present participle** wird durch **Anhängen von -ing** an den **Infinitiv** des jeweiligen Verbs gebildet. Beachte auch, dass einige Verben **keine progressive form** bilden.

Person	Langform	Kurzform	present participle
alle Personen	**will be** **will not be**	**'ll be** **won't be**	**playing (sleeping, working, …)**

Gebrauch des future progressive

Das future progressive wird verwendet für:

- Handlungen oder Ereignisse in der Zukunft, die sich **ohne weiteres Zutun ergeben** werden

You needn't wash the car. It'll be getting dirty tomorrow anyway in this weather.

- **länger andauernde Handlungen** oder Ereignisse zu einem zukünftigen Zeitpunkt

Formula One race – *Formel-1-Rennen*

Sorry, we can't meet tomorrow because I'll be watching the Formula One race.

Das future perfect

Bildung

Das **future perfect** wird für alle Personen im Singular und Plural folgendermaßen gebildet:

will + have + past participle

Person	Langform	Kurzform	past participle
alle Personen	**will have** **will not have**	**'ll have** **won't have**	**played (slept, worked, …)**

Gebrauch des future perfect

Das future perfect wird verwendet für

- Handlungen, die zu einem zukünftigen Zeitpunkt (z. B. Zeitangaben wie **by next Friday** oder **(by +) Nebensatz**) abgeschlossen sein werden.

I will have prepared my speech by next Friday.	*… werde … vorbereitet haben.*
By the time Mary gets up tomorrow William will have finished his nightshift.	*… wird William seine Nachtschicht beendet haben.*

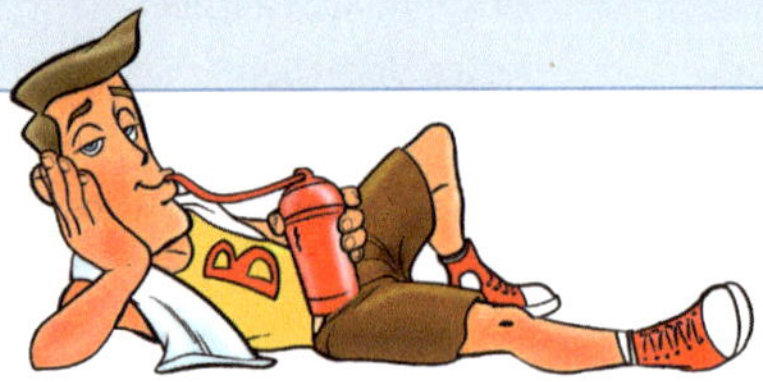

° Zukünftiges im Überblick

will-future	Vermutung über eine zukünftige Handlung/ein bevorstehendes Ereignis	**I'm sure Rita won't celebrate her 18th birthday at home. She'll probably book a party room.**
	spontane Entscheidung	**I need a break. — OK, I'll get some sandwiches.**
	Wettervorhersage (oder andere von äußeren Umständen abhängige zukünftige Ereignisse)	**It'll be sunny tomorrow morning but it'll start to rain later.**
going to-future	Vorhersage aufgrund von deutlichen Anzeichen	**Look, the birds are flying low. It's going to rain.**
	Plan/Idee für ein zukünftiges Ereignis	**We're going to spend our holiday in Italy this year.**
simple present	nicht vom Sprecher festgelegtes, feststehendes Ereignis/Fest	**New Year's Eve is on a Monday.**
	Fahrpläne, Stundenpläne	**The next bus to Rye is at 8.15.**
	Veranstaltungen	**The concert starts at 6 p.m.**
present progressive	feste Vereinbarung für eine zukünftige Handlung oder	**Mark's football team is playing against Luke's team next week.**
	beschlossenes Vorhaben	**I'm having my first party tonight.**
future progressive	Ereignisse, die zu erwarten sind bzw. sich ohne Zutun ergeben	**Where's Lucy? — I expect she'll be coming soon.**
	länger anhaltende Handlungen in der Zukunft	**This time tomorrow Caty will be flying to the Seychelles.**
future perfect	Ereignisse, die zu einem gewissen Zeitpunkt in der Zukunft abgeschlossen sein werden	**Mark will have finished his Spanish course by the end of June.**

SPRACHTIPP

Die Bedeutungen von going to-future und **present progressive** für Aussagen über Zukünftiges liegen sehr nahe beieinander. Oft sind beide Zeitformen möglich.

!

Im Gegensatz zum deutschen Präsens ist das **simple present** nur selten für zukünftige Handlungen möglich! Achte auf die Situation (Sprechabsicht)!

Vergleiche die folgenden Sätze. Alle beziehen sich auf etwas Zukünftiges und alle sind korrekt. Jedoch wird jeder Satz mit einer anderen Absicht gesprochen.

I'll arrive at ten o'clock.	Vermutung, Vorhersage
I'm going to arrive at ten o'clock.	Plan, Idee
I arrive at ten o'clock.	Ankunft laut Fahrplan
I'm arriving at ten o'clock.	festes Vorhaben
I'll be arriving at ten o'clock.	Ereignis, das sich ohne Zutun ergeben wird
I'll have arrived by ten o'clock.	in der Zukunft abgeschlossenes Ereignis

★ **1.** Bilde die entsprechenden bejahten bzw. verneinten Aussagen im **will-future.**

bejaht	**verneint**
1. I'm sure he'll come.	______
2. Marsha will spend the weekend in Madrid.	______
3. There'll be heavy showers at night.	______
4. ______	Mr and Mrs Hill won't leave early.

★ **2.** Lies die spontanen Äußerungen und ordne sie richtig zu.

OK. We'll go upstairs.

I'll get some from the supermarket.

Don't worry. I'll fix it for you.

I'll call the doctor.

fix – *reparieren*

be running a high temperature – *hohes Fieber haben*

toy car – *Spielzeugauto*

1. Bob is running a very high temperature.

______

2. Oh, no. We haven't got any eggs for the cake.

______

3. Be quiet, girls. We can't concentrate.

______

4. Look, my toy car is broken.

______

★★ **3.** Bilde Fragen mit dem going to-future.

1. Timo | meet | his girlfriend | again | ?

______

2. you | have | a party | for your birthday | ?

______

3. Dad | take a week off | ?

take a week off – *eine Woche freinehmen*

4. you and your friends | prepare | a surprise party | for Susan | ?

*** **4.** Was machst du am Wochenende? Plane für dich und deine Familie auf Englisch.

relax – *ausspannen*

1. *Ich werde ausspannen.*

2. *Am Samstag werden wir die Wohnung putzen.*

3. *Tim wird Fußball spielen.*

4. *Meine beste Freundin Nina wird in Hamburg sein.*

5. *Nina und ich werden ins Kino gehen.*

*** **5.** Lies dir Satz für Satz durch und überlege zuerst die Sprechabsicht. Übertrage dann mit der richtigen Zeitstufe ins Englische. Achtung: Hier werden alle 6 Möglichkeiten, im Englischen Zukünftiges auszudrücken, gebraucht.

1. *Heiligabend fällt dieses Jahr auf einen Freitag.*

Zeitstufe: __________

Englisch: __________

2. *Mutters Geburtstag ist nächsten Sonntag.*

Zeitstufe: __________

Englisch: __________

3. *Ich bin sicher, Oma und Opa kommen am Wochenende.*

Zeitstufe: __________

Englisch: __________

4. *Vielleicht gehen wir dann ins Restaurant.*
Zeitstufe: ______________________
Englisch: ______________________

5. *Mutter wird sowieso am Sonntag mit uns feiern.*
Zeitstufe: ______________________
Englisch: ______________________

boil over – *überkochen*

6. *Vorsicht, das Wasser! Es kocht gleich über!*
Zeitstufe: ______________________
Englisch: ______________________

7. *Bayern München spielt morgen gegen Manchester United.*
Zeitstufe: ______________________
Englisch: ______________________

8. *Ich fürchte, bis dahin wird sich das Wetter geändert haben.*
Zeitstufe: ______________________
Englisch: ______________________

*** **6.** Übertrage ins Deutsche.

SPRACHTIPP

Nicht jeder englische Satz im Futur muss im Deutschen mit Futur übersetzt werden!

1. Mum is going to meet her best friend on Sunday.
____

2. We're going to clean the windows tomorrow.
____

3. Wait a second, please. I'll write that down.
____

4. I'm sure you'll enjoy yourselves.
____

4 RELATIVSÄTZE

1. Wer war der Typ, der in die letzte Stunde reingeplatzt ist?
2. Das war Alex. Er ist der Neue aus der Parallelklasse.
3. Ist das der, der jeden Morgen mit dem Fahrrad kommt.
4. Nein, das ist der, dessen Moped direkt vor dem Eingang abgestellt ist.

Relativsätze (relative clauses) sind Nebensätze, die sich auf ein vorangegangenes Nomen bzw. eine Nominalgruppe im Hauptsatz beziehen. Englische Relativsätze können von einem Relativpronomen (relative pronoun) eingeleitet werden, in bestimmten Fällen aber auch ohne Relativpronomen gebildet werden. Man unterscheidet zwischen **notwendigen** und **nicht notwendigen Relativsätzen** (**defining** and **non-defining relative clauses**).

LERNTIPP

Nomen sind alle Substantive, Namen, Bezeichnungen, Städte, Länder, Flüsse usw. Bei einer Nominalgruppe handelt es sich um eine Gruppe aus mehreren Wörtern.

Relativpronomen

Who, which, that, whom und **whose** leiten Relativsätze ein, die sich auf das Subjekt (wer oder was?) oder das Objekt (wen oder was? wem? wessen?) des Hauptsatzes beziehen.

who	**nur bei Personen (wer, wen?)**
that	**bei Personen und Sachen (wer, wen, was?)**
which	**nur bei Sachen (was?)**
whom	**nur bei Personen (wen? wem?)**
whose	**bei Personen und Sachen (wessen?)**

SPRACHTIPP

whom wird vorwiegend in der Schriftsprache benutzt und klingt förmlich.

Alle englischen Relativpronomen sind unveränderlich (d.h. sie lauten im Singular und Plural immer gleich) und können sich gleichermaßen auf Wörter im Singular und Plural beziehen.

Beispiele für Relativpronomen als **Subjekt**

The child/the children who/that found 50 pence were happy.	*Das Kind, das.../Die Kinder, die....* (Nominativ: wer?)
The T-shirt/The T-shirts which/that we ordered last week haven't arrived yet.	*Das T-Shirt, das.../Die T-Shirts, die...* (Nominativ: was?)

Beispiele für Relativpronomen als **Objekt**

I've got a date with the guy who/whom/that I met in the pub last night.	*...dem Typ, den...* (Akkusativ: wen?)
I answered all the e-mails which/that I received.	*... alle E-Mails, die ...* (Akkusativ: was?)
I know the girl who/whom/that I gave your adress.	*... das Mädchen, dem ...* (Dativ: wem?)

Der Relativbegleiter **whose** (+ Substantiv) drückt **Besitz oder Zugehörigkeit** von Personen, Sachen oder Tieren aus. Er kann in notwendigen und nicht notwendigen Relativsätzen benutzt werden.

May I introduce you to Mr Jameson whose new book was published last week.	*Mr Jameson, dessen neues Buch ...* (Genitiv: wessen?)
There aren't many cities whose subways are as clean as Munich's.	*... Städte, deren U-Bahnen ...* (Genitiv: wessen?)

SPRACHTIPP

Verwende immer dann **which**, wenn du im deutschen Relativsatz ‚was' sagen würdest.

Das Relativpronomen **which** kann sich auch auf einen **ganzen Satz** oder einen **Sachverhalt** beziehen. Da der Relativsatz dann einen (zum Verständnis nicht notwendigen) Kommentar zum Hauptsatz darstellt, werden beide durch ein Komma getrennt. Das Relativpronomen **which** entspricht dann dem deutschen ‚was'.

During my trip to London I left the travel guide in a cafe, which was not very helpful.	*Auf meiner Londonreise habe ich den Reiseführer in einem Café liegen lassen, was nicht sehr hilfreich war.*

!

Beachte, dass diese verallgemeinernden Relativpronomen **kein Bezugswort im Hauptsatz** haben. Daher kann der Relativsatz auch zuerst stehen.

Besonderheit:
Who, **what** und **which** können mit **-ever** zu Relativpronomen mit der Bedeutung ‚jeder, der' oder ‚alles, was' bzw. ‚wer/was/welche(r, s) auch immer' erweitert werden .

There's somebody at the door. — Whoever it is, tell them I'm not at home.

Notwendige Relativsätze

Notwendige Relativsätze (defining relative clauses)

- werden durch Relativpronomen (**who, which, that**) eingeleitet.
- enthalten **Informationen**, die für das Verständnis des Hauptsatzes unverzichtbar, also **notwendig** sind.
- werden **nicht durch ein Komma** vom Hauptsatz abgetrennt.

	notwendiger Relativsatz	
Luke is the boy	**who/that won first prize in the talent competition.**	
The girl	**who(m)/that I love**	**loves another boy.**
All laptops	**which/that were bought before December**	**have to be returned.**

SPRACHTIPP

Bezieht sich der Relativsatz auf eine Sache, verwendet man eher das Relativpronomen **that** als which. Besonders häufig steht es nach **something, everything, nothing, all, the first, the last**.

I like **all** music **that** helps me to relax.

Notwendige Relativsätze ohne Relativpronomen: contact clauses

Nur im notwendigen Relativsatz **kann** unter bestimmten Umständen das Relativpronomen entfallen, und zwar nur:

- wenn das **Relativpronomen** nicht Subjekt des Relativsatzes ist, sondern die Funktion eines **direkten (Akkusativ-) Objekts** oder eines **Präpositionalobjekts** hat.

Contact clauses schließen (daher der Name) direkt an ihr Bezugswort an und werden als notwendige Relativsätze nicht durch Komma vom Hauptsatz getrennt. Häufig verwendet man sie in der Umgangssprache.

	notwendiger Relativsatz	
The performance	**(which/that) I saw yesterday was brilliant.**	*... die Vorstellung, die ...* (direktes Objekt: was?)
I booked the DJ	**(who(m)/that) Mary recommended .**	*... den DJ, den ...* (direktes Objekt: wen?)
Here are the books	**(which/that) you were asking for.**	*... die Bücher, nach denen* ...(Präpositionalobjekt: nach wem/was?)

recommend – *empfehlen*

Präpositionen im Relativsatz

Sind in notwendigen Relativsätzen auch Präpositionen enthalten, so sind mehrere Satzstellungen möglich. Vergleiche:

Look, there's the boy (who/that) you talked to yesterday.	*... Der Junge, mit dem ...*
Look, there's the boy to whom you talked yesterday.	
The newspaper article (which/that) we talked about in class was based on false information.	*... der Artikel, über den ...*
The newspaper article about which we talked in class was based on false information.	

- In notwendigen Relativsätzen mit **that** oder **who** und in **contact clauses** steht die Präposition immer **hinter** dem Verb.
- Im förmlichen Stil steht die Präposition oft vor dem Relativpronomen (z. B. **to whom, with whom, from whom, in which, about which**, etc.).
- **when** oder **where** können statt Präposition + Relativpronomen stehen, wenn Zeit oder Ort mit dem Bezugswort angegeben werden.

We saw the lake where (in which) Nessie is said to live.	*... den See, in dem ...*

Nicht notwendige Relativsätze

Nicht notwendige Relativsätze (non-defining relative clauses)

- enthalten zusätzliche **Informationen**, die für das Verständnis des Hauptsatzes entbehrlich, also **nicht notwendig** sind.
- können grundsätzlich **nicht mit that** eingeleitet werden. Hier müssen **who** (Personen) und **which** (Sachen und Tiere) verwendet werden. **Whom** kann für Personen als Objekt und nach Präpositionen stehen.
- werden durch **Kommas** vom Hauptsatz abgetrennt.
- werden vorwiegend in der **Schriftsprache** verwendet.

	nicht notwendiger Relativsatz	
Lisa,	**who lives next door,**	**does a lot of sports.**
The supermarket,	**whose opening hours are from 8 a.m. to 8 p.m.,**	**is a good place to meet people.**
My laptop,	**which I have been using for three years,**	**was a bargain.**

!

In nicht notwendigen Relativsätzen muss immer ein Relativpronomen stehen. Es kann nicht weggelassen werden!

SPRACHTIPP

In der Umgangssprache verwendet man eher zwei Hauptsätze:

Lisa lives next door. She works as a vet's assistant.

bargain - *Schnäppchen*

⋆ **1.** Setze das richtige **Relativpronomen** ein. Setze es in Klammern, wenn du es weglassen kannst.

1. I spent all day out in the sun ___________ was great.

2. Neil Armstrong was the first man ___________ walked on the moon.

3. I was the only person ___________ wasn't hurt in the accident.

4. My sister was the only one ___________ was able to give first aid.

5. Here is a list of e-mail addresses ___________ you must check.

6. Have you got a chair ___________ I can sit on, please?

7. Andrew ________ had been driving all day was tired and needed a break.

8. I was given this map by a man ___________ I met on the train.

⋆⋆ **2.** Bilde aus den zwei Hauptsätzen einen Hauptsatz mit **Relativsatz**. Vorsicht, es handelt sich um Sätze mit und ohne Relativpronomen!

1. I met Mrs Carter. She asked me to give you this parcel.

I met Mrs Carter who asked me to give you this parcel.

2. The man didn't know the way. This man was driving the bus.

____

3. This is Lilian Parker. I know her from the gym.

____

4. Lynn hated eating by herself. She hoped to have lunch with Louisa.

____

____

5. Nora knows the address. You need this address.

____

⋆⋆⋆ **3.** Übertrage die Sätze ins Deutsche.

1. There are so many things that I want to do.

____

2. Don't talk to people you don't know very well.

____

3. Dad is the sort of person who likes hard work.

4. I met a young man who works at Porsche.

5. The bills I have to pay every month are not very high.

6. I worked in Australia in 2004 which was a fantastic experience.

*** **4.** Übertrage die **Relativsätze** ins Englische. Entscheide selbst, ob ein **Relativpronomen** gebraucht wird oder nicht.

size – *Größe, Nummer*

1. *Das einzige Kleid, das mir wirklich gefällt, ist eine Nummer zu klein.*

trust – *(ver)trauen*

2. *Ich brauche einen Arzt, dem ich vertrauen kann.*

spoilt – *verwöhnt*

3. *Tina muss wieder auf die Kinder aufpassen, die so fürchterlich verwöhnt sind.*

camper – *Wohnmobil*

the four of us – *zu viert*

4. *Wir wollen ein Wohnmobil kaufen, in dem wir zu viert schlafen können.*

5. *Eltern, die beide arbeiten, müssen gute Organisatoren sein.*

complete disaster – *totaler Reinfall*

6. *Das Theaterstück, das wir gestern Abend gesehen haben, war ein totaler Reinfall.*

1 FALSCHE FREUNDE

Viele deutsche Wörter ähneln englischen Wörtern, aber oft ist die Bedeutung doch sehr unterschiedlich. Damit du nicht mit einer falschen Übersetzung ins Fettnäpfchen trittst, findest du hier verschiedene thematische Listen mit „Falschen Freunden" und den jeweils richtigen Übersetzungen.

Verben

to become	*werden*	*bekommen*	**to receive, to get**
to blame	*Schuld geben*	*(sich) blamieren*	**to make a fool of (oneself)**
to irritate	*jdn. verärgern*	*irritieren*	**to confuse**
to oversee	*beaufsichtigen*	*übersehen*	**to overlook, to miss**
to overhear	*zufällig mithören*	*überhören*	**not to hear**
to wonder	*sich etw. fragen*	*sich wundern*	**to be surprised**

Adjektive

actual(ly)	*eigentlich, tatsächlich*	*aktuell*	**current**
brave	*mutig*	*brav*	**good, well behaved**
consequent	*daraus folgend*	*konsequent*	**consistent**
decent	*anständig; angemessen*	*dezent*	**discreet, unobtrusive**
eventual(ly)	*schließlich*	*eventuell*	**possibly, possible**
engaged	*verlobt*	*engagiert*	**committed, dedicated**
familiar	*vertraut, bekannt*	*familiär*	**family ~, informal**
genial	*freundlich*	*genial*	**ingenious**
massive	*riesig, enorm*	*massiv*	**solid, strong**
ordinary	*gewöhnlich, normal*	*ordinär*	**vulgar, common**
plump	*rund(lich)*	*plump*	**clumsy, awkward**

pregnant	*schwanger*	*prägnant*	**concise, incisive**
self-conscious	*gehemmt, befangen*	*selbstbewusst*	**self-assured, self-confident**
sensible	*vernünftig*	*sensibel*	**sensitive**
sympathetic	*mitfühlend*	*sympathisch*	**pleasant, friendly**
thick	*dicht, zähflüssig; doof*	*dick*	**bulky, fat**

In der Schule

blackboard	*(Schul-)Tafel*	*schwarzes Brett*	**notice board**
floor	*Fußboden; Etage*	*Flur*	**corridor, hall**
gymnasium	*Turnhalle*	*Gymnasium*	~ **high school** (AmE), ~ **grammar school** (BrE)
high school	*weiterführende Schule*	*Hochschule*	**university, college**
map	*(Land-)Karte*	*Mappe*	**folder**
to mob	*jdn. umringen*	*mobben*	**to bully**
note	*Notiz*	*Note (Zensur)*	**mark, grade**
stuff	*Zeug, Sache*	*(Lehr-)Stoff*	**syllabus, material**

Bei der Arbeit

chef	*Koch, Köchin*	*Chef/in*	**boss**
concept	*Begriff, Idee*	*Konzept*	**draft, plan**
concurrence	*Übereinstimmung*	*Konkurrenz*	**competition, rivalry**
to control	*steuern*	*kontrollieren*	**to check, to inspect**
critic	*Kritiker/in*	*Kritik*	**criticism**
direction	*Richtung*	*Direktion*	**management, administration**
fabric	*Stoff (Gewebe)*	*Fabrik*	**factory**
housemaster	*Lehrer im Internat*	*Hausmeister/in*	**caretaker** (BrE), **janitor** (AmE)
to overtake	*überholen*	*übernehmen*	**to take on, to take over**
packet	*Verpackung*	*Paket*	**parcel**

pause	*Unterbrechung*	*Pause (Arbeit)*	**break**
personal	*persönlich*	*Personal*	**staff, personnel**
physician	*Arzt, Ärztin*	*Physiker/in*	**physicist**
prospects	*Aussichten*	*Prospekte*	**brochures, catalogues, leaflets**
to prove	*beweisen*	*prüfen*	**to check, to examine**
quote	*Zitat*	*Quote*	**rate, quota**
undertaker	*Leichenbestatter(in)*	*Unternehmer/in*	**entrepreneur**
warehouse	*Lager*	*Warenhaus*	**department store**

Finanzen

briefcase	*Aktentasche*	*Brieftasche*	**wallet**
caution	*Vorsicht; Warnung*	*Kaution*	**bail, deposit**
rate	*Kurs, Satz*	*Rate*	**instalment**
rent	*Miete*	*Rente*	**pension**
to spare	*jdn. (ver)schonen*	*sparen*	**to save, to make savings**
to spend	*ausgeben*	*spenden*	**to donate**

Medien und Kommunikation

also	*auch*	*also*	**therefore**
arguments	*Streits, Auseinandersetzungen*	*Argumente*	**reasons**
formula	*Formel*	*Formular*	**form**

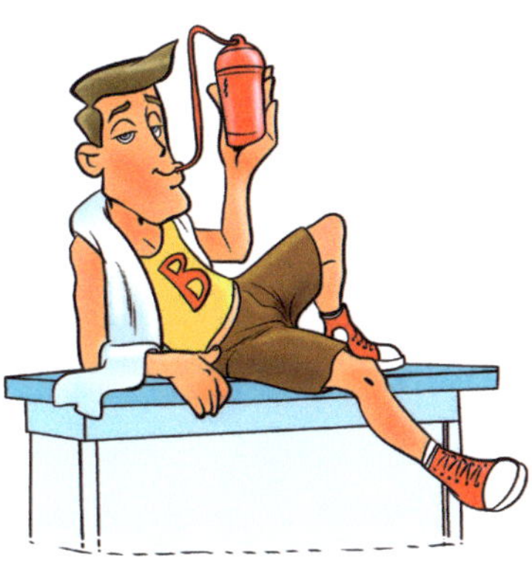

handy	*handlich*	*Handy*	**mobile phone** (BrE), **cell phone** (AmE)
meaning	*Bedeutung*	*Meinung*	**opinion**
photograph	*Foto*	*Fotograf/in*	**photographer**
Roman	*Römer/in, römisch*	*Roman*	**novel**

Gesundheit und Essen

card	*(Post-, Scheck-, Visiten-) Karte*	*(Speise)karte*	**menu**
flesh	*lebendes Fleisch*	*Fleisch (Essen)*	**meat**
marmalade	*Orangenmarmelade*	*Marmelade*	**jam** (BrE), **jelly** (AmE)
menu	*Speisekarte*	*Menü*	**(set) meal**
recipe	*Rezept (Kochen)*	*Rezept (Med.)*	**prescription**
sharp	*scharf (z.B. Klinge)*	*scharf (Essen)*	**hot**
station	*Bahnhof*	*Station (Med.)*	**ward**
tablet	*Tablette*	*Tablett*	**tray**

1. Ergänze in den folgenden Sätzen die jeweils richtige englische Übersetzung der deutschen Wörter in Klammern:

a. I ______________ many letters every week. (***bekommen***)

b. Going home is the most ________________ thing we can do. (***vernünftig***)

c. I had a huge ________________ with my boss. (***Auseinandersetzung***)

d. I would ____________ like to mention the environmental issue. (***auch***)

e. In the _______________ situation we cannot send Harry to Iraq. (***aktuell***)

f. This is a very ________________ topic. (***sensibel***)

g. ________________ we need to react now. (***also, deshalb***)

h. What do you want to ________________ when you finish school? (***werden***)

i. What is the ________________ problem? (***eigentlich, tatsächlich***)

BOXENSTOPP

Falsche Freunde lauern an allen Ecken, da hilft nur genaues Vokabellernen. Und im Übrigen solltest du dich nicht von ihnen einschüchtern lassen, denn es gibt auch viele „gute Freunde", der **apple** bleibt ein *Apfel*, die *Orange* ... Kennst du weitere falsche Freunde?

____

____

____

____

2 HÄUFIG VERWECHSELTE WÖRTER

Im Englischen gibt es viele Wörter, die trotz ähnlicher Grundbedeutung deutliche Bedeutungsnuancen aufweisen und daher in unterschiedlichen Zusammenhängen und Konstruktionen verwendet werden.

As oder like?

Die folgenden Bedeutungsunterschiede muss man unbedingt beachten:

She plays tennis like a professional.
Sie spielt Tennis wie ein Profi.
She plays tennis as a professional.
Sie spielt Tennis als Profi.
She plays tennis as well as a professional.
Sie spielt Tennis so gut wie ein Profi.

1. Setze in den folgenden Sätzen die Wörter **like**, **as** oder **as ... as** an der jeweils richtigen Stelle ein.

a. ______________ I mentioned, I'm going to change schools.

b. Leon would like to be ___________ famous _________ his favourite star.

c. You never listen. Talking to you is ________________ talking to a wall.

d. I have been waiting for something ________________ this for ages.

BOXENSTOPP

______________ bedeutet als Präposition *wie*. __________________ bedeutet als Präposition *als* oder in der Konstruktion **as ... as** (genau)so ... wie. **As tall as** heißt beispielsweise übersetzt ____________________.

Big, great oder large? Little oder small?

Bei diesen Adjektiven schleichen sich oft gemeine Fehler ein. Hier haben wir für dich die wichtigsten Unterschiede klargestellt.

Big und **large** beschreiben konkrete Objekte und Menschen:
a big man / a large building
ein großer, schwerer Mann / ein großes Gebäude
Beide Adjektive können aber auch bestimmte zählbare abstrakte Substantive beschreiben:
a big / large mistake / problem / order
ein(e) große(r/s) Fehler / Problem / Bestellung
Large ist dabei etwas förmlicher als **big**.

Great im Sinne von *groß* wird anders als **big** und **large** nur in Verbindung mit (meist unzählbaren) abstrakten Substantiven gebraucht:
great interest / news / progress
große(r/s) Interesse / Neuigkeiten / Fortschritt(e)
Hier wäre **big** oder **large** falsch.
In Verbindung mit konkreten Substantiven heißt **great** dagegen *großartig*:
a great man / book / idea
ein(e) großartige(r/s) Mann / Buch / Idee

Will man das Gegenteil von **big** und **large** in den oben genannten Fällen ausdrücken, verwendet man in der Regel **small**. **Little** drückt dagegen zusätzlich eine Verniedlichung, Sympathie oder Mitleid aus:

a small child	*ein kleines Kind*
a little child	*ein (süßes) kleines Kind*

Das korrekte Gegenteil zu **great** bei unzählbaren abstrakten Substantiven wäre **little** (im Sinne von *wenig*).
The news is of little interest.
Diese Nachrichten/Neuigkeiten sind von wenig/geringem Interesse.

2. Ergänze die folgenden Sätze mit **big**, **great**, **large**, **little** oder **small**. Aber aufgepasst: Jedes Wort kommt nur einmal vor!

a. Henry Ford was a ________________ (*großartig*) inventor.

b. A ________________ (*groß*) number of people came to the rock concert.

c. My grandmother lives in a ___________________ (*klein*) house.

d. There will be ___________________ (*wenig*) rain this week.

e. Tim's parents have got a house with a ______________ (*groß*) garden.

3. Entscheide in den folgenden Sätzen jeweils, welches Adjektiv richtig ist. Streiche dazu die falschen Ausdrücke einfach durch.

a. The government spends a **large** / **big** / **little** amount of money every year.

b. Crime is a **big** / **great** / **large** problem in Europe.

c. Mr Cooper is a **great** / **little** / **small** fan of English books.

d. Look at these **large** / **little** / **small** kittens! Aren't they cute?

e. When I was a **little** / **small** / **great** child, I was afraid of the dark.

BOXENSTOPP

Ergänze den untenstehenden Merksatz mit den folgenden Wörtern an der jeweils richtigen Stelle: **Big** - wenig - **Great** - Gegenteil - **large** - Little

________und ________________ beschreiben konkrete Objekte. **Small** ist das ____________________ von **big** und **large**. ________________ hingegen benutzt man eher um etwas zu verniedlichen, Mitleid oder Sympathie auszudrücken oder wenn man ________________ meint. _________ heißt *groß* in Verbindung mit (meist unzählbaren) abstrakten Substantiven.

Bored oder boring? Interested oder interesting?

Mit den Adjektiven **bored** und **interested** beschreibt man einen Gefühlszustand. Im Gegensatz dazu bezeichnen **boring** und **interesting** Menschen oder Dinge, die den Gefühlszustand verursachen. Beachte also die folgenden Bedeutungsunterschiede:

I'm bored.
Mir ist langweilig.
I'm boring.
Ich bin langweilig.

I'm interested in the new topic.
Ich bin an dem neuen Thema interessiert.
This is an interesting topic.
Das ist ein interessantes Thema.

4. Ergänze im folgenden Text die Wörter **bored**, **boring**, **interested** und **interesting** an der jeweils richtigen Stelle:

Yesterday at school I was really ____________________. I have never had such a ____________________ day at school. But in the afternoon I had an ____________________________ date with the new girl from my class. I think she's very ____________________ in me.

BOXENSTOPP

Bored heißt __________, während **boring** __________ bedeutet.
Interested übersetzt man mit __________, und **interesting** heißt auf Deutsch __________.

Lend oder borrow?

Borrow bezieht sich auf die Person, die etwas ausleihen will:
Can I borrow your bike? *Kann ich mir dein Fahrrad ausleihen?*

Lend bezieht sich auf die Person, die etwas gibt:
Can you lend me your bike? *Kannst du mir dein Fahrrad ausleihen?*

Merke dir einfach die folgenden Strukturen:

to borrow sth. from s.o.	sich etwas von jemandem ausleihen / borgen
to lend sth. to s.o. / to lend s.o. sth.	jemandem etwas ausleihen / borgen

5. In den folgenden Sätzen musst Du entscheiden, ob man jeweils **lend** oder **borrow** benutzt. Streiche jeweils das falsche Wort durch. Danach können wir den Fall schließen!

a. **Can you**	**borrow** / **lend**	**me you car? I'll give it back to you tomorrow.**
b. **If you**	**borrow** / **lend**	**my car, you have to be careful.**
c. **Tom**	**is lending** / **is borrowing**	**Jenny his new iPod.**
d. **Yesterday Karen**	**borrowed** / **lent**	**Paul's book.**

BOXENSTOPP

a) Ich benutze **lend**, wenn ich ______________________________

____

b) Ich benutze **borrow**, wenn ich ______________________________

____

Bring oder take?

Wird einem etwas *entgegengebracht*, dann heißt es **bring**:

Bring me the books.
Bring mir die Bücher.
Could you bring the parcel here?
Könnten Sie das Paket hierher bringen?

Take ist richtig, wenn es sich um eine Fortbewegung handelt oder um eine Bewegung zu einem Ort, an dem der Sprecher sich nicht befindet:

Will you take me to the station in the morning?
Bringst du mich morgen früh zum Bahnhof?
Jane is taking her son to the doctor.
Jane bringt ihren Sohn zum Arzt.

6. In den folgenden Sätzen hat sich jeweils ein falsches Verb eingeschlichen. Schreibe die Sätze mit dem richtigen Verb noch einmal darunter.

a. Mike brings his girlfriend out to a restaurant every weekend.

____

b. Pamela is bringing her daughter to the dentist.

____

c. Could you take me another glass of orange juice, please?

____

d. Can I take you anything to eat?

____

BOXENSTOPP

Man benutzt ______________________, wenn man etwas oder jemanden von einem anderen Ort hin zum Sprecher bringt.
Man benutzt ______________________, wenn etwas oder jemand an einen anderen Ort gebracht werden soll.

Can, could oder be able to?

Eigentlich ist der Gebrauch von **can**, **could** und **be able to** ganz einfach:

Wie alle Modalverben drückt **can** eine Vielzahl von Bedeutungen aus. Oft meint es *können* im Sinne einer allgemeinen Fähigkeit:
I can sing. *Ich kann singen.*

Could kann als Vergangenheitsform von **can** verwendet werden und drückt dann ebenfalls eine allgemeine Fähigkeit aus:
I could sing well when I was a child.
Ich konnte gut singen, als ich [noch] ein Kind war.

Zumeist wird **could** jedoch in einer konjunktivischen Bedeutung wahrgenommen:
We could go to the cinema if you like.
Wir könnten ins Kino gehen, wenn du möchtest.

Da man das Modalverb **can** in einer Reihe von Zeitformen nicht benutzen kann, weicht man in solchen Fällen auf die Alternativform **be able to** aus.
Will you ~~can~~ be able to finish your homework in time?
Wirst du deine Hausaufgaben rechtzeitig fertig bekommen können?

7. Ergänze in den folgenden Sätzen die jeweils richtige Form von **can, could** oder **be able to**. Aber aufgepasst: Achte dabei immer auf die richtige Zeitform der Verben! Außerdem kann es auch vorkommen, dass Du ein Verb verneinen musst.

a. Mike ______________ drive a motorbike, but he hasn't got one.

b. When I was 14, I ______________ regularly swim 400 metres in 4 minutes.

c. ______________ you ______________ finish your work yesterday afternoon?

d. Kim ______________ go to the training last week, but she ____________ come every week.

BOXENSTOPP

Das Modalverb ____________ verwendet man oft, um eine allgemeine Fähigkeit zum Ausdruck zu bringen.

Die Form ____________ benutzt man oft in einem konjunktivischen Zusammenhang. In diesem Fall drückt sie die Möglichkeit aus, etwas zu tun. ____________ kann aber auch als einfache Vergangenheitsform von ____________ verwendet werden.

Da ____________ eine Reihe von Formen nicht bilden kann (z.B. die Zukunft mit **will**, das Past perfect, oder den Infinitiv mit **to**) verwendet man ____________ als Ersatzform.

Carry oder wear?

Aufgepasst! Die beiden Verben **wear** und **carry** werden sehr häufig miteinander verwechselt. Eigentlich ist es aber gar nicht so schwer, die beiden Wörter auseinander zu halten, oder hast Du schon einmal versucht, dir ein Wörterbuch oder eine Handtasche ***anzuziehen***?

Wear bezieht sich auf Kleidungsstücke, die man ***an(gezogen)*** hat:
She's wearing a blouse and jeans.
Sie hat eine Bluse und eine Jeans an / Sie trägt ...

Für Kleidungsstücke oder z.B. Taschen, die in der Hand ***getragen*** werden, ist dagegen **carry** richtig:
Tim and Kevin always carry the dictionaries into the classroom.
Tim und Kevin tragen immer die Wörterbücher in den Klassenraum.

8. **Carry** weist Besonderheiten in der Schreibweise auf und **wear** ist ein unregelmäßiges Verb. In der folgenden Tabelle siehst Du die wichtigsten Besonderheiten der beiden Verben auf einen Blick. Kannst Du die fehlenden Formen selbst ergänzen?

Zeitform	carry	wear
Simple present	**I ________** **he/she/it carries**	**I wear** **he/she/it ________**
Present progressive	**she is carrying**	**I am ________**
Simple past	**we ________**	**they wore**
Past progressive	**they were ________**	**I was ________**
Present perfect	**you have carried**	**we have worn**
Past perfect	**I had ________**	**you had ________**

BOXENSTOPP

Man benutzt ____________, wenn es im weitesten Sinne um „Kleidung anziehen" geht. Man verwendet ____________, wenn man beschreibt, dass etwas in der Hand (oder auf der Schulter, dem Rücken, etc.) getragen wird.

Fit, match oder suit?

Bei den Verben **fit**, **match** und **suit** kann man schnell durcheinander kommen, da diese Verben im Deutschen alle mit passen übersetzt werden können, wo das Englischen für unterschiedliche Zusammenhänge nach einem jeweils anderen Verb verlangt. Diese Bedeutungsunterschiede muss man einfach lernen.

These trousers fit me.
Diese Hose passt mir [in Bezug auf die Größe].

These trousers match my sweater.
Diese Hose passt zu meinem Pulli [in Bezug auf die Farbe].

These trousers suit me.
Diese Hose steht mir [in Bezug auf das Aussehen].

When would it suit you?
Wann würde es dir passen [in Bezug auf die Zeit]?

9. Ergänze die folgenden Sätze mit der jeweils richtigen Form der Verben **fit, suit** oder **match**. Denke dabei auch immer an das **-s** in der 3. Person Singular!

a. Your wardrobe just doesn't ____________________ in my car.
b. The colour of the wall ____________________ the ceiling.
c. You can call me whenever it ______________ you.
d. Your new car really _________________ you!
e. I love to wear clothes that __________________ my hair colour.

BOXENSTOPP

Will man ausdrücken, dass etwas in Bezug auf die ________ passt, kann man **suit** verwenden. Darüber hinaus drückt das Verb aus, dass etwas in Bezug auf Aussehen und Stil gut zu etwas anderem passt.
Das Verb ________ benutzt man dagegen eher, wenn etwas in Bezug auf die Größe passt.
Und schließlich verwendet man ________ meist um auszudrücken, dass etwas in Bezug auf die Farbe zueinander passt.

Hear oder listen? See oder watch?

Die Verben **hear** und **see** beziehen sich auf eher *zufälliges, ungeplantes Hören und Sehen*, während **listen** und **watch** eine *bewusste, meist gewollte Tätigkeit* ausdrücken:

I heard a sudden noise. *Ich hörte plötzlich ein Geräusch.*
I saw Richard in town. *Ich sah Richard in der Stadt.*

I listened to the news / the music.
Ich hörte (mir) die Nachrichten / die Musik (an).
I watched an exciting film.
Ich sah (mir) einen spannenden Film (an).

Beachte folgende feststehende Wendungen:
to watch television, **to listen to the radio**

10. Entscheide, ob man **listen/watch** oder **hear/see** einsetzt.

a. ____________ to the tape recording and answer the following questions.
b. Can you ________________ the noise outside?
c. Let's ______________ that Brad Pitt movie tonight.
d. It's so dark. I can't ______________ you.

BOXENSTOPP

Wenn es um zufälliges, ungeplantes Hören und Sehen geht, benutzt man die Verben ____________ und ____________.
Wenn bewusstes oder gewolltes Hören und Sehen zum Ausdruck bringen will, verwendet man die Verben ____________ und ____________.

High oder tall?

Tall wird meist in Verbindung mit Sachen verwendet, die deutlich höher als breit sind (also z.B. für Menschen, Gebäude, Bäume, Türme, Schornsteine):

a tall person	**a tall TV tower**
eine große Person	*ein hoher Fernsehturm*

In anderen Fällen, z.B. bei ***Bergen*** oder ***Mauern***, wird eher **high** verwendet. Die meisten Dinge, die man im Deutschen als ***hoch*** bezeichnet, benutzt man im Englischen ebenfalls mit dem Adjektiv **high**:

a high level	**a high mountain**
ein hohes Niveau	*ein hoher Berg*

12. Streiche jeweils das Wort durch, das nicht passt:

a. a **high / tall** building
b. a **high / tall** rate
c. a **high / tall** man
d. a **high / tall** risk

BOXENSTOPP

Ergänze die folgende Tabelle mit Substantiven, die in Verbindung mit **high** bzw. **tall** benutzt werden. Wenn du dir dann später wieder einmal unsicher bist, ob man **tall** oder **high** verwendet, kannst du hier nachschauen!

high	tall
mountain, ...	person, tower, ...

Remind oder remember?

Die Wörter **remind** und **remember** werden oft verwechselt. Vor allem ist es verwirrend, dass im Deutschen **remember** reflexiv verwendet wird, im Englischen dagegen nicht.

Remember heißt *sich erinnern*, **remind** dagegen *jemanden (an etwas) erinnern*:
I can't remember her name.
Ich kann mich nicht an ihren Namen erinnern.
Remind me to phone Jane.
Erinnere mich daran, dass ich Jane anrufen muss.

12. Entscheide in den folgenden Sätzen jeweils, ob man **remind** oder **remember** einsetzen muss:

a. Tom wants to ____________ Jill to get him a new shirt for this evening.

b. Always ____________ to wear warm clothes when you go out.

c. I had to ____________ so many names on the list.

d. The pictures ____________ me of the good times we had.

BOXENSTOPP

Man benutzt **remind**, wenn man ____

______________________________________.

Man benutzt **remember**, wenn man ____

______________________________________.

Say oder tell?

Obwohl beide Verben ähnliche Bedeutungen haben, ist **say** allgemeiner, während **tell** meist den Sinn von ***informieren*** oder ***befehlen*** hat. Auch die möglichen Strukturen rund um beide Verben sind unterschiedlich.

Aufgepasst: vor einem Nebensatz ist oft nur **say** möglich:
She ~~told~~ said (that) she had a new job.
Sie erzählte / sagte, dass sie einen neuen Job habe.

Aber: vor einem Personalpronomen als Objekt funktioniert dagegen nur **tell**:
She ~~said~~ told me about her new job.
Sie erzählte mir von ihrem neuen Job.
They ~~said~~ told him to go home.
Sie sagten ihm, er sollte nach Hause gehen.

In der Regel braucht **tell** sowohl ein direktes als auch ein indirektes Objekt:
She never told me the real story.
Sie hat mir nie die wahre Geschichte erzählt.
*(**me** = direktes Objekt; **the real story** = indirektes Objekt).*

Die folgenden festen Ausdrücke sind Ausnahmen:
tell a joke / a story
einen Witz / eine Geschichte erzählen
tell a lie / the truth
lügen / die Wahrheit sagen

13. Entscheide in den folgenden Beispielen jeweils, welches Verb richtig ist. Beachte dabei die richtige Zeitform und streiche die falschen Antworten.

a. Your mother **said** / **tells** / **told** me not to disturb you.

b. Gerry **told** / **said** / **says** he would meet me at 7 o'clock in front of the cinema.

c. Could you **told** / **tell** / **say** us something about the English test, please?

d. Jim couldn't help me. He **told** / **said** / **tells** me to ask the teacher.

e. She **tells** / **said** / **says** her name was Janet.

f. I'd like to **say** / **told** / **tell** you something about my plans for the future.

BOXENSTOPP

Ergänze den Merksatz mit den folgenden Wörtern: Satzbau - informiert - allgemeinen - befiehlt

Say benutzt man eher in ____________________ Zusammenhängen. Mit **tell** ________________ man jemanden oder ___________________ etwas.

Außerdem muss man auf den _____________________ rund um die Verben **tell** and **say** achten, da dieser unterschiedlich ist.

Who oder where?

Das ist ein klassischer Anfängerfehler, der im Eifer des Gefechts auch Profis noch unterlaufen kann, da die vermeintliche Ähnlichkeit zwischen den deutschen und englischen Wörtern so groß ist. Es handelt sich hier schon fast um „Falsche Freunde".

Who und **where** werden häufig verwechselt. Wenn man dabei das Deutsche mit dem Englischen vergleicht, muss man hier „über Kreuz" denken.

Who ⟷ *wer*
Where ⟷ *wo*

14. Setze in den folgenden Sätzen jeweils **who** oder **where** ein:

a. I don't know __________ my keys are.

b. ______________ is the girl standing by the door?

c. Peter doesn't know __________ the entrance is.

d. ____________ is coming with me?

e. _____________ is my English book?

BOXENSTOPP

Who = ___________ **Where** = ___________

3 PROBLEMATISCHE VERBEN

Manche englische Verben bereiten Probleme in der Anwendung, da man sie genauso wie im Deutschen benutzen will.

Hier zwei Beispiele für ganz typische Fehler:

OK, I'll ~~make~~ do my homework!
In Ordnung, ich werde meine Hausaufgaben machen!
Waiter, may I ~~become~~ get a beefsteak, please?
Herr Ober, könnte ich bitte ein Beefsteak bekommen?

Sieh dir aber einfach einmal die folgenden Tabellen an und merke dir die problematischen Verben immer im konkreten Zusammenhang, dann kannst du eine ganze Reihe von typischen Fehlern vermeiden!

become

~~become~~ have a baby	*ein Baby bekommen*
~~become~~ get / receive a present	*ein Geschenk bekommen / kriegen*
become a teacher	*Lehrer/in werden*

do

do the washing / shopping	*die Wäsche / Einkäufe machen*
do well *gute Arbeit leisten/machen*	
~~make~~ do your hair / nails	*sich die Haare / Nägel machen*

get

get tired / old	*müde / alt werden*
~~get~~ have a baby	*ein Kind bekommen / haben*
Can I get a drink?	*Kann ich mir etwas zu trinken holen?*
Can I ~~get~~ have a drink?	*Kann ich etwas zu trinken bekommen?*
get married / divorced	*heiraten / sich scheiden lassen*
get something done	*etwas erledigen*

have

have breakfast / lunch	*frühstücken / zu Mittag essen*
have something done	*etwas machen lassen*

make

~~make~~ have an experience	*eine Erfahrung machen*
~~make~~ do / take a course	*einen Kurs machen*
~~make~~ do an internship	*ein Praktikum machen*
~~make~~ do homework	*Hausaufgaben machen*
~~make~~ take / sit an exam	*eine Prüfung machen / ablegen*
~~make~~ have / throw a party	*eine Party machen / ausrichten*
~~make~~ take a photo	*ein Foto machen*
make a phone call	*einen Anruf tätigen*
make an appointment	*einen Termin ausmachen*
make so do sth	*jemanden dazu zwingen etw. zu tun*

1. Sieh dir die folgenden deutschen Beispielsätze an und entscheide jeweils, welcher Satz die richtige Übersetzung ist. Streiche immer das Wort durch, das nicht passt!

a. *Jason macht seine Hausaufgaben.*

Jason	is making	his homework.
	is doing	

b. *Ich bekomme 10$ Taschengeld.*

I	get	10$ pocket money.
	become	

c. *Pamela möchte Anwältin werden.*

Pamela wants to	become	a lawyer.
	get	

d. *Mein Bruder lässt mich immer den Müll raus bringen.*

My brother always	makes	me take out the garbage.
	gets	

e. *Ich lasse meine Haare einmal im Monat schneiden.*

I	have	my hair cut once a month.
	become	

Einige Verben werden oft falsch verwendet, da sie ähnlich wie im Deutschen klingen. Man darf also **become** nicht mit dem deutschen Wort _________ verwechseln, und auch _________ bedeutet nicht immer ***machen***! Am besten merkt man sich die Verben **become**, **do**, **get**, **have** und **make** also immer im konkreten _________!

4 PROBLEMATISCHE ADJEKTIVE UND ADVERBIEN

Eigentlich bereiten Adjektive und Adverbien im Englischen kaum Probleme. Wo sich Adjektive im Deutschen immer an das zugehörige Substantiv anpassen, bleiben sie im Englischen in der Grundform immer gleich. Und wo im Deutschen die Unterscheidung zwischen Adjektiv und Adverb schwierig ist, weil die Formen gleich sind, ist die Unterscheidung aufgrund der Endung der Adverbien **-ly** im Englischen ganz einfach.

Wenn es nur nicht auch andere Formen und Ausnahmen gäbe, wie zum Beispiel: **Adverbien ohne -ly** oder **Adjektive, die auf -ly enden**, die Sonderfälle **good** und **well**, sowie einige Formen, die nur als Adjektiv oder Adverb auftreten können (**deadly**, **hardly**, **lately**, **shortly**).

Adverbien ohne -ly

Obwohl die meisten Adverbien durch Anhängen eines **-ly** an das Adjektiv geformt werden, gibt es eine ganze Menge Ausnahmen. Die folgenden Wörter werden in der angegebenen Bedeutung sowohl als Adjektiv als auch als Adverb gebraucht:

daily - *täglich*	**high** - *hoch*
early - *früh*	**late** - *spät*
fast - *schnell*	**low** - *niedrig*
hard - *hart*	**right** - *richtig*

1. Unterstreiche in den folgenden Sätzen zunächst das Adjektiv oder das Adverb und entscheide dann, ob das jeweilige Wort hier als Adjektiv oder als Adverb gebraucht wird:

a. She can run very fast. ___________

b. Janet is a fast runner. ___________

c. Mike got up early this morning. ___________

d. In his daily routine he always gets up at 7 o'clock. ___________

e. I had a bad accident in my early childhood. ___________

f. Julie has made the right decision. ___________

g. The newspaper is delivered daily. ___________

Adjektive, die auf -ly enden

Aufgepasst! Obwohl die folgenden Wörter auf -ly enden, handelt es sich hierbei um Adjektive und nicht um Adverbien:

cowardly - *feige*
lively - *lebendig*
lovely - *schön*
lonely - *einsam*
silly - *dumm / blöd*

Damit man solche Wörter überhaupt mit adverbialer Bedeutung verwenden kann, muss man sie mit Hilfe einer Umschreibung (**in a ... manner /way -** *in einer ... Art/Weise*) in den Satz einbetten:

She sang in a lovely way. — *Sie sang schön / auf schöne Weise.*
They reacted in a cowardly manner. — *Sie reagierten feige / auf feige Weise.*

Falsche Verwandte

Achtung! Die folgenden Wörter sehen zwar so aus, als wären sie die direkten adverbialen Verwandten von **dead** (*tot*), **hard** (*hart*, *schwierig*), **late** (*spät*) oder **short** (*kurz*).

Aber der Eindruck täuscht! Diese Wörter haben eine ganz eigene Bedeutung:

	Bedeutung	ausschließliche Verwendung
deadly	*tödlich*	Adjektiv
hardly	*kaum*	Adverb
lately	*in letzter Zeit*	Adverb
shortly	*bald, in Kürze*	Adverb

2. Welche Form passt? Streiche in den folgenden Sätzen das jeweils falsche Wort durch.

a. Last week he was bitten by a **dead** / **deadly** spider.
b. His brother had an accident last week. He is **deadly** / **dead** now.
c. He **hard** / **hardly** has time for any activities in the afternoon.
d. He works **hard** / **hardly** for his money.
e. Have you been to New York **lately** / **late**?
f. I was **late** / **lately** for school this morning.
g. We will **short** / **shortly** announce the results of the exams.
h. We will give a **short** / **shortly** report on the results.

Die Sonderfälle good und well

Das Adverb zu **good** ist **well**:

You speak English well.	*Du sprichst gut Englisch.*

Well kann aber im Sinne von ***in guter gesundheitlicher Verfassung*** auch als Adjektiv verwendet werden:

She's well.	*Ihr geht es gut.*

3. **Good** oder **well**? Setze in den folgenden Sätzen die jeweils richtige Form ein:

a. Michel is a ______________ dancer. He dances ___________.

b. I don't feel ___________, my head hurts.

c. Your English is very __________________!

d. I can't cook very _______________.

BOXENSTOPP

Es gibt verschiedene problematische Adjektive und Adverbien. Man kann diese aber in vier Gruppen einteilen:

Gruppe 1: Adverbien ohne **-ly** (Beispiel: ______________________________)

Gruppe 2: Adjektive auf **-ly** (Beispiel: ________________________________)

Gruppe 3: Falsche Verwandte (Beispiel: ______________________________)

Gruppe 4: Sonderfälle (Beispiel: ___________________________________)

Inhalt

Grammatik

Wortschatz

KLASSE 10

1 MODALE HILFSVERBEN

1 **Would** you **like** to go to the football match next Saturday?

2 Sure. **Shall** I **buy** the tickets?

3 No, you don't **need to**. I already have two tickets.

4 OK, I **can give** you the money then.

1. Würdest du nächsten Samstag gerne zum Fußballspiel gehen?
2. Oh ja. Soll ich die Tickets kaufen?
3. Nein, brauchst du nicht. Ich habe schon zwei Karten.
4. OK, ich kann dir dann das Geld geben.

Modale Hilfsverben

Modale Hilfsverben oder Modalverben (**modal verbs**, **modals**) erkennt man daran, dass ihnen immer ein Vollverb im Infinitiv folgt (außer in Kurzantworten). Es gibt sie nur in einer oder zwei Zeitformen; für die fehlenden Formen verwendet man **Ersatzformen**.

Die englischen Modalverben lauten:

present tense-Formen		past tense-Formen		deutsch
Langform/ Kurzform	verneinte Lang- und Kurzform	Langform/ Kurzform	verneinte Lang- und Kurzform	
can	**cannot/ can't**	**could**	**could not / couldn't**	*können*
will / 'll	**will not/ won't**	**would / 'd**	**would not / wouldn't**	*würden*
shall / 'll	**shall not/ shan't**	**should**	**should not / shouldn't**	*sollen*
may	**may not**	**might**	**might not / mightn't**	*dürfen*
must	**must not/mustn't**			*müssen*
need	**need not/needn't**			*brauchen*
		ought to (+ Infinitiv)	**ought not to / oughtn't to**	*dringend sollen*

!

will ≠ wollen!

Für das deutsche Modalverb **wollen** benutzt man im Englischen das Vollverb **want to + Infinitiv.**

!

must – *müssen*

mustn't – *nicht dürfen*

don't have to – *nicht müssen*

don't need to – *nicht brauchen (nicht müssen)*

Kennzeichen der modalen Hilfsverben

- Modalverben werden verwendet, wenn man mit seiner Aussage eine gewisse **Absicht** verfolgt (Bitte, Ratschlag, Aufforderung, Erlaubnis, Verbot usw.) oder eine **persönliche Einstellung** oder **Annahme** ausdrücken möchte.

Could you slow down a bit, please? I wouldn't drive so fast in this snow.

- Modalverben haben in allen Personen die gleiche Form.

Im **simple present** wird in der 3. Person Singular **kein s** angehängt.

Mike can do it for us. But Sheila may do it for us if she wants to.

! Vorsicht bei der scheinbaren Ausnahme need.

- Die verneinte Form wird **nicht** mit dem Hilfsverb **do**, sondern durch **Anhängen von not** (Kurzform **-n't**) gebildet.

Mike can't do it for us. Sheila shouldn't do it.

- Modalverben stehen bei der Bildung von **yes/no-questions** am Satzanfang.

Can you do this for me, please? — Must I really do it?

- Die past tense-Formen werden meist wie **Konjunktivformen** (dt. *könnte, würde, sollte* usw.) verwendet. Gelegentlich haben sie aber auch einfach Vergangenheitsbedeutung.

Can/could you help me, please?	*Kannst/Könntest du mir bitte helfen?*
She couldn't stay any longer.	*Sie konnte nicht länger bleiben.*

- Nach einem Modalverb folgt immer ein **Infinitiv ohne to**.

You may go and see your friend. But you must tidy up your room first.
She's so ill, she really ought to see a doctor.

! Vorsicht bei den Ausnahmen ought to.

Das Modalverb can/could

- Mit **can/could** kann man **Fähigkeiten** zum Ausdruck bringen, insbesondere bei **Verben der Wahrnehmung**. Die Ersatzform lautet dann **be able to**. Sie kann selbst auch im present und past tense verwendet werden.

I can't hear anything. We couldn't see very far because of the fog.
I've never been able to speak French properly.

- **Can/could** wird für **höfliche Fragen** und **Bitten (z. B. um Erlaubnis)** verwendet. Die Ersatzform lautet dann **be allowed to**. Auch **Vorschläge** sind möglich.

Can I have an apple, please? Please, could you close the door?
I don't think I'll be allowed to stay all night after the party.

- Mit **could + Infinitiv** bzw. **could have + past participle** kann man auch **Kritik** üben.

You could be more polite to your sister when you ask her to drive you.
You could have asked before you took my sweatshirt.

Das Modalverb will/would

Streng genommen ist **will/would** ein Hilfsverb zur Bildung des **will-future** und zur Bildung der **conditional-Formen**. Es gibt jedoch einige besondere Verwendungsformen:

- Mit **will/would you** kann man höflich um einen Gefallen bitten. **Would** ist dabei **höflicher** als **will**. Mit **I'll/we'll** kann man sich selbst anbieten, etwas zu tun. Ersatzformen für andere Personen und Zeitformen sind **be willing to** oder **be prepared to**.

Will you tell Mary to phone me?
We'll make a salad for the party.
Would you shut the door, please?
I hope Jamie is prepared to wait a while.

- Mit **would like to** kann man **Wünsche** ausdrücken oder danach fragen. Die Frage **Would you like to ...?** leitet meist **Angebote** oder **Einladungen** ein.

I'd like to go to Brighton on holiday.
Would you like to see the local gallery?

- Die **verneinte** Form **won't/wouldn't** wird manchmal im Sinne von **nicht wollen** benutzt. Dabei verwendet man **won't** für Gegenwart oder Zukunft, **wouldn't** für Vergangenes. Ersatzformen sind **refuse to, not be prepared to, not want to.**

I'd like to pick you up at the station, but the car won't start.
I asked him very politely, but he wouldn't tell me.
She has always refused to enter a plane.
Jimmy will not want to go skiing. You know he loves snowboarding.

SPRACHTIPP

Mit **will** werden manchmal auch **Annahmen**, mit **would frühere Gewohnheiten** zum Ausdruck gebracht:

Come on in. Mike **will** be happy to see you.

When I was a child we **would** go to the playground every Saturday.

SPRACHTIPP

Zur Äußerung von Wünschen bzw. Fragen danach kann man auch **want to** (oder förmlich **wish to**) verwenden.

Beachte, dass Fragen/Äußerungen mit **would (you) like to** höflicher sind als solche mit **want to**.

Das Modalverb shall/should

- Mit **shall** werden **höfliche Vorschläge** gemacht. Beachte, dass **shall** dann nur in der **1. Person Singular** und **Plural** verwendet werden kann:

Shall I get us some tea? **Shall we have stew for lunch?**

stew – *Eintopf*

- Mit **should** drückt man **Ratschläge**, **Verpflichtungen** und **Kritik** aus (dt. ‚sollte eigentlich').

You know, you should always ask before you borrow something.
You shouldn't eat so many sweets. It's bad for your teeth.

- Mit **should have + past participle** (dt. ‚hätte sollen') weist man auf einen **Fehler** oder ein **Versäumnis** hin.

You should at least have asked Peter before you took his bike!

SPRACHTIPP

Das deutsche ‚sollen' kann außerdem je nach Sprechabsicht folgendermaßen ausgedrückt werden:

be to – *sollen* (bei Auftrag, Vereinbarung)

I **am to** clean up my room today.

be said to,
be supposed to – *angeblich sollen*

She**'s said to/ supposed to** be from London.

Das Modalverb ought to

- Mit **ought to** wird eine **Verpflichtung** oder eine **dringende Notwendigkeit** ausgedrückt (dt. ‚sollte eigentlich', ‚sollte wirklich'), meist etwas stärker als mit **should**.

Terry ought to study regularly. **Ought we to stay a bit longer?**

Das Modalverb may/might

- Mit **may** bittet man höflich (**might**: sehr höflich) um **Erlaubnis** bzw. erlaubt man etwas. Entsprechend **verweigert** man mit **may not** eine **Erlaubnis**, besonders in **Kurzantworten** auf Fragen mit **may**. Als Ersatzform für past tense und andere Zeitformen verwendet man **be allowed to**.

May I have a cookie? No, you may not . But you may have an apple.
I wasn't allowed to have a dog when I was a child.

!

Für **may not** gibt es keine Kurzform!

- Mit **may** kann man in formellem Stil Wünsche formulieren.

May you both be very happy! Mögt ihr/Mögen Sie ... !

- **May** und **might** drücken eine **Möglichkeit** oder eine **Vermutung** aus (dt. ‚könnte (vielleicht)'). **Might** weist dabei auf eine **geringere Wahrscheinlichkeit** hin als **may.**

We may/might go to New Zealand at Christmas.

Das Modalverb must

- Mit **must** drückt man einen **starken Zwang** oder eine **Verpflichtung** aus. Bei **must** ist der Zwang/die Verpflichtung stärker als bei **should**. Die Ersatzform im past tense ist meist **had to**. Beachte, dass dann bei Fragen die **do-Umschreibung** verwendet werden muss!

I must go now, otherwise I'll miss the bus. — But you must try the fruit cake first.
He had to leave the concert early to catch the bus. — Did he have to run?

!

mustn't bedeutet **nicht dürfen** und nicht wie oft irrtümlich angenommen **nicht müssen!**

Für **Must I ...?** lauten die Kurzantworten Yes, you **must.**

oder

No, you **needn't.**

- Mit **must** lässt sich auch eine **starke Vermutung** ausdrücken. Es kann dann nicht durch **have (got) to** ersetzt werden.

It's ten o'clock. Then it must be the postman who's at the door.

Unterschied zwischen must und have to

Das Modalverb **must** und seine Ersatzform **have to + Infinitiv** haben im Gebrauch (nur im simple present) leicht unterschiedliche Bedeutung.

- Bei **must** hat das Subjekt den eigenen Wunsch oder das dringende Bedürfnis, etwas zu tun.

I must repair the computer. **We must invite Lisa.**

- Bei **have (got) to** kommt der Druck von außen. Die Person selbst möchte es vielleicht gar nicht tun, fühlt sich aber veranlasst zu handeln.

I have to repair the computer. **We have to invite Lisa.**

Das Modalverb need

Das Verb **need** kann als **Modalverb** und als **Vollverb** auftreten.

- Als **Modalverb** wird **need** meist nur in der **verneinten Form** in der Bedeutung von ‚**nicht müssen'/‚nicht brauchen'** benutzt. Auf needn't folgt wie bei den meisten anderen **modals** auch ein **Infinitiv ohne to**. Für andere Zeitformen verwendet man Formen von **not have to** als Ersatz. Seltener tritt **need** (bejaht) als **modal** auch in **Fragen** auf.

You needn't walk into town. I can give you a lift.
Need I bring a sleeping-bag?

Häufiger wird **need** als **Vollverb** benutzt. Es hat dann meist die Bedeutung von ‚**benötigen**'. Für **need** als Vollverb gelten alle Regeln wie für andere Vollverben auch:

- **do-Umschreibung** in Fragen und verneinten Sätzen

Do you need a pencil? - No thank you, I don't need one.

SPRACHTIPP

Es ist nicht falsch, **need** immer als Vollverb zu benutzen.

- need in der 3. Person Singular hat ein **s**

Sarah needs a new pair of jeans.

- **alle Zeitformen** können gebildet werden

Yesterday mum needed the car but tomorrow she won't need it.

- nach need kann ein Verb im **Infinitiv mit to** angeschlossen werden

I need to buy a new washing machine. But I don't need to buy a tumble-drier.

tumble drier – *Wäschetrockner*

Die selteneren Modalverben dare und used to

Das Verb **dare** kann (wie need) als **Modalverb** und als **Vollverb** auftreten.

- Als **Modalverb** wird **dare** (‚wagen', ‚sich trauen') nur in der **verneinten Form** und in **Ausrufen mit 'How ...!'** verwendet. Selten ist die past tense-Form **dared**. Es gelten die Regeln wie bei **need als Modalverb**, s. o.

She daren't walk home alone at night. **How dare you take my bike!**

- Als **Vollverb** benutzt man **dare** meist in **verneinten Sätzen** und **Fragen**. Es gelten ansonsten die Regeln wie bei **need als Vollverb**, s.o.

I wouldn't dare to touch that dog! **Did you really dare to play with him?**

Das Verb **used to** (+ Infinitiv) existiert nur in der past tense-Form und drückt eine **Gewohnheit** oder einen **Zustand** in der **Vergangenheit** aus (dt. ‚früher', manchmal auch ohne Übersetzung). Verneinte Formen sind **used not to, didn't use to, never used to**.

Jane used to take guitar lessons.
It didn't use to be so warm in summer a few years ago.

Ersatzformen für Modalverben

1 Great, since we are 18 we can stay out as long as we want to.

2 That's right, when we were younger, we had to fight for every hour.

1. Toll, seit wir 18 sind, können wir so lange ausbleiben, wie wir möchten.
2. Stimmt, als wir jünger waren, mussten wir um jede Stunde kämpfen.

Modalverben kommen nur im **simple present** und/oder **simple past** vor. Daher muss man in anderen Zeitstufen Ersatzformen mit gleicher oder sehr ähnlicher Bedeutung benutzen.

modal verb	Ersatzform
can, could	**be able to, be allowed to**
will, shall	**be going to (be prepared to, be willing to)**
may, might	**be allowed to**
must	**have to**
should, ought to	**be supposed to**
needn't	**not have to**
mustn't	**not be allowed to**

Bildung der Ersatzformen

Die Ersatzformen werden entweder mit **be** oder mit **have** gebildet.
Der Rest der Ersatzform bleibt bei der Zeitenbildung immer **unverändert**.
Auch nach den Ersatzformen folgt immer ein Infinitiv.

Ersatzformen mit **be**

	I	you/we/they	he/she/it
Simple Present	**am (not)**	**are (not)/aren't**	**is (not)/isn't**
Simple Past	**was(not)/ wasn't**	**were (not)/ weren't**	**was (not)/ wasn't**
Future	**will (not) be/ won't be**	**will (not) be/won't be**	**will (not) be/ won't be**
Conditional	**would (not) be/ wouldn't be**	**would (not) be/ wouldn't be**	**would (not) be/ wouldn't be**
unveränderliche Form	**able to, going to, allowed to, supposed to**		
+ Infinitiv	**come** to the party, **go** to town, **stay** at home, etc.		

Beachte, dass **have** im simple present und simple past für Verneinung und Frage die **do-Umschreibung** benötigt, **be** jedoch nicht.

Ersatzformen mit **have**

must

	I/you/we/they	he/she/it
Simple Present	**have/'ve to**	**has/'s to**
Simple Past	**had/'d to**	**had/'d to**
Future	**will/'ll have to**	**will/'ll have to**
Conditional	**would/'d have to**	**would/'d have to**
+ Infinitiv	**come to the party, go to town, stay at home, etc.**	

needn't

	I/you/we/they	he/she/it
Simple Present	**do not/don't have to**	**does not/doesn't have to**
Simple Past	**did not/didn't have to**	**did not/didn't have to**
Future	**will not/won't have to**	**will not/won't have to**
Conditional	**would not/wouldn't have to**	**would not/wouldn't have to**
+ Infinitiv	**come to the party, go to town, stay at home, etc.**	

Fragen mit Modalverben

Fragen mit **modals** und deren **Ersatzformen** werden nach dem gleichen Muster wie Fragen mit den Hilfsverben do oder have gebildet: Das (erste) Modalverb oder das (erste) Hilfsverb (bei den Ersatzformen) steht am Satzanfang vor dem Subjekt. **Fragewörter** werden den **modals** vorangestellt. Zur Bildung von **Kurzantworten** verwendet man das erste Modal- oder Hilfsverb aus der Frage, außer bei höflichen Fragen mit **would**.

Modalverb bzw. Ersatzform am Satzanfang:

Can you come to my party?	**Yes, I can./No, I can't.**
Have you been able to relax?	**Yes, I have./No, I haven't.**
May I invite my friends?	**Yes, you may./No, you may not.**
Will you be allowed to come?	**Yes, I will./No, I won't.**
Must I really eat the brussels sprouts ?	**Yes, you must./No, you needn't.**
Did you have to work?	**Yes, I did./No, I didn't.**
Would you like a cup of tea?	**Yes, please./No, thank you.**

brussels sprouts – *Rosenkohl*

Fragewort am Satzanfang:

Who can come to my party?	I think everybody can.
Why haven't you **been able to** relax?	Because I had so much work to do.
How many friends **may** I invite?	As many as you want.
When will you **be allowed** to come?	I don't know yet.
Why must I eat the brussels sprouts?	Because they are healthy.
How long did you **have to** work?	Until the early afternoon.
Would you **like** a cup of tea?	Yes, please./No, thank you.

Besondere Ausdrucksweisen mit Modalverben

Modals in der Konstruktion mit **have + past participle** können folgende Bedeutungsunterschiede zum Ausdruck bringen:

- Vermutungen über Ereignisse in der Vergangenheit:

Greta **will** have missed the train.	*Greta wird den Zug verpasst haben.*
Greta **may** have missed the train.	*Greta könnte den Zug verpasst haben.*
Greta **might** have missed the train.	*Greta könnte den Zug vielleicht verpasst haben.*
Greta **must** have missed the train.	*Greta muss den Zug verpasst haben.*
Greta **can't** have missed the train.	*Greta kann den Zug nicht verpasst haben.*

Nur **might** kann sowohl eine Vermutung als auch eine nicht eingetroffene Möglichkeit in der Vergangenheit ausdrücken.

- Nicht eingetroffene Möglichkeiten in der Vergangenheit:

Greta **would** have missed the train.	*Greta hätte den Zug verpasst.*
Greta **could** have missed the train.	*Greta hätte den Zug verpassen können.*
Greta **should** have missed the train.	*Greta hätte den Zug verpassen sollen.*
Greta **might** have missed the train.	*Greta hätte den Zug möglicherweise verpasst.*

Modals in der Konstruktion mit **be + present participle** können folgende Bedeutungen haben:

- Starke Vermutungen in der Gegenwart:

*Nick **must** be joking.*	*Nick macht bestimmt Witze.*
*Susan **must** be lying.*	*Susan lügt garantiert/höchstwahrscheinlich.*
*Nick **may** be joking.*	*Es kann sein, dass Nick Witze macht.*
*Nick **might** be joking.*	*Es könnte vielleicht sein, dass Nick Witze macht.*
Nick could be joking.	*Es könnte sein, dass Nick Witze macht.*

Vergleiche mit dem present progressive:

Nick is joking. – *Nick macht Witze.* (Tatsache)

Susan is lying. – *Susan lügt.* (Tatsache)

Vorsicht bei der Schreibweise:

lie – *lügen, Lüge*

She's lying. – *Sie lügt.*

* **1.** Ordne den deutschen Verben die englischen **Modalverben** zu.

wollen:	*nicht wollen:*
können:	*nicht können:*
sollen:	*nicht sollen:*
müssen:	*nicht müssen:*
brauchen:	*nicht brauchen:*
dürfen:	*nicht dürfen:*

** **2.** Setze die folgenden Aussagen in die Vergangenheit.

1. Mark **can explain** how the new gadget works.

____

2. Monica **mustn't walk** home on her own.

____

3. You **shouldn't ring** her up after 10 p.m.

____

4. **May** the children **have** some chocolate?

____

5. **Must** we **argue**?

____

6. You **needn't clean** my desk.

____

7. I **can't leave** her alone.

____

8. You **ought to post** those letters.

____

9. Do you **have to take** your little sister everywhere?

____

3. In welcher Zeitform steht die **Ersatzform** und welches **Modalverb** steckt jeweils dahinter?

Ersatzformform	**Zeitform**	**Modalverb**
will be able to	—	—
was allowed to	—	—
won't have to	—	—
was going to	—	—
didn't have to	—	—
were able to	—	—
will be supposed to	—	—
weren't allowed to	—	—
wouldn't be able to	—	—
will be allowed to	—	—

4. Ein Großvater unterhält sich mit seinem Enkel. Setze ein **Modalverb** oder eine **Ersatzform** in die Lücke.

When I was a young boy I *(musste helfen)* ________________ my parents on the farm in the afternoon. There was so much to do that I *(durfte nicht spielen)* ________________ with my friends. You are lucky. You *(kannst spielen)* ________________ football with your friends all afternoon. You *(solltest nicht sein)* ________________ angry if you *(musst helfen)* ________________ your parents from time to time. You *(darfst nicht vergessen)* ________________ that everybody in the family *(sollte beisteuern)* ________________ his or her share.

contribute one's share – *beisteuern*

5. Übertrage die folgenden Sätze ins Deutsche.

1. May I help you? ________________
2. I had asked you to clean the kitchen window only. You didn't have to clean all the windows.

____

____

3. After we had taken a break we were able to go on.

____

4. You might think I'm jealous, but I'm not.

____

5. Do you think I ought to ask for more money?

____

6. You mustn't park your car here.

____

7. I wouldn't allow the girls to stay up until midnight.

____

8. Linda's colleague was allowed to leave an hour earlier, but Linda wasn't.

____

★★★ **6.** Übertrage die Sätze ins Englische.

1. *Es ist 20 Uhr. Wir sollten die Nachrichten schauen.*

____

2. *Du brauchst mir nicht zu helfen. Ich kann es selbst tun.*

____

3. *Ich muss dir die neuesten Neuigkeiten erzählen.*

____

4. *Sollen wir dich abholen?*

____

5. *Wir könnten dich hinterher auch nach Hause bringen.*

____

6. *Du darfst Vater jetzt nicht stören.*

____

7. *Ich brauche einen neuen Job.*

____

2 PRONOMEN

1. *Oje, schau dir das Wetter an! Unser Flugzeug wird nicht pünktlich starten.*
2. *Keine Sorge, mein Bruder holt uns ab. Ich rufe ihn an und gebe ihm Bescheid, dass wir uns verspäten werden.*

Die Personalpronomen

SPRACHTIPP

Nach dem Subjekt eines Satzes fragt man: Wer oder was?

Nach dem Dativobjekt fragt man: Wem?

Nach dem Akkusativobjekt fragt man: Wen oder was?

Pronomen (pronouns) stehen für ein Wort (dt. Fürwort) und ersetzen einen Namen oder ein Substantiv. Die entsprechende Person oder Sache ist bekannt. Man möchte sie aber nicht wiederholen. Personalpronomen (personal pronouns) können Subjekt oder Objekt des Satzes sein. Je nachdem haben sie meist auch unterschiedliche Formen. (Übrigens: Die beiden Objektformen Akkusativ und Dativ sind im Englischen immer identisch.)

Subjekt (wer?)		Akkusativ-Objekt (wen?)		Dativ-Objekt (wem?)	
I	*ich*	**me**	*mich*	**me**	*mir*
you	*du/Sie*	**you**	*dich/Sie*	**you**	*dir/Ihnen*
he	*er*	**him**	*ihn*	**him**	*ihm*
she	*sie*	**her**	*sie*	**her**	*ihr*
it	*es*	**it**	*es*	**it**	*ihm/ihr*
we	*wir*	**us**	*uns*	**us**	*uns*
you	*ihr/Sie*	**you**	*euch/Sie*	**you**	*euch/Ihnen*
they	*sie*	**them**	*sie*	**them**	*ihnen*

Das englische ‚you' im Singular und Plural (deutsch: du/ihr) wird auch für das deutsche ‚Sie' (höfliche Anredeform) im Singular und Plural gebraucht.

Gebrauch der Personalpronomen als Subjekt und als Objekt

Justin, are you ready?	→	Wer? *du/Sie*
Justin, I'm waiting for you.	→	Wen? *dich/Sie*
Justin, I told you to hurry up.	→	Wem? *dir/Ihnen*
Where is Christine? Is she at home already?	→	Wer? *sie*
Sorry, I haven't seen her.	→	Wen? *sie*
Would you like to talk to her?	→	(mit) Wem? *ihr*
We can ask Susan for help.	→	Wer? *wir*
No, we can't. She invited us to her party.	→	Wen? *uns*
She can't help us at the weekend.	→	Wem? *uns*
Would you like to have a dog?		
It could easily live with you in your big house.	→	Wer? *er*
I can't afford it.	→	Wen? *ihn*
I can't give it a comfortable home. I have to work all day.	→	Wem? *ihm*

SPRACHTIPP

Im Englischen und Amerikanischen spricht man sich sehr viel häufiger mit dem Vornamen an. Der höfliche Umgangston wird aber durch den Vornamen und das ‚you' nicht gemindert.

Aufgepasst! Für Tiere und Gegenstände allgemein steht immer das sächliche Pronomen **it**! Nur für Tiere, zu denen man eine besondere Beziehung hat (z. B. Haustiere), verwendet man auch **he** oder **she**.

That's our dog Margie. She's afraid of fireworks.

Entsprechend kann auch für Dinge (z. B. Autos, Schiffe, Flugzeuge) das Pronomen **she** stehen (aber nicht **he**).

That's the Queen Mary 2. She's the largest ocean liner ever built.

Aufgepasst! Steht ein Pronomen alleine oder direkt nach dem Verb **be**, so muss die Objektform verwendet werden:

Did you call me so late last night or was it Melanie? — It wasn't me. It was her.	*Hast du mich gestern Abend so spät angerufen oder war es Melanie? Ich war es nicht. Sie war es.*
Who wants ice cream? — Me.	*... Ich.*

Besonderheiten

Nach den Verben **make, give, send, lend, pass, promise, sell, tell** und **show** stehen oft zwei Objekte bzw. Objektpronomen: ein Akkusativobjekt (direktes Objekt) und ein Dativobjekt (indirektes Objekt). Hier gibt es für die Objekte zwei Möglichkeiten der Wortstellung!

1. Das Dativ-Objekt steht **vor** dem Akkusativ-Objekt:

Subjekt	Prädikat	Dativ-Objekt	Akkusativ-Objekt
I	**can make**	**you**	**a cup of coffee.**
He	**gave**	**his wife**	**the keys.**
Mr Sams	**showed**	**Mrs Carrie**	**the new collection.**

2. Das Dativ-Objekt steht **hinter** dem Akkusativ-Objekt und wird mit **to** oder **for** angehängt:

Subjekt	Prädikat	Akkusativ-Objekt	Dativ-Objekt
I	**can make**	**a cup of coffee.**	**for you.**
He	**gave**	**the keys.**	**to his wife.**
Mr Sams	**showed**	**the new collection.**	**to Mrs Carrie.**

Achtung: nur bei dieser Wortstellung kann das Akkusativ-Objekt auch durch ein Pronomen ersetzt werden.

Subjekt	Prädikat	Akkusativ-Objekt	Dativ-Objekt
I	**can make**	**it**	**for you.**
He	**gave**	**them**	**to his wife.**
Mr Sams	**showed**	**it**	**to Mrs Carrie.**

SPRACHTIPP

Bei den meisten Verben wird das Dativobjekt mit **to** angeschlossen. Bei folgenden Verben wird das Dativobjekt mit **for** angeschlossen: **buy, cook, get, make, find,** etc.

Allgemeine Personalpronomen

1 They say that the Indian summer is the most beautiful season.

2 You never know. It may get quite cold at night.

1. Man sagt, dass der Indianersommer die schönste Jahreszeit ist.
2. Man kann nie wissen. Es kann nachts ziemlich kalt werden.

Die allgemeinen Personalpronomen (general personal pronouns) **one, you, they, people** (dt.: *man*) können für jede beliebige Person stehen. Sie werden verwendet, wenn man einen Sachverhalt verallgemeinert oder niemand Bestimmtes meint. **One** und **you** schließen dabei den Sprecher selbst mit ein, wohingegen **they** und **people** sich nur auf andere beziehen.

one für formale Aussagen:	
One shouldn't smoke here.	*Man sollte hier nicht rauchen.*
you für Umgangssprache:	
You can still use it.	*Man kann das noch gebrauchen.*
they / people für mehrere unbekannte Personen oder einen bestimmten Personenkreis:	
They should sit together and discuss the problems.	*Man sollte sich zusammensetzen und die Probleme diskutieren.*
People are expecting the final results tomorrow.	*Man erwartet die letzten Ergebnisse morgen.*

SPRACHTIPP

Typische Redewendungen sind z. B.:

One is as old as one feels.
Man ist so alt, wie man sich fühlt.

You can never tell.
Man kann nie wissen.

Die Possessivbegleiter

Possessivbegleiter (possessive determiners) geben Besitzverhältnisse an. Sie stehen wie ein Artikel vor dem Substantiv, ersetzen es aber nicht.

Singular:		Plural:	
my	*mein*	**our**	*unser*
your	*dein/Ihr*	**your**	*euer/Ihr*
his	*sein*	**their**	*ihr*
her	*ihr*		
its	*sein/ihr*		

Possessivbegleiter bleiben unverändert im Singular und Plural, z. B.:

Singular: **My brother is nice.**	*Mein Bruder ist nett.*
Plural: **My brothers are nice.**	*Meine Brüder sind nett.*

Possessivbegleiter bleiben unverändert im Akkusativ und Dativ, z. B.:

Akkusativ:	**I like my brother.**	*Ich mag meinen Bruder.*
Dativ:	**I always help my brother.**	*Ich helfe meinem Bruder immer.*

Folgende Formen dürfen nicht miteinander verwechselt werden:

Is this **your** car?
Ist das Ihr Auto?

Is this **her** car?
Ist das ihr Auto?

the car and **its** tyres
das Auto und seine Reifen

I've washed the car. **It's** clean now.
... Es ist jetzt sauber.

Beachte die Verwendung der Possessivbegleiter bei Kleidungsstücken, Körperteilen u. Ä.:

You won't need your swimsuit in Iceland, but you should take your backpack.	*... den Badeanzug* *... den Rucksack ...*
He cut his finger on a knife.	*Er schnitt sich den Finger an einem Messer.*

Soll die Zugehörigkeit zu etwas oder jemandem betont werden, kann der entsprechende Possessivbegleiter durch **own** (dt.: *eigen*) verstärkt werden. Dabei gibt es zwei Möglichkeiten der Satzkonstruktion:

1. **Possessivbegleiter + own + Substantiv**
2. **Substantiv + of + Possessivbegleiter + own**

Children have their own ideas.
Children have ideas of their own.
} *Kinder haben ihre eigenen Vorstellungen.*

Own muss immer mit einem Possessivbegleiter stehen:

I've got **my own** car now.

Ausdrücke wie ‚ein(e)/kein(e)/der (die, das) eigene' dürfen also nicht wörtlich ins Englische übersetzt werden.

Die Possessivpronomen

Wie Personalpronomen ersetzen auch Possessivpronomen ein Substantiv. Sie stehen **für** ein Substantiv mit Possessivbegleiter, das zuvor genannt wurde oder bekannt ist und können alleine stehen.

That's a nice coat. Is it yours? (anstatt: Is it your coat?)

Singular:		Plural:	
mine	*meines, meine, meiner*	**ours**	*unseres, unsere, unser*
yours	*deines, deine, deiner/ Ihres, Ihre, Ihrer*	**yours**	*euers/eures, eure, euer/Ihres, Ihre, Ihrer*
his	*seines, seine, seiner*	**theirs**	*ihres, ihre, ihrer*
hers	*ihres, ihre, ihrer*		
its	*seines, seine, seiner/ ihres, ihre, ihrer*		

Possessivpronomen bleiben im Englischen unverändert, egal ob das Substantiv, das sie ersetzen, im Singular oder Plural steht. Besonders häufig treten sie in Antworten auf Fragen mit **whose** zusammen mit dem Verb **be** auf.

Singular:	**Is this your book? — Yes, it's mine.** **Whose is this coat? — It's not hers.**
Plural:	**Are these your books?— Yes, they're mine.** **Whose are these shoes?— They're not hers.**

SPRACHTIPP

Diese Konstruktion funktioniert wie der doppelte Genitiv: He's a friend **of my sister's.**

Häufig wird im Englischen auch die Konstruktion **of + Possessivpronomen** benutzt.

Did I tell you about Lisa? **She's a friend of mine.**	... *Sie ist eine Freundin von mir.*
May I introduce you to Peter? **He's a colleague of ours.**	... *Er ist ein Kollege von uns.*

Die Reflexivpronomen

Reflexivpronomen sind rückbezügliche Fürwörter.
Sie beziehen sich zurück auf das Subjekt im Satz.
Im Deutschen sagt man: ich ... mich/mir, du ... dich/dir usw.

Personalpronomen	Reflexivpronomen	deutsch
I	**myself**	*ich ... mich/mir*
you	**yourself**	*du ... dich/dir bzw. Sie ... sich*
he	**himself**	*er ... sich*
she	**herself**	*sie ... sich*
it	**itself**	*es ... sich*
one	**oneself**	*man ... sich*
we	**ourselves**	*wir ... uns*
you	**yourselves**	*ihr ... euch bzw. Sie ...sich*
they	**themselves**	*sie ... sich*

!

Das Reflexivpronomen hat im Englischen stets eine andere Form als das Personalpronomen:

He introduced **them**.
Er stellte sie vor.

They introduced **themselves**.
Sie stellten sich vor.

Gebrauch der Reflexivpronomen

1. Reflexivpronomen werden gebraucht, wenn Subjekt (wer?) und Objekt (wen? wem?) im Satz die gleiche Person oder Sache sind.

Oh no, I've cut myself.	*Oh nein, ich habe mich geschnitten.*
Tina looked at herself in the mirror.	*Tina schaute sich im Spiegel an.*

!

Singular: yourself
Plural: yourselves

2. Reflexivpronomen werden im Englischen auch gebraucht, um den Verursacher einer Tätigkeit besonders hervorzuheben. Soll also im Satz ein Substantiv oder Pronomen besonders betont werden, stellt man ein Reflexivpronomen dahinter. Im Deutschen benutzt man das Wort „selbst“.

Leave her. She wants to do it herself.	*Lass sie. Sie will es selbst machen.*

SPRACHTIPP

Viele englische Heimwerkermärkte zeigen ein

DIY = Do it yourself!
Mach/Machen Sie es selbst!

Help yourself!
Bedien dich/ Bedienen Sie sich!

Enjoy yourself!
Viel Spaß!

Behave yourself!
Benimm dich/ Benehmen Sie sich!

!

Geht es um Gegenseitigkeit, kann kein Reflexivpronomen verwendet werden.

Soll das Subjekt betont werden, kann man das Reflexivpronomen auch ans Satzende stellen.

I spoke to the author herself at the reading.	*Ich sprach mit der Autorin selbst bei der Lesung.*
The children can tidy up their rooms themselves.	*Die Kinder können ihre Zimmer selbst aufräumen.*

3. Im Plural gibt es eine Besonderheit, die reziproken Pronomen (reciprocal pronouns).

each other, one another	*sich einander/gegenseitig, jeder dem anderen und jeder den anderen*
They looked at each other and smiled.	*Sie schauten sich an und lächelten.*
We give each other little presents for Christmas.	*Wir schenken uns zu Weihnachten kleine Geschenke.*
People should learn to listen to one another.	*Die Leute sollten lernen, sich/einander zuzuhören.*
Do you know each other?	*Kennt ihr euch? Kennen Sie sich?*

4. Es gibt Verben, die im Deutschen reflexiv benutzt werden, d. h. sie werden immer mit einem Reflexivpronomen benutzt. Bei der englischen Übersetzung ist das meist nicht so, wie die folgenden Beispiele zeigen:

sich streiten	*argue*
(sich) fürchten	*be afraid (of)*
sich (ver)ändern	*change*
sich beschweren über	*complain about*
sich konzentrieren (auf)	*concentrate (on)*
sich anziehen	*get dressed*
sich beeilen	*hurry*
sich (etwas) vorstellen	*imagine (sth.)*
sich freuen (auf)	*look forward (to)*
sich bewegen	*move*
sich (an etwas) erinnern	*remember*
sich setzen	*sit down*
sich fragen	*wonder*

Her parents never argue.	*Ihre Eltern streiten sich nie.*
Please, sit down.	*Bitte setz dich./Bitte setzen Sie sich.*

° Demonstrativpronomen und -begleiter

Demonstrativpronomen und -begleiter (demonstrative pronouns and determiners) weisen besonders betont auf jemanden oder etwas hin. Im Englischen gibt es eine Singular- und eine Pluralform, aber sie verändern ihre Form im Dativ oder Akkusativ nicht.

Singular:		**Plural:**	
this	*dieser/diese/dieses*	**these**	*diese*
that	*das bzw. jener/jene/jenes*	**those**	*jene*

Beachte:
this [ðis]
aber **these** [ði:z]

Gebrauch von this, that, these und those

This (Singular) und **these** (Plural) werden für räumlich, zeitlich oder geistig **nahe** Personen/Sachen verwendet (dt.: *dies hier*).

Watch this scene. It's brilliant.	*Schau dir diese Szene an. Sie ist fantastisch.*
These are the best films.	*Dies sind die besten Filme.*

That (Singular) und **those** (Plural) werden für räumlich, zeitlich oder geistig **weiter entfernte** Personen/Sachen verwendet (dt.: *jenes/dieses dort drüben*).

How much is that ring over there?	*Wie viel kostet der Ring dort drüben?*
And how much are those?	*Und wie viel kosten diese dort?*

This, that, these und those können als **Demonstrativbegleiter** vor Substantiven stehen. Sie können aber auch als **Demonstrativpronomen** allein stehen, wenn die Person(en) oder Sache(n) bekannt sind.

These colours are too dark.	*Diese Farben sind zu dunkel.*
Those are even darker.	*Jene sind sogar noch dunkler.*

Sollen zwei Personen oder Dinge einander gegenübergestellt werden, sagt man zuerst **this**, dann **that**. So kann man auch räumlich oder zeitlich Näheres von Entferntem unterscheiden.

This is my sister and that man over there is my brother.	*Dies ist meine Schwester und der Mann dort drüben ist mein Bruder.*
These oranges are from India and those over there are from Brazil.	*Diese Orangen sind aus Indien und diese/jene dort sind aus Brasilien.*

SPRACHTIPP

In der Umgangssprache kann man sowohl **this** als auch **that** verwenden, wenn es nicht um eine Gegenüberstellung geht.

he you you he I her it his you she he it they we

★ **1.** Setze die richtigen Personalpronomen oder Possessivbegleiter ein.

1. Mr Cranford is English. ______ is from Leicester.

2. ______ new office is in the city centre. ______ is next to the post office.

3. Mr Cranford's wife is Irish. ______ is from Cork.

4. ______ family is still in Ireland.

5. The Cranfords have got three children, two girls and one boy. ______ are always late in the morning.

6. Mr Cranford: "Sarah and Helen, where are ______ ?"

7. Sarah and Helen: " ______ are in the bathroom."

8. Mr Cranford: "And where is Alex? Is ______ ready?"

9. Sarah: " ______ don't know where ______ is."

10. Mr Cranford: "Hurry up. ______ must get the bus.

11. ______ doesn't wait for ______ ."

★ **2.** "At the market": Setze **this, that, these** oder **those** ein.

______ green apples are much cheaper than ______ green apples over there. Yes, and a pound of ______ tomatoes is also cheaper than a pound of ______ . What about a pineapple for our fruit salad? ______ pineapple looks good. No, ______ pineapple over there is much bigger. OK, let's take ______ one over there. And here are oranges from Brazil. Let's take five of ______ oranges. OK, ______ 's all then.

★★ **3.** Ersetze die vorgegebenen Personen, Gegenstände und Begriffe durch ein **Personalpronomen** und übersetze das Personalpronomen dann ins Deutsche.

	English	**German**
Mrs Craft	she	sie
Tim		
a fish		
Mr and Mrs Terence		
you and me		
my aunt		

our cat Tinker		
two e-mails		
Thomas and me		
Thomas and you		
Mrs Stone and her son		
the problems		
a chance		
a kindergarten		

BE: **kindergarten** – *Kindergarten*

AE: **kindergarten** – *Vorschule*

** **4.** Übersetze ins Englische. Verwende die Pronomen in den Kästchen für das **sie/Sie** in den folgenden Sätzen. Eines von ihnen wird 2 x benötigt.

she
they
you
her
it
them

1. *Die Tickets sind nicht da. Wo könnten sie sein?*

____

2. *Julian und sein Freund sind zu Hause. Sie spielen ein Computerspiel.*

____

____

3. *Hallo, Herr Baxter. Können Sie uns bitte helfen?*

____

4. *Meine Frau kann heute nicht kommen. Sie ist krank.*

____

5. *Deine Mutter kann dir helfen. Frag sie.*

____

6. *Was für eine schöne Blume! Stell sie bitte in den Garten.*

____

____

7. *Vielleicht können unsere Eltern uns ein bisschen Geld geben. Wir können sie anrufen.*

____

____

!

Beachte die Satzstellung im Englischen:

S-P-O

5. Welche der Pronomen für **sie** bzw. **Sie** aus Übung 4. entsprechen im englischen Satz jeweils einem Subjekt oder einem Objekt? Ordne ihnen die passenden grammatischen Begriffe **Personalpronomen Subjekt** oder **Personalpronomen Objekt** zu.

LERNTIPP

Nach dem Subjekt fragt man: Wer oder was?

Nach dem Objekt fragt man: Wen oder was?

1. Personalpronomen Subjekt
2. ______
3. ______
4. ______
5. ______
6. ______
7. ______

6. Setze in die Lücken **they're, their** oder **there** ein. Der Zusammenhang hilft dir bei der Entscheidung.

Vergleiche:

they're = they are (dt.: *sie sind*)

their (dt.: *ihr* (Plural))

there (dt.: *dort*)

Die Aussprache ist für alle drei gleich: [ðeə]

1. Betty and Anne Townsend live in London. ______ sisters.

2. They have a cat. ______ cat's name is Tickle.

3. The Townsends live in ______ own house but ______ not rich.

4. Margaret is ______ best friend. She lives over ______ .

5. Margaret's two children are very nice. ______ still students at a college nearby.

6. Margaret is talking to Anne about ______ new project.

7. "Hi, Margaret, where are the girls today?" — „Hi, Anne. ______ in the castle today. ______ 's an exhibition. ______ teacher told them to look at all the modern paintings and describe one of them."

8. "Well, I see. ______ was an article about that exhibition in the newspaper last week. The Brooks and ______ boys went ______ at the weekend. They were quite impressed."

7. Übersetze die Sätze ins Englische. Beachte dabei den richtigen Einsatz von Personal- und Demonstrativpronomen und -begleitern.

1. *Wir brauchen unsere Bücher.*

______

2. *Bitte gib mir die Tasche dort drüben. Es ist meine.*

______

3. *Das dort ist sein Geschenk. Dies hier ist deines.*

4. *Ich kann dir ihre Adresse geben.*

5. *Steven und Thomas, wo sind eure Handschuhe?*

gloves – *Handschuhe*

coat – *Mantel*

6. *Ist das mein Mantel? Ja, das ist Ihrer.*

7. *Ihren Reisepass, bitte!*

8. *Unsere Nachbarn sind in London. Ihre Kinder sind allein zu Hause.*

9. *Man kann nie wissen!*

** **8.** Ordne den angefangenen Sätzen das richtige Ende zu.

1. I can behave
2. The two girls looked at
3. The man couldn't repair the car
4. We have to help her. She can't help
5. They hate
6. Come on, Mark, you can do it
7. Michael and Steven, enjoy
8. Joanne and Julia, can I help you? No, thanks. We can do it
9. The Morgans built their house

___ A each other.
___ B ourselves.
___ C yourself.
___ D themselves.
___ E yourselves!
___ F myself.
___ G each other.
___ H himself.
___ I herself.

apologize – *sich entschuldigen*

! Im Deutschen reflexiv, im Englischen nicht!

look forward (to sth.) – *sich (auf etwas) freuen*

*** **9.** Übertrage die folgenden Sätze ins Englische.

1. *Ich möchte mich entschuldigen.*

2. *Du kannst dir das nicht vorstellen!*

3. *Meine Kinder verändern sich ständig.*

4. *Ich kann mich nicht an diesen Film erinnern.*

5. *Unsere Nachbarn freuen sich immer auf Besuch.*

6. *Ich ziehe mich immer nach dem Frühstück an.*

7. *Ihr Mann muss sich morgens oft beeilen.*

*** **10.** Übersetze die folgenden Sätze ins Englische. Entscheide dabei, ob du **Reflexivpronomen, each other** oder vielleicht noch etwas anderes benötigst.

1. *Susie hat das Fahrrad selbst repariert.*

2. *Meine Eltern haben sich gestern ein neues Auto gekauft.*

3. *Er schaute sich im Spiegel an.*

4. *Er schaute mich an.*

5. *Wir schauten uns an und mussten lachen.*

1 UNTERSCHIEDLICHE AUSSPRACHE BEI HOMOGRAPHEN

Aussprache

Die Aussprache im Englischen ist nicht immer so einfach, wie man vielleicht vermuten würde. Mit ein paar Tipps und Tricks kannst du jedoch tückische Aussprachefallen umgehen und deine Sprechweise der eines Muttersprachlers angleichen!

Homographe sind Wörter, die gleich geschrieben werden. Im Englischen gibt es eine ganze Reihe von Homographen, aber aufgepasst: Diese können auf unterschiedliche Weise ausgesprochen werden, und haben ganz verschiedene Bedeutungen!

Einsilbige Wörter

Hier eine kleine Auswahl einsilbiger Wörter, die unterschiedliche Bedeutungen haben, je nachdem, wie man sie ausspricht. Die folgenden Wörter muss man gleich in der richtigen Aussprache lernen:

	Aussprache 1	Aussprache 2
bow	[baʊ] *sich beugen*	[bəʊ] *Schleife*
close	[kləʊs] *nah*	[kləʊz] *schließen*
house	[haʊs] *Haus*	[haʊz] *unterbringen*
live	[lɪv] *leben, wohnen*	[laɪv] *live* (Konzert o. ä.)
read	[riːd] *lesen*	[red] Vergangenheitsform von **read**
row	[rəʊ] *Reihe, rudern*	[raʊ] *Streit, sich streiten*
tear	[teəʳ] *reißen*	[tɪəʳ] *Träne*
use	[juːs] *Verwendung*	[juːz] *verwenden*
wind	[wɪnd] *Wind*	[waɪnd] *aufziehen* (Uhr usw.)
wound	[wuːnd] *Wunde, verwunden*	[waʊnd] Vergangenheitsform von **wind**

Zweisilbige Wörter

Einige zweisilbige Wörter kann man im Englischen sowohl als Substantiv als auch als Verb benutzen. Dabei bestimmen Aussprache und Betonung, um welches Wort es sich jeweils handelt. Hier ein paar Beispiele:

	Substantiv	Verb
contract	['kɒntrækt] *Vertrag*	[kən'trækt] *zusammenziehen*
object	['ɒbʤɪkt] *Objekt*	[ɒb'ʤekt] *dagegen sein*
present	['prezᵊnt] *Geschenk*	[prɪ'zent] *präsentieren*
record	['rekɔːd] *Aufzeichnung*	[rɪ'kɔːd] *aufnehmen*
subject	['sʌbʤɪkt] *Subjekt, Thema*	[səb'ʤekt] *unterwerfen*

Wie du sicher bemerkt hast, liegt die Betonung in den oberen Beispielen bei Substantiven immer auf der ersten Silbe, und bei Verben auf der zweiten. Ähnliche Unterschiede gibt es z.B. bei den Wörtern **absent, abstract, combine, concert, conflict, console, content, desert, export, import, produce, rebel, refuse, reject, research, survey** und **suspect**.

1. Setze den fehlenden Betonungsstrich (') in der Lautschrift bei den folgenden Beispielen an der jeweils richtigen Stelle:

	Substantiv	**Verb**
a. **suspect**	[sʌspekt] *Verdächtiger*	[səspekt] *verdächtigen*
b. **survey**	[sɜːveɪ] *Übersicht*	[səveɪ] *begutachten*

Wie du siehst, ist es gut, die Betonung und Aussprache von Homographen immer in so genannten Minimalpaaren zu üben, also in Wortpaaren, die sich nur durch ein Merkmal unterscheiden. Die unterschiedlichen Bedeutungen der englischen Homographe kannst du dir leicht merken, wenn du zum Beispiel zuerst jeweils das Substantiv und dann das Verb laut aussprichst.

BOXENSTOPP

______________ sind Wörter, die gleich ______________ werden, aber unterschiedliche ______________ und ______________ haben. Einige zweisilbige Homographe kann man sowohl als ______________ als auch als ______________ verwenden, je nachdem, wie man sie ausspricht und betont. Dabei gilt meistens, dass Substantive auf der ______________ und Verben auf der ______________ Silbe betont werden.

2 HOMOPHONE

Homophone sind Wörter, deren Aussprache gleich ist, die aber ganz unterschiedlich geschrieben werden und verschiedene Bedeutungen haben. Im Englischen gibt es eine ganze Menge solcher Wortpaare. Hier haben wir einige der wichtigsten Fälle für dich zusammengestellt:

erstes Wort	Aussprache	zweites Wort
air - *Luft*	[eəʳ]	**heir** - *Erbe*
aisle - *Gang*	[aɪl]	**I'll** - *ich werde*
bare - *nackt*	[beəʳ]	**bear** - *Bär, tragen*
brake - *Bremse*	[breɪk]	**break** - *brechen, Pause*
desert - *verlassen*	[dɪ'zɜːt]	**dessert** - *Nachtisch*
flour - *Mehl*	['flaʊəʳ]	**flower** - *Blume*
hear - *hören*	[hɪəʳ]	**here** - *hier*
hour - *Stunde*	[aʊəʳ]	**our** - *unser*
knew - *wusste(st/t/n)*	[njuː]	**new** - *neu*
know - *wissen, kennen*	[nəʊ]	**no** - *nein, kein(e)*
one - *ein(e), eins*	[wʌn]	**won** - Vergangenheitsform von **win**
pair - *Paar*	[peəʳ]	**pear** - *Birne*
some - *etwas, einige*	[sʌm]	**sum** - *Summe*
son - *Sohn*	[sʌn]	**sun** - *Sonne*
suite - *Suite*	[swiːt]	**sweet** - *süß*
their - *ihr* (3. Pers. Pl.)	[ðeəʳ]	**there** - *dort, da* **they're** - *sie sind*
wear - *tragen* (Kleidung)	[weəʳ]	**where** - *wo*
wood - *Holz, Wald*	[wʊd]	**would** - *würde* usw.

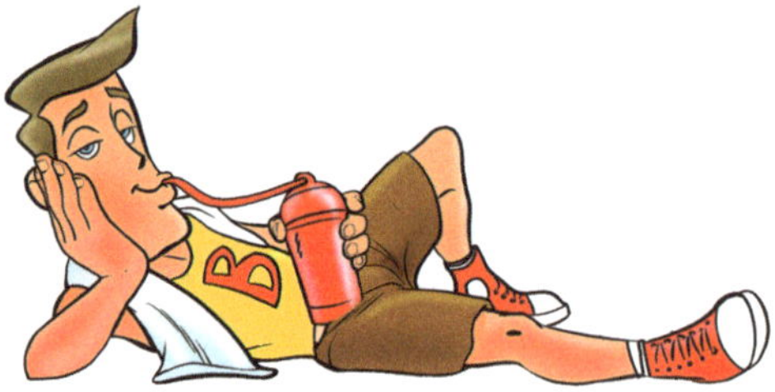

1. Ordne den englischen Begriffen jeweils die korrekte Aussprache in der Mitte zu.
Beachte dabei wieder, dass Homophone dieselbe Aussprache haben!

1. **here**	a. [swiːt]	2. **pair**
3. **hear**	b. [hɪəʳ]	4. **suite**
5. **sun**	c. [aʊəʳ]	6. **desert** (Verb)
7. **sweet**	d. [sʌn]	8. **our**
9. **son**	e. [dɪˈzɜːt]	10. **pear**
11. **hour**	f. [peəʳ]	12. **dessert**

BOXENSTOPP

______________ sind Wörter, die gleich ______________, aber unterschiedlich ______________ werden und dabei ganz andere Bedeutungen haben. Am besten lernt man die englischen Homophone als ____________, so kann man sie sich viel leichter merken!

3 SCHWIERIGE FÄLLE

Hier haben wir eine Reihe von allgemeinen Schwierigkeiten aufgelistet, die im Zusammenhang mit der englischen Aussprache immer wieder auftreten. Sieh dir die folgenden Fälle genau an und übe die Aussprache anhand der Beispiele, dann bist du schon bald Aussprache-Profi!

Wörter mit ough und augh

Wörter, in denen diese Buchstabenkombinationen vorkommen, sind oft sehr schwer auszusprechen, da **ough** und **augh** immer unterschiedlich gesprochen werden. Hier die wichtigsten Fälle auf einen Blick:

[ɔː]	**thought, ought, fought, taught, bought, caught, daughter**
[aʊ]	**bough, drought**
[əʊ]	**(al)though**
[uː]	**through**
[ə]	**thorough**
[ʌf]	**rough, tough, enough**
[ɒf]	**cough**
[ɑːf]	**draught, laugh**

Geschrieben o - aber ausgesprochen [ʌ]

Nicht immer wird ein **o** entweder als kurzes [ɒ] (wie in **dog**) oder als längeres [əʊ] (wie in **code**) ausgesprochen. Bei den folgenden Wörtern zum Beispiel spricht man das **o** an den markierten Stellen als [ʌ] (wie im Wort **cut**):

money	oven	government	one
colour	onion	London	nothing
done	comfort	month	stomach
son	company	mother	wonder
come	brother	none	worry

Nicht ausgesprochene Buchstaben

Im Englischen kommt es oft vor, dass ein geschriebener Buchstabe gar nicht ausgesprochen wird. Hier haben wir die häufigsten Stolperfallen für dich zusammengestellt, alphabetisch geordnet nach dem jeweils stummen Buchstaben:

b	**comb, dumb, lamb, debt**
h	**honest, honour, hour; where, why, when, which**
k	**knife** (bei allen Wortanfängen auf **kn-**)
l	**calm, could, half, should, talk, walk, would**
p	**pneumatic, psychology** (bei allen Wortanfängen auf **pn-** oder **ps-**)
t	**castle, Christmas, listen, often** (bei allen Wortendungen auf **-ction**)
u	**guess, guest, guide**
w	**who, whose, whole, write** (bei allen Wortanfängen auf **wr-**)

Die Aussprache von w und v

Das englische **w** ist ein so genannter Halbvokal, der je nach Position im Wort auf unterschiedliche Weise ausgesprochen wird. Ein englisches **w** wird aber niemals wie ein deutsches *w* gesprochen!

Am Wortanfang vor einem Vokal wird das **w** als konsonantischer *u*-Laut ausgesprochen:
west [west]

Innerhalb eines Wortes oder am Wortende wird das **w** eher vokalisch ausgesprochen:

tower [taʊəʳ]	**saw** [sɔː]
show [ʃəʊ]	**lawn** [lɔːn]

Der Buchstabe **v** wird dagegen im Englischen immer gleich ausgesprochen, phonetisch dargestellt als [v]. Er ist fast identisch mit dem deutschen *w*-Laut und darf daher auf keinen Fall wie ein englisches [w] ausgesprochen werden! Sonst kann man manche Wörter leicht verwechseln, wie zum Beispiel die folgenden:

Beispiel	Aussprache	Übersetzung
vest	[vest]	*Unterhemd, Weste*
west	[west]	*westlich, der Westen*

Die Aussprache des th

Das englische **th** führt immer wieder zu Problemen. Aber keine Sorge: Hier haben wir für dich eine kleine Anleitung zur Aussprache dieses schwierigen Lautes zusammengestellt:

Berühre mit deiner Zungenspitze die Rückseite der oberen Schneidezähne und spreche ein **s** aus, ohne die Zunge dabei zu bewegen. So entsteht das stimmlose (scharfe) **th** [θ]. Beim stimmhaften (weichen) **th** [ð] spürt man dazu eine stärkere Vibration der Stimmbänder im Kehlkopfbereich, analog zur Vibration beim weichen **s** im Deutschen Wort *lesen*. Die Zungenposition ist dabei dieselbe wie bei [θ].

Substantive, Verben, Adjektive und andere wichtige „Inhaltswörter", die mit **th** anfangen, haben in der Regel die stimmlose Variante [θ] (**theatre, think, thick, three**), während Bestimmungswörter, Konjunktionen und Pronomen eher mit [ð] anfangen (**the, this, though, that, they**).

Stimmhafte und stimmlose Wortendungen

Der Unterschied zwischen stimmhaften und stimmlosen Konsonanten ist im Englischen besonders wichtig, da sich dadurch eine Reihe von Bedeutungsunterschieden ergeben. Besonders als deutschsprachige(r) Sprecher(in) muss man sich bemühen, diese Unterschiede auch am Wortende zu beachten, denn im Gegensatz zum Deutschen gibt es hier im Englischen auch stimmhafte Konsonanten. In der folgenden Tabelle haben wir einige Fälle aufgelistet, bei denen dieser Unterschied sichtbar ist:

stimmlos	stimmhaft
pup [pʌp] *junger Hund* (**puppy**)	**pub** [pʌb] *Kneipe*
muck [mʊk] *Dreck*	**mug** [mʌg] *(Trink)becher*
extent [ɪk'stent] *Ausmaß*	**extend** [ɪk'stend] *erweitern*
price [praɪs] *Kaufpreis*	**prize** [praɪz] *Preis (Gewinn)*
teeth [tiːθ] *Zähne*	**teethe** [tiːð] *zahnen*
proof [pruːf] *Beweis*	**prove** [pruːv] *beweisen*

Die Intonation bei question tags

Kurze Frageanhängsel am Ende eines Aussagesatzes, die so genannten **question tags** (vergleichbar mit dem deutschen ***oder?*** bzw. ***nicht wahr?***), haben im Englischen zwei unterschiedliche Funktionen:

Manchmal bittet man seinen Gesprächspartner wirklich um Informationen, aber manchmal möchte man auch nur in seiner Aussage bestätigt werden.
Sieh dir das folgende Beispiel einmal an:
That's your new car, isn't it?
Das ist dein neues Auto, oder? / nicht wahr?

Ist man sich als Sprecher unsicher und möchte man tatsächlich eine Information, dann wird das **question tag** mit einer **Intonation nach oben** (also eher fragend) ausgesprochen.

Erwartet man als Sprecher mit dem **question tag** aber lediglich eine Bestätigung der eigenen Aussage, dann geht dabei die **Intonation nach unten** (bleibt also eher die eines Aussagesatzes).

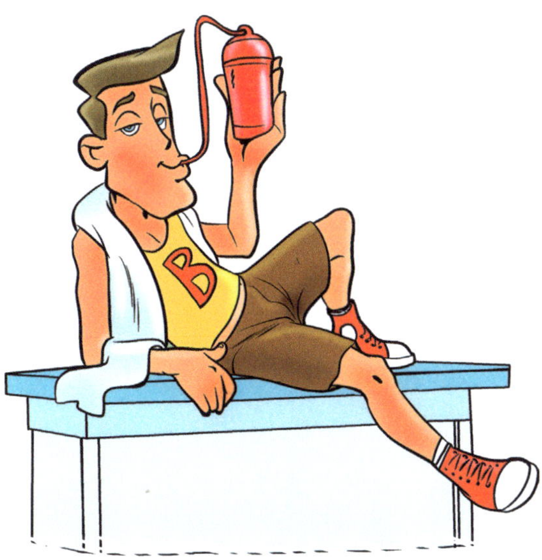

1. Kreuze in den folgenden Sätzen jeweils an, ob die Intonation des Frageanhängsels nach oben oder nach unten geht.

a. Du bist dir sicher, dass der Herr vor dir am Bahnschalter sein Buch vergessen hat:

Sir, this is your book, isn't it? ↑ ☐ ↓ ☐

b. Nun bist du dir nicht sicher, ob du im richtigen Zug sitzt:

This is the train to Oxford, isn't it? ↑ ☐ ↓ ☐

c. Ob du in Oxford noch den Anschlusszug nach London bekommst, ist fraglich. Vielleicht kann dir der Schaffner weiterhelfen:

We will make the 12 o'clock train to London, won't we? ↑ ☐ ↓ ☐

BOXENSTOPP

Es gibt eine Reihe von schwierigen Fällen bei der Aussprache im Englischen. Dabei fällt auf, dass die Aussprache eines Wortes manchmal stark von der geschriebenen Form abweicht: So werden zum Beispiel die Buchstabenkombinationen **ough** und **augh** ganz unterschiedlich ausgesprochen, in manchen Fällen Buchstaben auch ganz weggelassen, oder ein englisches **v** wird wie ein deutsches *w* gesprochen. Hast du dir die anderen Besonderheiten auch gemerkt? Notiere sie doch noch einmal hier:

____

____

____

____

____

REFERATE HALTEN

Inhalt

Hi... hello... errr... welcome...
now... eh... let's start... errr...
What was I going to say?

- Die passenden Worte finden
- Richtig gut vorbereiten und präsentieren
- Audiotrainer als Download unter www.pons.de/referate-englisch

Alles rund um Referate

- **Theorie-Kapitel „Referate"** – Hier wirst du auf deinem Weg zum präsentationsfähigen Referat begleitet. Schritt für Schritt wird jeder einzelne Aspekt genau beschrieben und erklärt: Wie plane und recherchiere ich richtig? Was ist ein geeigneter Referatsaufbau? Wie bereite ich mich auf den Auftritt vor und wie führe ich das Referat durch?

- **Tipps** – In den einzelnen Kapiteln findest du am Rand praxisnahe Tipps, die für die Vorbereitung und den Auftritt besonders nützlich sind und deinem Referat noch den letzten Schliff geben.

- **Checklisten** – Mit einem Häkchen markierte Checklisten stellen wichtige Punkte, die es zu beachten gilt, im Überblick dar.

- **Infoboxen** – Hier findest du zusätzliche Informationen zu spezielleren Bereichen des jeweiligen Themas. Infoboxen erkennst du an einem Ausrufezeichen.

Passende Worte für jeden Schritt

- **Wortlisten**[1] - Zu jedem einzelnen Referatsschritt findest du neben der Theorie auch ausführliche deutsch-englische Wortlisten mit dem benötigten Vokabular.
- **Sprechtraining** - Um einzelne Wendungen schnell und problemlos zu finden und zu üben, kannst du die Liste auf S. 442 benutzen. Die Reihenfolge der Wendungen entspricht der Reihenfolge im Theorieteil.
- **Audio-Download** - Für eine effektivere Vorbereitung und zum Trainieren der Aussprache stehen dir alle Sätze und Wendungen aus den Wortlisten als Download unter www.pons.de/referate-englisch zur Verfügung. Nummern neben den Wortlisten und im Index helfen dir bei der Orientierung. Alle Hörbeiträge wurden von englischen Muttersprachlern gesprochen.

Übung macht den Meister!

- **Übungen** - Am Ende findest du jeweils einen umfangreichen Übungsteil zu inhaltlichen Aspekten sowie zum Wortschatz. Nutze die Übungen, um dich selbst zu überprüfen und das Erlernte zu festigen. Die Lösungen dazu befinden sich auf S. 479.

Einem erfolgreichen Spurt ins Ziel steht jetzt nichts mehr im Weg.
Starte durch: Auf die Plätze, fertig, los!

Wir drücken dir die Daumen!

[1] Elemente in eckigen Klammern (z. B. Eigennamen) sind in den Wortlisten nur als Beispiel angegeben und können beliebig ausgetauscht werden.

1 READY: INHALTE SUCHEN UND AUFBEREITEN

1.1 Gut geplant ist halb gehalten – Die Vorarbeit

Wie erstelle ich einen Arbeitsplan?

Bevor du dich um inhaltliche Aspekte kümmerst und dich in die eigentliche Vorbereitung stürzt, solltest du dein Vorgehen planen. Nur dann kannst du abschätzen, wie viel Zeit du für die einzelnen Arbeitsschritte überhaupt zur Verfügung hast. Notiere dir den Referatstermin in deinem Kalender und erstelle dann einen Plan, wann du welchen Arbeitsschritt in Angriff nehmen und beenden willst. Du solltest dabei dein eigenes Arbeitstempo berücksichtigen und dir realistische Ziele setzen. Auch andere Termine (z. B. Klausuren und Ferien), die dich eventuell an einem zügigen Arbeiten hindern, solltest du in deine Planung mit einbeziehen.

Beginne rechtzeitig mit der Vorbereitung und plane Zeitpuffer ein.
So gerätst du nicht unter Druck.

Arbeitsphasen

BOXENSTOPP

Themenfestlegung: Sprich das Thema mit deinem Lehrer/Dozenten ab und wähle den Termin dafür möglichst früh, so dass eventuell noch ein zweites Treffen stattfinden kann.

Recherche: Wichtige Bücher, die du für deine Arbeit ausleihen möchtest, können entliehen sein, dann musst du möglicherweise wochenlang darauf warten. Plane entsprechend viel Zeit für diesen Schritt ein.

Materialbearbeitung: Das Sichten, Bewerten und Ordnen von Material erfordert Ruhe und Zeit. Mache dir gründlich Notizen und schreibe immer deine Quellen auf. Das erspart später unnötiges Suchen, wenn du einzelne Aspekte genauer nachschlagen musst.

Gliederung: Der Aufbau muss eventuell noch mit der Lehrperson abgesprochen werden. Vereinbare rechtzeitig einen Termin. Plane für Änderungen, die dann noch vorgenommen werden müssen, Zeit ein. Vielleicht musst du ein Teilthema neu recherchieren.

Ausarbeitung: Dies ist eine sehr intensive Arbeitsphase, in der du dich teils kreativ, teils analytisch mit den Inhalten auseinandersetzt. Rechne damit, dass dieser Prozess nicht immer zügig läuft. Ein paar Tage Abstand können dann gut tun, um mit neuem Schwung die Sache wieder anzugehen.

Letzte Vorbereitungen: Viele Kleinigkeiten können jetzt Zeit und Nerven kosten. Du musst Folien und Handouts kopieren, Geräte organisieren, etc. Dabei muss nicht immer alles glatt gehen: Hast du auch dann genug Zeit, wenn Kopierer oder andere technische Geräte streiken?

Wie präzisiere ich das Thema und definiere Ziele?

Das Thema des Referates ergibt sich in den meisten Fällen aus dem Unterricht und wird durch die Lehrperson vorgegeben. Mache dir zunächst eigene Gedanken zum Thema. Kläre für dich, welchen Bezug du zu diesem Thema hast und welche Aspekte du besonders reizvoll findest.
Gehe dann zu deinem Lehrer/Dozenten und kläre, inwieweit sich eure Vorstellungen treffen oder ergänzen. Besprich, wo der Schwerpunkt des Referates liegen soll und welche Bereiche unbedingt in deinen Ausführungen berücksichtigt werden müssen. Mache dir auch klar, für wen du dein Referat hältst und welche Informationen deine Zuhörer unbedingt brauchen.

TIPP:
Eine spontane Stoffsammlung (Brainstorming, Mind-Map usw.) hilft, sich an das Thema heranzutasten. Auch ein Lexikon gibt einen ersten Überblick.

Wenn du dein Thema selbst wählst, solltest du unbedingt auf den Umfang achten: Ist das Thema zu eng gewählt, langweilst du dein Publikum unter Umständen mit unnötigen Details und Spezialwissen. Ist das Thema zu weit gefasst, ist eine vertiefende Darstellung einzelner Aspekte unmöglich.
Bitte auch hier deine Lehrperson um ein beratendes Gespräch.

TIPP:
Im Zweifelsfall immer Rücksprache mit der Lehrperson halten!

Checkliste: Besprechung zur Themenfindung

- Wo soll der Schwerpunkt des Referates liegen?
- Was will ich mit meinem Referat erreichen?
- Welche Fragen und Unterthemen lassen sich formulieren?
- Welche Aspekte finde ich besonders spannend?
- Wie viel Zeit ist für die Durchführung des Vortrags vorgesehen?
- Gibt es Literatur, die mein Lehrer/Dozent mir empfehlen kann?
- Wann soll das Referat gehalten werden? Wie viel Zeit bleibt für die Vorbereitung?

1.2 Wer sucht, der findet – Die Recherche

Wo suche ich, was ich brauche?

Die Recherche ist ein wichtiger Schritt auf dem Weg zu einem guten und vor allem informativen Referat. Die Möglichkeiten, nach geeignetem Material zu suchen, sind vielfältig.

TIPP:
Stelle dir eine Liste mit Schlagwörtern zum Thema zusammen. So kommst du bei der Suche in der Bibliothek und im Internet schnell vorwärts.

Öffentliche Bücherei/Bibliothek: Der richtige Ort für die Recherche kann eine Bibliothek sein. Wenn du noch nicht mit den Gegebenheiten vertraut bist, lass dich vor Ort über das Bibliothekssystem informieren. Sowohl eine Suche nach thematischen Stichwörtern, als auch nach Autoren ist möglich. Du findest neben Fachbüchern, wissenschaftlichen Zeitschriften und aktueller Presse auch allgemeine Nachschlagewerke und Lexika.

Internet: Eine weitere Informationsquelle ist das Internet; das Problem ist hier aber, die gefundenen Seiten richtig einschätzen zu können und die verlässlichen Quellen von den zweifelhaften zu unterscheiden. Hierbei hilft es zum einen, sich eher auf Seiten von angesehenen Urhebern (Universitäten, Zeitschriften, Rundfunk) zu stützen. Zum anderen ist es ratsam, sich nicht nur auf eine Quelle zu verlassen, sondern mehrere zu vergleichen.

Checkliste: Die Nützlichkeit eines Buches schnell beurteilen
- Inhaltsverzeichnis lesen
- Index überfliegen
- Vorwort/Einführung anlesen
- zwei oder drei willkürlich ausgewählte Textpassagen anschauen

Wie notiere ich, was ich finde?

Während der Materialsuche erscheint es oft problematisch, die Informationen so zu notieren, dass sie später gut verarbeitet werden können.

TIPP:
Notiere immer auch die genaue Quelle der gefundenen Information, da du diese später ohnehin angeben musst.

Lesetechniken: Bei deiner Recherche geht es darum, möglichst schnell zu beurteilen, ob ein Text für dich relevant ist oder nicht. Verschaffe dir einen Überblick über den Inhalt, indem du die Seiten überfliegst und die Schlüsselwörter erfasst. Entscheide dann, ob es sich lohnt diesen Text genauer zu bearbeiten.

Texte exzerpieren: Markiere in den Texten, die du als wichtig erachtest, zentrale Stellen und schreibe dir zur eigenen Orientierung Überbegriffe an den Rand. Mache dir die Hauptgedanken des Textes klar und fasse diese in eigenen Worten zusammen.

TIPP:
Entnimm keine Textpassagen wörtlich, ohne sie als Zitate zu kennzeichnen.

Vorstrukturieren: Es bietet sich an, das Material in Mind-Maps oder Clustern thematisch vorzustrukturieren. Man sollte einzelne Aspekte, die man in Büchern, Zeitschriften oder im Internet findet, gleich so zusammenstellen, dass man sie später wieder findet und bei der Erarbeitung keinen Aspekt vergisst.

Zitieren: Notiere Zitate, die du womöglich in deinem Vortrag zur Verdeutlichung verwenden willst, mit genauen Quellenangaben (Autor, Titel, Jahr, Verlag, Seitenzahl).

Literaturverzeichnis anlegen: Du musst alle verwendeten Quellen angeben. Lege dir deshalb eine Liste an, auf der du die Angaben aller verwendeten Materialien notierst. Eventuell muss diese Liste auch abgegeben werden.

Checkliste: Literaturverzeichnis (Bibliografie)
- **Bücher**: Name, Vorname: *Titel*. Ort: Verlag, Jahr.
- **Zeitschriftenartikel**: Name, Vorname: „Titel". In: Name der Zeitschrift. Ausgabe. Ort: Verlag, Jahr. Seite.
- **Internetseiten**: vollständige Webadresse, in Klammern dahinter das Datum, an dem die Seite besucht wurde.
- Internetseiten werden separat von Büchern und Zeitschriften aufgelistet.
- Die Namen der Autoren werden alphabetisch sortiert.

Wie strukturiere ich, was ich verwenden will?

Mit dem Rohmaterial, das während der Recherche gesammelt wurde, wird nun eine endgültige Struktur erarbeitet. Du solltest dir noch einmal genau deine Themenformulierung und Zieldefinition anschauen. Überlege dir, welche der Informationen du tatsächlich auch verwenden willst bzw. solltest.

TIPP:
Lege am besten für jeden Unterpunkt ein eigenes Kartensystem an, das erleichtert das Zuordnen der verschiedenen Informationen.

Finde Überschriften zu Unterkapiteln und bringe diese in eine schlüssige Reihenfolge. Ordne dann dein Material diesen Unterpunkten zu (vgl. Kap. 3.2, S. 415). Überlege dir auch, mit welchen Medien du deine Inhalte präsentieren kannst: Welches Medium ist am besten geeignet, die einzelnen Aspekte verständlich zu machen und zu veranschaulichen?

BOXENSTOPP

Verschiedene Medien und ihre Einsatzmöglichkeiten

Die Tafel kann während deines Referates dafür genutzt werden, Äußerungen aus dem Plenum zu sammeln oder einige Stichpunkte zu notieren. Komplexere Schaubilder solltest du, wenn die Möglichkeit besteht, schon vor dem Vortrag anbringen oder dich für eines der anderen Medien entscheiden.

Flipcharts haben eine ähnliche Funktion wie die Tafel. Besonders eignen sie sich für Stichwortsammlungen und Skizzen. Man kann hier innerhalb kürzester Zeit verschiedene Aspekte auf einem jeweils neuen Blatt behandeln.

Poster haben den Vorteil, dass sie während des gesamten Referates präsent sind und auch darüber hinaus als Erinnerungsstütze und Ergebnis genutzt werden können.

Folien sind sehr flexibel einsetzbar, da sie vor dem Vortrag erstellt werden können, aber auch spontane Ergänzungen während des Referates zulassen. Achte auf die Schriftgröße und die Übersichtlichkeit.

Der Computer bietet die Möglichkeit, mit Powerpoint Grafiken, Bilder und Auflistungen zu erstellen und mit Hilfe des Beamers zu zeigen. Besonders wenn zahlreiche Bilder, Diagramme und Illustrationen eingesetzt werden sollen, ist dieses Medium sinnvoll. Achte aber auch hier darauf, dass deine Zuschauer Zeit brauchen, die Eindrücke aufzunehmen und zu verarbeiten.

Filme oder Filmsequenzen können einzelne Aspekte deines Themas eindrücklich veranschaulichen. Allerdings sollte der gewählte Ausschnitt genau auf das Thema abgestimmt sein und nur einen kleinen Teil deines Referates einnehmen. Nimm während deines Referates Bezug auf die gezeigten Szenen.

Tonträger können ähnlich wie Filme eingesetzt werden. Musik, Interviewausschnitte, Lesungen oder Ähnliches lockern den Vortrag auf und können als Ausgangspunkt oder Beispiel dienen.

2 STEADY: AUFTRITT VORBEREITEN

2.1 Ab in die Startlöcher – Vorbereitung und Visualisierung

Wie bereite ich mich auf meinen Auftritt vor?

Der Abend zuvor: Versuche, am Abend zuvor rechtzeitig mit allen Vorbereitungen fertig zu sein, so dass du genügend Schlaf bekommst. Ein ausgeschlafener Referent tritt wesentlich überzeugender und souveräner auf als ein übermüdeter.

Lampenfieber: Wenn du dich gut vorbereitet hast, gibt es eigentlich keinen Grund aufgeregt zu sein. Trotzdem ist es normal, ein gewisses Maß an Lampenfieber zu spüren. Oft hilft es, das Referat im Vorfeld vor Freunden oder auch nur vor dem Spiegel zu halten. Wenn dieser Probeauftritt gut läuft, legt sich die Nervosität von selbst.

Sei am Tag selbst pünktlich an Ort und Stelle. Plane lieber einen Zeitpuffer ein, damit du nicht zusätzlich unter Druck gerätst.

Nobody is perfect: Setze dich selbst nicht zu sehr unter Druck. Es ist kein Problem, wenn dir zwischendurch einmal kleine Fehler unterlaufen. Auch Versprecher wird niemand übel nehmen. Es ist vollkommen in Ordnung, sich bei Unsicherheiten an den Karteikarten zu orientieren, solange man nicht durchgängig abliest.

Wie bereite ich mein Material vor?

Kümmere dich rechtzeitig um die Anfertigung deiner Materialien. Kopiere Handouts und Folien mindestens einen Tag vor deinem Auftritt und nimm dir genügend Zeit, alles zu kontrollieren. Tippfehler schleichen sich schneller ein, als man denkt.
Überlege dir im Vorfeld, welche technischen Geräte du benutzen wirst und reserviere diese gegebenenfalls. Um frei sprechen zu können, solltest du dir nur Stichworte notieren. Ausformulierte Sätze verleiten dazu abzulesen und sind nicht übersichtlich genug. Bewährt haben sich Karteikarten. Lege dir am besten alle Materialien so zurecht, dass du direkt vor deinem Referat sicher sein kannst, alles in der richtigen Reihenfolge und vor allem komplett vorliegen zu haben.

Checkliste: Karteikarten

- für jeden neuen Aspekt eine eigene Karte benutzen
- Stichworte so knapp wie möglich halten
- groß und leserlich schreiben
- unterschiedliche Farben verwenden
- Schlüsselbegriffe markieren
- Karten nummerieren

Checkliste: Folien, Handouts und Plakate

- so wenig wie möglich, so viel wie nötig schreiben
- Gliederung übersichtlich gestalten
- grafische Elemente zur Veranschaulichung nutzen
- nicht zu viel auf eine Seite packen
- Schriftgröße nicht zu klein wählen (Handouts ca. 12 Punkt, Folien ab 16 Punkt)
- leserliche und einheitliche Schriftart benutzen
- Quellen angeben

3 GO: REFERATE DURCHFÜHREN

3.1 Auf los geht's los – Die Einleitung

Wie stelle ich mich vor und begrüße meine Zuhörer?

Hi, I know none of us want to be here, but Mrs. Stratford wants me to talk about this boring English guy called Shakesbeer …

> ***TIPP:***
> *Die Aufregung zu Beginn eines Referates bekommt man besser in den Griff, wenn man den Einstieg besonders gründlich vorbereitet und eventuell sogar auswendig lernt.*

Der erste Eindruck entscheidet – nicht alles, aber einiges: Er legt den Grundstein für eine gute und überzeugende Präsentation. Deshalb ist es noch vor Beginn des eigentlichen Referates wichtig, einen positiven Kontakt zum Publikum aufzubauen. Begrüße deine Zuhörer freundlich und teile ihnen durchaus auch mit, dass du dich über ihr Erscheinen freuen. Ein Publikum ist gerne bereit, sich auf das Kommende einzulassen, wenn es sich persönlich angesprochen fühlt und merkt, dass es dir Freude macht, dein Thema zu präsentieren.

Solltest du vor fremdem Publikum sprechen, ist es wichtig, dich und eventuelle Mitreferenten kurz vorzustellen: Nenne deinen Namen, eventuell deine Funktion und umreiße kurz, inwieweit du Experte für das von dir präsentierte Thema bist.

BOXENSTOPP

Richtiges Auftreten

Wichtig ist nicht nur, was du sagst, sondern auch wie du es sagst. Hier ein paar einfache aber sehr wirkungsvolle Tipps für dich:

Natürlich auftreten: Ziehe das an, worin du dich wohl fühlst. Dabei sollte die Kleidung gepflegt und dem Anlass angemessen sein.

Nervosität verbergen: Stehe aufrecht und unverkrampft, gehe nicht zu viel umher, wippe nicht.

Wichtiges betonen: Unterstreiche deine Ausführungen dezent mit Gestik und Mimik.

Kontakt zum Publikum: Vergiss nicht, dass du Zuhörer hast und halte Blickkontakt.

Positive Atmosphäre: Ein aufmunterndes Lächeln hilft dir, eine positive Atmosphäre im Raum zu schaffen.

Üben im Voraus: Finde das richtige Maß an Bewegung, Gestik und Mimik für dich heraus, indem du einen Teil des Referates einmal einem Freund präsentierst.

Download 1

Guten Morgen alle miteinander.	Good morning everybody.
Liebe Klassenkameraden ...	Dear classmates ...
Liebe Kommilitonen ...	Dear fellow students ...
Meine sehr verehrten Damen und Herren ...	Ladies and gentlemen ...
Ich begrüße euch sehr herzlich zu ...	Welcome to ...
Ich heiße euch herzlich willkommen.	I'd like to welcome you to ...
Schön, dass ihr alle heute morgen da seid.	Nice to see you all this morning.
Schön, dass ihr es alle geschafft habt her zu kommen.	I'm glad you could all make it.
Schön, dass ihr so zahlreich erschienen seid ...	I'm glad to be able to welcome so many of you ...

Download 2

Die meisten von euch kennen mich ja, ich bin ...	Most of you already know me, I'm ...
Für diejenigen, die mich nicht kennen, ich bin ...	For those of you who don't know me, I am ...
Ich möchte mich gerne kurz vorstellen.	Let me briefly introduce myself.
Mein Name ist ...	My name is ...
Ich heiße ...	I am ...
Ich bin Schüler der 10. Klasse.	I'm in year 10.
Ich bin Student im 3. Semester.	I'm a student in my third semester.
Ich bin ein Praktikant.	I'm doing work experience.
Heute steht hier mit mir ...	Here with me today is ...
Ich glaube, ihr kennt alle ...	I think you all know ...
Ich möchte gerne ... vorstellen.	I would like to introduce ...
Darf ich ... vorstellen:	May I introduce ...
Wir arbeiten schon lange zusammen an diesem Thema.	We have been working together on this topic for a long time.
Wir haben dieses Referat gemeinsam vorbereitet.	We prepared this presentation together.

Wir werden uns im Verlauf dieses Referates immer wieder abwechseln.	We'll be taking turns in giving this presentation.
Wir haben uns die Präsentation folgendermaßen aufgeteilt:	We have divided the presentation as follows:

Wie kläre ich technische und organisatorische Fragen?

I've got a bad cold so you won't hear me and I don't know how to switch on the light so you won't see me; but I'm here and I planned a three hour speech on Shakesbeard's plays ...

Bevor es mit der Präsentation richtig losgeht, ist es ratsam, noch einige technische und organisatorische Dinge zu klären und vorzubereiten.

Licht und Lesbarkeit: Achte darauf, dass das Licht im Vortragsraum hell genug ist, so dass du als Vortragender deine Aufzeichnungen gut lesen kannst; andererseits sollte es nicht so hell sein, dass die Zuschauer die Schrift auf dem OHP, Bildschirm oder Tafel nicht mehr lesen können. Teste dies am besten im Vorfeld und frage dein Publikum, ob alles gut sichtbar ist.

Lautstärke: Erkundige dich, ob deine Stimme oder die CD-Einspielung für alle Zuhörer laut genug und verständlich ist. Das vermeidet Unmut und Missverständnisse auf beiden Seiten.

Technische Probleme: Solltest du Probleme mit dem CD-Player, dem Tageslicht-projektor oder einem anderen Gerät haben, erkläre kurz die Lage und bitte um ein wenig Geduld.

Fragen: Wenn Fragen aus dem Publikum kommen, gibt es zwei Möglichkeiten der Handhabung: Entweder du lässt die Fragen immer dann stellen, wenn sie auftreten oder du verweist auf die Möglichkeit einer offenen Fragerunde am Ende deines Referates.

TIPP:
Wenn du dich beim Reden stark auf dein Konzept konzentrieren musst, lass die auftauchenden Fragen erst am Ende deines Vortrages stellen, so dass du den roten Faden nicht verlierst.

Zeitplanung: Sage, wie lange dein Referat ungefähr dauern wird. So können sich die Zuhörer darauf einstellen und unnötige Unruhe wird vermieden.

Handout: Du kannst das Handout vor dem Referat als Orientierungshilfe austeilen. Die Zuhörer haben dann die Möglichkeit, eigene Notizen zu ergänzen. Wenn du dein Handout nach dem Referat als Zusammenfassung austeilst, solltest du deine Zuhörer zu Beginn darauf hinweisen, dass sie nicht mitschreiben müssen, weil ein Handout mit den wesentlichen Informationen noch folgt.

Download 3

Ist es zu hell?	Is the light too bright?
Soll ich die Rollos herunterlassen?	Should I close the blinds?
Soll ich die Lichter dimmen?	Should I turn the lights down?
Ist die Präsentation auch hinten noch gut zu erkennen?	Can you see the presentation clearly in the back rows, as well?
Könnt ihr alle die Folie lesen?	Can you all read the transparency?
Hier vorne ist noch Platz. Vielleicht möchtet ihr noch etwas nach vorne kommen.	There's still room here at the front. Perhaps you'd like to move forward a little.
Könnt ihr mich überall gut verstehen?	Can you all understand me?
Spreche ich laut genug?	Am I speaking loudly enough?
Einen kleinen Moment, bitte. Die Technik spielt uns einen Streich.	One moment, please. The equipment is acting up.
Der CD-Spieler (der Videorekorder, der Computer) funktioniert nicht.	The CD player (video recorder, computer)* isn't working.
Es läuft gerade leider etwas anders als geplant, aber vielleicht können wir erstmal mit ... weitermachen.	Things aren't quite going to plan, unfortunately, but perhaps we can carry on with ... for the time being.
Entschuldigung für die kurze Unterbrechung, es geht sofort weiter.	I apologize for this brief interruption, we can carry on in a second.

Download 4

Unterbrecht mich ruhig, wenn etwas unklar sein sollte.	Please feel free to interrupt me if anything is unclear.
Meldet euch, wenn ihr eine Frage habt.	Just put your hand up if you've got a question.
Ihr könnt während der Präsentation jederzeit Fragen stellen.	You can ask questions at any time during the presentation.
Stellt Fragen immer gleich, wenn sie auftauchen.	Please ask questions as soon as they arise.
Ich beantworte eure Fragen am Ende des Referates.	I will answer your questions at the end of my presentation.
Es wird im Anschluss an die Präsentation genügend Zeit zur Diskussion geben.	There'll be plenty of time for discussion at the end of the presentation.
Alles in allem wird die Präsentation ungefähr zwanzig Minuten in Anspruch nehmen.	The whole presentation will take roughly twenty minutes

* Zusätzliche Varianten für einzelne Sätze und Wendungen sind in Klammern angegeben. Aus Platzgründen wurden bei den Tonaufnahmen nur die Grundvarianten aufgenommen.

Das Referat wird ungefähr eine Stunde dauern.	The presentation will take about one hour.
Es gibt ein Handout, das ich gleich austeile.	There is a handout which I will pass round in a moment.
Ich teile das Handout nach der Präsentation aus.	I will distribute the handout after the presentation.
Ihr bekommt ein Handout, deshalb müsst ihr nicht mitschreiben.	There will be a handout, so there's no need to take notes.

Wie steige ich in mein Thema ein?

The theme of Hamlet's famous speech is the afterlife. I hope you are all interested in the afterlife, if not - never mind. I wasn't, so I decided to tell you a few things about Shakesbear till the lesson is over.

Nenne das Thema und erläutere es gegebenenfalls kurz, bevor du mit dem Hauptteil loslegst. Sprich die Zuhörer direkt an. Der Einstieg soll das Interesse der Zuhörer wecken und möglichst spannend sein. Dies kann man auf unterschiedliche Art und Weise erreichen:

Begründung: Begründe kurz, warum du dich für dieses Thema entschieden hast, oder erläutere, warum das Thema für die Zuhörer wichtig ist.

Beispiel: Ein anschauliches oder witziges Beispiel bietet dem Zuhörer einen Anknüpfungspunkt und erleichtert den Einstieg ins Thema. Die Verbindung zum Thema darf dabei nicht aus dem Blickfeld geraten. Beispiele sollten deshalb klar verständlich sein und direkt zum Thema führen.

Ziel und Schwerpunkte: Gib an, worauf du im Laufe deines Referates hinauswillst und welches Ziel du dir vorgenommen hast. Provokante Thesen können die Aufmerksamkeit des Publikums fesseln. Bei sehr weit gefassten Themen empfiehlt es sich, Inhalte einzugrenzen und zu klären, welche Schwerpunkte du legst.

Aufbau: Erkläre in ein paar Stichworten, wie dein Referat aufgebaut ist. Dies schafft einen Überblick und informiert die Zuhörer darüber, was sie während des Vortrages erwartet. Zur besseren Orientierung kannst du den Aufbau auch auf einer Folie oder auf einem Handout darstellen.

TIPP:
Hilf den Zuhörern sich zu orientieren, indem du während deines Referates immer wieder Bezug auf deine Gliederung nimmst.

Download 5

Heute möchte ich über ... sprechen.	Today I want to talk about ...
Heute werde ich über ... sprechen.	Today I will talk about ...
Das heutige Thema ist:	Today's topic is:
Heute möchte ich mit euch ein interessantes (wichtiges, zentrales) Thema besprechen.	Today I want to introduce you to an interesting (an important, a central) topic.
Ich möchte euch in dieser Präsentation mit einem Thema vertraut machen, das ...	In this presentation I would like to introduce a subject to you which ...
... klingt vielleicht zunächst etwas langweilig (altmodisch). Ich hoffe aber, euch im Verlauf der Präsentation vom Gegenteil überzeugen zu können.	... at first might sound a bit boring (old-fashioned). However, I hope to change your minds during the course of my presentation.
Mich hat an diesem Thema besonders fasziniert (gereizt, bewegt, interessiert), dass ...	I was particularly fascinated (provoked, moved, interested) by this topic because ...
Ich interessiere mich schon lange für ...	I've been interested in ... for a long time.
In letzter Zeit hat dieses Thema an Aktualität gewonnen.	This subject has recently become very relevant.
Immer wieder hören wir in den Medien ...	Again and again the media reports ...
Es ist allgemein bekannt, dass ...	It's common sense that ...
Was hat dieses Thema eigentlich mit uns zu tun?	How does this topic actually relate to us?
Warum sollten wir eigentlich über dieses Thema sprechen?	Why do we have to talk about this subject at all?
Ihr habt euch sicher schon einmal gefragt, ...	You've probably asked yourselves before ...
Wie kommt es eigentlich, dass ...	How can it be that ...
Im Alltag begegnet uns immer wieder ...	Every day we come across ...
Dies ist ein Beispiel für ...	This is an example of ...
Das Ziel dieses Referates ist ...	The purpose of this presentation is to ...
Ich möchte zeigen, dass ...	I want to show that ...
Wir möchten belegen, dass ...	We want to prove that ...
Mein Ziel ist es zu erreichen, dass ...	My aim is to ...

Es ist wichtig über ... zu informieren.	It is important to inform people about ...
Ich möchte euer Interesse wecken für ...	I'd like to get you interested in ...
Ich würde gerne einen bisher noch wenig bekannten Aspekt in den Vordergrund stellen.	I would like to focus on an issue which has been given little attention up to now.
Es gilt, Vorurteile gegen ... aus dem zu Weg räumen.	It is necessary to get rid of prejudice against ...
Ich hoffe, dass ihr am Ende dieses Referates ... mit anderen Augen sehen werdet.	I hope that you will have a different view of ... by the end of this presentation.

Download 6

Ich möchte euch nun meine Gliederung vorstellen.	I would like to briefly present the structure of my presentation.
Ich habe den Vortrag in vier Abschnitte gegliedert.	I have divided this presentation into four different parts.
Ich werde in meinem Vortrag auf folgende Punkte eingehen:	I will present the following aspects:
Mein Fokus liegt auf ...	My focus is on ...
Ich setze folgende Schwerpunkte:	I will focus on ...
Zunächst werde ich auf ... zu sprechen kommen, dann sollen ... und ... folgen.	First I will talk about ... then ... after which ... will follow.
Zum Schluss werde ich ... ansprechen.	At the end I will mention ...
Abschließend werde ich ... ansprechen.	In conclusion, I will talk about ...
An dieser Stelle wird Raum für Fragen (eine Diskussion) sein.	And then there'll be time for questions (a discussion).
Anschließend haben wir noch ausreichend Zeit darüber zu diskutieren.	After the presentation there'll be enough time for discussion.

3.2 Jetzt geht's um die Wurst - Der Hauptteil

Wie präsentiere ich Inhalte und stelle meine Argumente vor?

As I said earlier on, I'm going to talk about Shakebear and his plays today. I thought that it is more fun not to talk about one play after the other but to mix them ... and let you guess at the end which of them I actually included in my talk.

Nach der Begrüßung und der ersten Darstellung deines Themas geht es nun darum, die Hauptinhalte, zentrale Fragen oder Thesen deines Referates detailliert zu erläutern. Dabei ist es wichtig, die Kerngedanken deutlich zu machen und eine übersichtliche Struktur zu schaffen.

> **TIPP:**
> *Sprich in kurzen, einfachen Sätzen. Zu komplizierten Satzkonstruktionen kann man als Zuhörer nur schwer folgen.*

Kerngedanken: Überlege dir im Vorfeld gut, welche Kerngedanken deine Zuhörer aus deinem Referat mitnehmen sollen. Konzentriere dich dabei auf das Wesentliche, da zu viele Informationen verwirren und die Gefahr besteht, dass die Zuhörer abschalten. Diese Auswahl ist eine der schwierigsten aber auch wichtigsten Aufgaben bei der Erstellung eines Referates: Durch die Wahl der Inhalte wird die Zielrichtung und der Schwerpunkt des Vortrages festgelegt. (vgl. Kap. 1.2, S. 404)

These aufstellen: Bei manchen Themenstellungen bietet es sich an, oder wird sogar erwartet, dass eine These formuliert wird. Eine These ist eine Behauptung, deren Richtigkeit noch zu klären ist. Es ist eine Aussage, über die es sich lohnt, länger nachzudenken und die durch verschiedene Argumente unterstützt oder entkräftet werden kann. Manchmal provoziert sie auch und steigert so das Interesse der Zuhörer. Findet sich bei der Vorbereitung eine solche These, kann der Aufbau des Hauptteiles durch die Abfolge von Pro- und Kontraargumenten gestaltet werden.

Reihenfolge: Lege eine Reihenfolge deiner ausgewählten Inhalte fest, die eine sinnvolle Struktur entstehen lässt. Bei historischen Themen ist es möglich, die Aspekte chronologisch zu ordnen. In anderen Fällen bietet es sich unter Umständen an, nach Themengebieten vorzugehen. Bei der Darstellung einer wissenschaftlichen Arbeit kann häufig die Struktur des Textes beibehalten werden. Wurde zu Beginn des Referates eine These aufgestellt, folgen nun die Pro- und Kontraargumente. Das Hauptargument ist am Ende eventuell besonders wirkungsvoll.

> **TIPP:**
> *Schreibe die einzelnen inhaltlichen Aspekte auf Kärtchen und schiebe diese so lange hin und her, bis du die optimale Abfolge gefunden hast.*

Checkliste: Aufbau einzelner Argumente

- Sind meine Argumente klar formuliert?
- Erkläre ich meine Argumente ausreichend?
- Sind die Begründungen nachvollziehbar und schlüssig?
- Habe ich genügend Fakten, um meine Argumente zu stützen?
- Habe ich genügend Beispiele, um meine Argumente zu veranschaulichen?

✓

Download 7

Wir sehen deutlich, dass ...	We can see clearly that ...
Folgender Gedanke ist zentral:	The following aspect is a central one:
Wir gehen von folgender Grundlage aus:	This is based on the assumption that ...
Dabei sind folgende Punkte besonders wichtig:	In this context, the following points are most essential:
Ein zentraler Aspekt ist ...	A crucial aspect is ...
Zwei Aspekte möchte ich besonders betonen:	I would like to emphasize two aspects in particular:
Wichtige inhaltliche Punkte sind ...	Important aspects are ...
Was ich damit sagen möchte, ist ...	What I'm saying is ...
Es liegt auf der Hand, dass ...	It is obvious that ...
Hier ist eine klare Tendenz zu erkennen.	An obvious tendency can be identified.
Es liegt nahe, die Aussagen dahingehend zu interpretieren ...	It would make sense to interpret the statements as follows:
Im Gegensatz zur allgemeinen Meinung, zeichnet sich eine andere Entwicklung ab.	In contrast to the general opinion, a different development can be seen.
In Anbetracht dieser Tatsachen ...	Considering these facts, ...
Es lässt sich trotzdem eine klare Entwicklung skizzieren ...	However, a clear development can be seen ...

Download 8

Lasst uns zunächst von folgender Annahme ausgehen:	Let's first assume that ...
Lasst mich zu Beginn folgende These aufstellen:	Initially, let me put forward the following hypothesis:
Ich behaupte, dass ...	I argue that ...
Folgende Hypothese werde ich in meinem Referat widerlegen:	I'm going to disprove the following theory in the course of my presentation:

Lasst uns als Arbeitshypothese erst einmal annehmen, dass ...	Let's start by assuming that ...
Ich möchte beweisen, dass ...	I want to prove that ...
Ich möchte in meinen Ausführungen diese These mit neuen Argumenten stützen.	In the course of my presentation I want to support this statement with new arguments.
Zunächst gehen wir von der Vermutung aus, dass ...	First we'll assume that ...
Aufgrund der bisher dargestellten Aspekte, gehe ich davon aus, dass ...	Based on the facts presented earlier, I assume that ...
Der bisherige Stand der Forschung lässt vermuten ...	The current research results give reason to believe ...
Bisher wurde immer davon ausgegangen, dass ...	Up to now it has always been assumed that ...
Ich halte die bisherigen Annahmen für falsch, weil ...	I consider the current assumptions to be wrong because ...
Ich möchte hiermit die These aufstellen ...	I would like to put forward the following theory:
Ich glaube, dass die Entdeckungen der letzten Jahre eher darauf hinweisen, dass ... als ...	I believe that the discoveries of the recent years point to ... rather than to ...

Download 9

Mein erstes Argument ist:	My first argument is:
Der erste Punkt, den ich anführen möchte, ist:	The first aspect I want to present is:
Zweitens ...	Secondly, ...
Und drittens sollte beachtet werden, dass ...	Thirdly, we should consider ...
Zunächst einmal möchte ich zeigen, dass ...	First I would like to show that ...
Ein weiteres Argument ist ...	A further argument supporting this theory is ...

Es muss aber auch erwähnt werden, dass ...	However, I should also mention that ...
Auch folgender Aspekt sollte nicht vergessen werden:	We should also not ignore the following:
Des Weiteren ...	Furthermore, ...
Außerdem ...	Besides, ...
Zudem ist wichtig, dass ...	In addition, it is important to ...
Darüber hinaus sollte erwähnt werden, dass ...	Additionally, we should mention that ...
Übrigens ...	Incidentally, ...
Nebenbei bemerkt ...	By the way, ...
Am Rande sei auch erwähnt, dass ...	In passing, let me mention that ...

Wie verknüpfte ich Inhalte und mache Zusammenhänge deutlich?

Well, that's a good question: what's the linking element of all that? ... errr ... well, I didn't get the connection myself ... I, too, thought that the stuff was strange in a way but hoped you could make a sense of it ...

Von Beginn deines Referates an sollte klar sein, wie die verschiedenen Aspekte miteinander zusammenhängen und wo die Verbindungen sind.

Gliederung transparent machen: Baue kleine Orientierungshilfen in dein Referat ein. Verweise immer wieder auf die Gliederung, lege bei Bedarf zwischendurch erneut die Gliederung auf Folie auf und mache so den roten Faden deutlich. Wenn du für die einzelnen Punkte einprägsame Überschriften findest, ist es sehr leicht, allein durch den Verweis auf eine dieser Überschriften deutlich zu machen, wo du dich befindest.

Übergänge gestalten: Zwischen den Informationsblöcken sollten kurze Zusammenfassungen des bereits Gesagten geliefert werden. Diese Zwischenfazits geben dem Zuhörer eine gewisse Sicherheit, die Inhalte wirklich verstanden zu haben und deuten an, dass man sich nun einem neuen Punkt zuwenden kann. Dieser neue Aspekt sollte ebenfalls durch eine kurze Ankündigung eingeleitet werden; das schafft weitere Orientierung.

Auf einen vorhergehenden Punkt verweisen: Sollten zwischen den einzelnen Aspekten Parallelen zu finden sein und sich Sachverhalte in ihrer Struktur ähneln, ist das eine wichtige Information für deine Zuhörer. Verweise deshalb auf diese Verbindungen und beziehe dich auf bereits genannte Punkte.

Download 10

Ich komme nun zu Punkt ...	I will now move on to ...
Damit möchte ich überleiten zu ...	Having said that, I want to go on with ...
Wir haben nun bereits die ersten drei Aspekte betrachtet.	We've already considered the first three aspects.
Diese Themen sind wichtig für den nächsten Punkt.	These issues are important for the next point.
Verbunden damit ist auch der nächste Bereich.	The next part is also related to this aspect.

Download 11

Bevor ich auf ... eingehe, möchte ich kurz festhalten ...	Before I move on to ..., I 'd like to repeat the following:
An dieser Stelle kann folgendes Zwischenfazit gezogen werden:	At this point we can draw the conclusion ...
Dies hat zur Folge ...	This has the effect ...
Auf der einen Seite ... auf der anderen Seite ...	On the one hand ... on the other hand ...
Jedoch ...	However, ...
Nichtsdestotrotz ...	Nevertheless, ...
Soweit also zu ...	This is all I want to say about ...
Was ... angeht, verhält es sich ähnlich (anders) ...	Regarding ..., the case is similar (different) ...
Es lässt sich natürlich auch anführen, dass ...	It can also be stated that ...
Andererseits ist festzuhalten, dass ...	On the other hand, it can be seen that ...
Das bringt mich auf einen anderen Aspekt.	This brings me to a different issue.
Dies führt mich zu meinem nächsten Punkt.	This leads me to my next point.
Ein weiterer wichtiger Punkt ist der Folgende:	The following aspect is another important one:
An dieser Stelle ist es auch interessant, dass ...	At this point it is also interesting to see that ...
Dabei sollte man auch beachten, dass ...	In this context we should also look at ...
Dabei darf nicht fehlen ...	In this context ... shouldn't be left out.
Gerne wird gesagt, dass ...	It is often said that ...

Hier aber gilt ...	In this case, however, ...
Dies ist zwar grundsätzlich richtig, aber ...	In general, this is right but ...
Es sollte ebenfalls erwähnt werden ...	It should also be mentioned that ...
Ganz ähnlich verhält es sich mit ...	A similar situation is ...
Ganz anders verhält es sich mit ...	The situation is quite different in the case of ...

Download 12

Hier kann eine Parallele zu ... festgestellt werden.	This is paralleled by ...
Dies erinnert an den vorherigen Punkt, der sich mit ... beschäftigte.	This brings to mind the previous issue which dealt with ...
Wie ich bereist erwähnte ...	As I have already mentioned ...
Dieser Punkt ist zu Anfang schon einmal diskutiert worden.	This point was already discussed at the beginning.
Um nochmals auf ... zurückzukommen:	To return to ... once more:
Und jetzt werden die anfangs erwähnten Punkte wieder wichtig.	And this is where the facts mentioned earlier become significant again.
Das scheint im Gegensatz zu meiner eingangs genannten These zu stehen.	This seems to contradict my original theory.
Vielleicht fragt ihr euch jetzt, hat er nicht gerade etwas ganz anderes behauptet?	You may be asking yourselves whether I didn't just say something completely different.
Ich kann euch versichern, dass dies kein Widerspruch zu ... ist.	I can assure you that this doesn't contradict ...
Nach dieser gründlichen Überprüfung und Abwägung der Argumente kann die Eingangshypothese nicht aufrechterhalten werden.	After carefully examining and weighing up the arguments, it is not possible to uphold the initial hypothesis.
Dies spricht für die anfangs aufgestellte These.	This supports the initial theory.
Damit ist unsere These bewiesen.	This proves our theory.

Wie baue ich Beispiele, Zahlen und Fakten ein?

Shakesbirth ... errr ... I think he was born in ... - well, around ... errr ... perhaps in the 16th century? Anyway, a long time ago, that's for sure.

Deine Thesen, Argumente und Ausführungen können erst dann wirklich überzeugen, wenn sie durch Beispiele, Zahlen und Fakten veranschaulicht und untermauert werden. Achte darauf, diese Information an den entsprechenden Stellen sinnvoll und im Zusammenhang in dein Referat einzubauen. Mache auch deutlich, was ein Schaubild zeigen und belegen soll. Behalte deinen Schwerpunkt im Auge und verliere dich nicht in Zusatzinformationen, die keinen wesentlichen Beitrag zum Hauptthema liefern.

Je nach Thema müssen unterschiedliche Informationen präsentiert werden:

Biografische Daten werden in chronologischer Reihenfolge präsentiert. Konzentriere dich auf wesentliche Eckdaten und beleuchte auch das geschichtliche Umfeld. Eventuell bietet sich ein Vergleich mit einer anderen historischen Person an.

TIPP:
Bilder der vorgestellten Personen und kurze Anekdoten aus ihrem Leben machen den Vortrag anschaulich.

Historische Ereignisse sollten in Bezug zum geschichtlichen Gesamtgeschehen gesetzt werden. Vergleiche beispielsweise die Entwicklung des von dir dargestellten Phänomens mit anderen Ländern und weise auf Zusammenhänge hin. Auch ein Vergleich mit der heutigen Zeit kann für viele Zuhörer das Verständnis erleichtern.

Zahlen und Fakten lassen sich ebenfalls gut vergleichen, um ihre Bedeutung zu verdeutlichen. Es hilft den Zuhörern, wenn du Zahlen in Relation setzt und Vergleichsgrößen bietest.

Statistiken lassen sich in Diagrammen anschaulich darstellen. Besonders komplexe Zusammenhänge solltest du auf jeden Fall visualisieren und erklären. Allerdings darfst du auch hier die Zuhörer nicht überfordern: Schaubilder sollten so einfach und übersichtlich wie möglich sein.

TIPP:
Gib den Zuhörern genug Zeit, ein Schaubild zu betrachten und zu verstehen. Für sie ist das Schaubild neu!

Checkliste: Umgang mit Beispielen, Zahlen und Fakten

- Habe ich für alle meine Ausführungen auch Belege?
- Reichen die Belege aus, um meine These zu stützen?
- Kenne ich die Quelle und habe ich sie angegeben (z. B. auf dem Handout)?
- Handelt es sich um eine verlässliche Quelle?
- Ist alles verständlich und klar dargestellt? Habe ich komplexere Zusammenhänge visualisiert?
- Ist die Fülle an Zahlen meinen Zuhörern noch zuzumuten?

Download 13

Dieses Beispiel zeigt, dass ...	This example shows that ...
An diesem Beispiel sehen wir ...	This example illustrates ...
Ein gutes Beispiel dafür ist ...	A good example for this is ...
Ich möchte ein paar Bespiele nennen ...	I would like to mention a few examples.
Lasst mich dies an einem kurzen Beispiel verdeutlichen.	Let me illustrate this with a little example.
Es gab beispielsweise einen Fall ...	There was, for example, a case ...
Vielleicht wird dies durch folgendes Beispiel klarer:	Perhaps this will become clearer in the following example:

Download 14

[Peter Brown] wurde im Jahr ... in ... geboren.	[Peter Brown]* was born in ...
[Peter Brown] starb im Jahr ... in ...	[Peter Brown] died in ...
Ich werde einige biographische Eckdaten zu ... nennen.	I'll give you some basic biographical facts about ...
Ich werde einen Überblick über den Lebenslauf von [Peter Brown] geben.	I'll give you a short résumé of [Peter Brown].
Im selben Jahr ...	In the same year ...
Dieses Ereignis war besonders prägend für ...	This incident was especially important for ...
Sein Lebensziel war es ...	His aim in life was to ...

* Elemente in eckigen Klammern (z. B. Eigennamen) sind in den Wortlisten nur als Beispiel angegeben und können beliebig ausgetauscht werden.

Download 15

Im Jahr ...	In ...
Die Situation sah folgendermaßen aus:	The situation was the following:
Im Jahr ... war die Situation besonders schwierig (günstig).	In ... the situation was particularly difficult (favourable).
Viele Faktoren beeinflussten ...	Many factors had an effect on ...
Die Gründe für diese Entwicklung waren vielfältig.	The reasons for this development were manifold.
Auch in anderen Ländern ...	In other countries ... also ...
Anders als heute gab es damals ...	Unlike today, in those times there was ...
Wenn wir die Situation mit der heutigen vergleichen, erkennen wir, dass ...	Comparing the historical situation with today's, it becomes clear that ...

Download 16

Ein paar Zahlen werden diese Befunde verdeutlichen.	A few figures will illustrate these results.
Die Zahl beträgt ...	The number is ...
Diese Zahl ist doppelt so hoch wie ...	The number (figure) is twice as high as ...
Dieser Wert lässt sich vergleichen mit ...	This amount (figure) can be compared to ...
Diese Größe ist vergleichbar mit ...	This quantity is comparable with ...
Die Zahl hat sich in zwei Jahren verdreifacht.	The figure (number, amount) has tripled in the last two years.
Das sind so viele wie ...	That's as many (much) as ...
Das sind weniger als ...	That's less (fewer) than ...

Download 17

Hier seht ihr ...	Here you can see ...
das Tortendiagramm / das Säulendiagramm / das Liniendiagramm	the pie chart / the bar chart / the line chart
Diese Statistik belegt ...	These statistics support ...
Dieses Schaubild zeigt, dass ...	This diagram shows that ...
ein Viertel / die Hälfte / ein Drittel / dreiviertel	a quarter / a half / a third / three quarters

23% der Menschen in [London] sind ...	23% of the people in [London] are ...
[Stratford] hat einen niedrigeren Prozentsatz an ... als London.	[Stratford] has a lower percentage of ... than [London].
Der Prozentsatz von ... in ... ist höher als im nationalen Durchschnitt.	The percentage of ... in ... is higher than the national average.
Ich möchte euch einige genaue Statistiken zeigen:	I would like to show you some detailed statistics:
Das Diagramm zeigt die ausgeprägte Tendenz an ...	The chart shows a clear tendency ...
Ich möchte euch besonders auf diese Graphik aufmerksam machen.	I would like to draw your attention to this diagram in particular.
Im Jahr 2004 lässt sich eine eindeutige Steigerung (ein steiler Abfall) feststellen.	In 2004, there was a marked increase (sharp fall).
An der Kurve kann man erkennen, wie der Verbrauch immer mehr ansteigt (absinkt).	This graph shows us how consumption continues to grow (fall).
Wenn man die Graphiken von 1998 und 2008 vergleicht, so kann man sehen, dass ...	If we compare the diagrams for 1998 and 2008, we can see that ...
Das ausgeglichene Verhältnis zwischen den grünen und roten Balken legt nahe, dass ...	The balanced ratio between the red and green bars suggests that ...
Das Ermutigende (Besorgniserregende) hier ist ...	The encouraging (worrying) thing here is ...
Die Zahlen sprechen hier eine eindeutige Sprache.	These figures convey a clear message.

Download 18

Grundlage für meine Überlegungen sind folgende Autoren:	I've based my assumptions on the following authors:
Ich stütze mich hierbei auf ...	I base this statement on ...
Als Quelle für mein Referat diente ...	One of the sources of my presentation is ...
Die Statistiken wurden von ... erstellt.	The statistics were compiled by ...
An dieser Stelle möchte ich auf die Untersuchung von [Peter Brown] hinweisen.	Here I would like to point out [Peter Brown's] study.

Wie gebe ich Meinungen an und zitiere Experten?

There is one man who thinks that this other man who wrote something about Shakesbill's plays was completely wrong and that in fact only that woman from Liverpool had really understood the true meaning of love.

Mache es sprachlich deutlich, wenn du nicht deine eigene Meinung, sondern die Meinung Anderer wiedergibst. Zitiere nur seriöse Wissenschaftler und Forscher, deren Meinung in der Fachwelt Gewicht hat. Wenn du wörtlich zitierst, musst du unbedingt den Namen des Autors nennen. Ein Vortrag wird spannender, wenn du Experten aus verschiedenen Lagern zu Wort kommen lässt, die du gegeneinander stellst und diskutierst.

TIPP:
Mache dich darauf gefasst, dass Nachfragen zu den von dir genannten Namen kommen. Die wichtigsten Dinge solltest du also über diese Personen wissen.

Übertreibe es aber nicht mit fremden Meinungen: Schließlich soll es ein von dir persönlich gestalteter Vortrag sein, in dem vor allem du selbst zu Wort kommst.
Du kannst auch Stimmungen in der Gesellschaft beschreiben oder landläufige Meinungen aufgreifen, um an diese anzuknüpfen oder sie zu widerlegen.

Download 19

[Peter Brown] vertritt die Meinung, dass ...	[Peter Brown] is of the opinion that ...
Laut [Peter Brown] ...	According to [Peter Brown], ...
[Peter Brown] zufolge ...	According to [Peter Brown], ...
[Peter Brown] meint ...	[Peter Brown] thinks ...
[Peter Brown] vermutet ...	[Peter Brown] assumes ...
[Peter Brown] ist der Auffassung ...	[Peter Brown] is of the opinion that ...
[Peter Brown] plädiert für (gegen) ...	[Peter Brown] is in favour of (against) ...
[Peter Brown] behauptet:	[Peter Brown] states:
Wie die Ministerin verlautbaren ließ ...	As the minister made known ...
[Peter Brown] weist immer wieder darauf hin, dass ...	[Peter Brown] repeatedly points out that ...
In seinem Aufsatz (Buch, Veröffentlichung) *[The British]* weist [Peter Brown] bereits darauf hin ...	In his article (book, publication) *[The British]*, [Peter Brown] has already pointed out ...

In diesem Zusammenhang möchte ich folgende Aussage von [Peter Brown] zitieren:	In this context I would like to quote [Peter Brown]:
Dazu hat [Peter Brown] folgendes gesagt:	In this context [Peter Brown] said:
Auch [Peter Brown] stellt in seinen Veröffentlichungen wiederholt diese These auf.	[Peter Brown] also repeatedly puts forward this theory in his publications.
Im Leitartikel der *Newsweek* vom 14.02.2008 wird ein wichtiger Aspekt angesprochen.	An important issue is addressed in *Newsweek's* leading article of 14.02.2008.
[Peter Brown] macht diese Beobachtung zum ersten Mal im Jahr 1996.	[Peter Brown] first made this observation in 1996.
Auf Seite 26 des Buches *[The British]* von [Peter Brown] aus dem Jahr 2003 finden wir folgende Bemerkung:	On page 26 of [Peter Brown's] book *[The British]* from 2003, we can find the following comment:
Dem widerspricht völlig ...	This is in complete contradiction to ...
Im Gegensatz zu dem, was [Peter Brown] in seinem Aufsatz *[The British]* behauptet, ...	Contrary to what [Peter Brown] says in his article *[The British]*, ...
Hiermit darf die These von [Peter Brown] als widerlegt gelten.	With this, [Peter Brown's] theory can be considered refuted.
Eine unbelegte Behauptung, die von [Peter Brown] in den Medien immer wieder verbreitet wird, ...	An unsubstantiated assertion that is frequently made in the media by [Peter Brown] is ...

Download 20

Es wird allgemein angenommen (vermutet) ...	It is generally accepted (assumed) that ...
Es kann kein Zweifel bestehen, dass ...	There can be no doubt that ...
Viele glauben ...	Many people believe ...
Oft wird gesagt, dass ...	It is often said that ...
Die öffentliche Meinung ist gegen (für) ...	Public opinion is against (in favour of) ...
Die Mehrheit (Minderheit) vertritt die Ansicht, dass ...	The majority (minority) is of the opinion that ...
Die Stimmung ist aufgeheizt (kühl, freundlich).	The atmosphere is heated (chilly, friendly).
Es herrscht eine starke Tendenz, dies so zu sehen.	There is a strong tendency to see it this way.
In wissenschaftlichen (informierten, politischen) Kreisen geht man davon aus ...	In scientific (informed, political) circles it is assumed that ...

Wie formuliere ich meine persönliche Stellungnahme?

Don't ask me what I think about all of this. I haven't read any of Shakesboy's plays.

Die persönliche Stellungnahme ist nicht immer unbedingt notwendig, kann aber dazu dienen, dem Vortrag eine eigene Note zu verleihen. Auch die Zuhörer zeigen in der Regel ein starkes Interesse an der Meinung des Vortragenden. Die persönliche Stellungnahme bietet sich besonders als Anknüpfungspunkt für Diskussionen an, in die das Publikum einbezogen werden soll.

Wenn du deine eigenen Gedanken und Ansichten zu einem Thema darlegen willst, mache deutlich, dass du jetzt deine eigene Position beschreibst. Achte darauf, dass sich deine Stellungnahme schlüssig aus den vorangegangenen Ausführungen ergibt und keine neuen Unklarheiten aufwirft. Begründe deine Position und nimm dabei vergleichend oder distanzierend Bezug auf zuvor genannte Argumente und Meinungen.

Download 21

Meiner Meinung nach ...	In my opinion ...
Ich glaube ...	I believe ...
Ich vermute ...	I suspect ...
Meines Erachtens ...	In my view ...
Ich bin der Ansicht, dass ...	I am of the opinion that ...
Wir sind der Meinung, dass ...	We think that ...
Wir sind der Auffassung, dass ...	We are of the opinion that ...
Was mich betrifft ...	As far as I'm concerned ...
Es steht für mich unzweifelhaft fest ...	In my view there is no doubt that ...
Ich halte es für sehr wahrscheinlich ...	I think it is very likely that ...
Ähnlich wie [Peter Brown] denke ich, dass ...	Like [Peter Brown], I think that ...
Ich kann mich der Meinung von [Peter Brown] anschließen.	I can only support [Peter Brown's] opinion.
Besonders überzeugend finde ich ...	... seems particularly convincing to me.
Dem kann ich unbedingt zustimmen.	I simply must agree with that.
Ich habe große Zweifel, ob ...	I very much doubt whether ...
Ich persönlich halte das für diskussionswürdig.	Personally, I think this is worth discussing.
Das Argument überzeugt mich nicht, weil ...	This argument doesn't convince me because ...
Im Gegensatz zu [Peter Brown] bin ich der Meinung, dass ...	Unlike [Peter Brown], I am of the opinion that ...

3.3 Ende gut, alles gut - Der Schluss

Wie fasse ich die Hauptpunkte zusammen?

I hope you won't forget all those interesting things about Shakesbeep. Perhaps I should better tell you everything all over again - just to be on the safe side.

TIPP:
Baue am Ende keine völlig neuen Gedanken und Argumente ein.

Der Schluss ist nicht nur ein Anhängsel, sondern auch das Finale deines Vortrags. Dieses Finale gilt es, möglichst kurz, prägnant und eindrücklich zu gestalten. Ziehe den Schluss nicht unnötig in die Länge - vor allem dann nicht, wenn du das Ende bereits angekündigt hast.

Versuche also nicht, sämtliche Argumente in Kurzform wiederzugeben, sondern zähle die wichtigsten Hauptpunkte deines Referates auf. Es könnte sich beispielsweise anbieten, dein Hauptargument in zugespitzter Form noch einmal auf den Punkt zu bringen. Ein Fazit oder eine Bewertung der Befunde sind weitere Möglichkeiten, um den inhaltlichen Teil des Referates abzuschließen und die einzelnen Aspekte zu bündeln.

Download 22

Lasst mich das Wesentliche noch einmal zusammenfassen.	Allow me to summarize the basic facts.
Ganz wichtig ist hier, dass ...	It is important here that ...
Zusammenfassend lässt sich sagen, dass ...	To summarize, we can say that ...
Abschließend möchte ich ...	Finally, I would like to ...
Nach sorgfältiger Abwägung der Argumente ...	After weighing up the arguments carefully, ...
Ich komme zu folgendem Schluss:	I arrive at the following conclusion:
Ich ziehe folgendes Fazit:	The conclusion I draw is:
Als Konsequenz aus meinen Ausführungen ergibt sich für mich ...	I conclude that ...
Lasst mich nun zu einer Bewertung kommen:	Allow me now to make an assessment:

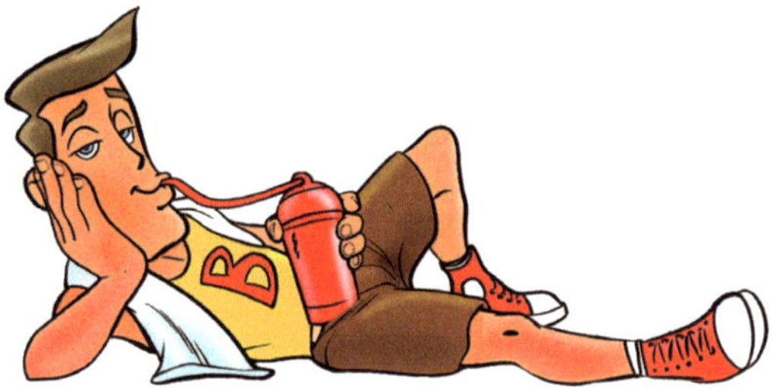

Wie beende ich die Präsentation?

Ok. That's it. Shakes-end.

Genauso wichtig wie eine freundliche Begrüßung ist auch ein gelungener Abschluss, der deutlich signalisiert, dass dein Referat beendet ist. Vergiss vor Erleichterung über den erfolgreich gehaltenen Vortrag nicht, dich angemessen bei deinen Zuhörern für die Aufmerksamkeit zu bedanken oder mit einem höflichen, an die Zuhörer gerichteten Schlusssatz, das Referat offiziell zu beenden.

Ich bedanke mich für eure Aufmerksamkeit.	Thank you for your attention.
Vielen Dank fürs Zuhören.	Thanks for listening.
Damit bin ich am Ende meines Vortrages angekommen.	I've now come to the end of my presentation.
Ich hoffe, das war hilfreich.	I hope that was helpful.
Ich hoffe, euch Denkanstöße (Diskussionsstoff) gegeben zu haben.	I hope that I have given you food for thought (something to discuss).
Ich hoffe, dass ich eine neue Sichtweise auf ... vermitteln konnte.	I hope that my presentation sheds a different light on ...
Ich hoffe, dass ich euch dieses Thema unter einem neuen Blickwinkel präsentieren konnte.	I hope that I have presented this topic from a new perspective.

Download 23

Wie rege ich Fragen an und gehe mit ihnen um?

Please don't ask any questions about Shakespie. I've told you everything I know.

Gib den Zuhörern am Ende auf jeden Fall die Gelegenheit, Fragen zu stellen. So hast du die Möglichkeit, Unklarheiten zu beseitigen und vertieft auf bestimmte Sachverhalte einzugehen.

Verständnisfragen: Zunächst sollten Verständnisfragen geklärt werden, damit jeder genau weiß, was gemeint ist. Lege gegebenenfalls eine Folie ein zweites Mal auf, um eine Problematik zu erläutern.

Weiterführende Fragen: Du solltest darauf gefasst sein, dass auch Fragen zu Themen kommen, die du in deinem Referat nur

TIPP:
Gib zu, wenn du auf eine Frage keine Antwort weißt und biete an, die Antwort herauszufinden und nachzureichen.

am Rande angeschnitten hast, oder dass tiefer gehende Erklärungen von dir erbeten werden. Es ist deshalb ratsam, möglichst viele Details zu kennen und sich die Zusammenhänge und Verbindungen zu verwandten Themen bereits im Vorfeld klar zu machen. Achte aber darauf, sehr spezielle Fragen Einzelner nicht zu ausführlich zu beantworten, um die übrigen Zuhörer nicht zu langweilen. Verweise eventuell auf Literatur, die sich näher mit diesem Thema befasst.

Diskussion: In manchen Fällen bietet sich eine Diskussion am Ende eines Referates an. Die bis dahin passiven Zuhörer erhalten die Möglichkeit, sich aktiv zu beteiligen, du dagegen solltest dich nun zurücknehmen und in die Rolle des Moderators schlüpfen. Deine Aufgabe ist es, die genannten Argumente und Stellungnahmen immer wieder zu bündeln, Dinge auf den Punkt zu bringen und durch geschickte Fragen die Diskussion am Laufen zu halten.

Download 24

Gibt es dazu Fragen?	Are there any questions?
Ist noch etwas unklar?	Is everything clear?
Für Fragen stehe ich gerne zur Verfügung.	I will be happy to answer any questions.
Falls es Fragen gibt, könnt ihr diese jederzeit stellen.	If you have any questions, you can interrupt me at any time.
Bitte scheut euch nicht zu fragen.	Please don't hesitate to ask questions.
Eine ausführlichere Beantwortung der Frage würde etwas zu weit führen.	Answering this question in detail would go too far.
Wenn ihr euch näher mit diesem Thema beschäftigen wollt, kann ich euch folgende Literatur empfehlen:	If you would like to know more about this topic, I can recommend the following titles:
Diese Frage würde ich gerne ins Plenum zurückgeben.	That's a question I would like to put to the audience.
Hiermit möchte ich die Diskussion eröffnen.	And now I would like to start the discussion.

4 ÜBUNG MACHT DEN MEISTER

4.1 Übungen zum Inhalt

Informationen finden und notieren

William Shakespeare

[1] Shakespeare, or "The Bard" (as he is often referred to), is considered one of the greatest playwrights of all times. His influence on later theatre productions and literature has been tremendous. Though we know a lot about his life, many details remain unknown.
[2] William Shakespeare was born in Stratford upon Avon in 1564. His parents were John Shakespeare and Mary Arden. He was raised in Stratford and at the age of 18 he married Anne Hathaway. The marriage was arranged in some haste, as Anne was already pregnant.
[3] It is not clear when Shakespeare started writing. All we know is that some of his plays were performed on a London stage by 1592. Shakespeare was involved in the acting company of the Lord Chamberlain's Men. In 1599 they built a theatre that Shakespeare was very closely associated with: The Globe. One of his earlier plays was the comedy 'A Midsummer Night's Dream'. In the early 1600s he wrote some of his most famous tragedies: 'Hamlet', ‚King Lear' and ‚Macbeth'.
[4] Shakespeare died a wealthy man in Stratford in 1616 and was buried there in Holy Trinity Church. His plays, however, didn't die with him. His works consist not only of almost forty plays, but also of poetry: Shakespeare wrote 154 sonnets, two narrative poems, and a number of other poems. Many later writers were influenced by Shakespeare: they quoted his works or copied his themes and style. Shakespeare left a lasting impression on writers, musicians and painters. Even Sigmund Freud, the psychoanalyst, drew on Hamlet to support his theories of human nature. Today, Shakespeare's work is repeatedly adapted, performed and reinterpreted throughout the whole world.

1 Ordne die Überschriften den einzelnen Abschnitten im Text zu!

☐ a) Shakespeare's influence

☐ b) Introduction#

☐ c) Shakespeare and the theatre

☐ d) Shakespeare's early life

2 Welche der folgenden **Fakten** über Shakespeare sind richtig? Welche sind falsch? Kreuze an!

	richtig	falsch
a) Shakespeare got married in haste, because Anne was underage.	☐	☐
b) Shakespeare was a famous writer.	☐	☐
c) Shakespeare was a wealthy man when he died.	☐	☐
d) Shakespeare started writing in 1592.	☐	☐
e) Shakespeare wrote plays and poems.	☐	☐
f) Shakespeare wrote over 60 plays.	☐	☐

3 Kreuze sieben der folgenden Wörter und Ausdrücke an, die du auf eine Karteikarte schreiben würdest, wenn du den Inhalt des Textes knapp wiedergeben müsstest!

- ☐ a) Stratford upon Avon in 1564
- ☐ b) was raised
- ☐ c) married Anne Hathaway
- ☐ d) haste
- ☐ e) acting company (Lord Chamberlain's Men)
- ☐ f) theatre
- ☐ g) The Globe
- ☐ h) was buried
- ☐ i) influence on themes and style
- ☐ j) impression on writers, musicians, painters
- ☐ k) Freud (Hamlet: human nature)
- ☐ l) theories

4 Ordne die oben gefunden Stichwörter und Wendungen den Oberbegriffen zu!

1) Shakespeare's life	2) Shakespeare and the theatre	3) Shakespeare's influence
________	________	________
________	________	________
________	________	________
________	________	________

Bibliographie erstellen

5 Ordne die Angaben auf der linken Seite ihren entsprechenden Bedeutungen auf der rechten Seite zu! Erstelle dann eine vollständige bibliographische Angabe!

a) ☐ PONS	1) Ort und Jahreszahl
b) ☐ Stuttgart: 2008.	2) Titel
c) ☐ *Shakespeare. The greatest playwright ever.*	3) Autor
d) ☐ Brown, Peter	4) Seitenangabe
e) ☐ S.12ff.	5) Verlag

4.2 Übungen zum Wortschatz

Die Einleitung

1 Welche der folgenden Wendungen eignen sich zur **Begrüßung** von Zuhörern in einer Klasse? Kreuze diese an!

- ☐ a) Good morning everybody.
- ☐ b) Ladies and gentlemen ...
- ☐ c) Dear classmates ...
- ☐ d) Hi ...
- ☐ e) Dear fellow students ...
- ☐ f) I'm glad you could all make it.
- ☐ g) I'd like to welcome you to ...
- ☐ h) At least you weren't late.
- ☐ i) Nice to see you all this morning.
- ☐ j) I'm glad to be able to welcome so many of you ...

2 Welche der folgenden Wendungen können Vortragende dazu verwenden, sich und ihren Mitreferenten den **Zuhörern vorzustellen**? Kreuze diese an!

- ☐ a) Let me briefly introduce myself.
- ☐ b) My hobbies are ...
- ☐ c) Here with me today is ...
- ☐ d) I'm a student in the third semester.
- ☐ e) We prepared this presentation together.
- ☐ f) I am ...
- ☐ g) My birthday is in May.
- ☐ h) My name is ...
- ☐ i) May I introduce ...
- ☐ j) I don't know him.

3 Zu Beginn deines Referates gibt es kleine **technische und organisatorische Probleme**. Wie reagierst du in welcher Situation? Finde die passende Wendung und trage den entsprechenden Buchstaben in der linken Spalte ein!

1) ☐ Es ist zu hell, um die Folie optimal lesen zu können.	a) I apologise for this brief interruption, we can carry on in a second.
2) ☐ Der CD-Player scheint nicht zu funktionieren.	b) There's still room here at the front. Perhaps you'd like to move forward a little.
3) ☐ Hinten müssen die Zuhörer bereits stehen, doch vorne ist noch genügend Platz.	c) One moment, please. The equipment is acting up.
4) ☐ Du bist dir nicht sicher, ob du auch überall verstanden wirst.	d) Should I close the blinds?
5) ☐ Die Lampe des Tageslichtprojektors muss gewechselt werden.	e) Do I speak loud enough?

4 Es ist wichtig, deinen Zuhörern einige **organisatorische Details** mitzuteilen; zum Beispiel, wann Fragen gestellt werden können oder ob es ein Handout geben wird. Setze die passenden Verben in die Lücken ein, so dass die Sätze Sinn ergeben!

give ask feel free be take distribute answer

1) Please ________________ to interrupt me if anything is unclear.
2) There'll ________________ plenty of time for discussion at the end of the presentation.
3) I will ________________ the handout after the presentation.
4) The presentation will ________________ roughly twenty minutes.
5) Please ________________ questions as soon as they arise.
6) I'll ________________ your questions at the end of my presentation.
7) Just ________________ a sign if you've got a question.

5 Die folgenden Wendungen können alle zur **Einleitung deines Themas** verwendet werden. Verbinde jene, die eine ähnliche Bedeutung haben und trage den entsprechenden Buchstaben in der linken Spalte ein!

1) ☐ Today I want to talk about ...	a)	Why do we have to talk about this subject at all?
2) ☐ Today I want to introduce you to an interesting topic.	b)	I want to prove that ...
3) ☐ How does this topic actually relate to us?	c)	In this presentation I would like to introduce a subject to you which is quite interesting.
4) ☐ I want to show that ...	d)	The purpose of this presentation is to ...
5) ☐ I hope that you will have a different view of that matter by the end of this presentation.	e)	In conclusion, I will talk about ...
6) ☐ At the end I will mention ...	f)	It is necessary to remove prejudices against ...
7) ☐ My aim is to ...	g)	Today's topic is ...

6 Welche der folgenden Wendungen kannst du nutzen, um den **Aufbau deines Referates** deutlich zu machen? Kreuze diese an!

- ☐ a) I have divided this presentation into four different parts.
- ☐ b) Everyday we come across ...
- ☐ c) I'd like to wake your interest in ...
- ☐ d) I would like to briefly present the structure of my presentation.
- ☐ e) At the end I will mention ...
- ☐ f) There will be a handout so that there's no need to take notes.
- ☐ g) First I will talk about ... then ... after which ... will follow.

Der Hauptteil

7 Du willst die **Kerngedanken** deines Referates darlegen. Übersetze die folgenden Wendungen, die du dazu verwenden kannst!

a) ______________________________
Wir gehen von folgender Grundlage aus:

b) ______________________________
Folgender Gedanke ist zentral:

c) ______________________________
Zwei Aspekte möchte ich besonders betonen.

d) ______________________________
Es lässt sich eine klare Entwicklung skizzieren ...

e) ______________________________
Wichtige inhaltliche Punkte sind ...

f) ______________________________
Was ich damit sagen möchte, ist ...

8 Du willst zu Beginn eine **These aufstellen**. Verbinde die passenden Satzanfänge mit den Satzenden und trage den entsprechenden Buchstaben in der linken Spalte ein!

1)	☐ Based on the facts presented earlier ...	a)	... I want to support this statement with new arguments.
2)	☐ I consider the current assumptions ...	b)	... it has always been assumed that ...
3)	☐ In the course of my presentation ...	c)	... to be wrong because ...
4)	☐ Up to now ...	d)	... give reason to believe ...
5)	☐ The current research results ...	e)	... the following theory ...
6)	☐ I would like to put forward ...	f)	... I assume that ...

9 Du willst ein **Argument anführen**, doch die Wendungen sind durcheinander geraten. Bringe die Elemente wieder in die richtige Reihenfolge!

1) ______________________________
argument / first / my / is ...

2) ______________________________
aspect / the / first / is ... / to present / I / want

3) ______________________________
I / also / however / should / that ... / mention

4) ______________________________
would / I / to show / first / that ... / like

5) ______________________________
to ... / it / important / is / in / addition

6) ______________________________
consider / thirdly / should / we / that ...

7) ______________________________
following: / we / ignore / should / also / not / the

10 Welche der folgenden Wendungen eignen sich ein (weiteres) **Argument anzuführen**? Kreuze diese an!

- ☐ a) Secondly ...
- ☐ b) Furthermore ...
- ☐ c) Strictly ...
- ☐ d) Additionally ...
- ☐ e) Funnily ...
- ☐ f) Incidentally ...
- ☐ g) By the way ...
- ☐ h) Firmly ...
- ☐ i) Besides ...

11 Du willst **Inhalte verknüpfen** und **Zusammenhänge deutlich machen**. Setze die fehlenden Wörter in die Lücken ein!

this leads | can draw | should also look | mentioned | different issue | quite different

1) At this point we ______________________ the conclusion ...
2) This brings me to a ______________________.
3) ______________________ to my next point.
4) It should also be ______________________ that ...
5) The situation is ______________________ in the case of ...
6) In this context we ______________________ at ...

12 Es ist sinnvoll, in deinem Referat **Bezüge zwischen einzelnen Punkten** deutlich zu machen und auf bereits genannte Aspekte zu verweisen. Bringe die richtige Übersetzung mit der jeweiligen Wendung zusammen!

1) ☐ Hier kann eine Parallele zu ... festgestellt werden.	a) To return to ... once more:
2) ☐ Wie ich bereits erwähnte ...	b) This supports the initial theory.
3) ☐ Um nochmals auf ... zurückzukommen:	c) This is paralleled by ...
4) ☐ Dieser Punkt ist zu Anfang schon einmal diskutiert worden.	d) And this is where the facts mentioned earlier become significant again.
5) ☐ Ich kann euch versichern, dass dies kein Widerspruch zu ... ist.	e) This proves our theory.
6) ☐ Dies spricht für die anfangs aufgestellte These.	f) As I have already mentioned ...
7) ☐ Vielleicht fragt ihr euch jetzt, hat er nicht gerade etwas ganz anderes behauptet?	g) This point was already discussed at the beginning.
8) ☐ Und jetzt werden die anfangs erwähnten Punkte wieder wichtig.	h) You may be asking yourselves whether I didn't just say something completely different.
9) ☐ Damit ist unsere These bewiesen.	i) I can assure you that this doesn't contradict ...

13 Welche der folgenden Wendungen eignen sich, die **Quellen deiner Arbeit anzugeben**? Kreuze diese an!

- ☐ a) I base this statement on ...
- ☐ b) My neighbour says ...
- ☐ c) The statistics were compiled by ...
- ☐ d) Here, I would like to point out the following study:
- ☐ e) Last night I had a dream ...
- ☐ f) Years ago I read in a magazine that
- ☐ g) The main source of my presentation is ...
- ☐ h) I've based my assumptions on the following authors:

14 Du willst in deinem Referat verschiedene **Fakten, Statistiken und Zahlen angeben**. Finde die passenden Wendungen zu den vorgegebenen Situationen!

1) ☐	Du willst ein Beispiel anführen.	a) Comparing the historical situation with todays, it becomes clear ...
2) ☐	Du präsentierst ein Schaubild.	b) A few figures will illustrate these results.
3) ☐	Du nennst Gründe für eine Entwicklung.	c) The reasons for this development were manifold.
4) ☐	Du vergleichst zwei Situationen.	d) The situation was the following:
5) ☐	Du beschreibst eine Situation.	e) A good example for this is ...
6) ☐	Du gibst Zahlen zur Illustration an.	f) One of the sources of my presentation is ...
7) ☐	Du machst auf eine Graphik aufmerksam.	g) Here, I would like to point out [Peter Brown's] study.
8) ☐	Du gibst die Quelle deiner Arbeit an.	h) This diagram shows that ...
9) ☐	Du machst auf eine weitere Untersuchung aufmerksam.	i) I would like to draw your attention to this diagram in particular.

15 Welche der folgenden Wendungen sind geeignet, um **Meinungen anzugeben**? Kreuze an!

- ☐ a) According to ...
- ☐ b) I assume ...
- ☐ c) I see ...
- ☐ d) She is in favour of ...
- ☐ e) He thinks ...
- ☐ f) We are of the opinion that ...
- ☐ g) He is nice.
- ☐ h) He points out that ...

16 Du formulierst deine **persönliche Stellungnahme**. Mit welchen Wendungen stimmst du anderen zu, mit welchen machst du einen anderen Standpunkt deutlich? Kreuze an!

	Zustimmung	Widerspruch
1) I can only support his opinion.	☐	☐
2) This argument doesn't convince me because ...	☐	☐
3) Like Peter, I think that ...	☐	☐
4) I simply must agree with that.	☐	☐
5) I very much doubt whether ...	☐	☐
6) Personally, I think this is worth discussing.	☐	☐
7) ... seems particularly convincing to me.	☐	☐
8) Unlike Peter, I am of the opinion that ...	☐	☐

Der Schluss

17 Zum Schluss deines Referates willst du die **Hauptpunkte nochmals zusammenfassen**. Welche Übersetzung passt zu welcher Wendung?

1) ☐ Ganz wichtig ist hier, dass ...	a) I conclude that ...
2) ☐ Lasst mich das Wesentliche noch einmal zusammenfassen.	b) It is important here that ...
3) ☐ Als Konsequenz aus meinen Ausführungen ergibt sich für mich ...	c) Allow me to summarise the basic facts.
4) ☐ Lasst mich nun zu einer Bewertung kommen.	d) Allow me now to make an assessment.
5) ☐ Zusammenfassend lässt sich sagen, dass ...	e) To summarise, we can say that ...

18 Welche der Wendungen ist geeignet, deinen **Vortrag** zu **beenden**? Kreuze pro Dreiergruppe jeweils zwei mögliche Wendungen an!

1) ☐ a) Thank you for your attention.
☐ b) Thank God, it's over.
☐ c) Thanks for listening.

2) ☐ a) That's it.
☐ b) I hope that was helpful.
☐ c) I've now come to the end of my presentation.

3) ☐ a) I hope that I have presented this topic from a new perspective.
☐ b) I hope that you liked me and my fantastic way of presenting the topic a lot.
☐ c) I hope that my presentation sheds a different light on ...

19 Nach deinem Referat ist es wünschenswert, **Fragen anzuregen** und mit diesen geschickt umzugehen. Verbinde die Satzanfänge mit den jeweiligen Satzenden!

1) ☐	I will be happy ...	a) ... to ask questions.
2) ☐	Please don't hesitate ...	b) ... would go too far.
3) ☐	That's a question I would like ...	c) ... you can interrupt me at any time.
4) ☐	And now I would like ...	d) ... to start the discussion.
5) ☐	Answering this question in detail ...	e) ... to know more about this topic, I can recommend the following titles.
6) ☐	If you would like ...	f) ... to put to the audience.
7) ☐	If you have any questions ...	g) ... to answer any questions.

Referate halten

Zuhörer begrüßen

Download 1

Good morning everybody.
Dear classmates ...
Dear fellow students ...
Ladies and gentlemen ...
Welcome to ...
I'd like to welcome you to ...
Nice to see you all this morning.
I'm glad you could all make it.
I'm glad to be able to welcome so many of you ...

Sich vorstellen

Download 2

Most of you already know me, I'm ...
For those of you who don't know me, I am ...
Let me briefly introduce myself.
My name is ...
I am ...
I'm in year 10.
I'm a student in my third semester.
I'm doing work experience.
Here with me today is ...
I think you all know ...
I would like to introduce ...
May I introduce ...
We have been working together on this topic for a long time.
We prepared this presentation together.
We'll be taking turns in giving this presentation.
We have divided the presentation as follows:

Technische Fragen klären

Download 3

Is the light too bright?
Should I close the blinds?
Should I turn the lights down?
Can you see the presentation clearly in the back rows, as well?
Can you all read the transparency?
There's still room here at the front. Perhaps you'd like to move forward a little.
Can you all understand me?
Am I speaking loudly enough?
One moment, please. The equipment is acting up.
The CD player (video recorder, computer) isn't working.
Things aren't quite going to plan, unfortunately, but perhaps we can carry on with ... for the time being.
I apologize for this brief interruption, we can carry on in a second.

Organisatorische Fragen klären

Download 4

Please feel free to interrupt me if anything is unclear.
Just put your hand up if you've got a question.
You can ask questions at any time during the presentation.
Please ask questions as soon as they arise.
I will answer your questions at the end of my presentation.
There'll be plenty of time for discussion at the end of the presentation.
The whole presentation will take roughly twenty minutes
The presentation will take about one hour.
There is a handout which I will pass round in a moment.
I will distribute the handout after the presentation.
There will be a handout, so there's no need to take notes.

Ins Thema einsteigen

Download 5

Today I want to talk about ...
Today I will talk about ...
Today's topic is:
Today I want to introduce you to an interesting (an important, a central) topic.
In this presentation I would like to introduce a subject to you which ...
... at first might sound a bit boring (old-fashioned). However, I hope to change your minds during the course of my presentation.
I was particularly fascinated (provoked, moved , interested) by this topic because ....
I've been interested in ... for a long time.

This subject has recently become very relevant.
Again and again the media reports ...
It's common sense that ...
How does this topic actually relate to us?
Why do we have to talk about this subject at all?
You've probably asked yourselves before ...
How can it be that ...
Every day we come across ...
This is an example of ...
The purpose of this presentation is to ...
I want to show that ...
We want to prove that ...
My aim is to ...
It is important to inform people about ...
I'd like to get you interested in ...
I would like to focus on an issue which has been given little attention up to now.
It is necessary to get rid of prejudice against ...
I hope that you will have a different view of ... by the end of this presentation.

Download 6

Referatsaufbau vorstellen

I would like to briefly present the structure of my presentation.
I have divided this presentation into four different parts.
I will present the following aspects:
My focus is on ...
I will focus on ...
First I will talk about ... then ... after which ... will follow.
At the end I will mention ...
In conclusion, I will talk about ...
And then there'll be time for questions (a discussion).
After the presentation there'll be enough time for discussion.

Download 7

Inhalte präsentieren

We can see clearly that ...
The following aspect is a central one:
This is based on the assumption that ...
In this context, the following points are most essential:
A crucial aspect is ...
I would like to emphasize two aspects in particular:
Important aspects are ...
What I'm saying is ...
It is obvious that ...
An obvious tendency can be identified.
It would make sense to interpret the statements as follows:
In contrast to the general opinion, a different development can be seen.
Considering these facts, ...
However, a clear development can be seen ...

Download 8

Argumente vorstellen

Let's first assume that ...
Initially, let me put forward the following hypothesis:
I argue that ...
I'm going to disprove the following theory in the course of my presentation:
Let's start by assuming that ...
I want to prove that ...
In the course of my presentation I want to support this statement with new arguments.
First we'll assume that ...
Based on the facts presented earlier, I assume that ...
The current research results give reason to believe ...
Up to now it has always been assumed that ...
I consider the current assumptions to be wrong because ...
I would like to put forward the following theory:
I believe that the discoveries of the recent years point to ... rather than to ...

Download 9

Referate strukturieren

My first argument is:
The first aspect I want to present is:
Secondly, ...
Thirdly, we should consider ...
First I would like to show that ...

A further argument supporting this theory is ...
However, I should also mention that ...
We should also not ignore the following:
Furthermore, ...
Besides, ...
In addition, it is important to ...
Additionally, we should mention that ...
Incidentally, ...
By the way, ...
In passing, let me mention that ...

Orientierungshilfen geben

Download 10

I will now move on to ...
Having said that, I want to go on with ...
We've already considered the first three aspects.
These issues are important for the next point.
The next part is also related to this aspect.

Zwischenfazits ziehen und überleiten

Download 11

Before I move on to ..., I 'd like to repeat the following:
At this point we can draw the conclusion ...
This has the effect ...
On the one hand ... on the other hand ...
However, ...
Nevertheless, ...
This is all I want to say about ...
Regarding ..., the case is similar (different) ...
It can also be stated that ...
On the other hand, it can be seen that ...
This brings me to a different issue.
This leads me to my next point.
The following aspect is another important one:
At this point it is also interesting to see that ...
In this context we should also look at ...
In this context ... shouldn't be left out.
It is often said that ...
In this case, however, ...
In general, this is right but ...
It should also be mentioned that ...

A similar situation is ...
The situation is quite different in the case of ...

Auf Vorangegangenes verweisen

Download 12

This is paralleled by ...
This brings to mind the previous issue which dealt with ...
As I have already mentioned ...
This point was already discussed at the beginning.
To return to ... once more:
And this is where the facts mentioned earlier become significant again.
This seems to contradict my original theory.
You may be asking yourselves whether I didn't just say something completely different.
I can assure you that this doesn't contradict ...
After carefully examining and weighing up the arguments, it is not possible to uphold the initial hypothesis.
This supports the initial theory.
This proves our theory.

Beispiele einbauen

Download 13

This example shows that ...
This example illustrates ...
A good example for this is ...
I would like to mention a few examples.
Let me illustrate this with a little example.
There was, for example, a case ...
Perhaps this will become clearer in the following example:

Biographische Daten nennen

Download 14

[Peter Brown] was born in ...
[Peter Brown] died in ...
I'll give you some basic biographical facts about ...
I'll give you a short résumé of [Peter Brown].
In the same year ...
This incident was especially important for ...
His aim in life was to ...

Download 15

Historische Ereignisse darlegen

In ...

The situation was the following:

In ... the situation was particularly difficult (favourable).

Many factors had an effect on ...

The reasons for this development were manifold.

In other countries ... also ...

Unlike today, in those times there was ...

Comparing the historical situation with today's, it becomes clear that ...

Download 16

Zahlen und Fakten einbauen

A few figures will illustrate these results.

The number is ...

The number (figure) is twice as high as ...

This amount (figure) can be compared to ...

This quantity is comparable with ...

The figure (number, amount) has tripled in the last two years.

That's as many (much) as ...

That's less (fewer) than ...

Download 17

Statistiken erläutern

Here you can see ...

the pie chart / the bar chart / the line chart

These statistics support ...

This diagram shows that ...

a quarter / a half / a third / three quarters

23% of the people in [London] are ...

[Stratford] has a lower percentage of ... than [London].

The percentage of ... in ... is higher than the national average.

I would like to show you some detailed statistics:

The chart shows a clear tendency ...

I would like to draw your attention to this diagram in particular.

In 2004, there was a marked increase (sharp fall).

This graph shows us how consumption continues to grow (fall).

If we compare the diagrams for 1998 and 2008, we can see that ...

The balanced ratio between the red and green bars suggests that ...

The encouraging (worrying) thing here is ...

These figures convey a clear message.

Download 18

Quellen angeben

I've based my assumptions on the following authors:

I base this statement on ...

One of the sources of my presentation is ...

The statistics were compiled by ...

Here I would like to point out [Peter Brown's] study.

Download 19

Meinungen angeben und zitieren

[Peter Brown] is of the opinion that ...

According to [Peter Brown], ...

According to [Peter Brown], ...

[Peter Brown] thinks ...

[Peter Brown] assumes ...

[Peter Brown] is of the opinion that ...

[Peter Brown] is in favour of (against) ...

[Peter Brown] states:

As the minister made known ...

[Peter Brown] repeatedly points out that ...

In his article (book, publication) *[The British]*, [Peter Brown] has already pointed out ...

In this context I would like to quote [Peter Brown]:

In this context [Peter Brown] said:

[Peter Brown] also repeatedly puts forward this theory in his publications.

An important issue is addressed in *Newsweek's* leading article of 14.02.2008.

[Peter Brown] first made this observation in 1996.

On page 26 of [Peter Brown's] book *[The British]* from 2003, we can find the following comment:

This is in complete contradiction to ...

Contrary to what [Peter Brown] says in his article *[The British]*, ...

With this, [Peter Brown's] theory can be considered refuted.

An unsubstantiated assertion that is frequently made in the media by [Peter Brown] is ...

Download 20

Allgemeine Auffassungen angeben

It is generally accepted (assumed) that ...
There can be no doubt that ...
Many people believe ...
It is often said that ...
Public opinion is against (in favour of) ...
The majority (minority) is of the opinion that ...
The atmosphere is heated (chilly, friendly).
There is a strong tendency to see it this way.
In scientific (informed, political) circles, it is assumed that ...

Download 21

Die eigene Meinung formulieren

In my opinion ...
I believe ...
I suspect ...
In my view ...
I am of the opinion that ...
We think that ...
We are of the opinion that ...
As far as I'm concerned ...
In my view there is no doubt that ...
I think it is very likely that ...
Like [Peter Brown], I think that ...
I can only support [Peter Brown's] opinion.
... seems particularly convincing to me.
I simply must agree with that.
I very much doubt whether ...
Personally, I think this is worth discussing.
This argument doesn't convince me because ...
Unlike [Peter Brown], I am of the opinion that ...

Download 22

Hauptpunkte zusammenfassen

Allow me to summarize the basic facts.
It is important here that ...
To summarize, we can say that ...
Finally, I would like to ...
After weighing up the arguments carefully, ...
I arrive at the following conclusion:
The conclusion I draw is:
I conclude that ...
Allow me now to make an assessment:

Download 23

Das Referat beenden

Thank you for your attention.
Thanks for listening.
I've now come to the end of my presentation.
I hope that was helpful.
I hope that I have given you food for thought (something to discuss).
I hope that my presentation sheds a different light on ...
I hope that I have presented this topic from a new perspective.

Download 24

Fragen anregen und darauf reagieren

Are there any questions?
Is everything clear?
I will be happy to answer any questions.
If you have any questions, you can interrupt me at any time.
Please don't hesitate to ask questions.
Answering this question in detail would go too far.
If you would like to know more about this topic, I can recommend the following titles:
That's a question I would like to put to the audience.
And now I would like to start the discussion.

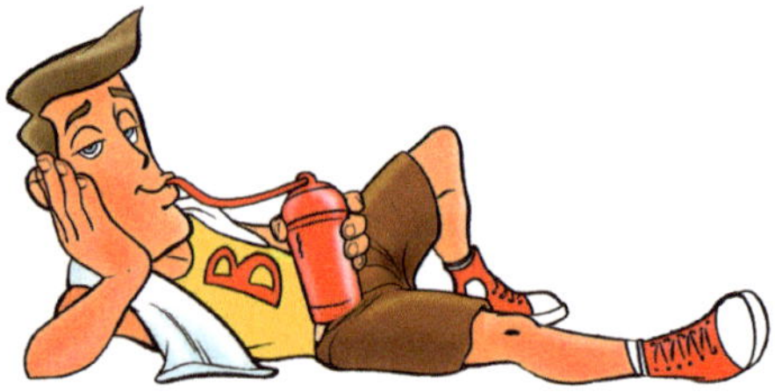

Lösungen

GRAMMATIK

1 DAS VERB *TO BE*

S. 12 •
am, 'm, is, is, are, are, 're

S. 12 Boxenstopp
Langformen: I am, you are, he is, she is, it is, we are, you are, they are; *Kurzformen:* I'm, you're, he's, she's, it's, we're, you're, they're

S. 12 ••
1. is **2.** are **3.** is **4.** is **5.** is **6.** are

S. 13 •••
1. It is very hot today. **2.** The bottles are empty. **3.** It is Monday today. **4.** The grandparents are on holidays.

S. 13 •
1. is not **2.** are not **3.** isn't **4.** aren't

S. 13 Boxenstopp
Die Formen von *to be* werden verneint, indem man *not* hinter das Verb stellt.

S. 14 ••
1. isn't / is **2.** isn't **3.** isn't **4.** is / isn't **5.** aren't **6.** am not / am

S. 14 •••
1. Tim isn't eleven years old. **2.** Linda is a very beautiful girl. **3.** This book isn't interesting. **4.** New York and London are big cities. **5.** Your favourite TV show is on. **6.** My grandparents aren't very old.

S. 15 •
1. How are you? **2.** And how are you? **3.** Who is your German teacher? **4.** Where is my German book? **5.** Is this your book? **6.** What's your name?

S. 15 Boxenstopp
Nach den Fragewörtern *how, who, what, where* oder *when* steht immer eine Form von *to be*. Gibt es keine Fragewörter, steht die Form von *to be* gleich am Anfang des Satzes.

S. 15 ••
1d, **2c**, **3a**, **4b**

S. 16 •••
1. Who is your teacher? **2.** When is school over? **3.** What is your sister's name? **4.** Where is the post office? **5.** How is the birthday party? **6.** Is the homework too difficult?

2 PERSONALPRONOMEN

S. 16 •
Singular: I, she, you *Plural:* we

S. 17 Boxenstopp
Langform: I am, you are, he is, she is, it is, we are, you are, they are *Kurzform:* I'm, you're, he's, she's, it's, we're, you're, they're

S. 17 ••
1. They are in the garden. **2.** He is Tina's brother. **3.** She likes to play table tennis with Freddy. **4.** It is under the table.

S. 18 •••
1. you **2.** He **3.** she **4.** We **5.** We **6.** I **7.** they **8.** She **9.** you **10.** It

S. 18 •
him, you, me, you, it, them

S. 18 Boxenstopp
me, you, him, her, it, us, you, them

S. 19 ••
1. She wants to read it. **2.** They like him. **3.** It sees it in the yard. **4.** He reads it. **5.** He wants to meet her.

S. 19 •••
1. us **2.** them **3.** me / it **4.** it **5.** him **6.** you **7.** you **8.** it **9.** them **10.** me

3 DAS SIMPLE PRESENT

S. 20 •
gets up, arrives, starts, have, is, play

S. 20 Boxenstopp
Grundform, *to*, *-s*, regelmäßig, oft, *always*, *often*

S. 21 ••
1. visit **2.** always does **3.** go **4.** normally stay **5.** sometimes like

S. 21 •••
1. gets up **2.** fetches **3.** picks up **4.** takes **5.** like **6.** is **7.** get **8.** drives **9.** takes **10.** checks **11.** finds **12.** ask

S. 21 •
1e, **2c**, **3a**, **4b**, **5d**

S. 22 Boxenstopp
don't, *does not*, Infinitiv

S. 22 ••
1. Nick doesn't go shopping. **2.** We don't write a lot at school. **3.** In the evening Lucy doesn't watch TV. **4.** The weather in England isn't sunny. **5.** Sammy and Robert don't play football every Saturday.

S. 23 •••
1. Sarah doesn't live in Nottingham. Kim lives in Nottingham. **2.** Sarah's parents don't make her a birthday cake. Sarah's grandma makes her a birthday cake. **3.** Mrs O'Brien doesn't come from Germany. Sarah comes from Germany. **4.** German children don't wear school uniforms. English children wear school uniforms. **5.** Sarah doesn't play the guitar. Sam plays the guitar.

S. 23 •
1. Do I **2.** Do you **3.** Does he **4.** do we **5.** do you **6.** do they

S. 23 Boxenstopp
do, does, Subjekt, Infinitiv, Vollverbs, *where, what*

S. 24 ••
1. Does it always rain in England? **2.** Do British people drink a lot of tea? **3.** Do children like sweets? **4.** When does Jeremy do his homework? **5.** Where do your grandparents live?

S. 24 •••
1. Where do you come from? **2.** Where do you want to go on vacation? **3.** When do you do your homework? **4.** When do you play basketball? **5.** How do you get home from school? **6.** How do you like your teacher? **7.** What do you do on Saturday? **8.** What do you like to eat?

4 DAS PRESENT PROGRESSIVE

S. 25 •
are spending, is buying, is looking, is waiting, are ... doing, are ... buying, 'm reading

S. 25 Boxenstopp
Gegenwart, gerade dabei ist, Form von *to be (am – is – are)*, Infinitiv, Verbs, *to, -ing, just, (right) now, at the moment*

S. 26 ••
1. She is talking to her friend. **2.** Luke is swimming in a lake. **3.** We are hiding under the table. **4.** Lane is kissing Tom. **5.** The grandparents are watching TV. **6.** You are talking to Frances. **7.** I'm riding my bike.

S. 26 •••
1. Sarah is reading a book. **2.** Sam is doing his homework. **3.** Sarah isn't sleeping. **4.** Sam is playing tennis with his brother. **5.** Sarah isn't talking to her grandmother. **6.** Sarah and Sam aren't eating pizza.

S. 27 •
2. isn't **3.** playing **4.** Are **5.** he is **6.** Yes

S. 27 Boxenstopp
Eine Frage im Present Progressive stellst du, indem du die Form von *to be* mit dem Subjekt vertauschst. Die Kurzantwort besteht dann nur aus *yes* oder *no*, dem Subjekt und der passenden Form von *to be*.

S. 28 ••
1. Is he playing a game? **2.** Are they visiting London? **3.** Is the cat sleeping in its basket? **4.** Is she going to the playground? **5.** Are we writing a test now?

S. 28 •••
1. Are you listening to rock music? **2.** Is she playing basketball? **3.** Are they reading a book? **4.** Are you talking to a friend on the phone? **5.** Am I watching a film?

S. 29 •
Simple Present: Does he play, he doesn't *Present Progressive:* what is your brother doing, He is playing, what are you two doing, We are studying

S. 29 Boxenstopp
Simple Present: often, always, sometimes, never, usually, every... *Present Progressive:* (right) now, at the moment

S. 30 ••
1. are swimming in the sea **2.** goes **3.** eats **4.** plays **5.** talk **6.** is cleaning **7.** ride **8.** isn't baking

S. 30 •••
1. lives **2.** works **3.** gets up **4.** goes **5.** has **6.** walks **7.** is **8.** wears **9.** goes **10.** takes **11.** is standing **12.** are walking **13.** speak **14.** don't speak **15.** help **16.** speaks **17.** likes

5 DAS SIMPLE PAST

S. 31 •
dreamed, was, saw, came, saw, was, looked, landed, came, said, was, had, gave, filled, flew, was

S. 31 Boxenstopp
Vergangenheit, Ereignissen, Handlungen, abgeschlossen, *-ed*, Infinitiv, lernen

S. 32 ••
Regelmäßige Verben: to dream – dreamed, to look – looked, to land – landed, to fill – filled
Unregelmäßige Verben: to be – was, to see – saw, to come – came, to say – said, to have – had, to give – gave, to fly – flew

S. 32 •••
1. went **2.** put **3.** carried **4.** won

S. 33 •
1c, 2e, 3a, 4d, 5f, 6b

S. 33 Boxenstopp
didn't (did not), Infinitiv, gleich, *to be, wasn't, weren't*

S. 33 ••
1. didn't go **2.** weren't **3.** didn't get **4.** didn't sleep **5.** wasn't **6.** didn't like

S. 34 •••
1. wanted **2.** wasn't **3.** went **4.** made **5.** told **6.** weren't **7.** explained **8.** didn't listen **9.** played **10.** felt **11.** didn't want **12.** carried **13.** was **14.** thought **15.** didn't have **16.** cleaned **17.** found

S. 34 •
1b, 2a, 3d, 4c, 5f, 6e

S. 35 Boxenstopp
did, was/were, Subjekt, *when, where, what, who*

S. 35 ••
1. Did he play the piano this afternoon? **2.** When did they leave the house? **3.** Did she want a book for her birthday? **4.** Where did you stay on the class trip?

S. 36 •••
1. Did you get **2.** did **3.** liked **4.** Did you stay **5.** weren't **6.** looked **7.** found **8.** Did she see **9.** showed **10.** Did she read **11.** wrote **12.** didn't **13.** didn't think **14.** was **15.** said

6 DIE SATZSTELLUNG IN AUSSAGESÄTZEN

S. 36 •
1. *Subjekt:* my sister *Verb:* reads **2.** *Subjekt:* we *Verb:* play **3.** *Subjekt:* Karen and Jenny *Verb:* must do **4.** *Subjekt:* you *Verb:* 're **5.** *Subjekt:* I *Verb:* 'm meeting

S. 37 Boxenstopp
allen, Subjekt, Verb, Objekt, Ortsangaben

S. 37 ••
1. I play tennis every Saturday. **2.** We do our homework in the afternoon. **3.** They often listen to music. **4.** I always go to the city centre by bus. **5.** My parents never go to the cinema.

S. 38 •••
1. They always have breakfast together. **2.** Every Saturday my sister goes for a walk in the park. **3.** I'm painting a beautiful picture.

7 FRAGEWÖRTER

S. 38 •
1. What - Was? **2.** Where - Wo? **3.** When - Wann? **4.** How many - Wie viele? **5.** Why - Warum? **6.** Who - Wer? **7.** Which - Welche/r/s?

S. 38 Boxenstopp
Bei Fragen mit einem Fragewort und einer Form von *to be* gilt folgende Regel: Zuerst kommt das Fragewort und dann die Form von *to be*.

S. 39 ••
1. where **2.** what **3.** how **4.** how **5.** what **6.** where **7.** who **8.** how **9.** who **10.** what

S. 39 •••
1. Who are you? **2.** How old are you? **3.** Where is she from? **4.** How old is the girl? **5.** Where is Marc? **6.** Who is his teacher? **7.** What is this? **8.** Where is the bag? **9.** What colour is your pen? **10.** Where are we? **11.** What is this?

8 DIE MODALEN HILFSVERBEN

S. 40 •
can, can't, can, can't, can, can't, can, mustn't, needn't, can

S. 40 Boxenstopp
can - können, can't - nicht können, must - müssen, mustn't - nicht dürfen, needn't - nicht müssen

S. 41 ••
1. falsch **2.** richtig **3.** falsch **4.** richtig **5.** falsch

S. 41 •••
1. can't write **2.** mustn't stay **3.** can jump **4.** needn't get up / can sleep **5.** must bring

S. 41 •
Subjekte: Sally, Marc *Hilfsverb:* can
Vollverben: give, buy

S. 42 Boxenstopp
nach, vor, zwischen

S. 42 ••
1. Can you dance with me? **2.** Can you be nice to your sister Delilah? **3.** Can they play in the garden? **4.** Can he sit next to me?

S. 43 •••
1. Can old people run 400 metres in one minute?
2. Can you help me with my Maths homework?
3. Can you give me the bag from the table?
4. Do you know when Sam can help me?
5. Can you carry so many books?

9 DIE ARTIKEL

S. 43 Boxenstopp
1. ein **2.** eine **3.** Konsonant **4.** Vokal

S. 44 ••
a: funny uncle, swimming pool, tennis racket, brilliant game, right answer, silly exercise, great CD, good idea
an: answer, easy question, orange folder, Indian friend, old CD, English book, empty bottle

S. 44 •••
1. a **2.** an **3.** a / a **4.** an **5.** a **6.** an / a

S. 45 Boxenstopp
bestimmte, männliche, weibliche, Plural, Vokal

S. 45 ••
[ðə]: the best pizza, the sea side, the classroom, the uniform, the girl from England, the unit, the tidy room
[ði:]: the answer, the ocean, the example, the orange folder

S. 46 •••
1. [ði:] 2. [ðə] 3. [ði:] 4. [ðə] 5. [ðə]

10 *HAVE GOT* UND *HAS GOT*

S. 46 •
I've got, you've got, he's got, she's got, it's got, we've got, you've got, they've got

S. 46 Boxenstopp
Wenn man ausdrücken möchte, dass man etwas hat oder besitzt, dann benutzt man im Englischen *have got* oder (bei *he*, *she* und *it*) *has got*.

S. 47 ••
1. Have you got a new school bag? - Yes, I have. / No, I haven't. **2.** Has your family got a house? - Yes, we have. / No, we haven't. **3.** Have your friends got a dog?

- Yes, they have. / No, they haven't. **4.** Has your mother got a car? - Yes, she has. / No, she hasn't. **5.** Have your grandparents got pets? - Yes, they have. / No, they haven't. **6.** Has your father got a computer? - Yes, he has. / No, he hasn't.

S. 47 • • •
1. No, they haven't. They've got comics. **2.** Yes, she has. But she hasn't got a cat. **3.** No, they haven't. They've got a bicycle. **4.** No, she hasn't. She's got a brother. **5.** Yes, he has. But he hasn't got a new DVD. **6.** No, they haven't. They've got inline skates. **7.** No, she hasn't. She's got a book.

11 *WOULD LIKE TO* UND *WANT TO*

S. 48 Boxenstopp
Man benutzt *would like to*, wenn man höflich sein will. *I would like to...* bedeutet *Ich möchte gerne...* und *I want to...* übersetzt man im Deutschen mit *Ich will...*

S. 49 • •
1c, **2b**, **3d**, **4a**

S. 49 • • •
1. would like to **2.** want to **3.** wants to **4.** would like to

12 SINGULAR UND PLURAL

S. 49 •
mouse - mice, sandwich - sandwiches, box - boxes, child - children, fish - fish, foot - feet, sheep - sheep, class - classes, country - countries, woman - women, postcard - postcards, tooth - teeth, potato - potatoes, knife - knives

S. 50 Boxenstopp
1. *z.B.* postcard - postcards **2.** *z.B.* box - boxes **3.** *z.B.* country - countries **4.** *z.B.* knife - knives **5.** *z.B.* sheep - sheep **6.** *z.B.* child - children

S. 50 • •
1. postcard - postcards **2.** box - boxes, sandwich - sandwiches, class - classes, potato - potatoes **3.** country - countries **4.** knife - knives **5.** sheep - sheep, fish - fish **6.** child - children, mouse - mice, foot - feet, woman - women, tooth - teeth

S. 51 • • •
1. fish **2.** cats **3.** children **4.** sheep **5.** mice **6.** feet **7.** CDs **8.** countries

13 *THERE IS* UND *THERE ARE*

S. 51 •
1. There are **2.** There is **3.** There is **4.** There are

S. 52 Boxenstopp
there is, Personen, Dinge, Singular, Plural, *there are*, ist, sind

S. 52 • •
1. In unserer Klasse ist ein neues Mädchen. **2.** In meinem Zimmer ist ein Monster. **3.** Da sind zwei grüne Bücher auf meinem Bett.

S. 52 • • •
1. There are **2.** There isn't **3.** There are **4.** there is **5.** There are **6.** there is **7.** there aren't **8.** there are

14 *MUCH, MANY* UND *A LOT OF*

S. 53 •
1c, **2d**, **3a**, **4b**

S. 53 Boxenstopp
Much steht vor nicht zählbaren Substantiven, und *many* steht vor zählbaren Substantiven. Beide Mengenangaben werden hauptsächlich in Fragen und verneinten Aussagesätzen benutzt. In bejahten Aussagesätzen wird dagegen meist *a lot of* oder *lots of* verwendet.

S. 53 • •
1. many **2.** much **3.** many **4.** much **5.** many **6.** much

S. 54 • • •
1. a lot of **2.** many **3.** a lot of **4.** much **5.** much **6.** many

15 DEMONSTRATIVBEGLEITER

S. 54 Boxenstopp
This und *these* verwendet man zusammen mit Substantiven, die sich in der Nähe des Sprechers befinden. Und umgekehrt benutzt man *that* und *those* bei Substantiven, die etwas weiter weg sind.

S. 55 • •
1. Marc, would you like these comics here or those over there? **2.** I would like to have these comics, please. **3.** Ok. And do you like this cake? **4.** No, I like that cake over there. **5.** Are those girls over there at your school? **6.** No, those over there aren't. But this girl here is.

S. 55 • • •
1. This pullover here is too big for you, but that pullover is okay. **2.** Oh look, right here! Aren't these posters beautiful? **3.** Just look over there! Can you see those beautiful flowers? **4.** I like this green cap and these blue sneakers much better than that black cap and those grey tennis shoes over there.

16 DER *S*-GENITIV UND DER *OF*-GENITIV

S. 55 Boxenstopp
gehört, Personen, Lebewesen, 's, Apostroph

S. 56 • •
1. Marc's **2.** neighbours' **3.** girls' **4.** dog's **5.** boys' **6.** boys' **7.** cat's **8.** Sam's **9.** teacher's children's **10.** These are the childrens lunchboxes

S. 56 • • •
1. der Freund meines Bruders **2.** der Freund meiner Brüder **3.** die Freunde meiner Brüder **4.** die Freunde meines Bruders **5.** der Korb der Katzen **6.** die Körbe der Katze **7.** die Körbe der Katzen **8.** der Korb der Katze

S. 57 Boxenstopp
Im Gegensatz zum *s*-Genitiv wird der *of*-Genitiv nur bei Sachen verwendet, sowohl im Singular als auch im Plural.

S. 57 • •
1. Die Tür des Hauses ist grün. **2.** Die Stühle der 5. Klasse sind neu **3.** Die Farbe des Tisches ist blau. **4.** Die Preise der T-Shirts sind hoch.

S. 57 • • •
1. C is the third letter of the alphabet. **2.** Today is the first day of the week. **3.** The park is at the end of the road. **4.** The colour of the socks is green. **5.** The name of the street is Marble Lane.

WORTSCHATZ

1 MEIN KÖRPER

S. 58 •
(3) tail - *Schwanz* / (6) horn - *Horn* / (7) beak - *Schnabel* / (11) tusk - *Stoßzahn* / (14) fin - *Flosse* / (19) wing - *Flügel*

S. 59 • •
1. hair - *Haare* **2.** eyebrow - *Augenbraue* **3.** eyes - *Augen* **4.** ears - *Ohren* **5.** mouth - *Mund* **6.** chin - *Kinn* **7.** nose - *Nase* **8.** cheek - *Wange* **9.** teeth - *Zähne* **10.** tongue - *Zunge* **11.** lips - *Lippen*

S. 60 • • •
Erste Übung: **1.** run **2.** kick **3.** watch **4.** clap **5.** hear **6.** smell **7.** shout **8.** shake

Zweite Übung: *mouth:* sing / eat / speak / drink
feet: run / kick / stomp / dance
hands: beat / grasp / write / knock

2 IN DER WELT DER TIERE

S. 61 •
Waagerecht: elephant, bird, kangaroo, cow, cock, hippo, hen, duck, hamster, mouse, monkey, giraffe, rabbit
Senkrecht: cat, ox, pig, dog, horse, rat, fish

S. 62 • •
pets: mouse, hamster, dog, cat, rabbit, bird, rat, guinea pig *farm animals:* cow, ox, horse, cock, hen, pig, duck *zoo animals:* kangaroo, monkey, hippo, giraffe, fish, lion, crocodile, snake, elephant

S. 63 • • •
1f, **2b**, **3i**, **4e**, **5a**, **6j**, **7c**, **8g**, **9d**, **10h**

3 IN DER SCHULE

S. 65 • •
Erste Übung: **1b**, **2c**, **3f**, **4a**, **5d**, **6e**
Zweite Übung: **1.** rubber **2.** ruler **3.** pencil sharpener **4.** workbook **5.** lunch box **6.** exercise book **7.** scissors

S. 66 • • •
Erste Übung: **1.** chalk **2.** teacher **3.** dustbin **4.** blackboard **5.** satchel **6.** classmate **7.** desk **8.** sponge **9.** chair **10.** pupil

Zweite Übung: **1.** Stand up **2.** Open **3.** read **4.** listen to **5.** sing **6.** wipe **7.** draw **8.** Erase **9.** write down **10.** Learn

4 ZU HAUSE

S. 67 Boxenstopp
Immer wenn ein Wort im Singular auf *-f* endet, wird die Mehrzahl mit *-ves* gebildet.

S. 68 • •
Erste Übung: **1e**, **2c**, **3g**, **4a**, **5d**, **6b**, **7f**

Zweite Übung: **1.** sofa **2.** stove **3.** bunk bed **4.** toys **5.** TV set **6.** table **7.** chairs **8.** double bed **9.** armchair **10.** lamp

S. 69 • • •
1. lay the table **2.** walk the dog **3.** make the bed **4.** does the washing **5.** cleans the windows **6.** does the washing-up **7.** tidies up **8.** folds the washing **9.** waters the flowers **10.** does the shopping **11.** do the cooking **12.** reads the newspaper

5 MEINE FAMILIE UND ICH

S. 71 • •
mother and father, brother and sister, grandmother and grandfather, great grandfather and great grandmother, aunt and uncle, nephew and niece, wife and husband, cousin and cousin, daughter and son

S. 72 • • •
1. husband **2.** wife **3.** son **4.** parents **5.** brother **6.** son **7.** daughter **8.** sister **9.** cousin **10.** parents **11.** grandparents **12.** aunt **13.** uncle **14.** niece **15.** nephew **16.** Hier bist du selbst gemeint!

6 DATUM UND UHRZEIT

S. 73 •
1. School trip to London **2.** Delilah's birthday **3.** Daddy's birthday **4.** Christmas Day **5.** Boxing Day

S. 73 • •
1. second **2.** August **3.** week **4.** autumn **5.** Tuesday **6.** night

S. 75 ••
1. Morgen **2.** Mittag **3.** Nachmittag **4.** Abend **5.** Nacht **6.** Montag **7.** Dienstag **8.** Mittwoch **9.** Donnerstag **10.** Freitag **11.** Samstag **12.** Sonntag **13.** Januar **14.** Februar **15.** März **16.** April **17.** Mai **18.** Juni **19.** Juli **20.** August **21.** September **22.** Oktober **23.** November **24.** Dezember **25.** Frühling **26.** Sommer **27.** Herbst **28.** Winter

S. 75 •••
Erste Übung: **1b**, **2c**, **3a**, **4d**

Zweite Übung: **1.** a.m. **2.** p.m. **3.** a.m. **4.** p.m. **5.** p.m. **6.** a.m.

7 ESSEN UND TRINKEN

S. 75 •
1. eggs **2.** tea **3.** ham **4.** beans **5.** sausages **6.** toast **7.** cereals **8.** butter **9.** marmalade **10.** coffee

S. 76 ••
1g, **2a**, **3e**, **4b**, **5h**, **6f**, **7c**, **8d**

S. 77 ••
1. Kim's pizza is with broccoli, mushrooms and peppers. **2.** Delilah's pizza is with ham and pineapple.

S. 78 •••
1. Erbsen **2.** Karotten **3.** Zwiebeln **4.** Nudeln **5.** Äpfel **6.** Birnen **7.** Bananen **8.** Orangensaft **9.** Kartoffelchips **10.** Tomaten **11.** Hühnchen **12.** Schweinefleisch **13.** Rindfleisch **14.** eine Tafel Schokolade

8 IM STRASSENVERKEHR

S. 78 •
1. bus **2.** van **3.** train **4.** bike **5.** plane **6.** car **7.** lorry **8.** roller skates

S. 79 ••
Erste Übung: **1.** run **2.** drive **3.** cycle **4.** walk **5.** ride **6.** go

Zweite Übung: **1.** cycles **2.** rides **3.** goes **4.** drives **5.** walk **6.** run

S. 80 •••
Erste Übung: **1.** traffic lights **2.** crossroads **3.** underpass **4.** zebra crossing

Zweite Übung: **1.** by **2.** on **3.** on **4.** in **5.** off **6.** around

9 AUS DER WELT DER TECHNIK

S. 81 •
Waagerecht: Internet, microwave, toaster, stereo
Senkrecht: telephone, mouse, remote

S. 82 ••
1. coffee machine / toaster **2.** dishwasher / fridge **3.** washing machine / drier **4.** stereo / speakers **5.** TV set / DVD player **6.** mp3-player / headphones **7.** telephone / fax machine

S. 83 •••
1. to surf the internet: Marc may surf the internet after his homework is done. **2.** to write an e-mail: Kim writes an e-mail to her cousin in India. **3.** to print something out: Now I have to print it out. **4.** to play a CD: They play a CD with great music. **5.** to turn down the stereo: She shouts, "Turn down the stereo!" **6.** to turn up the stereo: When her mother leaves the house, Delilah turns up the stereo again. **7.** to call somebody: She wants to call somebody from a quiet place. **8.** to fax an order: But you can also fax an order. **9.** to switch something on: Switch on the TV set! **10.** to switch/turn something off: Switch/Turn off the light, please!

10 PRÄPOSITIONEN

S. 84 •
upon, at, next to, across, on, in, with, in front of, behind, in, up, in, down, to, before, after, inside

S. 85 ••
Erste Übung: **1.** above **2.** between **3.** below **4.** beside

Zweite Übung: **1.** into **2.** in **3.** in **4.** into **5.** in **6.** into

S. 85 •••
1. after midnight **2.** before dinner **3.** behind the house **4.** at 4 o'clock **5.** in front of the tree **6.** on Wednesday

S. 86 •••
1. at **2.** on **3.** over **4.** into **5.** under **6.** in **7.** on **8.** after **9.** between **10.** before

KLASSE 6

GRAMMATIK

1 DIE SATZSTELLUNG IM ENGLISCHEN

S. 90 •
1. Last week (Z) my sister (S) went (V) to Paris (OT).
2. My grandmother (S) is knitting (V).
3. My uncle (S) married (V) my aunt Patty (O) 20 years ago (Z).
4. Tim (S) bought (V) me (O) a flower (O) yesterday (Z).
5. Yesterday (Z) my mother (S) bought (V) a new shirt (O).
6. My mother (S) bought (V) a new shirt (O) in the shop (OT) yesterday (Z).

S. 90 Boxenstopp
(Zeit) Subjekt Verb (Objekt) (Ort) (Zeit)

S. 91 ••
Erste Übung:
1. Some people never go to church. **2.** Carol is reading a magazine in her room. **3.** The Americans celebrate California Day every year. **4.** Phillip writes her a little

message every day. *Oder:* Every day Phillip writes her a little message. **5.** The Millers always go swimming in summer.

Zweite Übung:
1. richtig **2.** falsch - She went to Venice last summer.
3. richtig **4.** falsch - Valerie goes to school every day.

S. 91 •••
1. Mary goes to the cinema every Tuesday.
2. Lara and Sophie turned 13 last week.
3. Millie is reading a book in her room at the moment.
4. I never watch TV before 6 o'clock in the evening.

2 DIE ZEITEN

S. 92 Boxenstopp
Das Simple Present verwendet man für *regelmäßige* Ereignisse und *nie eintretende Ereignisse*. Hierzu gehören auch Berufsbezeichnungen und Hobbies. Auch *wissenschaftliche Fakten* werden mit dem Simple Present ausgedrückt. Das Present Progressive verwendet man für *gerade ablaufende Ereignisse*.

S. 92 ••
1. are speaking **2.** works **3.** is Sandra doing / is repairing **4.** cry **5.** watch **6.** circles

S. 93 ••
1. richtig **2.** falsch - I am reading a book.
3. falsch - Water boils at 100 degrees Celsius.
4. richtig **5.** falsch - My mother never waters them.

S. 93 •••
1. What are you doing? Are you writing an e-mail? **2.** Frank plays football. It's his hobby. **3.** Where is Michael? - He is taking his dog for a walk. **4.** Susan and Manuel like computer games. **5.** Miriam goes to school by bike every morning. **6.** The sun rises every day.

S. 94 ••
1. has been **2.** have found **3.** have you done / have broken **4.** has lived **5.** have never been **6.** have known **7.** has played **8.** have had **9.** Have you ever seen **10.** have not yet finished **11.** has lived

S. 95 ••
Erste Übung:
1. since **2.** for **3.** since **4.** since **5.** for **6.** since **7.** since **8.** since **9.** since **10.** for

Zweite Übung:
1. Laura has invited friends from school.
2. She has invited her family.
3. She has not made 2 cakes for the party.
4. She has bought sweets.
5. She has not cleaned her room.
6. She has not thought of little presents for the guests.
7. She has chosen the music for the party.

S. 96 •••
1. I have known Robert for 8 years.
2. My mother has never been to Australia.
3. My mother has not yet been to Australia.
4. What have you done? - I have broken my leg.
5. Look! Mike has finished his picture.
6. We have lived here for ages.
7. The Connors have had this car since 1991.

S. 96 •
was / was born / died / married / was / had / got / was / made

S. 97 ••
Erste Übung:
1. to go - went **2.** to walk - walked **3.** to talk - talked
4. to see - saw **5.** to be - was, were **6.** to do - did
7. to sing - sang **8.** to feel - felt **9.** to say - said
10. to drink - drank

Zweite Übung:
1. left **2.** wrecked / stranded **3.** tried **4.** was / counted **5.** found / named **6.** taught / converted **7.** taught

S. 98 •••
1. One minute ago it was dark.
2. I got a lot of presents for my birthday yesterday.
3. Mary visited her aunt in New York last week.
4. Daniel Defoe wrote a lot of stories in his life.
5. We went to England last year.
6. We had lunch 20 minutes ago.
7. I had no time yesterday.
8. When he was young, he was very small.

S. 98 Boxenstopp
Noch einmal zur Erinnerung: Das *Simple Past* beschreibt Handlungen, die in der Vergangenheit abgeschlossen sind. Das *Present Perfect* beschreibt dagegen Handlungen, die noch Auswirkungen auf die Gegenwart haben, also noch nicht abgeschlossen sind. Auch das *Ergebnis* einer Handlung kann im Present Perfect stehen.

S. 99 ••
Erste Übung:
Signalwörter für das Simple Past: last weekend, last holiday, yesterday, in 1891, half an hour ago
Signalwörter für das Present Perfect: (not) yet, ever, never, already, for many years

Zweite Übung:
Signalwörter für das Present Perfect: (not) yet, ever, never, already, for many years
Signalwörter für das Simple Past: last weekend, last holiday, yesterday, in 1891, half an hour ago

Dritte Übung:
Übersetzung Signalwörter Present Perfect: (not) yet - noch nicht, ever - jemals, never - niemals, already - schon, for many years - seit vielen Jahren
Übersetzung Signalwörter Simple Past: last weekend - letztes Wochenende, last holiday - letzten Urlaub, yesterday - gestern, in 1891 - im Jahr 1891, half an hour ago - vor einer halben Stunde

S. 100 ••
1. bought **2.** Have you ever watched **3.** have been **4.** has been **5.** washed **6.** have lived **7.** learnt

8. Have you ever seen **9.** has done **10.** finished
11. haven't finished **12.** haven't done

S. 100 •••

1. Have you ever played golf?
2. John has been ill since Monday.
3. I haven't been there for a long time / ages.
4. I saw him yesterday.
5. I have known Claudia for ages.
6. Three weeks ago we met a nice lady on the underground.
7. I have just had lunch.

S. 101 Boxenstopp

Das *Past Progressive* wird mit einer Form von *(to) be* im Simple Past *(was / were)* + **ing**-Form gebildet. Die Verneinung im Past Progressive wird mit *wasn't / weren't* + **ing**-Form gebildet.

S. 101 ••

1d, **2b**, **3c**, **4b**, **5a**, **6b**, **7a**, **8d**, **9b**, **10b**

S. 102 ••

1. When Martin phoned, we were preparing dinner.
2. It was a wonderful day. The sun was shining, the children were playing.
3. What were you doing at 10 o'clock? – I was helping my brother with his homework.
4. Yesterday Susan was playing table tennis and Jim was playing football.

S. 102 •••

1. When I came home my mother was standing in the kitchen, my brother was playing the piano, my father was reading the paper and my granny was cleaning the house.
2. The show started when we were entering the room.
3. What were you doing at seven o'clock? At seven o'clock I was preparing dinner.
4. It was a wonderful party. The guests were dancing, the music was playing and the sun was shining.

S. 103 Boxenstopp

Die Zukunft mit *going to* wird für zukünftige Ereignisse verwendet. Ganz besonders für solche Ereignisse, die geplant sind und auf die man selbst Einfluss hat.

Auch für Vorhersagen benutzt man die Zukunft mit *going to*, aber nur wenn es deutliche Anzeichen dafür gibt, dass ein Ereignis auch tatsächlich eintritt. Gebildet wird die Zukunft mit *going to* so:

Simple Present von
to be (am [not] / are [not] / is [not]) + *going to* + Infinitiv

S. 104 ••

Erste Übung:

1. Ich werde alle meine Freunde aus der Schule einladen.
2. Meine Mutter macht mir mein Lieblingsessen.
3. Wir werden so viel Spaß haben.

Zweite Übung:

1. I'm going to sit on that chair.
2. We are going to fly to Brazil next summer.
3. They are going to meet the Queen in London.
4. It is going to rain.
5. He is not going to watch a movie tonight.
6. They are going to sell their car.
7. We are going to have fun.
8. She is not going to go to a concert.
9. This is going to be a nice day.
10. I am not going to buy you this thing.

S. 105 ••

1. Are you going to bake cookies for your mother?
2. Is he going to go to Paris next summer?
3. Are we going to spend the rest of the day in this shopping center?
4. Am I going to read all those books until next week?
5. Is she going to water the plants this afternoon?
6. Are they going to play soccer?
7. Is it going to snow soon?

S. 105 •••

1. We are going to make pizza tonight.
2. Sally is going to visit her aunt in Mexico in summer.
3. I am not going to go to Sally before 9 o'clock.
4. My father is going to build a swimming pool behind the house.

S. 106 •

will be, will be, will appear, will be

S. 106 ••

1. will help **2.** will find **3.** will hold

S. 107 ••

1. Plan **2.** Vorhersage mit deutlichen Anzeichen
3. Vorhersage **4.** Spontane Entscheidung
5. Vermutung **6.** Vorhersage **7.** Vermutung **8.** Plan

S. 107 •••

1. will get **2.** am going to get **3.** will freeze **4.** will be

S. 108 •••

1. I hope you will win. **2.** We are all going to watch the football game tomorrow. **3.** Don't worry about the keys. I'm sure you are going to find them. **4.** Sorry, there is no more room for you in my car, Lucy. – No problem, I'll take her with me.

3 IF-SÄTZE TYP I

S. 108 •

If I win the jackpot, I will buy a new house.

S. 109 ••

Erste Übung: **1f**, **2c**, **3e**, **4g**, **5a**, **6d**, **7b**.

Zweite Übung:

1. Your mother will like it if you buy her roses.
2. If you eat those mushrooms, you will / can die.
3. If I see him, I will give him something.
4. We won't / can't / needn't go home if the weather gets better.
5. I won't say hello if I meet her.
6. If you put sugar into it, it will taste sweeter.

7. Sue will / can / must buy a house if she wins the lottery.

Dritte Übung:
1. If I see him, I will greet him.
2. You will win if you play.
3. If he speaks English, I can understand what he says.
4. If I lose it, she will be very angry.
5. You can fix the vase with glue if you break it.

S. 110 •••
Erste Übung:
1. If you mow the grass, you will get 10 euros.
2. If you tell any more lies, I will get angry.
3. If you read in bad light, you will ruin your eyes.
4. If you speak slowly, I can understand you.

Zweite Übung:
1. I will get very angry if your dog bites me.
2. If we leave now, we will be there at 4 o'clock.
3. If you eat a lot of sweets, you will get fat.
4. You can save money if you turn the heating off.

4 QUESTION TAGS

S. 110 •
1. wasn't it **2.** do you

S. 110 Boxenstopp
1. Ist das Verb im Aussagesatz bejaht, dann ist das question tag verneint.
2. Ist das Verb im Aussagesatz verneint, dann ist das question tag bejaht.

S. 111 ••
Erste Übung:
1e, **2b**, **3f**, **4a**, **5g**, **6c**, **7d**

Zweite Übung:
1. isn't it **2.** doesn't she **3.** wasn't she **4.** didn't you
5. did you **6.** doesn't he **7.** doesn't she

S. 112 ••
1. haven't you / isn't it **2.** wasn't it / isn't it
3. didn't you / don't they

S. 112 •••
1. shall we **2.** aren't I **3.** will you **4.** will you
5. shall we **6.** aren't I **7.** will you

5 ADJEKTIVE UND ADVERBIEN

S. 113 •
The elephant is taller than the mouse.

S. 113 Boxenstopp
1. groß / so groß wie **2.** größer als **3.** am größten

S. 114 ••
Erste Übung:
1. more seriously - the most seriously
2. higher - the highest
3. more boring - the most boring
4. more important - the most important
5. bigger - the biggest
6. more peaceful - the most peaceful
7. colder - the coldest

Zweite Übung:
1. Dieses Auto ist teurer als das hier.
2. Marys Haus ist das größte in unserer Stadt.
3. Dein Zimmer sieht sauberer aus, seit du es aufgeräumt hast.
4. Hamburger sind genauso gut wie Cheeseburger.
5. Ein Sofa ist viel bequemer als ein Stuhl.

S. 115 •••
1. Lena is younger than Phillip.
2. Juice tastes better than water.
3. Maths is more complicated than English.
4. Mary is taller than John.
5. My grades are worse than your grades.
6. Health is more important than money.
7. Sydney is further / farther away than London.

6 DAS GERUND ALS SUBJEKT UND OBJEKT

S. 115 •
1. Sally likes dancing.
2. Tom likes playing football.
3. Steven likes collecting stamps.

S. 116 Boxenstopp
Das gerund wird aus dem Infinitiv eines Verbs + *-ing* gebildet. Wenn das gerund als Subjekt gebraucht wird, dann steht es meistens am Satzanfang und ihm folgt meistens eine Form von *(to) be*. Vor einem gerund steht im Englischen kein Artikel!
Achtung bei der Schreibung: Konsonanten werden am Wortende oft verdoppelt (*sit* → *sitting*), und ein -e am Verbende fällt weg (*like* → *liking*).

S. 116 ••
Erste Übung:
1. Subjekt **2.** Objekt **3.** Objekt **4.** Subjekt

Zweite Übung:
1. playing **2.** swimming **3.** being **4.** sitting **5.** stopping
6. singing **7.** loving **8.** going **9.** doing **10.** riding

S. 117 ••
1. Reading books is my hobby.
2. I hate cycling.
3. We all love playing cards.

S. 117 •••
1. I hate writing letters.
2. Swimming is fun.
3. Marcy likes dancing.
4. He enjoys watching TV alone / on his own.

7 POSSESSIVPRONOMEN UND POSSESSIVBEGLEITER

S. 118 •
"Oh no, it's raining. I have forgotten my umbrella." - "Here, take mine."

S. 119 • •
Erste Übung:
1. Possessivbegleiter **2.** Possessivbegleiter
3. Possessivpronomen **4.** Possessivpronomen
5. Possessivbegleiter **6.** Possessivpronomen
7. Possessivbegleiter **8.** Possessivbegleiter
9. Possessivpronomen **10.** Possessivbegleiter

Zweite Übung:
1. These are not my shoes. Mine are black.
2. Sally gave me her umbrella. Mine was at home.
3. Her teacher is nicer than yours.
4. Can I use your phone? Mine is broken.
5. Where are your parents? Hers are over there.
6. Is this my new bike? Yours looks much nicer.
7. Whose are these? Mine or yours?
8. She has finished her tea. Does she want to have mine now?

S. 120 • • •
1. Conny gave me my book back yesterday.
2. Is this your child? - No, this is my niece.
3. This is my ice cream. You have already eaten yours.
4. Whose bike is this? - It is mine.
5. Is this your laptop or hers? -It's hers.

8 PERSONALPRONOMEN

S. 120 •
"I know you, don't I? You are the guy that helped me with my bags. We talked for a while. Do you remember?" - "Yes, of course. I remember you. It was a pleasure to help you."

S. 121 • •
Erste Übung:
1. Objektpronomen **2.** Objektpronomen
3. Subjektpronomen **4.** Objektpronomen
5. Subjektpronomen **6.** Objektpronomen
7. Subjektpronomen **8.** Objektpronomen
9. Subjektpronomen **10.** Objektpronomen

Zweite Übung:
1. I have got sandwiches with me.
2. Are you crazy?
3. They are very much in love.
4. She has taken her dog along. Perhaps we can play with it.
5. Tom wrote me an e-mail yesterday. He said that he would like to see me.
6. Can you help me carrying them to the station?
7. They are swimming in a line. Can you see them?
8. This is our son Charles. He is eleven years old. Our daughter's name is Sammy. Charles likes her very much. They often play together. It is nice watching them.
9. Can you give them back to me, please?
10. What is she doing? Are those her kids? I've never seen them together.

S. 122 • • •
1. She asks them. **2.** He sees him. **3.** We see us. **4.** She loves her. **5.** It is empty. **6.** They are looking for it. **7.** They met us yesterday. **8.** Timmy? Are you looking for him? **9.** Is he looking for them?

9 PRÄPOSITIONEN

S. 123 • •
1. The bird is in the cage.
2. The cat is on the sofa.
3. The mouse is under the bed.
4. The child is in front of the computer.
5. The picture hangs over the bed.
6. The dog sits next to the desk.

S. 124 • •
Erste Übung:
1. after **2.** before **3.** behind **4.** on **5.** between **6.** into **7.** at

Zweite Übung:
1. by **2.** in front of **3.** into **4.** in - from - until **5.** between **6.** at

S. 124 • • •
1. I go to school by bike.
2. Our house is in front of the church.
3. We go home between 7 and 8 o'clock.

10 RELATIVSÄTZE

S. 125 Boxenstopp
Who wird nur für Personen *(Der Mann, der ...)* gebraucht und *which (Die Uhr, die ...)* nur für Gegenstände. *That* kann für beide Fälle verwendet werden. *Whose* wird im Deutschen mit *wessen* oder *dessen/deren* übersetzt *(Die Frau, deren Mann ...)*. Alle Relativpronomen sind im Singular und Plural gleich.

S. 126 • •
Erste Übung:
1. who / that **2.** whose **3.** who / that **4.** whose
5. which / that **6.** which / that **7.** who / that

Zweite Übung:
1. Sally told us a story (which / that) I couldn't believe.
2. Tim has got a dog which / that is black.
3. Harry is a good boy who / that can't tell a lie.
4. We have a nice flat (which / that) I like.

Dritte Übung:
1. that (contact clause) **2.** who **3.** which (contact clause) **4.** that / which (contact clause) **5.** that / which (contact clause)

S. 127 •••
1. I have an aunt who / that lives on a farm.
2. This is the man whose sister has got 5 children.
3. The woman (who / that) I saw was alone.

11 SOME UND ANY IN AUSSAGEN UND FRAGESÄTZEN

S. 127 Boxenstopp
Man benutzt *some* oder *any* im Englischen, um eine unbestimmte Menge oder Anzahl auszudrücken. Übersetzt werden beide Ausdrücke ins Deutsche mit *etwas, ein paar* oder *einige*. *Some* benutzt man in bejahten Sätzen. Bei Fragen und Verneinungen wird dagegen meistens *any* verwendet. *Some* kann jedoch auch bei Fragen verwendet werden, wenn man eine höfliche Bitte *(Can I have some butter, please?)* oder ein höfliches Angebot *(Would you like some tea?)* formuliert.

S. 128 ••
Erste Übung:
1. some **2.** any **3.** some **4.** some **5.** some **6.** any **7.** any **8.** any **9.** some **10.** some

Zweite Übung:
1. Sally hasn't got any friends.
2. I cannot see any birds in the sky.
3. Would you like some sugar?
4. Can I have some milk, please?
5. We haven't got any newspapers.
6. Do you know any people from Japan?
7. My father has got some tools in the garage.

S. 129 •••
1. Do you have any advice for me?
2. Could you give me some salt, please?
3. Would you like some sugar?
4. I haven't got any pets.
5. Can you buy some butter?

12 MODALVERBEN

S. 129 •
1. Ich kann nicht zu deiner Party kommen.
2. Ich muss meiner Schwester helfen.
3. Sie muss eine Präsentation halten.
4. Wir können uns ein anderes Mal treffen.
5. Du darfst mich nicht zurückrufen.
6. Meine Eltern müssen nicht wissen, dass...

S. 130 ••
1. Darf ich diese DVD haben?
2. Du musst nicht mehr sagen.
3. Er darf nicht raus gehen.
4. Kannst du aufstehen?
5. Du darfst diese Tür nicht öffnen.
6. Der Kiwi kann nicht fliegen.
7. Du musst hier nicht länger bleiben.

S. 131 ••
1. cannot **2.** can **3.** have to **4.** need not **5.** must not **6.** Can

S. 131 •••
1. You must not enter the house. **2.** must invite Sarah **3.** need not **4.** can go

13 ZEICHENSETZUNG

S. 132 ••
1. I will ask her what happened to her grandmother, but I think she won't tell me.
2. Henry went shopping. He bought apples, a loaf of bread, a bottle of wine and a toothbrush.
3. If you leave your cat out there, it will die.
4. My mother was talking to my sister while I was upstairs.
5. I went to see my grandmother in Chicago, and my wife visited her friends in Australia.
6. She had a lot of fun and he was bored.
7. If I see him, I will tell him that you want to speak to him.
8. While you were away, someone called on the phone.
9. She met an old man, a lot of Japanese tourists with cameras, and a small child that was looking for its mother.
10. Before she wrote this great novel, no one knew who she was.

S. 133 ••
1. Tom said, "Come here!"
2. "If you listen to what the teacher says," my mother said, "you will get good grades."
3. "What's up?" asked Martin.
4. "I want to know," Charles said, "who left the front door open."
5. My aunt asked, "Is there any mail for me today?"

S. 133 •••
1. "Who is there?" asked Maria.
2. "It is," he said, "a friend."
3. Verena asked, "Where are you?"

WORTSCHATZ

1 ZAHLEN

S. 134 •

one	**three**	**two**	four
two	four	three	**one**
three	one	four	two
four	two	**one**	three

S. 135 ••
Erste Übung:
1. twenty-three **2.** forty-four **3.** eighty-seven **4.** thirteen **5.** nineteen **6.** fifty-six **7.** one hundred and one **8.** sixty **9.** nine **10.** one hundred and forty-eight

Zweite Übung:
1. thirty-five **2.** sixty-four **3.** one hundred **4.** eleven **5.** fifty **6.** twelve **7.** twenty-five **8.** eighty-one

S. 136 •••
1. first **2.** last but one **3.** thirty-five **4.** nine **5.** first **6.** second **7.** third **8.** last **9.** forty **10.** twenty-five

2 WORTBILDUNG

S. 136 • und S. 137 ••
1. misunderstood - falsch verstehen
2. unmusical - unmusikalisch
3. non-metal - nicht metallisch
4. biweekly - zweiwöchentlich / alle zwei Wochen
5. prepaid - vorbezahlt
6. semiannual - halbjährlich
7. antifreeze - Frostschutz
8. unclouded - unbewölkt
9. misbehave - nicht benehmen
10. monosyllabic - einsilbig

S. 138 ••
1. tricolour **2.** semiliquid **3.** mishear **4.** unfinished **5.** preschool **6.** nonsense **7.** anticlockwise **8.** counterweight **9.** bisyllabic **10.** monotonous

S. 138 •••
1. semiautomatic **2.** trisyllabic **3.** unbelievable **4.** misinterpret **5.** preheat **6.** semiannual **7.** antifreeze **8.** counterattack **9.** miscalculate

S. 139 •
1A, 2V, 3N, 4N, 5A, 6A, 7V, 8N, 9V

S. 139 •• und S. 140 ••
Nomen: warmth (Wärme), freedom (Freiheit), development (Entwicklung)
Adjektive: washable (waschbar), childish (kindisch), frightening (Angst einflößend)
Verben: activate (aktivieren), darken (abdunkeln), simplify (vereinfachen)

S. 140 •••
1. light - Licht - lighten - erhellen
2. symbol -Symbol - symbolize - symbolisieren
3. free - frei - freedom - Freiheit
4. emotion - Gefühl - emotionless - gefühlslos
5. organ - Orgel - organist - Organist
6. king - König - kingdom - Königreich
7. sick -krank - sicken - erkranken
8. bore - langweilen - boring - langweilig
9. dark - dunkel - darkness - Dunkelheit
10. feel - fühlen - feeling - Gefühl

S. 141 •
1. toothbrush **2.** goldfish, birthday **3.** football, baseball **4.** handbag, bathroom **5.** policeman

S. 141 ••
toothbrush (Zahnbürste), goldfish (Goldfisch), birthday (Geburtstag), football (Fußball), baseball (Baseball), handbag (Handtasche), bathroom (Badezimmer), policeman (Polizist)

S. 142 ••
1. classroom **2.** strawberry **3.** keyboard **4.** waterfall **5.** sunshine **6.** windmill **7.** fireman **8.** headache **9.** afternoon **10.** flowerpot

S. 142 •••
1. skyscraper **2.** blackboard **3.** teapot **4.** handball **5.** butterfly **6.** grandmother **7.** pencil case **8.** toothbrush **9.** grasshopper **10.** houseboat

3 IN DER SCHULE

S. 143 •
maths / English / science / history / geography / music / French / German / PE

S. 144 ••
Waagerecht: rubber, school bus, biro, chalk, desk, glue, timetable, homework
Senkrecht: blackboard, teacher, pupil, pen, book, ruler, pencil case

S. 145 •••
1. Sit down, please.
2. Nimm die Kreide.
3. Can you open the window, please?
4. Where is your pencil case?
5. Gehe ins Büro des Direktors.
6. Kannst du bitte die Tür schließen?
7. Wenn du die Antwort weißt, hebe deinen Arm.
8. Mr Hill is ill today.

4 EUROPA

S. 145 •
Ländernamen: **1.** France **2.** Italy **3.** Greece **4.** Sweden **5.** Spain **6.** Switzerland **7.** Belgium
Adjektive: **1.** French **2.** Italian **3.** Greek **4.** Swedish **5.** Spanish **6.** Swiss **7.** Belgian

S. 146 ••
1. German **2.** Switzerland **3.** Italy **4.** Spanish **5.** French **6.** Norway **7.** Greek **8.** Belgium **9.** Austrian **10.** English **11.** Portugal **12.** Danish **13.** Swedish **14.** Finland

S. 147 •••
1. Italian **2.** Turkey **3.** France **4.** England **5.** French **6.** Greece **7.** Austrian **8.** Spanish **9.** English **10.** Switzerland

5 IN DER STADT

S. 148 •
1. Altstadt **2.** geradeaus **3.** Ampel **4.** Ausfahrt

S. 149 ••
Erste Übung:
stationery: pens, glue, envelopes
confectionery: chocolate bars, jelly bears, chewing gum
dairy products: milk, yogurt, cheese

Zweite Übung:
1e, **2h**, **3d**, **4f**, **5c**, **6a**, **7b**, **8j**, **9g**, **10i**

S. 150 •••
Client:	Good morning.
Shop assistant:	Good morning, Madam. How can I help you?
Client:	I'm looking for a pair of trousers.
Shop assistant:	Sure, Madam. What size do you take?
Client:	I take size 12.
Shop assistant:	Here you are, Madam. What do you think?
Client:	I think it's too small. I need a bigger size.
Shop assistant:	How about these ones here?
Client:	These are perfect. I'll take them. How much are they?
Shop assistant:	They are on sale. Just £29.90, Madam.
Shop assistant:	*(At the cash desk)* That's £29.90 then, Madam.
Client:	Here you are.
Shop assistant:	Thank you very much. That's 10 pence change for you.

6 FUN TIME

S. 150 •
1. LKW **2.** Glühbirne **3.** Armbanduhr
4. schweizerisch **5.** gemischt **6.** Plätzchen
7. in die Hand nehmen **8.** sauer eingelegt **9.** Paprika

S. 151 ••
Humpty Dumpty saß auf der Mauer,
Humpty Dumpty fiel von dort herunter,
all des Königs Pferde und all des Königs Männer,
konnten Humpty Dumpty nicht wieder zusammenbauen.

S. 152 ••
elementary school (Grundschule)
look out for (pass auf ... auf)
interrupt (unterbrechen)
upset (verwirrt)
shrug one's shoulders (mit den Achseln zucken)

S. 152 •••
1. small talk **2.** one in a million **3.** Excuse me
4. too big to ignore

7 DAS WETTER

S. 153 •
1. Temperatur **2.** Richtung **3.** North **4.** Northeast
5. Southeast **6.** West

S. 154 ••
Wortschlange 1: cloudy, sleet, sunny, shower, forecast, blizzard
Wortschlange 2: lightning, rain, storm, thunder, snow, weather

S. 155 ••
London: Low: -10°C High: -2°C
Sheffield: Low: -5°C High: +2°C
Los Angeles: Low: +20°C High: +32°C
Hong Kong: Low: +16°C High: +25°C

8 FAMILIE

S. 157 •
1. father **2.** cousin **3.** son **4.** aunt **5.** sister **6.** daughter
7. nephew **8.** uncle **9.** brother **10.** mother

S. 158 ••
1. daughter **2.** nephew **3.** aunt **4.** niece **5.** brother
6. son **7.** cousin **8.** mother **9.** grandfather **10.** sister

S. 158 •••
1. falsch – My sister's son is my nephew. **2.** richtig
3. richtig **4.** falsch – The children of my father's brother are my cousins. **5.** falsch – My mother's father is my grandfather. **6.** richtig

9 BERUFE

S. 159 •
Berufsbezeichnungen stehen im Englischen mit dem *Simple Present*.

S. 159 ••
Waagerecht: bus driver, cleaner, dentist, policeman, secretary, plumber, carpenter, doctor

Senkrecht: hairdresser, waitress, postman, chef, nurse, farmer, teacher

S. 160 ••
bus driver (Busfahrer/-in), cleaner (Reinigungskraft), dentist (Zahnarzt/-ärztin), policeman (Polizist), secretary (Sekretär/-in), plumber (Klempner/-in), carpenter (Schreiner/-in), doctor (Arzt/Ärztin), hairdresser (Friseur/-in), waitress (Kellnerin), postman (Postbote), chef (Koch), nurse (Krankenpfleger/-in), farmer (Landwirt/-in), teacher (Lehrer/-in)

S. 160 •••
1c, **2i**, **3e**, **4a**, **5g**, **6b**, **7d**, **8j**, **9f**, **10h**

KLASSE 7

GRAMMATIK

1 DIE ZEITEN DER GEGENWART

S. 164 •

1. gets up **2.** has **3.** likes **4.** likes **5.** leave **6.** starts **7.** finish **8.** does **9.** surfs **10.** stay **11.** don't have **12.** are eating **13.** are having **14.** is reading **15.** is listening **16.** is wondering **17.** are you doing **18.** are being **19.** is Jenny coming **20.** are looking **21.** is going **22.** are laughing **23.** are not going

S. 164 Boxenstopp

Simple Present	Present Progressive
sometimes	right now
never	at the moment
usually	just
always	Look!
often	Listen!
on Saturday	now
every week	still

S. 165 • •

Erste Übung:

1. Where exactly do you live in Germany? **2.** When do you get up in the morning? **3.** What do you like for breakfast? **4.** Do you have a pet? **5.** Who is taking care of your dog at the moment? **6.** How do you feel being in New York?

Zweite Übung:

1. is doing / does **2.** is having / has **3.** is playing / practices **4.** is going / buys **5.** have / are going

S. 166 • • •

So könnte deine Unterhaltung lauten:

1. Hey. How are you doing? Can I help you? **2.** Hi. I'm looking for a new coat. **3.** And what size do you normally wear? **4.** My German size is M... **5.** Have a look at this nice red coat then. **6.** What does it cost? **7.** It's sales time and I can offer it to you for only $ 39,90. **8.** Great! Where could I try this coat on? **9.** This changing room here is free. **10.** I like this coat very much, but it doesn't fit. **11.** I'm sorry, but this is the last coat we have... **12.** Well, that's too bad. Good bye!

2 DIE ZEITEN DER ZUKUNFT

S. 167 •

1. My older brother will be 18 in June.
2. I'm sure he'll have a party, but that's still a secret.
3. Can you promise you won't tell anybody about it?
4. Look at Mr Mills, he is going to shout soon.
5. If we are too noisy he is going to give us detention.
6. We're going to have to be quieter next lesson.

S. 167 Boxenstopp

Man verwendet die Zukunft mit **will**, um Handlungen in der Zukunft auszudrücken, auf die man **keinen Einfluss** hat und auch, um **Vermutungen** über die Zukunft anzustellen. Die Zukunft mit **going to** verwendet man dagegen, wenn man **sicher** ist, dass etwas geschehen wird, weil es bereits erste **Anzeichen** dafür gibt, oder weil man die feste **Absicht** hat, etwas zu tun.

S. 168 • •

Erste Übung:

1b, **2c**, **3a**

Zweite Übung:

1. On Monday we're doing skateboarding all day.
2. On Tuesday we're having a judo competition.
3. On Wednesday we're playing tennis after lunch.
4. On Thursday we're going swimming at the public pool.
5. On Friday, aerobics is starting at 8:30 a.m.

Dritte Übung:

1. By Monday I will have done skateboarding.
2. By Tuesday I will have had a judo competition.
3. By Wednesday I will have played tennis.
4. By Thursday I will have swum at the public pool.
5. By Friday aerobics will have started.

S. 168 • • •

1. I'm going to study hard this weekend.
2. My mum will have learned three times with me until then.
3. By Wednesday I will have read through my English folder twice.

3 DIE ZEITEN DER VERGANGENHEIT

S. 169 •

1. was **2.** did he get **3.** turned **4.** hasn't had **5.** didn't want **6.** did he get **7.** gave **8.** have you ever done **9.** went **10.** was **11.** have never done

S. 169 Boxenstopp

Mit dem **Simple Past** drückt man aus, dass eine Handlung in der Vergangenheit **abgeschlossen** wurde und **vorbei** ist. Mit dem **Present Perfect** betont man, dass sich etwas in der Vergangenheit abgespielt hat, das **jetzt** (in der Gegenwart) **noch spürbar** ist. Bestimmte Zeitangaben (z.B. **already, never, just, (not) yet**) zeigen, dass es sich um einen **Zeitraum** handelt, der von der Vergangenheit bis in die Gegenwart reicht.

S. 170 • •

Erste Übung:

1. Lukas had prepared lots of snacks **before** his birthday party started.
2. When all of his guests had arrived, they all sang him a song.
3. After Lukas had thanked them for singing, they had a great party together.

Zweite Übung:
1. After Lukas had done his homework he invited his friends.
2. I had already finished my book when I went to the party.
3. After I had phoned Maria she came to the party.

Dritte Übung:
1. was / had decorated **2.** came / had sent **3.** had gone / were **4.** had baked / tasted **5.** had put out / could

S. 171 •••
1. When Lucy arrived at the bus stop at 6 p.m., the bus had already left.
2. After the next bus had arrived at 6:15 p.m., Lucy got on the bus.
3. Before Lucy took the wrong bus at 6:25 p.m., she had already bought her ticket.

4 MODALE HILFSVERBEN

S. 171 •
1b, 2c, 3a

S. 172 Boxenstopp
1. Mit **can** kann man ausdrücken, dass jemand **in der Lage ist / fähig ist** etwas zu tun. Die Ersatzform lautet **be able to**.
2. Mit **can / may** kann man ausdrücken, dass jemand etwas tun **darf**. Die Ersatzform lautet **be allowed to**.
3. Mit **must** kann man ausdrücken, dass etwas **notwendig ist**. Die Ersatzform lautet **have to**. Mit **needn't** kann man ausdrücken, dass etwas **nicht notwendig ist**. Die Ersatzform lautet **not have to**.

S. 172 ••
1. are able to **2.** are allowed to / aren't allowed to
3. have to / don't have to **4.** are allowed to
5. aren't allowed to

S. 173 •••
Hier einige mögliche Lösungen:
1. Teachers must wear school uniforms. **2.** Pupils may read comics. **3.** Teachers can write SMS messages to pupils. **4.** Pupils needn't do homework. **5.** Teachers mustn't give homework.

5 VOM AKTIV INS PASSIV

S. 173 •
1. Subjekt des Aktivsatzes: *the teacher*
2. Subjekt des Passivsatzes: *Eric*

S. 174 ••
1. Peanut butter is spread on one slice of bread. **2.** Jelly of Jam are spread on the other slice of bread. **3.** Slightly less jelly than peanut butter is used **4.** The two pieces of bread are put together. **5.** The sandwich is cut in half for easier eating. **6.** Sandwiches are loved **7.** Sandwiches were loved. **8.** Sandwiches have been loved. **9.** Sandwiches had been loved. **10.** Sandwiches will be loved.

S. 175 ••
Erste Übung:
1. My juice was drunk up by Stella and Jonas.
2. My money was taken by somebody...!
3. The same meal was ordered by Philip!
4. My hamburger was eaten by the dog!
5. The coffee was spilled all over the table by my parents.
6. The bill wasn't brought by the waiter!

Zweite Übung:
1. The meals are prepared by the cook.
2. The guests are welcomed by the waiter.
3. The dishes are washed by the waitress.
4. The drinks are mixed by the bar keeper.
5. The table is set by the waitress.

S. 176 •••
1. The waiter showed **the bill** (Sache) to **my mother** (Person).
a. (Person) My mother was shown the bill by the waiter.
b. (Sache) The bill was shown to my mother by the waiter.
2. My dad gave **the bar keeper** (Person) **a tip** (Sache).
a. (Person) The bar keeper was given a tip by my father.
b. (Sache) A tip was given to the bar keeper by my father.
3. The waitress brought **coffee** (Sache) to **all of us** (Person).
a. (Person) All of us were brought coffee by the waitress.
b. (Sache) Coffee was brought to all of us by the waitress.

6 DAS GERUND

S. 176 •
1. I can imagine buying expensive things. **2.** I would enjoy travelling to New York. **3.** I would prefer having a personal assistant. **4.** I wouldn't mind owning my own chauffeur.

S. 177 Boxenstopp
vermeiden - (to) avoid, *mögen* - (to) like, *hassen* - (to) hate, *vermissen* - (to) miss, *beenden* - (to) finish, *vorschlagen* - (to) suggest, *üben* - (to) practice, *sich auf etwas freuen* - (to) look forward (to)

S. 177 ••
Erste Übung:
1b Winning (Subjekt) the next tennis match is my biggest dream!
2a I like playing (Objekt) tennis a lot.
3c Winning (Subjekt) just one tournament once a year isn't enough for me.

Zweite Übung:
obwohl - in spite of, *durch, wenn, indem* - by, *ohne* - without, *bevor, vor* - before, *nach, nachdem* - after, *(an)statt* - instead of

S. 178 ••
1. In spite of going home now, I will call you.
2. Before leaving the party, please have a drink.
3. John always tells jokes without laughing.
4. Instead of lying, you should always tell the truth.
5. By taking the train you won't get into a traffic jam then.

S. 178 •••
Dear player,
Remember the tennis match on Saturday! **Playing** tennis in a competition is fun. And we always need motivated players in our tournament! **Winning** this Saturday's match could bring you to a training camp in the US. So why don't you invite your friends, too? The matches this weekend need to have lots of support to become a really big event. We look forward to **seeing** you at the tennis court!

7 PRONOMEN ALS OBJEKT

S. 179 •
1. his **2.** their **3.** your **4.** my **5.** our **6.** Its **7.** her **8.** your

S. 179 Boxenstopp

Personal-pronomen	Possessiv-begleiter	Possessiv-pronomen
I	my	mine
you	your	yours
he	his	his
she	her	hers
it	its	its
we	our	ours
you	your	yours
they	their	theirs

S. 180 ••
Erste Übung:
1. Hi. My (Begleiter) name is Jimmy.
2. Look at those CDs. They are all ours (Pronomen).
3. And these books? - They belong to Mum and Dad. They are theirs (Pronomen).
4. This is Ann's and Mary's sister. Her (Begleiter) name is Mona.
5. Mandy, what's your (Begleiter) tutor's name again?
6. We've got a new cat. Its (Begleiter) colour is black.
7. This is Brad's flat. Its (Begleiter) rooms are rather small.
8. I like singing. And our (Begleiter) music classroom is very nice.
9. What about these shoes? - They are mine (Pronomen)!
10. Bob's sister is eleven years old. His (Begleiter) best friend is eleven, too.
11. Whose books are these? Are they yours (Pronomen)?
12. These are their (Begleiter) books. They're fantastic!
13. Whose lunch box is this? Is it his (Pronomen)?
14. Is this your (Begleiter) friend? I know him, too.
15. Whose exciting book is this? - It's hers (Pronomen).
16. Don't eat these biscuits. They are not yours (Pronomen).

Zweite Übung:
1e, **2f**, **3a**, **4c**, **5d**, **6b**

Dritte Übung:
1. He loves her. **2.** She loves him. **3.** They don't like them. **4.** Read it.

S. 181 •••
1. Ich kann **dir/ euch/ Ihnen** den Weg zum Supermarkt sagen.
2. Wir können **dich/ euch/ Sie** nicht auf dem Foto entdecken.
3. Hier ist ein Ball. Warum spielst du nicht **damit**?
4. Jerry ist da. Lasst uns mit **ihm** reden.
5. Meinen Vater? Ja, lasst uns **ihn** fragen.

8 DIE REFLEXIVPRONOMEN

S. 181 •
1. I taught **myself** **5. You** can help **yourselves**
2. he hurt **himself** **6. we** usually enjoy **ourselves**
3. she only thinks of **herself**
7. They enjoy **themselves**
4. It's cleaning **itself**

S. 182 Boxenstopp
1. Tom und Perry betrachten sich im Spiegel.
2. Tom und Perry sehen sich gegenseitig an.
Wenn du ausdrücken möchtest, dass etwas **zwischen** mehreren Personen wechselseitig geschieht, so musst du **each other** verwenden. Im Deutschen kann **each other** mit *sich*, *gegenseitig* oder *einander* wiedergegeben werden.

S. 182 ••
1. richtig **2.** falsch **3.** falsch **4.** falsch **5.** richtig

S. 183 ••
sich (ver)ändern - (to) change, *sich anziehen* - (to) get dressed, *sich beeilen* - (to) hurry, *sich bewegen* - (to) move, *sich entscheiden* - (to) decide, *sich entspannen* - (to) relax, *sich ereignen* - (to) happen, *sich erinnern* - (to) remember, *sich fühlen* - (to) feel, *sich öffnen* - (to) open, *sich (hin)setzen* - (to) sit down, *sich treffen* - (to) meet, *sich trennen* - (to) split up, *sich verirren* - (to) get lost

S. 183 •••
1. Look at yourselves.
2. My brother and I bought ten new CDs.
3. We do our hair ourselves.

4. Well, I taught myself. But my mum and her friend didn't, they taught each other.
5. The people in my family see each other very often.
6. My brother and I were looking after ourselves when my parents went on holiday.
7. Nick and his friends meet at school every day.
8. I tried to see where the cat was - but it didn't move.

9 ADJEKTIV UND ADVERB

S. 184 •

Adjektive: angry, hungry, crazy, happy, holy, dirty, bloody, dry, easy, friendly, chilly
Adverbien: rarely, internationally, exactly, sadly, loudly, positively, slowly, carefully, fully

1. Generally people go to bed at halpast ten. **2.** Mike's mother spoke to him **angrily**. **3.** Anne has **definitely** decided to quit basketball. **4.** Susan **particularly** liked the end othe movie. **5.** Nina **suddenly** began to sing. **6.** Megan ate the burger **hungrily**.

S. 184 Boxenstopp

*Verben, die eine **Sinneswahrnehmung** beschreiben:* to taste, to feel, to smell, to sound
*Verben, die einen **Zustand** oder eine **Eigenschaft** beschreiben:* to look, to stay, to seem, to be

S. 185 ••

Erste Übung:

1. When Scott did his camping expedition, he didn't **really** like it.
2. The weather was **terrible** and he felt **cold** most of the time.
3. During the day the weather was better and Scott and his friends **happily** walked up the hills.
4. The last hill was very **steep** and it was very **hard** for them to reach the top.
5. The girls and boys also had to cook on their own and the food tasted **good** most of the time.
6. When they started to walk, Scott couldn't walk very **fast**.
7. Unfortunately, he also got some blisters and they had to climb **slowly**.
8. When they came back from their trip, Scott felt **happy** to **finally** be back home.

Zweite Übung:

1. Scott cannot run fast.
2. He cannot play the guitar quietly.
3. He can sing beautifully.
4. He can tell stories well.
5. He cannot cook well.
6. He can laugh loudly.

S. 185 •••

1. Scott is a good friend of mine.
2. Unfortunately, he couldn't hike for long during our trip.
3. "Could you please walk more slowly," he said. "I have got blisters."
4. He had to walk really carefully.
5. When we waited for him, he smiled happily.

10 ADJEKTIVE ALS NOMEN

S. 186 •

1. In my favourite book the **good** always win over the **bad**.
2. "Nightmare" is not a film for the **nervous**!
3. The playground in the schoolyard isn't only for the **young**.
4. Tell a joke to the **sad** and they will laugh.

S. 186 Boxenstopp

a. Blinde haben oft einen guten Hörsinn.
b. Margaret half dem blinden Mann über die Straße.

1. Wenn man von einer ganzen **Gruppe** von Menschen spricht, kann das Adjektiv als Nomen verwendet werden. Es steht dann mit dem **bestimmten Artikel**.
2. Wenn man von **einzelnen Personen** spricht, muss das Adjektiv durch ein **Nomen** (z.B. **woman, girl, man, boy, people, ...**) ergänzt werden. Anders als im Deutschen kann das Adjektiv hier also nicht alleine stehen.

S. 187 ••

Erste Übung:

1. The **little girl** has lost her parents.
2. The **sick man** was taken to hospital.
3. The **blind man** doesn't have a guide dog.
4. I saw a **famous person**.

Zweite Übung:

1d, **2e**, **3a**, **4b**, **5c**

Dritte Übung:

1. Reporters in Hollywood like to interview **the famous**.
2. Doctors must always help **the sick**.
3. In nature only **the strong** survive.
4. Some people are always jealous of **the rich**.
5. Big boys sometimes make fun of **the weak**.

S. 188 •••

1. The old woman drank a cup of tea.
2. A blind man was waiting at the bus stop.
3. We can learn a lot from the old.
4. The little boy drew a picture.

11 DIE ARTIKEL

S. 188 •

Goal is a very popular magazine with **the** young and sporty in the UK. In it you will find many articles about **the** different football clubs in Britain. And there is usually an interview with a star from **the** world of (the) sport. In (the) last month's edition there was an article about the football world cup of the year 1966 in England. (The) time goes by so quickly. The last world cup took place in 2006.
Jim has got **a** pair of new football trainers. He had bought them for **a** match on Saturday, but then he couldn't play. Why? Well, his older brother is **a** football

coach at Jim's club. He is five years older than Jim, he has **a** car and he usually drives to the matches by (a) car. He then takes Jim's bag with him because it's **a** heavy bag. But on (a) Saturday he left home early after (a) breakfast and Jim couldn't give him his bag with the shoes in it. That's why Jim couldn't play on that day. He was **an** athlete without trainers.

S. 189 Boxenstopp

1. Der **bestimmte** Artikel **the** zeigt an, dass etwas näher bestimmt ist. Nomen können z.B. durch einen Relativsatz oder eine Ergänzung mit **of** näher bestimmt werden. Der **bestimmte** Artikel steht nicht, wenn von Personen und **Dingen** ganz allgemein gesprochen wird.
2. Der **unbestimmte** Artikel **a / an** wird im Englischen meistens genauso verwendet wie im Deutschen. Nur in wenigen Fällen unterscheidet sich der Gebrauch, so z.B. bei **Berufsbezeichnungen** und feststehenden Wendungen.

S. 189 ••

1. on TV **2.** to have a headache **3.** at work **4.** most people **5.** to be in a hurry **6.** on the radio
7. to play the guitar **8.** on the telephone

S. 190 ••

1. Bill is a taxi driver. He goes to work by taxi.
2. Uncle Joe is a teacher. He goes to work by bike.
3. Mandy is a manager. She goes to work by car.
4. Monica is a shop assistant. She goes to work by train.
5. Lewis is a doctor. He goes to work by bus.

S. 190 •••

1. SURPRISE: Lucky lottery winners on TV.
2. TEACHERS PROTEST: Under these circumstances pupils can't learn at school.
3. DANGEROUS: Eating lemons may lead to having **a** headache.
4. ON THE NEWS: People who play music are happier.
5. STAR TALK: More interviews with **the** famous five.

12 DIREKTE UND INDIREKTE REDE

S. 190 •

Helen: "Our class trip **starts** on Friday."
Chris: "We'**ll fly** to Dublin just one day after my birthday."
Mary Ann: "I **don't want** to visit any museums!"
Benny: "I **want** to visit St. Patrick's Cathedral."

S. 191 Boxenstopp

1. Helen said that **their** class trip **started** on Friday.
2. Chris said that **they would** fly to Dublin just one day after **his** birthday.
3. Mary Ann said that **she didn't** want to visit any museums.
4. Benny said **he wanted** to visit St. Patrick's Cathedral.

S. 191 ••

1. his **2.** her **3.** their **4.** them **5.** their **6.** his **7.** their
Lösung: Trinity (Hotel)

S. 192 ••

The kids **told** their parents that they...
1. **took** a class trip to Dublin that year.
2. **were planning** everything for the trip on their own.
3. **had** already **booked** their tickets.
4. **had prepared** the trip with a guide book and by using the internet.
5. **hadn't imagined** that Dublin was such a beautiful place.
6. **would get** back to Dublin some day.
7. **could** always **visit** the friends they made there again.

S. 192 •••

	Direkte Rede	Indirekte Rede
1.	Simple Present	Simple Past
2.	Present Progressive	Past Progressive
3.	Present Perfect	Past Perfect
4.	Simple Past	Past Perfect
5.	Past Perfect	Past Perfect
6.	*will*-future	*would*
7.	*can*	*could*

13 INDIREKTE FRAGEN

S. 193 •

1c, **2d**, **3e**, **4a**, **5b**

S. 193 Boxenstopp

Gibt es in der direkten Rede kein Fragewort, dann wird der Nebensatz in der indirekten Rede mit **if** oder **whether** eingeleitet (im Deutschen: ..., *ob* ...).

S. 193 ••

1. Mein Vater fragte mich, was ich gemacht habe, bevor ich ins Bett gegangen sei.
2. Er wollte wissen, warum ich heute Morgen nicht ausgeschlafen habe.
3. Er wollte auch wissen, wann ich ins Bett gegangen sei.
4. Er fragte mich, von wem ich geträumt habe.
5. Er fragte mich, ob ich später als Mitternacht ins Bett gegangen sei.

S. 194 ••

Erste Übung:

1. George **told / asked** Mike to return the books to the library.
2. Jill's mother **told / advised** her to take a hot bath because she was so wet.
3. The coach **told / advised** his team to practice more.
4. The dentist **warned / asked** the patient to keep still.
5. The police officer **warned / advised** us not to cross the road here.

Zweite Übung:

1. Return the books to the library, please!
2. Take a hot bath - you are so wet!
3. You should practice more!
4. Please keep still!
5. Don't cross the road here!

S. 194 •••

1. I asked you to get a classic CD.
2. I warned you not to lose it.
3. I remember that I reminded you to pack it.
4. Well, dear, I advised you to get here earlier!

14 RELATIVSÄTZE

S. 195 •

a. richtig **b.** falsch **c.** richtig **d.** richtig **e.** richtig **f.** richtig **g.** falsch

S. 195 Boxenstopp

1. coach **2.** referee **3.** baseball **4.** racket **5.** goalkeeper

S. 196 ••

Erste Übung:

1. Ice skating is a sport **which / that** you can only do in winter.
2. Athletes **who / that** can run fast are always good at track & field.
3. Lots of people **who / that** don't do sports still enjoy watching it on TV.
4. Top athletes work with personal trainers **whose** task is to coach them.
5. This is the famous man **whose** homerun will always be remembered in baseball.
6. The Super Bowl is a football event on TV **which / that** Americans enjoy every year.

Zweite Übung:

1. Ice skating is a sport you can only do in winter.
2. The Super Bowl is a football event on TV Americans enjoy every year.

S. 38 •••

1. The coach, whose team won the championship, is happy.
2. The goal that the striker scored was brilliant!
3. The team whose captain can't play today is fighting to win.
4. This woman here that coaches us twice a week is our coach.
5. Rugby is a rough sport that is rather popular in Britain, Australia and France.

15 TEMPORALSÄTZE

S. 197 •

Waagerecht: as, when, after, as soon as
Senkrecht: while, until, before, since

S. 197 Boxenstopp

1. as - *als* **2. before** - *bevor* **3. until** - *bis* **4. when** - *wenn / als* **5. while** - *während* **6. after** - *nachdem* **7. since** - *seit(dem)* **8. as soon as** - *jedes Mal, wenn*

Man verwendet **while** und **when** im Sinne von *als* für einen Vorgang, der sich abspielte, während etwas anderes passierte. Dabei verwendet man **when** meist für gleichzeitige, länger andauernde Vorgänge. **As** verwendet man ebenfalls im Sinne von *als*, allerdings um hervorzuheben, dass etwas in einem bestimmten Zeitraum geschah.

S. 198 ••

Erste Übung:

1. Bye, Marta! Please ring me **when** you get home.
2. The garden is wet this morning, it must have rained **during** the night.
3. Would you look after the cat **when** I'm on holidays?
4. Why don't you go shopping **while** you are waiting for your bike to be repaired?
5. I watched **as** the policemen examined the crime scene.
6. The phone rang just **when** I was getting into the tub.

Zweite Übung:

1. When her guests arrived, she had just prepared a nice dinner.
2. When I played football, I broke my leg.
3. When you go to bed, please turn off the lights.

S. 198 •••

1. I'll cook you dinner **when** I come home.
2. I'll e-mail you **when** I arrive.
3. She won't speak to her boyfriend **until** he apologizes.
4. Every night **before** I go to bed, I brush my teeth.
5. Don't forget to pack your suitcase **before** you go to the airport.
6. I want to graduate from school **as soon as** possible.

16 IF-SÄTZE

S. 199 •

1. If you **set** the table, I**'ll do** the washing up.
2. If I **asked** you to help me with the laundry, **would** you **help** me?
3. If you **finish** your homework early tonight, you **may watch** your favourite TV show.
4. If you **had tidied up** your room, you **would have found** the keys earlier.
5. You **would become** more fluent in English if you **spent** more time in England.
6. If you **had worn** your rain coat, you **wouldn't have got** so wet.

Satz	Verbform im **if**-Satz	Verbform im Hauptsatz
1.	Simple Present	Zukunft mit *will*
2.	Simple Past	Conditional
3.	Simple Present	*may*
4.	Past Perfect	Conditional Perfect
5.	Simple Past	Conditional
6.	Past Perfect	Conditional Perfect

S. 200 Boxenstopp

Im Bedingungssatz **Typ 1** hält der Sprecher die Bedingung für **realistisch**. Im **if**-Satz steht das **Simple Present**, im Hauptsatz steht meist die Zukunft mit **will** oder ein modales Hilfsverb (**can, must, may**, etc.)

Im **if**-Satz **Typ 2** steht das **Simple Past**. Es drückt jedoch nicht aus, dass die Handlung in der Vergangenheit stattgefunden hat, sondern es beschreibt eine **unwahrscheinliche** Handlung. Im Hauptsatz steht das **conditional** (**would** + **Infinitiv**).
Beim Bedingungssatz **Typ 3** weiß der Sprecher, dass die Bedingung nicht **erfüllbar** ist, weil es sich um eine Situation handelt, die in der Vergangenheit liegt und bereits vorbei ist. Im **if**-Satz steht das **Past Perfect**, im Hauptsatz das **Conditional Perfect** (**would** + **have** + **past participle**).

S. 201 ••

1. If he **had** studied for the test, he **would** have passed it.
2. She **would** have understood you if you **had** spoken English.
3. I **would** have written you a postcard if I **had** had your address.
4. If you **had** listened to the radio, you **would** have heard the news.
5. If you **had** dropped the vase, it **would** have broken.

S. 201 •••

1. We **would have swum** in the sea last summer if there **hadn't been** so many sharks there.
2. If she **had taken** the bus, she **would not have arrived** on time.
3. I **wouldn't go** to school by bus if I **had** a driving licence.
4. We **would be** stupid if we **didn't tell** him the truth. Let's talk to him!
5. If I **were** you, I **wouldn't go** to school today – you're ill!
6. If my dad **hadn't lost** the keys, he **could have opened** the door.

WORTSCHATZ

1 HÖFLICHKEITSFORMEN

S. 202 •

Waagerecht: sorry, rude, help, polite, thanks
Senkrecht: apologize, please, nevermind

S. 203 ••

1. What would you like to know?
2. I'm sorry, but there isn't any dessert left for you.
3. Could you please open the window?
4. Thank you very much for carrying that heavy bag for me!

S. 204 ••

1d, **2e**, **3f**, **4b**, **5a**, **6c**

S. 204 •••

1c, **2b**, **3b**, **4c**, **5b**

2 SIGHTSEEING IN LONDON

S. 205 •

1a, **2b**, **3a**, **4a**, **5b**, **6a**

S. 205 Boxenstopp

1. sightseeing **2.** hotel booking **3.** asking for the way **4.** travelling **5.** going out for a meal

S. 206 ••

1. must see **2.** visit **3.** take **4.** guide book **5.** ticket **6.** waterfront **7.** travelcard **8.** queue

S. 207 ••

1. **Could** I take pictures in this museum?
2. Where's the next **supermarket**?
3. How **far** is **the museum**?
4. How much does it cost to **enter**?
5. What time does the museum **open** on the weekend?
6. Is the **museum** open on **Mondays**?

S. 207 •••

1. Ich würde gerne das Britische Museum besuchen, weil es interessanter als das London Eye ist.
2. Obwohl der Eintritt sehr teuer ist, ist Madame Tussauds wirklich einen Besuch wert.
3. Das Sherlock Holmes Museum ist billiger als der Tower of London.
4. Bist du schon einmal in Camden Town gewesen?

3 HOTEL GEBUCHT?

S. 208 •

1. help **2.** dates **3.** nights **4.** rooms **5.** bathroom **6.** breakfast **7.** double **8.** need **9.** booking

S. 209 ••

1. double room **2.** dining room **3.** room service **4.** en-suite

S. 209 •••

Dear Sir or Madam,
I'd like to book a double room for my parents. They are looking for a bed and breakfast accommodation for 3 nights (from August 1 to August 4). They will arrive by car at 5 p.m. on August 1, and they will leave Edinburgh on August 4 after breakfast. Do your rooms have en-suite facilities? And what are the costs per room and per night? Thank you for your immediate reply.
Yours faithfully ...

4 WEGBESCHREIBUNGEN

S. 210 •

1. "**Excuse** me, how do I **get** to the cinema?"
2. Go **straight on**.
3. Turn **left** at the corner.
4. Then take the **second** road on your **right**.
5. **Continue** to the **end** of the road.
6. **Turn** left there.
7. The cinema is on your **left, next to** the castle.

S. 211 Boxenstopp

1. on the left **2.** on the right **3.** straight on **4.** opposite **5.** near **6.** next to **7.** between **8.** at the end (of) **9.** on / at the corner **10.** behind **11.** in front of **12.** (just) around the corner

S. 212 • •

1c: Ampel **2e:** Kreuzung **3f:** Kreisverkehr **4a:** Zebrastreifen **5b:** Vorfahrtstraße **6d:** Einbahnstraße

S. 212 • • •

1. Go straight on.
2. Turn right at the second (set of) traffic lights.
3. Cross the intersection.
4. Go on to the roundabout.
5. Turn left behind the petrol station.
6. Stop at the end of the road.
7. There's a parking lot in front of you.
8. You have arrived at the swimming pool.

5 ÖFFENTLICHE VERKEHRSMITTEL

S. 213 •

1h: Tom is going to Spain by lorry.
2e: Jack and Lisa are going shopping by car.
3g: Miguel is visiting his family py plane.
4f: Mr and Mrs Jones are on their honeymoon by ferry.
5a: Clarisse is going to see the doctor by bus.
6b: Mary-Ann is visiting Canada and the USA by coach.
7d: Robin goes to school by bike.
8i: Martin is going to Hyde Park on foot.
9c: Grandpa and grandma are going to Vienna by train.

S. 214 Boxenstopp

plane: luggage check-in, information desk, lost and found
train: platform, track, schedule, ticket counter, station
bus: double-decker, bus stop
taxi: driver, taxi rank, black cab

S. 214 • •

1. Does this train go to New York?
2. How long is the flight to Denver?
3. When does the bus to Seattle leave?
4. When do we arrive in Philadelphia?
5. Where can I catch a taxi?

S. 215 • •

1. Where is the ticket counter, please?
2. How much are two tickets to Boston, please?
3. A return ticket to New Orleans, please.

S. 215 • • •

1. I'd like two return tickets to London, please.
2. Yes, that's for today. / No, it's for ...
3. We'd like to leave Cambridge in the morning.
4. First class, please.
5. Can I pay by credit card?
6. Do I have to make a reservation?
7. OK. I'd like to confirm the reservation then, please.
8. Here you are. Thank you.

6 IM RESTAURANT

S. 216 •

1e, **2d**, **3a**, **4c**, **5b**, **6f**

S. 216 • •

1. table **2.** menu **3.** hungry **4.** order **5.** fish and chips **6.** drinks **7.** dessert **8.** bill

S. 217 • • •

So könnte deine Unterhaltung mit dem Kellner lauten:

Waiter: Hello. Are you ready to order?
You: Yes. I'd like a nice breakfast. Would you bring me a bagel with cream cheese, please?
Waiter: A bagel with cream cheese. What kind of jam would you like with that?
You: What kinds do you have?
Waiter: We have strawberry, blackberry, apricot and cherry.
You: In this case I'll have the blackberry jam, please.
Waiter: Alright. And would you like a cup of coffee with your breakfast?
You: Yes please. I'll have a coffee with sugar and cream.

7 SMALL TALK

S. 218 •

1e, **2b**, **3f**, **4c**, **5d**, **6a**

S. 219 Boxenstopp

1. I see. **2.** Really? **3.** Exactly. **4.** Yes, I know. **5.** Oh no! **6.** Right,

S. 219 • •

I fell over and slipped on this icy ground which caused the accident.

S. 220 • •

1. You know, yesterday I was at the movies and I really liked the film.
2. Actually I didn't go to the swimming pool on Thursday or something because I lost my ticket, you know.
3. We really had to wait until they were all gone, you know. And it was actually dark when we got home.

S. 220 • • •

1. Really? Haven't you ever lost a game?
2. Definitely! I bought it at a very exclusive store in Paris!
3. Oh no! Didn't you lock it properly?
4. Right! I also prefer summertime to winter.
5. Exactly. People are waiting for us there.

8 FAMILIENLEBEN

S. 221 •

1. uncle **2.** parents **3.** great-grandparents **4.** niece **5.** son **6.** grandfather **7.** cousin **8.** me

S. 221 Boxenstopp

Enkel	grandson	*Enkelin*	grand-daughter	*Enkelkind*	grandchild
Großvater	**grandfather**	*Großmutter*	grandmother	*Großeltern*	grandparents
Urgroßvater	great-grandmother	*Urgroßmutter*	**great-grandmother**	*Urgroßeltern*	great-grandparents
Vater	**father**	*Mutter*	mother	*Eltern*	**parents**
Sohn	son	*Tochter*	daughter	*Kinder*	children
Bruder	brother	*Schwester*	**sister**	*Geschwister*	brothers and sisters

Ehemann	husband	*Ehefrau*	**wife**	*Eheleute*	couple
Onkel	uncle	*Tante*	aunt	*Verwandte*	**relatives**
Neffe	nephew	*Nichte*	niece		
Cousin	**cousin**	*Cousine*	cousin		

S. 222 ••

1. Sarah Burton is the daughter of Michael and Susan Royal. She is the wife of John Burton. She is the mother of Simon and Becky Burton.
2. Michael Royal is the husband of Susan Royal. He is the father of Sarah Burton and Jane Miller. He is the grandfather of Simon, Becky, Jim and Wendy.
3. Wendy Miller is the daughter of Jane and Tom Miller. She is the sister of Jim Miller. She is the granddaughter of Michael Royal.

9 DIE WELT DES SPORTS

S. 223 •

1c, **2f**, **3b**, **4a**, **5d**, **6e**

S. 224 Boxenstopp

Sportart	Ort	Ausrüstung
aerobics	gym	music
baseball	pitch	bat
basketball	arena	basket
football	stadium	goal
rugby	field	helmet
swimming	pool	goggles
tennis	court	racket
track and field / athletics	track	running shoes

S. 224 ••

indoor activities: squash, badminton, table tennis, swimming, judo, volleyball, basketball, gymnastics
outdoor activities: cycling, skiing, tennis, climbing, football, golf, cricket, baseball, windsurfing, rugby, riding, running

S. 225 •••

1. favourite **2.** play **3.** go **4.** best **5.** play **6.** good **7.** do **8.** real **9.** play **10.** really

10 DIE WELT DER MEDIEN

S. 225 •

1a, **2b**, **3b**, **4a**, **5c**

S. 227 •••

1b. Before you can talk on the phone, you need to pick up the receiver.
2d. With a mobile phone you can't only talk, but you can also text messages.
3a. You can leave a message on an answering machine if the person you're calling is not at home.
4c. If the line is busy, you better hang up the phone.
5e. When calling somebody abroad, you must dial an extra area code before dialling the telephone number.
Klasse 8

S. 227 • •

Text message	Englische Übersetzung	Deutsche Übersetzung
GR8 2 CU. TLK 2 U 2MORO. Mick	**1.** Great to see you. Talk to you tomorrow, Mick.	**a.** Schön, dich zu sehen. Wir sprechen uns morgen, Mick.
THX FYI. I CALL U L8R. Nina	**2.** Thanks for your information. I call you later, Nina.	**b.** Danke für deine Info. Ich ruf dich später an, Nina.
DF, RUOK? Tim	**3.** Dear friend, are you okay? Tim.	**c.** Lieber Freund, geht's dir gut? Tim.
IDK, MY SISTER IS HERE. I CY L8R. Mel	**4.** I don't know. My sister is here. I see why later, Mel.	**d.** Ich weiß es nicht. Meine Schwester ist da. Warum, finde ich später heraus, Mel.
GR8 2 HEAR. ILU 4EVER. Sandra	**5.** Great to hear. I love you forever. Sandra.	**e.** Schön, das zu hören. Ich werde dich immer lieben, Sandra.
NP. HAND. CM 2MORO. Sam	**6.** No problem. Have a nice day. Call me tomorrow. Sam.	**f.** Kein Problem. Einen schönen Tag noch. Ruf mich morgen an. Sam.
CU IN SCHOOL. GB. Will	**7.** See you in school. Good bye, Will.	**g.** Bis (morgen) in der Schule. Tschüß, Will.
Y CAN'T U COME? WB. Steve	**8.** Why can't you come? Write back, Steve.	**h.** Warum kannst du nicht kommen? Schreib mir, Steve.

KLASSE 8

GRAMMATIK

1 IF-SÄTZE (S. 236-238)

1.
1. need, ask, **2.** do, don't have, **3.** burn, stay, **4.** get, is.

2.
1. will (oder can) play/'ll play, **2.** will (oder may) catch/'ll catch, **3.** will (may, can) travel/'ll travel, **4.** (can) come **5.** will (oder can) call/'ll call, **6.** will (oder can) go and get/'ll go and get.

3.
1. would have to eat/'d have to eat, **2.** booked, **3.** would do/'d do, **4.** would know/'d know, **5.** wouldn't be at work, **6.** were

4.
1. would have called/'d have called, **2.** wouldn't have known, **3.** would have understood/'d have understood, **4.** would have lived/would have been living, **5.** would have paid for, **6.** had not wished for/hadn't wished for.

5.
1. will spend/'ll spend, **2.** would go, **3.** had not taken/ hadn't taken, **4.** would not ask/wouldn't ask, **5.** had, **6.** don't do, **7.** wouldn't have had, **8.** won't pass, **9.** would have loved/'d have loved.

6.
erfüllbare Bedingung: **2.** If she says silly things about me, I'll be angry.
schwer erfüllbare Bedingung: **1.** If she said silly things about me, I would be pretty angry.
unerfüllbare Bedingung: **3.** If she had said silly things about me, I would have been pretty angry.

7.
1. If I find your ring, I'll call/phone you.
2. If you asked Tom for € 3,500, what would he say?
3. I'll come with you if you wait a moment/second.
4. If you like, I'll get you a job in this company.
5. If I were afraid of flying, I would have/'d have a big problem with my job.
6. If I had had more time, I would have gone/'d have gone jogging more often.

2 GERUNDIUM UND INFINITIV (S. 245-247)

1.
1. Our children enjoy watching TV on Saturday evenings./ *Unsere Kinder genießen es, samstagabends Fernsehen zu schauen.*
2. Do you miss earning your own money?/ *Vermisst du es, dein eigenes Geld zu verdienen?*
3. Learning a foreign language can be very useful./ *Das (Er)lernen einer Fremdsprache kann sehr nützlich sein.*
4. Playing golf is an expensive hobby in Germany./ *Golfspielen ist in Deutschland ein teures Hobby.*

2.
1. Sailing is fun. **2.** Driving on the left is not difficult. **3.** Playing football is our son's biggest hobby. **4.** I'm interested in learning a foreign language.
5. My boss prefers drinking tea in the morning.
6. I love watching TV on Sundays. **7.** I started jogging two weeks ago.

3.
1. to chat/chatting, **2.** travelling, **3.** to take, **4.** talking to, **5.** buying, **6.** eating, **7.** to speak, **8.** to laugh/ laughing, **9.** catching, **10.** to see.

4.

enjoy, I'm afraid of (be afraid of), don't miss, love, don't like, hate	flying.
decided, promised, offered, hope	to come earlier next time.
decided, promised, offered, don't like, love, hate	to book the Westminster Hotel in London.
decided, don't like, love, hate	to argue with my best friends.
enjoy, don't miss, love, don't like, hate	smoking in trains.
enjoy, I'm afraid of (be afraid of), don't miss, love, don't like, hate	living in the city.
enjoy, don't miss, love, don't like, hate	eating in Italian restaurants.

5.

1. *Julie hörte mit dem Klavierspielen auf, als sie 18 Jahre alt war.*
   Julie hörte [mit irgendetwas] auf und spielte Klavier/um Klavier zu spielen, weil sie an diesem Tag noch nicht geübt hatte.
2. *Die Sekretärin/der Sekretär vergaß, dass sie/er die Reservierung storniert hatte.*
   Die Sekretärin/der Sekretär vergaß, die Reservierung zu stornieren.
3. *Ein hübscher Garten heißt, fast jeden Tag darin zu arbeiten.*
   Aber ich will dich wegen deines Gartens wirklich nicht kritisieren.
4. *Erinnerst du dich, dass du mit Helen über ihre Lebensversicherung gesprochen hast?*
   Denk dran, mit Helen über ihre Lebensversicherung zu sprechen.

3 DAS CONDITIONAL (S. 251)

1.

1. *Wir könnten Valerie fragen. Sie wüsste, was zu tun ist.* **2.** *Lass uns am Sonntag fahren. Am Sonntag wäre nicht so viel Verkehr.* **3.** *Würdest du diese Musical-Tickets für 40 Pfund kaufen?* **4.** *Großmutter hätte es nicht geschafft zum Arzt zu gehen. Ich habe sie hingebracht.* **5.** *Sie hätten 3 Millionen Euro gewonnen, wenn sie den Jackpot geknackt hätten.*

2.

1. I'd share/I would share a flat with you. **2.** Tom would like to go/travel to Australia together with Lena. **3.** We wouldn't have won the race if it had rained. **4.** I wouldn't have thought that you are thirty already! **5.** We'd rather move away from here. **6.** Thomas wouldn't have asked you.

4 INDIREKTE REDE (S. 257-258)

1.

1. had renovated the office very quickly. **2.** could organize the next meeting. **3.** had definitely closed the door. **4.** had visited many European countries. **5.** would rain tomorrow. **6.** had been living in Hamburg for five years. **7.** had already talked about that problem several times. **8.** had been no snow/hadn't been any snow in Germany that year. **9.** were going to sell their house.

2.

1. her children always walk to school. **2.** I never work at weekends. **3.** Aboriginals live in Australia. **4.** he would prepare the dinner. **5.** each village in Great Britain has at least one pub. **6.** Ireland has got beautiful beaches. **7.** she had read so many fantastic books.

3.

1. had (any) time to go out. **2.** whether/if I could repair his/her alarm clock. **3.** how long I would need for that. **4.** whether/if I wanted him/her to pick me up. **5.** why I wasn't listening. **6.** whether/if he/she had upset me. **7.** he/she was sorry, he/she hadn't meant to pressure me.

4.

1. Kim asked me to go home. **2.** Luke advised me to open the window. **3.** Tom asked me not to wait for him. **4.** Sheila told me not to miss the new film. **5.** Ben warned me not to forget my umbrella.

5 DER ARTIKEL (S. 263-264)

1.

the office, the aunt, the eyes, the earring, the hour.

2.

1. der; **2.** die; **3.** den; **4.** Der, des; **5.** dem; **6.** Die.

3.

1. a, an; 2. an, a; 3. a, a; 4. an, a; 5. an, a; 6. an, a; 7. a, a.

4.

a: safe underground, young uncle, clever agent, new argument, useful book, brilliant idea, high building, fantastic office
an: English flag, interesting film, ugly house, angry man, old church, early flight, orange juice

5.

- holiday, - France, the French Alps, a skiing course, - Marc, a Frenchman, - summer, a sailing instructor, the Mediterranean Sea, the Super Sail School, - Lake Windermere, - English, the Smiths, - skiing, - famous sights, the Mont Blanc, a bus, the hotel, the foot, the mountain, - October, - April, - Mondays, the Christmas holidays, - school.

6.

1. **Half the students** of our class went to Madame Tussaud's last summer.

2. **All the people** in our bus had booked tickets in advance.
3. Everybody else stood in a queue for **half an hour**.
4. **What a surprise** to see the new James Bond actor already there!
5. **Quite a lot** of people took a photo of him.
6. Everybody spent **twice the amount** of money they had planned.
7. **Both the photos and the souvenirs** were very popular.

6 SOME UND ANY (S. 269-270)

1.

1. some, **2.** any, **3.** any, **4.** any, **5.** some, **6.** any, **7.** some

2.

1. *überall in Deutschland,* **2.** *nichts Besonderes,* **3.** *Irgendetwas Neues?* **4.** *einige Probleme,* **5.** *Irgendwelche Vorschläge?* **6.** *mitten im Niemandsland/ Nirgendwo,* **7.** *Keine Ahnung.* **8.** *Alles in Ordnung.* **9.** *(den) ganzen Tag,* **10.** *die ganze Zeit*

3.

somewhere, any, everything, anything, some, some, anybody, somebody.

4.

1. I haven't got/I don't have any interesting hobbies.
2. We can't do anything.
3. You shouldn't tell anybody the truth.

5.

1. *Ich habe niemanden um Hilfe gebeten.*
2. *Keine Nachrichten sind gute Nachrichten.*
3. *Wir wussten nichts über die Katastrophe.*

6.

1. Did you hear anything last night/yesterday evening?
2. I have made a few photos. You can see very little on them.
3. Why didn't you tell everybody (about it)?
4. All neighbours are curious. (vgl. "all the neighbours" – *„alle unsere (oder sonstwie bestimmten) Nachbarn"*)

WORTSCHATZ

1 AMERICAN ENGLISH & BRITISH ENGLISH

Unterschiede im Wortschatz

1. a. AmE, b. BrE, c. AmE, d. BrE, e. AmE, f. BrE, g. BrE, h. BrE

Rechtschreibung

2. jewelry – realised – aluminium – centre – center – practice – defense – maneuvers – travellers – offence – cheques

Boxenstopp

-or, -nse und **-er** – z.B. **gray** (AmE) / **grey** (BrE) - *grau*, **tire** (AmE) / **tyre** (BrE) - *Autoreifen*

Grammatik

Boxenstopp

Variante 1: **Have** wird als Vollverb benutzt. – *Variante 2:* **Have** wird durch **have got** ersetzt. – **Got** ist die Partizip-Perfekt-Form von **get** im **britischen Englisch**. – **Gotten** verwendet man als Partizip-Perfekt-Form im **amerikanischen Englisch**.

2 LEICHT VERWECHSELBARE WÖRTER

1. a. effect, b. affect, c. break, d. dessert, e. brake
2. a. its, b. it's
3. a. Whose, b. Who's

Boxenstopp

klingen – Bedeutung – geschrieben – **brake** und **break**, **desert** und **dessert**, **its** und **it's** usw.

KLASSE 9

GRAMMATIK

1 DIE GEGENWART (S. 291-296)

Übungen zum Simple Present

1.

(1) works, (2) likes, (3) gets up, (4) takes, (5) collect, (6) put, (7) drives, (8) starts, (9) leaves, (10) puts, (11) walks, (12) enjoys, (13) takes, (14) are, (15) finishes

2.

2. Sarah cooks large meals but she doesn't like the washing up.
3. Nick and Sam go fishing but they don't eat the fish.
4. Alice loves shopping but she doesn't spend much money.
5. I (+ Grundform, + don't + Grundform).
6. Justin surfs the Internet but he doesn't go into chat rooms.

3.

1. often	*oft*
2. always	*immer*
3. usually	*gewöhnlich, normalerweise*
4. never	*nie*
5. sometimes	*manchmal*

4.

1. Judy gets up at 6.30 every morning.
2. She usually has breakfast at home.
3. She sometimes buys a sandwich at the baker's next door.
4. Judy always takes the underground to school.
5. School is often out at four/4 o'clock.

6. She sometimes meets a friend after school.
7. Judy normally does her homework in her room in the evening.
8. She goes to bed every night at ten/10 o'clock.

5.

1. *Wer zuerst kommt, mahlt zuerst.*
2. *Neue Besen kehren gut.*
3. *Er benimmt sich wie ein Elefant im Porzellanladen.*
4. *Was Hänschen nicht lernt, lernt Hans nimmermehr.*
5. *Darauf kannst du Gift nehmen.*
6. *Ende gut, alles gut.*
7. *Ausnahmen bestätigen die Regel.*
8. *Wahre Freunde erkennt man in der Not.*
9. *Geld regiert die Welt.*
10. *Keine Nachricht ist eine gute Nachricht.*
11. *Es gehören immer zwei dazu.*
12. *Morgen ist auch noch ein Tag.*
13. *Wo ein Wille ist, ist auch ein Weg.*

Übungen zum present progressive

6.

1. is talking to, **2.** are drinking, **3.** are standing, **4.** is telling, is laughing, **5.** is dancing, **6.** 's/is saying, **7.** 's/is wearing

7.

1. is cutting, **2.** are teaching, **3.** are operating, **4.** are controlling, **5.** is flying, **6.** are selling, **7.** is tying, **8.** is driving

8.

simple + progressive form: understand, run, talk, work, carry, get, read, tell, try, make, watching
nur simple form: hate, see, want, like, smell, notice, know, think, imagine

9.

It's Monday afternoon. What a day! The sun **isn't shining**. It's **raining** cats and dogs. Mr Spencer is **sitting** in his office. He **isn't talking** on the phone. He's **writing** a report. His secretary is **writing** an e-mail. But not everybody is **working**. A young girl in a building across the street is **daydreaming**. She **isn't doing** her homework although she has a lot to do. And Mr and Mrs Frazer from next door **are going** for a walk in the park. They **aren't wearing** their rain coats. But they are **having** an umbrella each. Their dog Colin is **enjoying** the walk. He's **chasing** a rabbit.

10.

John: Hello, Martin. How are you? What are you doing?
Martin: Hi, John. Well, Sandra is working on the computer and I'm preparing myself for the maths exam tomorrow. And what are you doing?
John: I'm lying on my bed and I'm watching TV. Can we go to school by bike together tomorrow morning?
Martin: Yes, good idea. Let's meet at the station at eight o'clock.
John: Ok. See you then. Have fun studying maths. Bye.
Martin: Thanks. See you tomorrow. Bye.

11.

1. always gets up, is getting up; **2.** is writing, usually creates; **3.** sometimes works, is working; **4.** 'm looking for, need

2 DIE VERGANGENHEIT (S. 309–322)

Übungen zum simple past

1.

Waagerecht, **1.** Zeile (v.l.): said – say, was – be; **2.** Zeile: went – go; **5.** Zeile: read – read; **6.** Zeile: told – tell; **7.** Zeile: swam – swim, ran – run; **9.** Zeile: sold – sell, won – win. **Senkrecht**, **1.** Spalte (v.l.): stood – stand; **2.** Spalte: wrote – write; **3.** Spalte: wore – wear; **5.** Spalte: had – have, drank – drink; **6.** Spalte: ate – eat, came – come; **7.** Spalte: saw – see, threw – throw; **8.** Spalte: built – build; **9.** Spalte: took – take.

2.

When I **was** a child life **was** quite different. We **lived** in a small house in the country and we **had** a big garden. We **spent** most of the time outside. My father **went** to work every morning and Mum **stayed** at home. She **had** to look after us. We **were** three boys and a girl. When Dad **came** home he **took** a shower first and then he **played** with us. That **was** always great fun. Our parents **insisted on** having dinner together. We **liked** that. My mother **cooked** wonderful meals and my father often **told** funny stories. After that Mum **put** us to bed and everybody **listened** to her brilliant good night stories. Those **were** great times.

3.

1. came, didn't wake up, **2.** didn't answer, heard, **3.** invited, agreed, didn't want, **4.** moved, didn't have.

4.

1. Did you get your driver's licence last week?
2. Did your parents buy that house in Florida?
3. Did your mum do the computer course?
4. Did she tell you about that funny teacher?
5. Was Henry successful in his Maths test?
6. Did Mary like the detective story you gave her?
7. Did your friends prepare a surprise party for you?

5.

1. *Wo wart ihr?* Where did you go?
2. *Was habt ihr dort gemacht?* What did you do there?
3. *Wo habt ihr gewohnt?* Where did you stay?
4. *Wir waren in einem Hotel.* We stayed in a hotel.
5. *Wie fandest du das Hotel?* What did you think about the hotel?
6. *Ich fand es hervorragend.* I thought it was brilliant.
7. *Mir gefiel die Aussicht sehr.* I loved the view.

8. *Wie war das Wetter?* What was the weather like?

6.
1. Were you at the travel agency? Yes, I was.
2. Was Jennifer there, too? No, she wasn't.
3. Did you speak to her? Yes, I did.

Übungen zum past progressive

7.
1. was snoring, **2.** was sleeping, **3.** were telling, **4.** was reading, **5.** were burning, **6.** was lying, **7.** was running, **8.** was striking

8.
1. I was sleeping. **2.** Rita/She was answering an e-mail. **3.** The people/They were grumbling about public transport. **4.** Lucy/She was listening to her new CD. **5.** The dinner guests/They were eating their dessert. **6.** Gina's/Her husband/ He was working on his computer. **7.** Those young people/They were demonstrating for human rights.

9.
1. Lukas was dancing on the table. **2.** Tim was throwing a sponge at Nico. **3.** Four boys were playing cards. **4.** Simone was standing on a chair next to them. **5.** Three girls were drawing pictures on the board. **6.** Nina and Patrick were leaning out of the window. **7.** Toby and Kim were fighting on the floor. **8.** Susan was shouting at her friend.

10.
1. und **2.** While Lukas was dancing on the table, Tim was throwing the sponge at Nico.
3. und **4.** While four boys were playing cards, Simone was standing on a chair next to them.
5. und **6.** While three girls were drawing pictures on the board, Nina and Patrick were leaning out of the window.
7. und **8.** While Toby and Kim were fighting on the floor, Susan was shouting at her friend.

11.
Yesterday Jeannie had to go to work by train because her husband needed the car. When she arrived at the station, lots of people were already waiting on the platform. The train was late. Some people were nervously walking up and down while others were talking about the delay. Fortunately Jeannie found a vacant seat on a bench. While she was reading her morning paper, the woman next to her opened her bag. She was making a lot of noise while she was searching for something. Finally she stopped with a deep sigh. "Is everything OK?" Jeannie asked her. "Yes, thanks," she replied with a smile. "I was just thinking about my new flat when I thought I had left the keys at home. But I hadn't." "Lucky you", Jeannie said as the woman waved a bunch of keys in her hand.

12.
1. *Als Jeannie am Bahnhof ankam, warteten schon viele Leute auf dem Bahnsteig.*
2. *Einige gingen nervös auf und ab, während sich andere über die Verspätung unterhielten.*
3. *Während Jeannie ihre Morgenzeitung las, öffnete die Frau neben ihr ihre Tasche.*
4. *Sie machte eine Menge Geräusche, während sie nach irgendetwas suchte.*
5. *Ich habe gerade über meine neue Wohnung nachgedacht, als ich dachte, ich hätte meine Schlüssel zu Hause vergessen.*
6. *„Sie Glückliche", sagte Jeannie, als die Frau mit ihrem Schlüsselbund in der Hand winkte.*

Übungen zum present perfect simple

13.
1. broke, broken, **2.** answered, answered, **3.** sent, sent, **4.** saw, seen, **5.** cost, cost, **6.** buy, bought, **7.** speak, spoken, **8.** watch, watched, **9.** do, did, **10.** make, made, **11.** invite, invited, **12.** catch, caught

14.
1. taught, taught, **2.** paid, paid, **3.** thought, thought, **4.** began, begun, **5.** read, read, **6.** brought, brought, **7.** got, got, **8.** fought, fought

15.
1. Yes, I have. **2.** No, I haven't. **3.** Yes, he has. **4.** Yes, I have. **5.** No, it hasn't. **6.** Yes, they have.

16.
1. have won, **2.** has restored, **3.** haven't seen **4.** haven't heard, **5.** has done, **6.** hasn't failed, **7.** haven't been **8.** have been

17.
1. yet/*Hast du schon den neuesten Krimi von Elizabeth George gelesen?* **2.** yet/*Nein, ich habe ihn noch nicht gelesen.* **3.** so far/*Was hast du bisher geschrieben?* **4.** just/*Ich bin gerade mit den ersten zwei Abschnitten fertig.* **5.** ever/*Hast du jemals frei lebende Elefanten in Afrika beobachtet?*
6. never/*Nein, ich war überhaupt noch nie in Afrika.* **7.** already/*Aber ich habe schon welche in einem Safaripark in Frankreich gesehen.*

18.
2. They haven't put the rubbish in the bin.
3. They have bought some apples, yoghurt and two pizzas.
4. They have done their homework.
5. They haven't tidied up their rooms.
6. They have hoovered the ground floor.
7. They have locked the front door.
8. They haven't gone to bed before midnight.

19.
1. have you spoken, spoke, **2.** have you taken, took,
3. have you gone out, haven't done,
4. have you noticed, haven't, haven't been,
5. has (your sister already) ordered, has, ordered

Übungen zum present perfect progressive

20.

1. have been, **2.** have been, **3.** has been, **4.** has been, **5.** has been, **6.** have been, **7.** have been, **8.** have been

21.

1. Zeitpunkt, since, **2.** Zeitpunkt, since, **3.** Zeitpunkt, since, **4.** Zeitraum, for, **5.** Zeitpunkt, since, **6.** Zeitraum, for, **7.** Zeitraum, for.

22.

1. *Herr Hunt wartet schon seit halb fünf auf seine Frau.* **2.** *Der Briefträger trägt die Briefe schon seit dem frühen Morgen aus.* **3.** *Zwei Männer reparieren den Bürgersteig schon seit letzten Dienstag.* **4.** *Victor und seine Freunde joggen (schon) seit einer halben Stunde um den Sportplatz.* **5.** *Melissa schaut schon seit 8 Uhr Fernsehen.* **6.** *Unsere Kinder sammeln schon seit fünf Jahren Autogramme.* **7.** *Frau Colin korrigiert schon seit zwei Stunden Arbeiten.*

23.

present progressive: are repairing, am travelling, isn't driving
simple past: wished, didn't want, understood
present perfect simple: have printed, hasn't read, has written
present perfect progressive: haven't been teaching, has been living, have been waiting

24.

1. We've been/We have been living in this flat for 15 years. **2.** I've/I have just renovated it. Now it looks like new again. **3.** I've been/I have been learning English since 1980 and I still don't know everything.

Übungen zum past perfect simple

25.

Last year we <u>had asked</u> our neighbours to look after the house and the garden while we were staying in Italy for a fortnight. When we came back two weeks later we couldn't believe what we saw. The letterbox was bursting because they <u>hadn't emptied</u> it. The lawn in the garden was brown because they <u>hadn't watered</u> it. And all the lovely plants in the garden! What a shame. We were so surprised because our neighbours <u>had</u> always <u>made</u> such a positive impression on us. After the first shock we went over to them. But they weren't at home. In the evening we received a phone call from the neighbours' son. And then we understood: Mr Hill and Mrs Hill <u>had had</u> an accident and were both still in hospital. We weren't annoyed any longer and visited them. They were pleased to see us and very sorry at the same time but that wasn't important anymore. They're wonderful neighbours.

26.

1. *Letztes Jahr hatten wir unsere Nachbarn gebeten, auf unser Haus und den Garten aufzupassen, während wir für zwei Wochen in Italien waren.* **2.** *Der Briefkasten platzte aus allen Nähten, weil sie ihn nicht geleert hatten.* **3.** *Der Rasen im Garten war braun, weil sie ihn nicht gesprengt hatten.* **4.** *Wir waren so überrascht, weil unsere Nachbarn immer einen so guten Eindruck auf uns gemacht hatten.* **5.** *Herr und Frau Hill hatten einen Unfall gehabt und waren beide noch im Krankenhaus.*

27.

1. started, had checked; **2.** remembered, had told; **3.** presented, had drawn; **4.** suggested, had read; **5.** had missed, had to wait; **6.** had gone, noticed, had left; **7.** didn't keep, had promised, **8.** arrived, had already treated.

28.

1. Before Marian started to work at the office she had already taken the kids to school. **2.** She didn't tell me that her boyfriend had left her. **3.** After we had booked our flight we bought a travel guide. **4.** He told me how he had broken his arm. **5.** Ted couldn't get into the house yesterday because he had left the keys at school.

Übungen zum past perfect progressive

29.

1. had been working, **2.** had been reading, **3.** had been living, **4.** had been working, **5.** had been following.

30.

1. Mr Turner had been watching TV all the time. **2.** Mrs Cook had smelled the fire and called the fire brigade. **3.** Mrs Joyce said that somebody had knocked at her door beforehand. **4.** But she hadn't opened the door. **5.** Mr and Mrs Stilton had been eating dinner. **6.** Some people said that they had had a headache. **7.** Others said that they hadn't noticed anything.

3 DIE ZUKUNFT (S. 328–330)

1.

1. I'm sure he won't come.
2. Marsha won't spend the weekend in Madrid.
3. There won't be heavy showers at night.
4. Mr and Mrs Hill will leave early.

2.

1. I'll call the doctor. **2.** I'll get some from the supermarket. **3.** OK. We'll go upstairs. **4.** Don't worry. I'll fix it for you.

3.

1. Is Timo going to meet his girlfriend again?
2. Are you going to have a party for your birthday?
3. Is Dad going to take a week off?
4. Are you and your friends going to prepare a surprise party for Susan?

4.

1. I'm going to relax. **2.** We are going to clean the flat on Saturday. **3.** Tim is going to play football. **4.** My best friend Nina is going to be in Hamburg. **5.** Nina and I are going to go to the cinema.

5.

1. simple present/Christmas Eve falls on a Friday this year.
2. simple present/It's mother's birthday next Sunday.
3. will-future/I'm sure grandma and granddad will come at the weekend.
4. will-future/Maybe we'll go to a restaurant then.
5. future progressive/Mum will be celebrating with us on Sunday anyway.
6. going to-future/Careful, the water. It's going to boil over.
7. present progressive/Bayern München is playing against Manchester United tomorrow.
8. future perfect/I'm afraid the weather will have changed until then.

6.

1. *Mama trifft am Sonntag ihre beste Freundin/ihren besten Freund.* **2.** *Wir putzen morgen die Fenster.*
3. *Warte mal eben. Ich schreibe das auf.*
4. *Ich bin sicher, ihr werdet euch amüsieren.*

4 RELATIVSÄTZE (S. 335-336)

1.

1. which, **2.** who/that, **3.** who/that, **4.** who/that, **5.** (which/that), **6.** (which/that), **7.** who, **8.** (who/ whom/that)

2.

2. The man who/that was driving the bus didn't know the way.
3. This is Lilian Parker who/whom I know from the gym.
4. Lynn, who hated eating by herself, hoped to have lunch with Louisa.
5. Nora knows the address (that) you need. (Auch möglich: Nora knows which address you need.)

3.

1. *Es gibt so viele Dinge, die ich tun möchte.*
2. *Sprich nicht mit Leuten, die du nicht so gut kennst.*
3. *Papa ist der Typ Mensch, der harte Arbeit mag.*
4. *Ich habe einen jungen Mann getroffen, der bei Porsche arbeitet.*
5. *Die Rechnungen, die ich jeden Monat bezahlen muss, sind nicht sehr hoch.*
6. *(Im Jahr) 2004 habe ich in Australien gearbeitet, was eine tolle Erfahrung war.*

4.

1. The only dress (which/that) I really like is a size too small. **2.** I need a doctor (who/whom/that) I can trust. **3.** Tina again has to look after those children who/that are terribly spoilt. **4.** We want to buy a camper, which the four of us can sleep in/ in which the four of us can sleep. **5.** Parents who/ that both work have to be good organizers. **6.** The play (which/that) we saw yesterday evening was a complete disaster.

WORTSCHATZ

1 FALSCHE FREUNDE

1. a. get; b. sensible; c. argument; d. also; e. current; f. sensitive; g. Therefore; h. become; i. actual

Boxenstopp

Zum Beispiel: *brav* - **brave** (*mutig*), *Gift* - **gift** (*Geschenk*), *Gymnasium* - **gym(nasium)** (*Sporthalle*), *still* - **still** (*noch*) und viele mehr!

2 HÄUFIG VERWECHSELTE WÖRTER

As oder like?

1. a. As, b. as ... as, c. like, d. like

Boxenstopp

Like - As - genauso groß wie

Big, great oder large? Little oder small?

2. a. great, b. large, c. small, d. little, e. big
3. *Richtig*: a. large, b. big, c. great, d. little, e. small

Boxenstopp

Big - large - Gegenteil - Little - wenig - Great

Bored oder boring? Interested oder interesting?

4. bored - boring - interesting - interested

Boxenstopp

gelangweilt - langweilig - interessiert - interessant

Lend oder borrow?

5. *Richtig*: a. lend, b. borrow, c. is lending, d. borrowed

Boxenstopp

a) sagen will, dass ich jemandem etwas ausleihe, b) sagen will, dass sich jemand etwas ausleiht

Bring oder take?

6. a. brings → **takes**, b. bringing → **taking**, c. take → **bring**, d. take → **bring**

Boxenstopp

bring - take

Can, could oder be able to?

7. a. can, b. could, c. Were you able to, d. was able to - cannot

Boxenstopp

can - could - Could - can - can - be able to

Carry oder wear?

8. *Simple present:* I **carry**, he/she/it **wears**; *Present progressive:* I am **wearing**; *Simple past:* we **carried**; *Past progressive:* they were **carrying**, I was **wearing**; *Past perfect:* I had **carried**, you had **worn**

Boxenstopp

wear - carry

Fit, match oder suit?

9. a. fit, b. matches, c. suits, d. suits, e. match

Boxenstopp
Zeit - fit - match

Hear oder listen? See oder watch?
10. a. Listen, b. hear, c. watch, d. see

Boxenstopp
hear - see - listen - watch

High oder tall?
11. *Richtig*: a. tall, b. high, c. tall, d. high

Boxenstopp
high: mountain, costs, heel, potential, ...
tall: person, tower, fence, ladder, tree, ...

Remind oder remember?
12. a. remind, b. remember, c. remember, d. remind

Boxenstopp
ausdrücken will, dass jemand jemanden an etwas erinnert. - sagen will, dass sich jemand an etwas erinnert.

Say oder tell?
13. *Richtig*: a. told, b. said, c. tell, d. told, e. said, f. tell

Boxenstopp
allgemeinen - informiert - befiehlt - Satzbau

Who oder where?
14. a. where, b. Who, c. where, d. Who, e. Where

Boxenstopp
Who = *Wer* **Where** = *Wo*

3 PROBLEMATISCHE VERBEN

1. *Richtig*: a. is doing, b. get, c. become, d. makes, e. have

Boxenstopp
bekommen - make - Zusammenhang

4 PROBLEMATISCHE ADJEKTIVE UND ADVERBIEN

Adverbien ohne -ly
1. a. fast - Adverb, b. fast - Adjektiv, c. early - Adverb, d. daily - Adjektiv, e. bad - Adjektiv, early - Adjektiv, f. right - Adjektiv, g. daily - Adverb

Falsche Verwandte
2. *Richtig:* a. deadly, b. dead, c. hardly, d. hard, e. lately, f. late, g. shortly, h. short

Die Sonderfälle good und well
3.a. good - well, b. well, c. good, d. well

Boxenstopp
Gruppe 1: z.B. **daily**, *Gruppe 2:* z.B. **lively**, *Gruppe 3:* z.B. **deadly**, *Gruppe 4:* **good** und **well**

KLASSE 10

1 MODALE HILFSVERBEN UND IHRE ERSATZFORMEN (S. 373-375)

1.
wollen: will; **nicht wollen**; will not/won't; **können**: can; **nicht können**: cannot/can't; **sollen**: shall/should; **nicht sollen**: shall not/shan't; should not/shouldn't; **müssen**: must; **nicht müssen**: do not have to/don't have to, need not/needn't; **brauchen**: need; **nicht brauchen**: do not have to/don't have to, need not/needn't; **dürfen**: may; **nicht dürfen**: must not/mustn't

2.
1. Mark could explain how the new gadget worked.
2. Monica wasn't allowed to walk home on her own.
3. You weren't supposed to ring her up after 10 p.m.
4. Were the children allowed to have some chocolate?
5. Did we have to argue?
6. You didn't have to clean my desk.
7. I couldn't leave her alone./I wasn't able to leave her alone.
8. You were supposed to post those letters.
9. Did you have to take your little sister everywhere?

3.

Ersatzform	Zeitform	modal verb
will be able to	future	can
was allowed to	simple past	may, can
won't have to	future	must
was going to	simple past	will, shall
didn't have to	simple past	must
were able to	simple past	can
will be supposed to	future	should
weren't allowed to	simple past	may, can
wouldn't be able to	conditional	can
will be allowed to	future	may, can

4.
had to help, wasn't allowed to play, can play, shouldn't be, have to help, must not forget, should contribute.

5.
1. *Darf ich dir/Ihnen helfen?*
2. *Ich hatte dich gebeten, nur das Küchenfenster zu putzen. Du musstest nicht alle Fenster putzen./Du hättest nicht alle Fenster putzen müssen.*
3. *Nachdem wir eine Pause eingelegt hatten, konnten wir weitermachen.*
4. *Du könntest vielleicht denken, dass ich eifersüchtig bin, aber ich bin es nicht.*

5. *Denkst du, ich sollte um mehr Geld bitten?*
6. *Du darfst dein/Sie dürfen Ihr Auto hier nicht parken.*
7. *Ich würde den Mädchen nicht erlauben, bis Mitternacht aufzubleiben.*
8. *Lindas Kollege/Kollegin durfte eine Stunde eher gehen, aber Linda nicht.*

6.
1. It's eight o'clock. We should watch the news.
2. You needn't help me. I can do it myself.
3. I must tell you the latest news.
4. Shall we pick you up?
5. We could bring you home afterwards, too.
6. You mustn't disturb father now.
7. I need a new job.

2 PRONOMEN (S. 384-388)

1.
1. He, **2.** His, It, **3.** She **4.** Her, **5.** They, **6.** you, **7.** We, **8.** he, **9.** I, he, **10.** You, **11.** It, you.

2.
These green apples are much cheaper than those green apples over there. Yes, and a pound of these tomatoes is also cheaper than a pound of those. What about a pineapple for our fruit salad? This pineapple looks good. No, that pineapple over there is much bigger. OK, let's take that one over there. And here are oranges from Brazil.
Let's take five of these oranges. OK, that's all then.

3.
Mrs Craft: she/sie; Tim: he/er; a fish: it/er; Mr and Mrs Terence: they/sie; you and me: we/wir; my aunt: she/sie; our cat Tinker: he oder she/er oder sie; two e-mails: they/sie; Thomas and me: we/wir; Thomas and you: you/ihr; Mrs Stone and her son: they/sie; the problems: they/sie; a chance: it/sie; a kindergarten: it/er.

4.
1. The tickets are not here. Where could they be? **2.** Julian and his friend are at home. They are playing a computer game. **3.** Hello, Mr Baxter. Can you help us, please? **4.** My wife can't come today. She is ill. **5.** Your mother can help you.
Ask her. **6.** What a nice flower. Put it in the garden, please. **7.** Maybe our parents can give us some money. We can/could phone them.

5.
1. Personalpronomen Subjekt, **2.** Personalpronomen Subjekt, **3.** Personalpronomen Subjekt, **4.** Personalpronomen Subjekt, **5.** Personalpronomen Objekt, **6.** Personalpronomen Objekt, **7.** Personalpronomen Objekt.

6.
1. They're, **2.** Their, **3.** their, they're, **4.** their, there, **5.** They're, **6.** their, **7.** They're, There, Their, **8.** There, their, there.

7.
1. We need our books.
2. Give me the bag over there, please. It's mine.
3. That is his present. Here is yours./ Yours is here.
4. I can give you her address.
5. Steven and Thomas, where are your gloves?
6. Is that my coat? Yes, that's yours.
7. Your passport, please!
8. Our neighbours are in London. Their children are alone at home.
9. You can never tell!

8.
1F, 2A, 3H, 4I, 5G, 6C, 7E, 8B, 9D.

9.
1. I would like to excuse myself. **2.** You can't imagine that! **3.** My children are constantly changing. **4.** I can't remember this film. **5.** Our neighbours always look forward to visitors. **6.** I always get dressed after breakfast. **7.** My husband must often hurry in the morning.

10.
1. Susie repaired the bike herself. **2.** My parents bought a new car yesterday. **3.** He looked at himself in the mirror. **4.** He looked at me.
5. We looked at each other and had to laugh.

AUSSPRACHE

1 UNTERSCHIEDLICHE AUSSPRACHE BEI HOMOGRAPHEN

1. a. [ˌsʌspekt] *Verdächtiger,* [səˈspekt] *verdächtigen;* *b.* [ˌsɜːveɪ] *Übersicht,* [səˈveɪ] *begutachten*

Boxenstopp
Homographe - geschrieben - Aussprachen - Bedeutungen - Substantiv - Verb - ersten - zweiten

2 HOMOPHONE

1. a. [swiːt] - 4. suite / 7. sweet, b. [hɪər] - 1. here / 3. hear, c. [aʊər] - 8. our / 11. hour, d. [sʌn] - 5. sun / 9. son, e. [dɪˈzɜːt] - 6. desert (Verb) / 12. dessert, f. [peər] - 2. pair / 10. pear

Boxenstopp
Homophone - ausgesprochen - geschrieben - Minimalpaare

3 SCHWIERIGE FÄLLE

1. a. Intonation nach unten, b. Intonation nach oben, c. Intonation nach oben

Boxenstopp
Den Buchstaben **o** kann man auf unterschiedliche Arten aussprechen, z.B. als [ɒ] (wie in **dog**), als [əʊ] (wie in **code**) oder als [ʌ] (wie in **cut**). - Eine Reihe von Buchstaben, sind im Englischen stumm, werden also nicht ausgesprochen. - Das **th** kann man auf

zwei Arten aussprechen: Entweder als stimmhaftes [ð] (wie in **breathe**) oder als stimmloses [θ] (wie in **breath**). – Anders als im Deutschen gibt es im Englischen auch **stimmhafte Wortendungen**. – **Question tags** werden je nach Intention des Sprechers unterschiedlich betont.

REFERATE HALTEN

ÜBUNGEN ZUM INHALT

1.
a) 4, b) 1, c) 3, d) 2

2.
richtig: b), c), e); falsch: a), d), f)

3.
a), c), e), g), i), j), k)

4.
1) a, c; 2) e, g; 3) i, j, k

5.
a) 5, b) 1, c) 2, d) 3, e) 4
Brown, Peter: Shakespeare. The greatest playwright ever. PONS, Stuttgart: 2008. S.12ff.

ÜBUNGEN ZUM WORTSCHATZ

1.
a), c), e), f), g), i), j)

2.
a), c), d), e), f), h), i)

3.
1) d, 2) c, 3) b, 4) e, 5) a

4.
1) feel free, 2) be, 3) distribute, 4) take, 5) ask, 6) answer, 7) put

5.
1) g, 2) c, 3) a, 4) d, 5) f, 6) e, 7) b

6.
a), d), e), g)

7.
1) This is based on the assumption that ...; 2) The following aspect is a central one:; 3) I would like to emphasise two aspects (in particular):; 4) A clear development can be seen ...; 5) Important aspects are ...; 6) What I'm saying is ...

8.
1) f, 2) c, 3) a, 4) b, 5) d, 6) e

9.
1) My first argument is ...; 2) The first aspect I want to present is ...; 3) However, I should mention that ...; 4) First I would like to show that ...; 5) In addition, it is important to ...;
6) Thirdly, we should consider ...; 7) We should also not ignore the following:

10.
a), b), d), g), j)

11.
1) can draw, 2) different issues, 3) this leads, 4) mentioned, 5) quite different, 6) should also look

12.
1) c, 2) f, 3) a, 4) g, 5) i, 6) b 7) h, 8) d, 9) e

13.
a), c), d), g), h)

14.
1) e, 2) i, 3) c, 4) a, 5) d, 6) b, 7) h, 8) f, 9) g

15.
a), b), d), e), f), h)

16.
Zustimmung: 1), 3), 4), 7);
Widerspruch: 2), 5), 6), 8)

17.
1) b, 2) c, 3) a, 4) d, 5) e

18.
1) a+c, 2) b+c, 3) a+c

19.
1) g, 2) a, 3) f, 4) d, 5) b, 6) e, 7) c

Bildnachweis

Seite 65: 1. fotolia.de/ Carola Schubbel, 2. fotolia.de/ awfoto, 3. istockphoto.com/ Floortje, 4. fotolia.de/ Marc Dietrich, 5. fotolia.de/ Finetti, 6. istockphoto.com/ Marie-france Bélanger; **Seite 80**: 1. fotolia.de/ deepwhite, 2. fotolia.de/ contour99, 3. fotolia.de/ RW-Design, 4. istockphoto.com/ ooyoo; **Seite 81**: Toaster: fotolia.de/ frankoppermann, Mikrowelle: istockphoto.com/ Matjaz Boncina, Stereoanlage: istockphoto.com/ Matjaz Boncina, Fernbedienung: fotolia.de/ felix, Telefon: istockphoto.com/ Matjaz Boncina, Maus: shutterstock.com/ fotohunter; **Seite 232**: istockphoto.com/ YinYang; **Seite 239**: istockphoto.com/ Geoff Kuchera; **Seite 248**: istockphoto.com/ Imre Cikajlo; **Seite 252**: fotolia.de/ Mareen Friedrich; **Seite 259**: istockphoto.com/ webphotographeer; **Seite 265**: istockphoto.com/ Brandon Laufenberg; **Seite 286**: istockphoto.com/ Skip O'Donnell; **Seite 294**: istockphoto.com/ Oleg Prikhodko; **Seite 297**: istockphoto.com/ Galina Barskaya; **Seite 323**: istockphoto.com/ Chris Schmidt; **Seite 331**: istockphoto.com/ Lisa Klumpp; **Seite 335**: istockphoto.com/ dieter Spears; **Seite 364**: fotolia.de/ Michael Flippo; **Seite 374**: istockphoto.com/ John Cowie; **Seite 376**: istockphoto.com/ Elena Korenbaum; **Seite 384**: Äpfel: istockphoto.com/ Zolnerovichs, Ananas: Avenue Images/ IT Stock Free, Tomaten: istockphoto.com/ Paul Johnson